THE FEDERALISTS
AND THE ORIGINS
OF THE
U.S. CIVIL SERVICE

THE FEDERALISTS AND THE ORIGINS OF THE U.S. CIVIL SERVICE

Carl E. Prince

New York · New York University Press · 1977

Library of Congress Cataloging in Publication Data

Prince, Carl E.
    The Federalists and the origins of the U.S. civil service.

    Bibliography: p.
    Includes index.
    1. Federal Party. 2. Civil service—United States—
History. 3. Patronage, Political—United States—
History. I. Title.
JK2306.P75   329'.1'009033   76-53708
ISBN 0-8147-6570-X

Library of Congress Catalog Card Number: 76-53708
ISBN: 0-8147-6570-X

Manufactured in the United States of America

For Liz and Jon

Contents

Illustrations

Introduction

The Federalist party, long known as "the party of the aristocracy," was very much a political movement that drew its lifeblood from the middle class of postrevolutionary America. Viewed from the perspective of its relationship to the first American civil service, the majority party of the 1790s takes on a different coloration. To a marked degree the Federalists * were led by men made by the American Revolution, party managers who had little in common, political affiliation apart, with the well-established, old-line landed and merchant gentry. This grass-roots leadership in communities across the nation, in turn, provided a solid identifiable nucleus that reinforced a "party of the people" image that challenges current stereotypes of federalism. This reality helps to explain a long-standing historical paradox: how a presumably arrogant, elitist party of organized placemen remained in power for a dozen years by drawing on the popular support of free voters at all levels of government. Ideology may have been one factor providing public tone to the party's image, but another source of input was the public perception

* For a definition of what I mean by the term Federalist, see note 1, chapter 11.

of local Federalist leaders as men like other men, federal employees deriving from backgrounds rendered extraordinary not so much by elite status as by previous patriotic service in the American Revolution.

The United States Constitution reordered and strengthened the federal government and, in so doing, called into existence the first United States civil service. I have investigated that civil service as the foundation of this study of Federalist party political behavior, testing the assumption that the national Federalist leaders exploited the service both to reward local party loyalty and build party organization.

The civil service, in fact, formed a haven for party cadre (party managers at state and local levels), thus virtually professionalizing secondary leadership by individually linking status and pecuniary rewards to the success of the national party. The more than two thousand federal officeholders named by Presidents Washington and Adams in the dozen years the Federalists reigned between 1789 and 1801 were rarely drawn from the much-studied luminaries of the era; rather, many were individuals relatively unknown to history who held more or less responsible jobs at the second or third levels of federal administration, remained residents of their towns and villages and, in general, formed the backbone of the Federalist party establishment in virtually every state.

The newly established civil service of the 1790s seemingly had little in common with the vast bureaucracy that exists today. The original federal establishment lacked the structure, depth, range and traditions of today's civil service. The staffs within its components were smaller and much more decentralized than those of today, and the service's operations were much more personalized and closer to the daily lives of most Americans. Nevertheless, even in its incipient stages, the various elements of the first civil service carried out some functions that would be surprisingly familiar to today's society. This was true of the four major components of the new civil service discussed here: the customs service, the internal revenue service, the post office department and the judicial establishment. Together these units formed an important part of the newly expanded federal authority conferred by the Constitution. Moreover, even in its fledgling years the promise of the service's continued future growth and authority were clearly visible.

I have found political and biographical information on more than one-third of that first civil service, enough data to suggest some revisions of existing stereotypes of the Federalists. The party was not the uncentralized, loose-jointed political mechanism that historians have almost universally concluded it was. Partly because of its connection with the first federal service, the new party in most states matured rapidly into a highly professional, tightly knit cluster at the state and local levels, closely aligned with and led by the national leadership at Philadelphia. This in turn has led me to broadly reinterpret the political roles of national figures like Washington, Hamilton, Adams, Pickering, and others. These towering figures were, in fact, deeply conscious of the party organizations that kept them in office and very much aware of the role the civil service played in maintaining the Federalists generally in power.

I have also attempted to evaluate the link between the Constitutional Federalist movement of the 1780s and the Federalist party in the 1790s. When compared to the former, the latter notably broadened its social and political base via the civil service, drawing into its professional embrace significant second-line leadership from the urban, small town, and rural middle classes * of America. Nevertheless, the post-1789 Federalist party also clearly incorporated into its organization—and into the civil service—many of the men responsible for the success of the Constitutional movement of the Confederation era.

The "new" Federalists appeared in town after town in every section of the nation precisely because the Federalist party cadre coincided so extensively with federal office-holders. Customs collectors and subordinate customs officers along the entire Atlantic seaboard, postmasters in the interior towns, supervisors, inspectors, and collectors of internal rev-

---

* See chapter 11 for guidelines I followed for ascriptions of class and status to individuals.

enue, federal judges, district attorneys, and marshals were all very much in evidence as local party leaders in an era when their paying federal positions not only did not disqualify them from politics but really made them both more politically visible and potent. This development by 1801 had helped to forge the Federalist party into as professional and modern a political movement in its own way as its Republican adversary. There may very well have been cogent ideological reasons, manifest before 1800, behind the demise of the Federalists, but it is doubtful if responsibility for their downfall can any longer be laid at the door of inferior or backward organization.

Parts of this study have appeared in the *Journal of American History* and the *Journalism Quarterly,* and I am grateful to both for permission to reproduce that material here in changed and expanded form. I also want to acknowledge the assistance rendered by grants from the American Association for State and Local History and from the Arts and Science Research Fund of New York University. A faculty fellowship from the National Endowment for the Humanities provided the better part of a year's leave to research this study. I want to acknowledge also the co-operation of Haifa University and the Hebrew University, Jerusalem, Israel. Both institutions so arranged my lecture schedule, when I was a visiting member of their respective faculties in 1972–73, as to give me plenty of time to write.

Professors Patricia Watlington and Norman Risjord shared the results of their research with me, augmenting significantly what I could learn about Kentucky and Virginia respectively. Ronald Milos, my assistant for a year when I taught at Seton Hall University, helped me to prepare the quantitative data contained in the last chapter. Dr. Dennis P. Ryan and Professors Patricia U. Bonomi, Richard H. Kohn, and Bernard Sternsher have read parts of the manuscript, and I have benefited greatly from their insights and encouragement. I want to acknowledge a really special debt to my colleague Professor David M. Reimers. His cogent reading of the entire manuscript caused me to look at it with renewed perspective and brought me to change things around considerably.

Professor Richard P. McCormick's friendship and professional counsel remain an important motivating force for me, and I am glad to be able to acknowledge this once more. My wife Sue, a feminist whose views I share, had some trepidations about my reference here to her constant support of my work, but the fact is she remains both my best critic and my major source of inspiration. My children Elizabeth and Jonathan will be delighted to see their names in print and are aware of the deeply felt reasons for this book's dedication.

March 11, 1977

THE FEDERALISTS
AND THE ORIGINS
OF THE
U.S. CIVIL SERVICE

CHAPTER ONE

The View from Philadelphia

Recently historians have begun to examine and appreciate the advances made by the Federalist party as a political organization. Federalist parties in the states appeared soon after 1789, sometime before their Jeffersonian Republican counterparts. In large measure these early parties responded to the goals and leadership of Alexander Hamilton, but the Federalist entity was by no means his creation alone. The Washington administration was a Federalist administration, and this often overlooked fact explains much about what followed in the states in the wake of the general's election in 1788. The new national government's insistence on support for, and loyalty to, the new Constitution as a *sine qua non* for appointments created a political test for officeholding at all echelons of that government. This course of action, moreover, in turn sustained, indeed underwrote, the creation of strong Federalist party machinery in the states. To understand the patterned mosaic of that machinery, it is important to understand both the policies and attitudes of the key figures in the Federalist administrations and the operation of the new civil departments of government in the states.

Historians usually assert that George Washington tried very hard to rise above political combat while he was president. It is true that he rarely answered political attacks and never engaged in anything that might be construed as partisan activity. Washington, moreover, granted his cabinet officers broad discretion in making subordinate appointments, another fact that students of his administration have fixed on in describing the limitations he imposed on himself. While this was abstractly true, and while most involved Americans took Washington's presidential political sheltering as an article of faith, in practices governing day-to-day appointment procedures it didn't work that way at all. Washington made it clear, for example, that he approved a policy generally excluding former Antifederalists from office. Perhaps his reasons were not so much political as statesmanlike in his own mind; that is, he viewed his primary function to be the launching of an enduring administration under the Constitution. But in practice, this goal led to the president's tolerance of political intolerance in the matter of filling subordinate offices, and resulted in the early creation of a political test for officeholding. The man who rigidly interpreted and enforced presidential wishes in this matter, indeed the man who either made or influenced most nominations in practice, was Alexander Hamilton. It should be remembered that Hamilton always functioned under a broad presidential mandate. Given Hamilton's completely different views, Washington's outlook, though prompted mainly by a desire for stability and loyalty within the new federal establishment, contributed immensely to the politicization of the federal civil service and in sequence to the creation of a strong, entrenched, relatively professional Federalist party.

The president, in fact, did not always delegate his appointive authority. There are several known instances where he himself accepted a political standard in making appointments, often by acting directly on the advice of others who suggested the imposition of such a criterion. So in spite of a frequently expressed desire to base nominations to office on the principle of fitness only, the president either looked the other way when purely political appointments were made, or succumbed more directly to inevitable political pressures.

The best example of a modification in Washington's initial impartial attitude centered on his appointment of William Paca as the United States district judge for Maryland in 1789. Paca was the president's third and virtually the last available qualified choice for the post. The chief executive, nevertheless, was reluctant to name him even after two others had refused the post. The reason? Although Paca had finally voted for ratification in the Maryland Ratifying Convention of 1788, he had been openly hesitant about doing so and had long been identified with the opponents of a strong central government. The president, explaining his views to his Maryland-based confidant and former aide-de-camp James McHenry, disclosed that the prospective jurist's "sentiments have not been altogether in favor of the General Government, and a little adverse on the score of Paper [money] emissions, etc." He apologized for naming Paca but, the president noted, he had been forced to settle.[1]

James McHenry and other influential Federalists, meanwhile, generally urged a political test on Washington. They were confident that their advice would carry weight, whatever high-road statements the president might make about fitness being the only yardstick for office; their confidence was not misplaced. McHenry, on whom Washington relied for advice on federal appointments in Maryland, always placed political considerations first in suggesting people to the president. There is no instance, moreover, where a McHenry-sponsored applicant was not appointed. The Maryland Federalist recommended one applicant to the president as a man who "has been particularly my friend in my opposition to those who thought differently from me respecting the present government." Another applicant, according to the former aide, was one "who exerted himself in his county in support of the rights of property." In recommending only the appointment of Constitutional Federalists, McHenry cautioned Washington in 1791 "that the old leaven [antifederalism] is by no means exhausted, and that it will be used on every promising occasion to foment the public mind." Therefore, political criteria for nominations to office must continue in force. "I can assure you," the Marylander wrote Washington in recommending three customs appointments, "that it will give great joy to the federalists of this town [Baltimore]. The cause in this place owes much to them and their friends." [2] Washington was almost always noncommittal in reply, but by his subsequent nominations to the civil service it is clear he took to heart McHenry's advice.

United States Supreme Court Justice William Paterson recommended the successful applicant for a high federal office in New Jersey in a letter forwarded by a United States senator to the president in 1791. In it Paterson indicated that he was "well acquainted with [Aaron Dunham's] character, which in both a political and personal sense is extremely fair and good. He is a Federalist; this Fact in his Character ought not in my opinion to be overlooked." [3] This sort of urging was difficult for the chief executive to ignore. Because he cherished his image as a chief executive who frowned on political differences, Washington was reluctant go to on record by either initiating or acquiescing in a political test. Usually the president's concurrence in a political nomination was passed on verbally to the concerned parties, as in the case of William Richardson's appointment in 1793. In this instance, William Perry had all but been appointed an inspector of internal revenue in Maryland. His signed commission was about to be forwarded by the president when he discovered what Hamilton had overlooked: that Perry was a Republican, named over a somewhat less qualified applicant (Richardson) who was a Federalist. According to Hamilton, the president instructed him verbally to drop the nomination of Perry through the auspices of the Treasury Department and passed on to him Richardson's commission instead. It is clear that Hamilton willingly took whatever public responsibility there was over the last-minute change, accepting an onus that clearly belonged with the president. [4]

Washington agreed to a systematic exclusion of Antifederalists from office (and, after a while, Republicans as well) in almost all states. In some states this political proscription, and the reasons for it, is clearer and more easily documented than in others. In New York, for example,

Washington protected Hamilton's local flank by excluding
Antifederalists—and later Republicans like the lower-manor
Livingstons—from federal office.[5] In Vermont, a new state
whole politics could not at first be clearly gauged,
Washington permitted Federalist Jeremiah Wadsworth, an
outsider from Connecticut but a long-time friend, to guide
him in making appointments. Wadsworth invoked political
criteria repreatedly in his long memo to the president, and
Washington acted on them to appoint only Federalists to all
key federal offices.[6]

The clearest example of Washington's deliberate invoca-
tion of political affiliation as virtually the exclusive measure
for making appointments occurred in Antifederalist Rhode
Island. Depending on the advice of key local Federalists like
Jeremiah Olney, Jabez Bowen, and John Brown, Washington
not only involved himself directly in the appointive process
to insure that Federalists would gain all the key federal
offices at his command, in one instance he also agreed to
demote one incumbent Antifederalist customs officer as the
transition from state to federal customs took place. In a
troublesome political state the president was taking no
chances on the loyalty of the second line of federal authority.
Indeed, Theodore Foster, an Antifederalist and the new
United States senator from Rhode Island, wrote Washington
that his turning out "antis" and replacing them with
Federalists indicated the appearance of a political test for
appointment. This was something, Foster reminded the president, the latter had repeatedly foresworn. The chief executive's actions, Foster concluded, continued to "give occasion
for Mistrust." [7]

Alexander Hamilton had a great deal of room in which to
operate within the flexible leadership structure created by
Washington. Given that the president's definition of "fitness"
for office comprehended the yardstick of "political orthodoxy," as Carl Russell Fish observed more than a half
century ago, it was possible for the treasury secretary, superb
administrator that he was, to insinuate himself ever more
deeply into the appointive process.[8] This was something
Washington probably encouraged because he found it politi-

cally advantageous to himself. Moreover, as Leonard White
has concluded, Washington "as a leading Federalist had observed the conflict between Jefferson and Hamilton, and it
must be assumed knew well the dominant position of the
latter in the councils of their common party." So it was that
the New Yorker "remained the dynamic center of the
Federalist party to whom President Washington . . . turned
for advice." [9]

Protestations apart, the president did nothing to prevent
the application of political criteria for officeholding in practice and on occasion directly contradicted his own oft-
verbalized commitment to impartiality. Hamilton found this
anomalous situation quite satisfactory. What usually occurred
when the matter of appointments in the states came up was
that Washington would delegate to Hamilton the task of
finding candidates upon whom he as president would ultimately pass judgment. The Virginian wrote in 1794, "I never
decide in the first moments . . . a Successor [to office]; being
desirous (and having so determined from the beginning of
my administration) always, to obtain a full knowledge of circumstances before I either nominate, or . . . appoint, Persons to Office." [10]

Because the preponderance of offices fell under the direct
administration of the Treasury Department anyway, and because Hamilton could always be counted on to discreetly
relay politically acceptable nominees to the president,
Washington turned to Hamilton to seek out possible appointees in a vast majority of the nominations to the first civil
service. So it was that the treasury secretary, sometimes
working with the president, but most often operating on his
own, developed extensive autonomy in the appointments
process by gaining control over the screening function within that process. The rapid politicization of the civil service
that ensued made George Washington at least a passive
agent in the growth of Federalist political hegemony in the
nation.

Alexander Hamilton's political power owed much to the
extended allegiance he commanded among federal officers in

the states. It was a loyalty he cultivated with both his usual intensity and careful planning. Even as the new government was taking shape, Treasury Secretary-designate Hamilton received some hard-headed advice from the eminently political Stephen Higginson. The elitist Massachusetts merchant warned the new cabinet minister to limit federal officeholding to those who had supported constitutional reform and continued to favor the administration. Such men, Higginson observed, would not be tempted by the cries of "clamorous popular leaders" and so would not endanger the government. Appointment of men who did not line up openly on the side of the government was a source of instability. "Such conduct in government [nominations to office without regard for political views] has a direct tendency to increase the Evil it is intended to prevent." Political toleration "encourages others to act the same part" in opposition to the government and "the number of opposers is by this means generally increased." This key figure in the Essex Junto claimed to have learned this lesson the hard way. In Massachusetts, Higginson pointed out, "I am sure we have been cursed with Insurgents [Shays's Rebellion] and Antifederalists by such conduct." [11]

Advice like that surely fed Hamilton's instincts. Other shrill cries of alarm convinced the secretary of the need for active political discretion. For example, soon after Rhode Island ratified the Constitution, Jeremiah Olney warned Hamilton that powerful Antifederalist forces in the state, led by Governor Arthur Fenner and the two newly elected Antifederalist United States senators, were going to move to ensure that "anti" revenue officers would be appointed. Hamilton intervened successfully to head off this real or imagined effort to "have all the *Ante* Revenue officers of the State reappointed." These *"Bitter* and *Uniform* opposers of the Constitution," Hamilton felt, must be (and were) prevented from gaining federal patronage. [12]

Hamilton's political role from 1789 on hardly needs recounting here, but it is instructive to note that the new secretary had years before carefully worked out a rationale governing appointments under a strong central government. As early as 1782, Hamilton suggested the line of conduct he would implement a decade later: "The reason of allowing Congress [e.g., the central government] to appoint its own officers of the Customs [and] Collectors of the taxes . . . is to create in the interior of each State, a mass of influence in favor of the Federal Government." It would be possible to build loyalty, Hamilton added, "by interesting such a number of individuals in each State, in support of the Federal Government, as will be counterpoised to the ambitions of others, and will make it difficult to unite the people in opposition to the first and necessary measures of the Union." [13]

This clearly summed up Hamilton's view of the civil service in the years 1789–95. Experience dictated some refinements to his view of the federal establishment over the years, but essentially the political leader followed his own early precepts. He remained as politically aware of the civil service's role in 1793 as he had ten years earlier. Hamilton cautioned a customs collector in a major port not to be too strict in administering the customs laws, for "in special cases a degree of relaxation" might be in order; "the good will *of the Merchants is very* important in many senses" after all.[14]

The secretary of the treasury carefully worked out his official relationship with Washington in matters touching on appointments. Inasmuch as fully three-quarters of the subordinate jobs were in Treasury, this was absolutely necessary.[15] For appointments in Hamilton's ministry, the president usually permitted his secretary wide latitude to "make the necessary enquiries into the fitness" of candidates. Hamilton as a matter of common practice presented names of potential Treasury Department appointees to Washington, along with his notes, opinions, and recommendations. These were invariably accepted. On the other hand, when Washington received requests for appointment to fill openings, he turned the correspondence over to his chief minister. On one revealing occasion in 1790, the president wrote that "these papers are not intended to influence your opinion in favor of these persons further than as they may serve to form a comparison of their merits with other candidates." If one did not know

who was the writer and who the recipient, it might appear
that the secretary was writing to the president and not the
reverse.[16]

When others took this relationship for granted, as sometimes happened, and wrote directly to Hamilton, he was
scrupulously careful to avoid the appearance of usurpation of
authority. He protected his flank by perserving the president's image. Simon Gross, captain of the Maryland revenue
cutter, wrote Hamilton in 1791 informing him that his first
mate had resigned and suggesting a replacement. Hamilton
wrote back that all suggestions for a new appointment go
directly to Washington, for "this is a power . . . which can be
exercised only by the President of the United States." [17]

Regard for the niceties did not prevent the secretary of the
treasury from expanding his power in other ways. Using the
good offices of his Treasury Department subordinates in the
Providence customshouse in 1793, for example, Hamilton involved himself directly in the appointment of the United
States attorney for Rhode Island, an office that fell under the
administrative jurisdiction of Thomas Jefferson and the State
Department.[18]

At a time when Citizen Genêt set out to charter American
vessels as privateers, and in the midst of the ensuing domestic crisis in 1793, Hamilton went over Jefferson's head once
again. The treasury secretary informed his friend Richard
Harison, United States attorney for New York, that, whatever
the secretary of state's instructions, Harison was to seize a
recently chartered privateer either by civil or military force.
Hamilton added that a cabinet decision to that effect had just
been made with instructions that the State Department implement it, but he did not trust either Jefferson's dispatch or
forcefulness in the matter. That Hamilton could instruct
Harison, who was Jefferson's subordinate, was an indication
of where the loyalties of the civil service resided.[19] Jefferson's vigorous protests at what he considered Hamilton's
usurpation of authority did little to change matters, for
Hamilton had laid the groundwork carefully by earlier securing the president's permission to have the customs collectors
act as agents (Jefferson called them spies) to inform the fed-

eral government of possible infractions of American neutrality. To implement this earlier unrelated directive, all that remained was for a customshouse officer to inform Harison. When this occurred Harison, already alerted by the treasury secretary, acted.[20]

These two examples of the usurpation of Jefferson's authority may well have hastened his departure from the government. At any rate, it is clear that an unwritten but very effective relationship between Washington and Hamilton had developed, in which the latter was given wide if subtle latitude to use the federal service to strengthen the government's hand politically.

By the time John Adams moved up to the presidency, the politicization of the federal service was an accomplished fact. This did not dismay Adams. Washington's successor was much more openly partisan than the general had been, or as Leonard White felicitously put it, "direct reference to party attitude . . . became more common and less concealed." [21]

Like Hamilton, John Adams had developed some strong views on the matter of appointments long before he came to power. In a 1787 letter to Jefferson discussing the new Constitution, Adams made clear his conception of executive control of the civil service. "I would . . . have given more power to the president, and less to the Senate," Adams noted with regard to appointments. "The nomination and appointment to all offices, I would have given to the president, assisted only by a privy council of his own creation; but not a vote or voice would I have given to the Senate or any senator unless he were of the privy council." [22] In fact, his worst fears of Senate interference were realized during his tenure as president. Adams believed "the Senate was less friendly to him than to his predecessor." If the Congress were to limit him in making appointments, Adams felt at the beginning of his term, "the executive authority" would be rendered "a nose of wax." [23]

John Adams, as his outlook made clear, directly involved himself in the nominating process, much more so in fact than did his predecessor, who had been just as concerned but much more given to finessing his interest and involvement.

Adams was a strong executive. It was rare even for a sometimes disloyal but often weak-willed Oliver Wolcott, Jr.,
Adams's inherited secretary of the treasury, to attempt to
guide Adams's course of action. The irascible New Englander, Page Smith has disclosed, "devoted a disproportionate amount of time trying to assure himself that the best
candidate for each position received the appointment." And,
Smith concluded, "he clearly preferred applicants who were
firm supporters of the government." [24]

John Adams made no bones about naming Federalists to
office, but more importantly, he openly encouraged his subordinates to act politically. The president, moreover, did not
hesitate to remove Republicans from office wherever and
whenever they were found. "Political principles, and discretion, will always be considered, well weighed, in all appointments" Adams informed his treasury secretary. Occasionally he went further. Chafing under the sustained as-
saults of the Philadelphia *Aurora* in 1799, Adams told Secretary of State Timothy Pickering to pass the word down the
line to United States Attorney for Pennsylvania William
Rawle: "If Mr. Rawle does not think this paper libelous,"
Adams wrote, "he is not fit for his office; and if he does not
prosecute it, he will not do his duty." [25] If political involvement by a federal civil servant benefited the wrong side,
however, Adams's views changed. In justifying to Boston's
Federalist Customs Collector Benjamin Lincoln his removal
of several Portsmouth, New Hampshire, customs officers, the
president wrote: "the representations to me of the daily language of several officers at Portsmouth, were so evincive of
aversion, if not hostility, to the national Constitution and
government, that I could not avoid making some
changes. . . . If the officers of government will not support
it," Adams concluded, "who will?" [26]

Political orthodoxy was a precept to which the second president strictly adhered in initiating appointments. Adams
made this clear within a month of taking office. John Gibbons
was rejected as a possible surveyor of customs at Savannah,
Georgia, in 1797 specifically because he had earlier signed a
petition denouncing Jay's Treaty.[27] When Elbridge Gerry
sought a job in the revenue service for William Lee, the pres-

ident, although a close friend of Gerry's, responded, "Mr. Lee is represented to me as a Jacobin, who was very busy on the wrong side. His pretensions, however, shall be considered with all others impartially, if I should make any appointments." At risk of engaging in anticlimax, it should be noted that Lee was not appointed.[28] After the customs collector at Norfolk, Virginia, died in 1797, Adams, openly for political reasons, appointed Otway Byrd, a Federalist, over much better qualified (by Adams's own admission) Daniel Bedinger, a Jeffersonian.[29]

Although John Adams inherited most of his civil service from his predecessor, there were opportunities available in the course of his term to exercise his strong-handed control over patronage. Manning Dauer offers overwhelming evidence that Adams systematically proscribed Republicans from nominations to the upper ranks of the provisional army established at the height of the Franco-American crisis of 1798.[30] Congress's enactment of a direct federal property tax in 1798, a result of the same crisis, opened to Adams many civil appointments in the lower reaches of the federal government. Some political opponents even saw in the new tax proof of Adams's rank opportunism: Adams "had the assistance of so many Pens and a Vast Number of Tongues and they all Expected their Reward," noted one Republican. To satisfy this host of political allies, Adams's men were alleged to have concluded that "a direct tax and stamp act will make Roome for more officers; by this time all the yelpers was Nearly put into office with good Salaries." [31]

There was some feeling among Adams's contemporaries that political considerations dominated his thinking in making nominations. Stephen Higginson, not normally one of the president's admirers, wrote with approval in 1800 that Adams's "patronage has been indeed very efficacious" in preparing the way for the coming election. Among other deserving Federalists, Higginson noted, Harrison Gray Otis "expected to receive his reward" and was not disappointed.[32] When a North Carolina Jeffersonian expressed a desire to be recommended to the president for an office in 1798, he was told in a letter, a copy of which was forwarded to Adams: "I cannot suppose that any person antifederal can be agreeable to the executive." [33] Frederick Muhlenberg, late a Republican congressman, felt it was necessary to apologize to President Adams for his opposition to the administration when he applied for the post of collector of customs for Philadelphia—a job he didn't get until Thomas Jefferson gave it to him.[34]

Adams's personal attention to nominations even penetrated to the point of making political distinctions among Federalists. By the end of 1797, Manning Dauer points out, Adams was naming party moderates who were "anathema to most Federalists." This meant in practice that early on in the Adams administration the Hamilton wing of the party was as proscribed as were the Jeffersonians. While obviously this could not apply retroactively to the multitude of Hamilton supporters already in office, it could and did affect new appointments. This development from the outset of Adams's administration generated schism in the ranks of the reigning party. A good example of the new president's procedure manifested itself after only a month in office; it involved Adams's handling of the powerful and lucrative post of collector of customs for New York City. Treasury Secretary Oliver Wolcott, Jr., Hamilton's protégé and successor, solicited candidates from Hamilton, then out of office and living in New York, and the latter's two close associates William Seton and Robert Troup. Four possible nominees were suggested by this triumvirate. Adams was shown the high Federalists' recommendations, but the chief executive instead appointed Joshua Sands to fill this critical and politically powerful vacancy. Sands was on nobody's list, but he could be counted upon to further the interests of the Adams Federalists in the city.[35] Because he inherited much of the existing civil service, Adams's opportunities to use patronage to enhance his authority were curtailed. Nevertheless, not the least of the New Englander's important presidential attributes was his heavy-handed attention to those second-line offices that did become vacant during his term.

The several departments of government were directly responsible to policy-making officials like Washington, Hamilton, and Adams. The two departments that together employed the majority of civil officeholders in the states were part of the Treasury establishment: the customs service and the internal revenue service.* The other two functioning civil service centers with large establishments in the states were the federal judiciary and legal establishment subsumed under the Department of State, and the Post Office, operating more or less autonomously in the Federalist era and directly answerable only to the postmaster general (who did not yet have cabinet rank) and the president.† All of these agencies were drawn into the party vortex.

The customs service, operating in fourteen states by 1792, claimed 146 officers and 332 subordinates. Officers with executive responsibility included collectors of customs, naval officers (really deputy collectors and always civil appointees despite the confusing designation), surveyors of customs, and civilian masters (captains) of the revenue cutters. Subordinate positions, in practice usually filled by the collector, included revenue cutter crews, inspectors of customs (popularly known as "tidewaiters" in eighteenth-century vernacular), gaugers, weighers, measurers, and boatmen. Only the largest ports were served by a full complement of officers. Medium-sized ports usually functioned without a naval officer and cutter. Smaller ports were administered only by a collector; some of the smallest only by a surveyor. Subordinate customs personnel, of course, were most in evidence in the large and medium-sized harbors. By the time the Federalist era ended in 1801, the number of inferior employees in the 71 ports of entry had risen to 944, although the roster of officers had not increased much.[36]

The officers at the top of the service in the states exerted

*The commissioners of loans and later the commissioners of the direct land tax of 1798 were also attached to the Treasury Department. The latter two were not large enough to form "departments" by themselves and were administered directly by the secretary of the treasury.

† There were a few federal civil appointees from the War and Navy Departments also carrying out their duties in their respective states.

great political leverage because of their prestige, income, and the deference paid them. But their major source of power derived from a more mundane source, namely, that the officers, particularly the collectors, made subordinate appointments in a rapidly expanding department. These officers, moreover, took home handsome incomes deriving from salaries and fees, continued without exception to reside in their native communities, and were not barred from politics either by law or custom. All in all, the customs service constituted the best official reservoir for political cadre. This potential was not lost on Federalist leaders. James McHenry was not telling Alexander Hamilton anything new when he wrote in 1792 that the collector's office "possesses vast influence, and ought not to be given away lightly." [37]

McHenry's observation was borne out in Boston, for example, where Benjamin Lincoln presided over the customshouse. Lincoln had served in the uppermost echelons of the Continental army, figured significantly in the repression of Shays's Rebellion, and filled the office of secretary of war in the Confederation government. As collector in one of America's largest ports of entry, he was a prominent Massachusetts Federalist leader. The portly Lincoln named dozens of underlings; there was, according to one contemporary account, "but one republican under all his appointments as collector" in the 1790s. This was the claim of a petition forwarded to James Madison soon after Jefferson's inauguration. If the petitioners exaggerated the political importance of the collector's office when they claimed that "within two years [of Lincoln's replacement by a Republican] . . . the party shall rise with brilliance and show the Southern states that we are not lost," nevertheless their view of the politicization of the office was accurate enough.[38] Philadelphia was also singled out. President Jefferson was called upon "to release this city from injuries . . . sustained by the abuses of the department of the Customs to the grievous wrong of men who offended only in being republicans." [39]

The politicization of the customs service was not limited to large ports with huge complements of men. The relative political impact of a partisan collector was the same or greater for smaller ports with fewer employees. Dighton, Massachusetts, was a case in point: "We beg leave to invite your attention to the collector's office in Dighton," two local Republicans wrote to Secretary of the Treasury Gallatin in 1805. Hodijah Baylies, the Federalist collector, "is a gentleman of adequate talents and for ought we know unchargeable with any immoral or official misconduct." He was guilty, however, of being "a decided and we believe a sentimental federalist and of course his official influence is against us. Our wish is to have that influence for us." The complainants concluded that "the removal of the present officer will be an act of public justice and sound Policy." [40] The customs service functioned ably and efficiently in the Federalist decade, as Leonard White has concluded. But it is also true that it was put together knowingly as a vehicle for sustaining emergent Federalist cadres in the states.

The growth pattern evident in the customs service applied to the first internal revenue service as well. The latter was called into existence by the passage of the excise levy of 1791, although its complement of officers and subordinates was filled slowly as a result of well-known complications in implementing the excise tax. By the time Alexander Hamilton retired in 1795, however, he had appointed 36 officers and 183 subordinate employees. Once again, while the number of senior supervisors and inspectors of the revenue did not materially change by 1801, the ranks of the subordinate collectors and auxiliary officers swelled to 533.[41]

Unlike customs personnel, excise collectors were great travelers, with each inspector and his collectors canvassing their respective districts within a state almost continuously. The officers, according to Hamilton, were "important" and "respectable." [42] The political potential of the service, moreover, was not lost on either the Federalists or their opponents. "The State has been so harassed with those [who] would be called Federal Officers," wrote Republican Senator James Jackson of Georgia in 1801, "from the . . . Collectors and Supervisors down to the . . . excise understaffers." [43] Henry Miller, Pennsylvania's supervisor, was accused by a Jeffersonian congressman of being "active against us to the last degree." [44] The same was true in neighboring New Jersey. "It is a well known fact in New Jersey," wrote Governor-elect Joseph Bloomfield, that Aaron Dunham, supervisor of the revenue for the state, "has gone all lengths to support the late election [in 1800] of our political opponents, more by the characters and electioneering abilities of his Deputys in the several countys, than by his own influence." [45] Virtually identical allegations were made for other states. Republican Pierce Butler of South Carolina was incensed over the fact that in 1800 "all the petty Excise officers [were sent] posting through the State to try to prevent the Election of such Men to the State Legislature as were of Republican principles." [46] The decade-long history of this first United States internal revenue service is in part the history of an organized agency of the government devoting itself to the perpetuation of Federalist power.

The post office also was an obvious haven for political activists. The service initially functioned as a quasi-independent agency, in practice subject only to nominal presidential control. The aberration derived from the fact that, under the Federalist administrations, the postmaster general did not have cabinet rank. The two Federalist presidents simply set down some general guidelines to determine appointments and more or less left the choice of local postmasters to the postmaster general. The latter administered his department without responsibility to any cabinet officer.

The three postmasters general under the Federalists were Samuel Osgood, a holdover until 1791 from the Confederation government; Federalist Timothy Pickering, who served from 1791 to 1795; and Joseph Habersham, a Georgia Federalist who occupied the office from 1795 to 1801. The post office grew from well under 100 postmasters at the end of the Confederation to about 200 in 1791. There followed a period of rapid expansion so that by the end of 1800, the number of postmasters had risen to 824. Virtually every city, town, village, and hamlet boasted its own post office.[47] Timothy Pickering headed the department expertly during its greatest period of growth, always making sure that Federalist interests were looked after. Joseph Habersham, who took over in 1795, did not depart from the standard of political preference so clearly laid down by his predecessor. By 1801 the Federalist cadre had been bolstered extensively throughout the nation at the most local of levels by the addition of hundreds of Federalist postmasters.

Federalist newspaper editors were particularly favored with post office nominations. The appointment was valuable to printers, not so much because of the remuneration which was often little enough, but because of the advantages the local post office provided for cheap or even free delivery of papers. Post officers, moreover, received franking privileges that postmaster-editors employed in a variety of business-connected ways.[48] As early as 1790 two congressmen protested against attempts "to build up a Court Press" by permitting the postmaster general to introduce regulations allowing some newspapers, owned by postmasters, privileged circulation through the mails. Timothy Pickering admitted "it is true divers postmasters are printers of newspapers," virtually all of them Federalist.[49] It was no wonder that Jefferson complained to Madison that under Pickering the post office had become "a source of boundless patronage to the executive." [50]

For the historian, Timothy Pickering's chief virtue was his candor. He wrote to an applicant for the postmastership at Marblehead, Massachusetts: "I should not think it expedient for you to receive it on account of [your Republican] political sentiments." He added, to clarify that which needed no clarification, "I think myself bound to discharge [the public trust] . . . by introducing to public beneficial situations honest men *who have claims on the public* for their service in effecting the establishment of a government." [51]

By the end of the decade the post office, the Jeffersonians felt with some justice, had become a Federalist "engine." "The Post Offices in this part of the United States [New England]," Ephraim Kirby wrote in 1801, "have for years past been almost universally in the hands of violent political partizans." Another Republican accused the last Federalist postmaster general, Joseph Habersham, of permitting "the most partisan discrimination" in post offices in Philadelphia,

Newport, Albany, and "several of the eastern towns." [52] Complaints like these arrived in Washington in a steady stream around the time Jefferson took his oath of office.

Several postmasters were accused of delaying or misplacing communications between Republican activists; others were alleged to have opened mail and passed on their contents to those Federalists who could make the best use of the information. One Pennsylvania postmaster, reported a western Pennsylvania Republican leader, was guilty of "the suppression or mislaying of the votes for electors in 1796." [53] These accusations were substantially true. Political action by postmasters, either directly involving abuse of their post office powers or their functioning as party activists outside their official stations, was widespread during the Federalist decade.

Not even the new judicial establishment was immune to the political virus. The fact that initially it fell within Secretary of State Thomas Jefferson's bailiwick did not limit the Federalists' penetration of the judiciary. Hamilton seems effectively to have frozen Jefferson out of the selection process while at the same time he involved himself deeply. Most of the appointments, those of the "midnight" variety in 1801 excepted, occurred well before Hamilton left public office.[54] Indeed, the initial establishment of sixty-three superior officers was completed before 1792 and grew only slightly thereafter. The roster of federal officials included United States district judges, district attorneys, marshals, and court clerks for each state. There were also an unknown number of deputy marshals and lawyers employed by the case in the marshals' and district attorneys' offices respectively.

All of the judicial officers, with the possible exception of the court clerks, were politically active. Federal judges in the 1790s repeatedly handed down decisions that were politically motivated, a serious claim and one that can be well documented. The judicial substructure, functioning under the authority of the United States district court judges in the states, displayed equally overt political leanings. Political power was a hallmark of the offices of both the United States district attorney and the United States marshal. The federal

attorney for a given state was responsible for prosecuting
federal cases (for example, violations of the neutrality laws),
compiling evidence on all government suits originating in his
state (e.g., violations of customs laws), and farming out investigations to lawyers whose fees he assigned at his discretion.
The marshal was charged with empaneling grand and petit
juries for government cases (for example, in trials under the
Sedition Act), and controlled extensive personal patronage in
that he designated all assistant marshals in his state. Both
positions, in short, were highly visible, highly political
posts.[55] The judicial branch was no less susceptible to
Federalist political infiltration than were the revenue
branches and the Post Office.

The pattern established here involved a vast majority of the
first civil service. For the purposes of Alexander Hamilton
and John Adams, and perhaps also for George Washington,
the federal service offered shelter to a paid political cadre
devoted to keeping the "ins" in. Some men were appointed
to prestigious and profitable posts by the two Federalist presidents because they either aided the Federalist Constitutional cause of the 1780s or the party in the 1790s; others
most certainly became active in the party because they were
the recipients of appointments they wanted to keep. Some
undoubtedly became believers ex post facto or were simply
grateful. Whatever the cause, the result was clear. The first
federal civil service became a fountainhead of relatively professional Federalist party leadership. The new United States
customs service, established in 1789, sheltered a large component of that leadership

CHAPTER TWO

The Customs Service: Massachusetts

The Constitution of 1787, by empowering the federal government to regulate commerce, foreordained the creation of the United States customs service. In maritime Massachusetts this was seized on as an opportunity to build local Federalist party cadres in the commonwealth's many ports. From Dighton and New Bedford at the extreme southern end of the commonwealth, where federal customs stations were first established in 1789, to the several ports in Essex County at the Bay State's northern tip, the Massachusetts coastline was dotted with fine harbors. United States ports of entry were also placed at Nantucket Island, Barnstable, and Plymouth in the Cape Cod area. Moving further north, Boston, still the first port of the New World, housed America's largest initial customs establishment. Salem and neighboring Beverly, treated as a single administrative unit for customs purposes were, along with Marblehead, Gloucester, and Newburyport, anchorages that sustained eighteenth-century Essex County's dominant economic and political position in the commonwealth.

The federal employees who presided over the commerce of these Massachusetts towns were men whose names are

21

only dimly if at all recalled nearly two centuries later. Supported by the national administration in Philadelphia, but laboring in the shadows of the well-known placemen who formed the first line of Federalist leadership in postrevolutionary Massachusetts, these customs officers and their subordinates nevertheless anchored the local Federalist parties in a dozen of the commonwealth's most populous towns and cities. Using their influence and positions with a full measure of commitment, these cadremen formed the backbone of the Federalist establishment in the harbor towns. There were forty-three customs officers and nearly a hundred subordinates whose influence radiated outward, so the customshouses formed a nearly professional series of foundation blocks upon which local Federalist parties rested. The Federalist-oriented customs service was one factor that contributed to the Bay State's status as a national party bellwether.

And if Massachusetts was the rock on which American federalism was founded, Essx County was the keystone for the commonwealth.[1] Just as this coastal county dominated commerce, so did its Federalist elite dominate politics. Whether or not the Essex Junto continued to act cohesively in the 1790s remains an open question. Nevertheless, its members—or former members—continued to exercise extensive statewide political power. George Cabot, John Lowell, Timothy Pickering, Stephen Higginson, Jonathan Jackson, and Benjamin Goodhue were all politically ubiquitous in the Federalist decade.

There were also Boston Federalists who counted. John Hancock remained a major party leader until his death in 1793. Harrison Gray Otis matured into an important influence in Federalist circles midway through the decade. Authority derived also from the patronage and esteem commanded by moderate Federalist Benjamin Lincoln, Boston's collector of customs. Lincoln, especially close to the national administration, was not infected by the increasing political rigidity of the Essex group in the waning years of the Federalist decade.

In spite of the moderation of Lincoln, the occasional independence of Otis, or the continuing stubborn opposition of aging, virtually partyless Sam Adams, the Federalist party comprised more than merely "a combine of little cliques and personal connections." Massachusetts, in short, contained a Federalist party in the modern sense of that term, and its ability to moderate and reconcile internal conflicts was the strongest indicator that this was so. It housed inconsistencies that would have broken lesser political organisms: "Celebrated for its aversion to factions, it nevertheless became an organized political power," James Banner has written. "Acclaimed as the champion of strong central government, it fathered the first coherent regionalist movement in the nation's history. . . . Enemies of doctrines, dogmas and theories, it gave rise to a commanding ideology."

Among the primary dispensers of this ideology were the collectors and, in the larger ports, the naval officers and surveyors of customs. These men were generally the cardinal party leaders in place along the Massachusetts coastline. As cadremen possessing both prestige and local visibility, they set the grass-roots patterns of Federalist political activity.

This generalization clearly applied to the two United States ports of entry on Massachusetts' south shore: Dighton at the head of Fall River, and the premier whaling port of New Bedford. Both were bustling harbors in the 1790s, each presided over by a Federalist collector who supervised a staff that he appointed. The two ports, moreover, typically provided their superior officers with annual incomes in the neighborhood of $1,000 for work that was for the most part performed by subordinates.

The customs collector at Dighton, appointed by President Washington in 1789, was Hodijah Baylies, "a decided and . . . sentimental federalist." Baylies had graduated from Harvard in 1777 and immediately entered the Continental army. He rose to the rank of major, serving with distinction until the end of the war. Afterward he turned to the management of the family ironworks in New Bedford, an occupation that did not interfere with his customs duties. Baylies remained active in the Massachusetts chapter of the Society of the Cincinnati, an allegiance he shared with many other Federalist officeholders.

Given the combined weight of his elite background and high customs office, the former Continental army officer emerged as Dighton's leading Federalist. The customshouse in turn became the center of local Federalist activity. When Thomas Jefferson was elected, town Republicans pointed out that for more than a decade the collector at Dighton, his subordinates, and "those under their influence" had formed the nucleus of the Federalist party in town. "Some of them [customs officials]," a Republican lamented, "at different times on days of Elections have been Violent in their Conduct and very indecent in the Language" toward the minority party. Baylies, although relatively moderate himself, nevertheless led a group of party men who were not. His official influence was keenly felt and widely deplored by Dighton Republicans, although no one questioned his official competence. Even Baylies's political enemies conceded that "he is a gentleman of adequate talents and for ought we know unchargeable with any immoral or official misconduct." Widely respected in the town and possessed of significant patronage, Baylies was the effective leader of the local Federalist majority for twenty years, and was not untypical of the second rank of Federalist management in the commonwealth.[2]

Much the same could be said for the port collector in nearby New Bedford. In the 1790s that town both attracted its share of the European trade and remained, as it had for nearly a century, the first whaling port of the New World. Edward Pope presided over an apparently unrestrained cadre of Federalist officials. Not only was Pope himself deeply involved in local politics, but "all the appointments he made in his District . . . to all the lesser customs offices" also derived from party ranks. Like Baylies, Pope possessed enormous local prestige in an age of deference. He was descended from a family of original settlers in the town and was frequently described as "one of the most prominent citizens" of New Bedford.

The collector operated a general store on the waterfront, an occupation he continued to pursue during his long tenure in office, and he also remained a judge on the county court of common pleas. Like many of the merchants in town, Pope was a Quaker, so he had not served in the military during the War for Independence. He had been involved locally in the Whig cause, however. The extended nature of Pope's engagements in the Federalist decade led to charges of incompetence and "inattention to the duties of office" leveled at him by his political opponents, and it was true that he left most of the customs routine to his deputies. Federalist party leadership was one of the most important of his many extracurricular commitments. During the election campaign of 1800, for example, Pope, presiding at a New Bedford Federalist meeting, described Jefferson as "a man of infamous character, a man of no religion and who wishes the destruction of all religion, and all good government." Needless to say, demands for the collector's removal followed hard on the news of Jefferson's election.[3]

The ports of entry on and near Cape Cod also drew their political leadership from the customshouses. Plymouth clearly was the most notoriously Federalist harbor town in the area, according to contemporary accounts.[4] Here William Watson presided over a committed group of party-oriented tidewaiters. By the 1790s, Plymouth was well on its way to recovery after the nearly disastrous decline of its commerce during the American Revolution. This first Massachusetts settlement rapidly restored a home fleet that specialized in the Mediterranean trade, while husbandry and fishing operated side by side as other economic mainstays in the former Pilgrim colony.[5]

The collector of customs at Plymouth was also acknowledged locally as the head of the Plymouth Junto, the euphemistic label with which the local Federalist party was tagged. William Watson was a venerable man by the 1790s, absolutely dependent on his customs service income. The collector had been born in 1730 to one of Plymouth's first families. He graduated from Harvard in 1751, returned to his native town, eventually built a fine mansion, and took his place as an "indispensable town father." Watson was a staunch Whig prior to 1776. His son entered the Continental army after the war broke out, and the elder Watson was both a colonel in the local militia and part owner of a privateer. He was a member of the county Committee of Correspondence and held many civil offices in the quarter century following 1763. His reputation as a revolutionary supporter was so widespread that Watson was one of relatively few honorary inductees taken in by the Society of the Cincinnati.

For all his honors and family connections, however, Watson perpetually "had a hard time finding cash." Watson and Ephraim Spooner opened a tannery in Plymouth in 1777. The uncertainties of the Confederation era took its toll, and the operation struggled on only until 1788, when its owners went bankrupt. With the aid of his son-in-law John Davis, a rising Federalist star and the United States attorney for Massachusetts in the Washington administration, Watson was able to secure the Plymouth customshouse appointment from the federal government. He filled lesser customs offices with men who eventually acquired local reputations as party activists.

These subordinates clearly took their cue from the collector. Watson, fellow townsman Henry Warren alleged to President Jefferson in 1802, was a "bitter federalist" in customs business, one who "winked at the fraud of [merchant followers in] his party." Several charges like this, although unprovable, did provide excuse enough for Jefferson to clean out the entire customs staff simply by removing Watson and appointing a Republican in his place. Whether or not the Plymouth customshouse enforced the law selectively and loosely, Watson's Plymouth Junto was from 1789 an effective example of a professionally rooted local Federalist party that, closely tied to the town elite, nevertheless cut deeply and fully into the economic and social spectrum of Plymouth.[6]

The harbor at Boston, thirty-five miles away, dwarfed that of Plymouth. It remained the busiest port in the nation for most of the Federalist decade. The city's customshouse employed over fifty men under the astute supervision of Collector Benjamin Lincoln, "one of the foremost men of the state." Lincoln had been a Continental army general, the secretary for war in the Confederation government, and the man who led the troops who put down Shays's Rebellion. After ratification, he emerged as a moderate force in the complex configuration of Massachusetts Federalist politics. Having been granted the Boston customshouse, an inviting place which he badly needed, Lincoln in the early 1790s "became a valued correspondent of Hamilton," whose economic program, he wrote the treasury secretary, was vital "for the political salvation of this country." Before 1798, Lincoln was a confidant of Stephen Higginson, Jonathan Jackson, and other key men in the Essex Junto. He worked closely as well with men like John Hancock of Boston and Theodore Sedgwick of Berkshire County in the west. Finally, for the entire decade he remained close to John Adams, who was never really trusted by many Massachusetts high Federalists.

If there was a liaison then, a single connecting figure to link the diverse components of Massachusetts federalism for most of the 1790s, that person was Benjamin Lincoln. It was to Lincoln that Treasury Secretary Hamilton frequently turned in soliciting political information and recommendations for the Bay State. And it was the portly general whom Adams often consulted for advice and help throughout the decade. In 1798 the president asked Lincoln to approve before nomination all prospective appointments to the new American provisional army. Among other suggestions made in the course of his response, the customs collector, signaling his own shifting politics and perhaps gauging the turn of Adams's mind, advised the president not to appoint Hamilton to a command in that army. Innately moderate himself, Lincoln by 1798 had turned away both from Hamilton and the high Federalists. He agreed to head a Boston Federalist committee that publicly endorsed Adams's foreign policy in 1798, at a time when Essex Federalists bitterly opposed that policy.

It was only at this time that Lincoln's long-standing working alliance with the Essexmen began to weaken. But while relations between the collector and the junto clearly cooled, they never wholly broke down. Lincoln was far too subtle and astute a politician to allow that to happen. In deference to his popularity, moreover, criticism of the Boston collector by Essex County Federalists was either muted or privately expressed. Timothy Pickering wrote to a friend, for example, that Lincoln's talents were "overrated." In 1800, after two years of friction among Massachusetts Federalists, Lincoln made a pilgrimage to Adams in Philadelphia to attempt conciliation of all factions prior to the presidential canvass. Stephen Higginson, mistrusting the collector's motives, alleged that Lincoln "will play cunning, but will join in anything to get rid of Hamilton." Through all of the many changes in political fortune during the decade, including the rise and demise of Alexander Hamilton, the increasing schism in both Massachusetts and national Federalist circles between Adams men and the high Federalists, and even including the trauma caused by Jefferson's victory in 1800, Lincoln retained a public reputation for moderation, independence of mind, and integrity. In short, in the eyes of the Massachusetts public, he was a man "above all party politics." This in the face of the fact that most of his subordinates in the customshouse were, by Lincoln's own admission, involved Federalists.[7]

Thomas Jefferson, nevertheless, was reluctant to remove this major figure who always kept a token handful of Republicans in his customshouse, providing a thin leavening of bipartisanship. So an accommodation was worked out in 1802 which permitted Lincoln to keep his office. In return, the incumbent promised Jefferson he would grant subordinate positions to Republicans as the posts became vacant, and repress the more obvious Federalist activities of the zealous lower ranks in the service. Lincoln also publicly acknowledged his past political errors. Predictably, Boston Republicans were not convinced by Lincoln's forced mea culpa of 1802: "I have never attempted to controul your political creed," Lincoln announced to his subordinates, "or influence any of your votes in the choice of officers at any of our public meetings." He promptly negated the inference that his customshouse sheltered no political creed, however, when he added: "If any of you [customs employees] . . . villified the Chief Magistrate of the Union [Jefferson] in terms rude and indecent . . . I have to ask that you will in future recollect that there is an infinite difference between Right and propriety of exercising that Right." He would, he said candidly, no longer be able to protect the positions of active Federalists in the public employ.[8]

The heaviest commercial concentration outside of Boston centered on the sprawling coastline of Essex County in the northeastern reaches of the commonwealth. Here the "codfish aristocracy" presided over mercantile, fishing, and shipbuilding interests, and here the Essex Junto both ruled the county's politics and exerted enormous influence over the rest of the commonwealth. Eleven customs officers and forty subordinates served the six closely concentrated ports of entry. Essex County constituted a virtually urban area and housed a fascinating and complex eighteenth-century society. The ports of Salem, Beverly, Marblehead, Gloucester, Ipswich, and Newburyport, moreover, drew on miniature hinterlands and together formed very much a common sea-oriented economy. It was the unusually heavy concentration of commerce, and thus of customs facilities, that after 1789 helped not only to invigorate an emergent Federalist party but also to revitalize the authority of the county's ruling junto.

Was there an Essex Junto operative in the Federalist decade? David H. Fischer makes a good case for the negative. It may well be that the junto's influence in greater Massachusetts had slipped badly by the 1790s, but there are strong indications that on its own turf in Essex County at least, its grip on local affairs was as strong as ever. Timothy Pickering's 1797 claim that "he had never heard the term" Essex Junto before is not credible. Certainly the local Jeffersonians had.

Essex Republican leader Henry Warren virtually demanded of Thomas Jefferson in 1802 that he remove Salem Customs Collector Joseph Hiller "for being in league with the Essex Junto." Perhaps Warren was engaging in polemics to dramatize his case, but in light of other evidence that is not likely. All eleven Essex County customs officers subject to presidential appointment in 1789 were named in conformity to specific junto desires. In a remarkable display of political engineering, Essex County Congressman Benjamin Goodhue, a central figure among the Essexmen, sent the newly inaugurated first president a list of eleven Federalists to fill every higher customs office in the six Essex ports, and Washington named them all. Not only had Goodhue made clear that he was speaking for a consensus of Essex Federalist leaders, but his perfect eleven for eleven was a feat rarely duplicated in other places in the nation. Congressmen, senators, governors, Federalist managers of various grades in the nation for the most part were content if one-half to three-quarters of their recommendations were placed in nomination by George Washington.

Fischer makes the telling point that in 1788 the Essexmen were unsuccessful in attempting to name a United States senator for Massachusetts. But collectively a year later they dictated the choices to fill the customs appointments in the county. Moreover, as Fischer himself points out, the junto was successful in 1790 in naming George Cabot, one of their own, to fill another United States Senate vacancy. Nor had the situation changed by mid-decade. Congressman Goodhue and Senator George Cabot wrote Secretary of the Treasury Oliver Wolcott, Jr., in 1795 "recommending" William Tuck as the new customs collector at Gloucester. This was not in itself unusual; what was different about this recommendation was its imperious tone. "I will thank you to have it [the appointment] soon accomplished," Goodhue wrote Wolcott. "Please to notify me of it as soon as possible that I may communicate it to him." The secretary and presumably the president complied, and Tuck was named, informed not by presidential communication but by word from the congressman. Perhaps it is possible to read too much into the form of address, but the supreme confidence of the communication does not leave much room for doubt that Cabot, Goodhue, and other influential Essexmen fully anticipated that their wishes would be complied with.

Certainly New England Republicans always ranked the junto high on their scale of evils. In the midst of the presidential campaign of 1800, for example, a New England newspaper queried: "Americans, do you wish to . . . resign your rights, suffer an ESSEX JUNTO to dispose of your property and engross the places and emoluments of the state . . . ?" Another Republican sheet at the same time claimed the junto was responsible for the "wretched situation" of Massachusetts politics. It is at least debatable then, whether or not a junto existed in the Federalist era. It is incorrect to conclude that "the myth had been invented" to suit Republican needs. At least the germ of reality existed to justify the "myth." In any event, even if the junto existed only in the minds of Republicans, this had the impact of imposing it as a reality on Massachusetts politics in the 1790s.[9]

If there was some doubt about the contemporary term Essex Junto, there was no doubt about what the "codfish aristocracy" was all about. It conjured up a late eighteenth-century vision of a commanding economic gentry centered on Salem. Paired with neighboring Beverly, where only a surveyor of customs was stationed, Salem was designated a major port of entry by the United States Treasury Department and was allocated a full complement of officers and subordinate federal employees. Joseph Hiller, one of the most politically talented of Essexmen, presided there as collector. In one way he did not fit the stereotype of the typical juntoman in that he was not at all adverse to politicking openly. In fact, if the junto could be said to have had an executive administrator, it probably was Hiller. Among his twenty appointees in two ports, there was not a single Jeffersonian. The customs posts were held by local Federalist party men who looked to Hiller for direction.

The collector had settled in Salem around the time of the Revolution. A major in the local militia during the war, he inherited some money and became prominent in Salem in the years following the Revolution. Hiller, according to Stephen Higginson, possessed "integrity, accuracy and [a] faculty of exerting rigidly the duties of his office without giving offence." His political activities, however, gave a great deal of offense. Jacob Crowninshield reported in 1801 that Hiller was the chief financial supporter and political contributor to "an abusive federal gazette in this town [the Salem

Figure 1. Two eighteenth-century coasting vessels.

Figure 2. Crowninshield's wharf, Salem port, in 1798.

Gazette] which is continually and systematically engaged in the work of slander and defamation" against the Republicans generally and Crowninshield in particular. Branding Hiller "a decided Federalist," Jefferson removed him in 1802. Hiller claimed at the time that he resigned, but Albert Gallatin noted decisively in his government file that he "was certainly removed." [10]

The other Salem customs officers were also party men. William Pickman, the naval officer, and Bartholemew Putnam, the surveyor of customs, were both important local Federalists. Pickman, according to Congressman Goodhue, was from "one of the best families in the Town"—tainted, however, by its loyalism during the Revolution. The naval officer's father had made the family fortune before the war, and the clan's allegiance to the Loyalist cause seemed not to have disturbed either its wealth or social position. William, a merchant and shipowner, helped to ease the stigma of an English association when, late in the war, he publicly recanted his loyalism and permitted a vessel he owned to enter the lists as an American privateer. By the mid-1780s Pickman was a member of the Massachusetts legislature, maturing into an important figure in the Federalist cause in Essex County. His political leverage derived from his leadership of a close-knit political clan. "He is decidedly opposed to the [Republican] government," a local Jeffersonian reported in 1802, "and all his near relations and friends (particularly those bearing the same name) are most violently hostile to Mr. Jefferson." [11]

The third officer at Salem port was Surveyor Bartholemew Putnam. Older than Hiller and Pickman, Putnam prior to the Revolution was first a ship's officer and finally a ship's master. By the time war broke out, Putnam owned a vessel of his own and was active both in the local militia and as a privateer operating out of Salem. Related by marriage to Timothy Pickering, he like Pickman presided over an extended Federalist family in the town. Both Pickman and Putnam were assailed by local Jeffersonians for their political activities in the 1790s; both men, it is clear, aided the collector in exerting pressure on subordinates in the customshouse to campaign for the Federalist party. [12]

The Newburyport customshouse, north of Salem, was eventually molded into a Federalist enclave. As such, it helped to neutralize politically a marginally Republican town.[13] In 1789, however, the Essex Federalist leadership made a bad mistake when it designated Stephen Cross the collector of customs at Newburyport. Cross, like most of his townsmen, favored ratification of the Constitution, but when strong support for an emerging Jeffersonian interest materialized in the town thereafter, Cross and his family found their way into the Republican camp. Given the local independence, visibility, and patronage of the post, local Federalists concluded that Cross had to go.

Stephen Cross was a member of a well-to-do and highly respected Newburyport family. He and his brother were the third generation to operate a family shipbuilding business. Stephen had served in several local offices and on the local Committee of Correspondence prior to and during the Revolution. His firm built two frigates for the Continental Congress during the war. During the Confederation period and for many years afterward, Cross was a member of the Massachusetts legislature. In 1783, moreover, he was named collector of customs at Newburyport by the commonwealth of Massachusetts, a post he retained at the behest of the junto after ratification. George Cabot remarked in 1802 that Essex Federalists personally held him in high esteem in spite of his politics.

Thus his removal for "misconduct" from the customs post in 1792 by Alexander Hamilton and George Washington is suspect. Cross, who Jefferson returned to office in 1802, claimed he had been dismissed for political reasons. Repeated requests from Cross to Hamilton for the specific instances of his misconduct were never satisfactorily answered by the secretary. He was told only that he was guilty of obtaining larger customs fees than the law allowed, but neither explanation nor details of this allegation ever followed. A demand by Cross, finally, for a real investigation into the nature of his misconduct was also turned down, and he was neither prosecuted nor sued for recovery of public monies or violations of federal law. Cross himself claimed that he "gave

Satisfaction to all [in the office] until Mr. Hamilton had got his plan in some forwardness, in concert with those of the Essex Junto in this town, and they supposing me to have considerable influence and finding me a stubborn Republican and what little influence I had would be improved against them, thought it necessary to destroy it by obtaining my removal and disgrace." The collector believed he was removed for political reasons only, and wrote Jefferson that he was a victim of Federalist persecution, a conclusion with which Jefferson agreed.[14]

The first act of Edward Wigglesworth, the new collector in 1792, was to dismiss Ralph Cross, Stephen's Republican brother who was a weigher and gauger of customs. Coincidently, Ralph at the time of his removal was "discovered to connive at smuggling or practising deceit in the weight or measure of dutied goods," according to George Cabot. Besides, he was a man "much below Stephen in reputation; indeed his truth or integrity would be very little trusted in the part of the country where he lives."

There was an irony in all this. Stephen Cross's Federalist successor, Edward Wigglesworth, was accused of "poor arithmetick" in customshouse higher mathematics in 1795 and had to be removed himself. Wigglesworth immediately declared bankruptcy and thus avoided federal prosecution for recovery of allegedly embezzled customs receipts. No effort was made to invoke existing debtor laws either, and Wigglesworth, in fact, soon picked up a revolutionary pension.

At the time of his appointment, Wigglesworth certainly seemed a good bet. In addition to his credentials as a Federalist, he was a Harvard graduate, the son of a Puritan clergyman, and a member of an old Newburyport family. Politically he was active in the Cincinnati, a firm supporter of ratification, and a close associate of Massachusetts Federalist leader Jonathan Jackson. Wigglesworth, moreover, had been an active patriot prior to the Revolution and had served as a colonel in the Continental army through most of the war. In short, though his pedigree was impeccable, his management of the customshouse proved intolerable. In 1795, Essex

Federalists finally got a customs collector they could live with in the person of Dudley Tyng.[15]

A lawyer by profession, Tyng was active in the local Presbyterian church and related by marriage to United States District Court Judge John Lowell, an important Federalist. After the protracted difficulties at the Newburyport customshouse, first with a Jeffersonian, then with an incompetent at the helm, Tyng was selected with great care. Stephen Higginson was charged with gaining a firm political commitment from Tyng, and was subsequently able to report to Senator George Cabot that the candidate acknowledged his "obligation for this attention to him." Cabot in turn pressed the nomination on the national administration—a nomination that clearly derived from a junto alive and well in Newburyport, if Higginson's involvement had any meaning—and Tyng was appointed. Higginson's prediction to Cabot that Tyng "will certainly prove a most valuable acquisition" was borne out by the collector's extended political involvement in customshouse politics. He was among those early marked for removal in Jefferson's first term because of his "hostility to Republican principles." [16]

An important stabilizing factor for the Federalist party in the town was the fact that the second and third officers of the customshouse, Jonathan Titcomb the naval officer and Michael Hodge the surveyor, were both good party men. Titcomb was part of an elite family. He had served as a colonel in the Continental army, and after the war was a general in the Massachusetts militia and a member of the state legislature. The naval officer had been elected as a Federalist to the Massachusetts Ratifying Convention in 1788 and was active in other ways in support of the Constitutional movement. He continued to be politically involved in Newburyport during the Federalist decade.[17]

Michael Hodge also derived from a prominent family. He was a merchant before and during the Revolution. Although he remained precariously in business after the war, Hodge was clearly affected by the economic uncertainties of the Confederation. Consequently, the customs post, gained both by the intercession of his cousin United States Senator Tris-

tram Dalton and the support of the Essex Junto, clearly provided welcome financial relief in 1789. He repaid his friends
with remarkable political energy, remaining consistently and
emphatically for the next decade a man of "pure public principles." Even Hodge's friends complained that he was "a
morose, unpleasant man in the office," but no Federalist
could fault his political efforts. He was described later as "a
high party man, generally very active in all the elections, and
using his influence against the republicans." Especially visible during the prolonged difficulties surrounding the collector's post at Newburyport, Hodge filled what otherwise
might have been a dangerous political void for the junto.
"Mr. Hodge is an open enemy to Mr. Jefferson," wrote one
Republican seeking his removal; he "is very violent in opposition," wrote another, "and keeps no bounds in his conduct." Perhaps because he was an old man in 1801 and not
the first officer in the port, Jefferson did not remove him. He
stayed on, an unreconstructed Federalist in one of the few
Republican ports in New England, until 1809 when he resigned in protest against the embargo.[18]

The Maine plantations, like Newburyport, generally
aligned with the Republicans. Sparsely settled and restive
under Massachusetts rule, Maine's settlers drifted into Republican ranks after ratification, although there were reser-
voirs of Federalist strength, especially in some of the larger
Maine ports. The national administration made a special effort to pass on key customs posts to local Federalists.

This was the case, for example, in the small Republican
port at York. The first collector was moderate Federalist
Richard Trevett, who occupied the office until his death in
1793. Trevett, a seaman before the Revolution, was an incumbent customs officer under the state dating back to the
first years of the Confederation. He had been an active patriot, serving on his local Committee of Correspondence prior
to the Revolution and commanding a privateer during the
war. He was frank to describe his post as a "sinecure," and a
local historian aptly characterized the federal customs job as
a "snug harbor for local politicians."[19]

Joseph Tucker assumed Trevett's office in 1793. Tucker, like his predecessor, clearly derived from a middling family. He was a fisherman at the time of his appointment, operating his own modest boat out of York. He clearly held a high place, Federalist though he was, in the affections and trust of his Republican townsmen. An enlisted man in the Continental army, Tucker had been wounded at Bemis Heights. On his recovery he was breveted a lieutenant and given the relatively inactive berth of paymaster of a Massachusetts brigade. At the time of his federal appointment, he represented his district in the Massachusetts General Court (the legislature). From 1795 onward, moreover, he was elected annually the York town clerk. Tucker, finally, was active in the Massachusetts chapter of the Society of the Cincinnati. The evidence indicates that his personal stature and leadership were the key factors behind both the small Federalist organization and the survival of a vigorous Federalist minority in the community and surrounding hinterland.[20]

Another port of entry was established in 1800, twenty miles up the coast at Kennebunk. Unlike York, Kennebunk was a Federalist town. Jonas Clark, a rather unsuccessful storekeeper, was given the office. Financial difficulties apart, he had a great deal going for him. His daughter was married to highly placed Massachusetts Federalist Nathan Dane's son, and Clark himself had a decade-long record of Federalist activity behind him at the time of his appointment. Clark had been the prime mover in convening a town meeting to acclaim the still controversial Jay Treaty in 1796. Two years later he was one of a committee that called another meeting, this one to endorse Adams's foreign policies and in particular to denounce Americans who were partial to France. A local Republican described Clark as "a man who is systematically opposed to a republican government and who has zealously exerted his abilities to oppose it." At a July 4 celebration after Jefferson's inauguration the collector, perhaps anticipating his own fate, toasted: "John Adams, the ex President—when vice prevails and imperious men bear sway the post of honour is the private station." Clark, his political enemies noted, was "dangerous to the political rights of such a free government" and he was indeed consigned to his "post of honour." [21]

Portland was far and away the largest port serving the Maine plantations. If there was an urban center in Maine, it was Portland, which formed the hub of Federalist party activity for the entire Maine district. The port itself was increasingly active, with tonnage increasing steadily each year. The customshouse employed only seven in 1792, but by the end of the decade that total had more than trebled to twenty-three. The collector's income doubled in the same period, from $545 in 1792 to $1,139 in 1801.

Nathaniel Fosdick was the man who both presided over this growth and skimmed off the increasing emoluments of office. Under thirty at the time of his appointment in 1789 and a native of Salem, he had pursued a not very successful career as a merchant after his graduation from Harvard in 1779. Described as a "high-toned Federalist," he was extremely active in local politics and was well thought of as a customs officer, even by his opponents. However, Fosdick was an acknowledged leader of the Federalist interest in the town, and one who exploited his position to the utmost. At political meetings "Mr. Fosdick was often a leader in the debate, and was the most vociferous in his personal invectives" against Republicans. A Republican army officer stationed at Portland alleged, just prior to the collector's removal in 1803, that, after Jefferson's election had been verified, Fosdick had attempted to incite the American troops at Portland to mutiny. Clearly an exaggeration, it is, nevertheless, an indicator of the deep local political feelings Fosdick aroused. The office has "not only made him rich," another opponent said, "but very impudent and bold in his unqualified opposition" to anything Republican.

Fosdick's supporters pointed out that he was a good collector, that only his "political character and conduct have been arraigned," and that after Jefferson's inauguration he acted "with perfect decency, prudence and respect." Nevertheless, Levi Lincoln of Massachusetts, Jefferson's attorney general, singled out Fosdick as one of the most blatantly political of the Massachusetts collectors, a signal honor in a state in which the customs service was so party oriented. Friends of the collector wrote Jefferson, on the one hand pleading with the president that Fosdick was actually in very modest circumstances and needed the post to support his large family, and on the other hand demanding for him "the right of every man to meet his accusers face to face." Nothing helped; Fosdick was removed and departed Portland to resettle in Salem.[22]

The subordinate positions in the Massachusetts customshouses were filled mostly by middle-class Federalists. This characteristic of the less visible, lower federal service contrasted sharply with the generally elite composition of the higher civil service. Social and economic distinctions apart, however, the tidewaiters were as deeply committed to the Federalist party as were their superiors in the federal establishment. The political involvement of federal employees of the customshouses at New Bedford and Plymouth provides examples in depth.

Edward Pope's subordinates in the New Bedford customshouse, according to one townsman, "continued to be very mischievous" during the Federalist decade. "All the subordinate offices have been filled with men decidedly and avowedly" Federalist, claimed this spokesman for the town's Republican minority. Even allowing for exaggeration, control of the inferior offices "gives them an additional influence to effect their designs." And contrary to traditional views of Federalist politicking, these designs were sometimes of a most sophisticated nature. Robert Earl, an inspector of customs at New Bedford from 1789 through 1801, annually denounced Jefferson in particular and the Republican party in general at the New Bedford town meetings. At the election of 1800, Earl "took his stand by the side of one of the Select men who stood up to receive the Votes as they were put into the hat, and made use of every Indecent expression he could think of to those he found put in a Vote on the Republican side." Robert Earl was not alone in his efforts. William Tobey, both an inspector of customs and the New Bedford postmaster, was described as an "extreme party man," one of several customs employees so singled out.[23]

William Watson also chose his subordinates in the Plymouth customshouse with an eye to political impact. His tidewaiters were at different times accused of mismanagement, delinquency, and misconduct, but the main thrust of Republican strictures involved their politicking. The collector's first order of business in 1789 was to designate Ephraim Spooner, his newly bankrupt former partner, as the port's gauger of customs. Spooner, a tanner by trade, derived from a Plymouth family that, though of long standing, was far from affluent and significantly less notable than were the Watsons.

Another Federalist appointee, William Goodwin, started out as an inspector of customs in 1789, and became the local postmaster and collector of the internal revenue as well in the next few years. He clearly earned his offices, for Goodwin early replaced Spooner as Watson's political right hand. "The post officer" in Plymouth, Republican Henry Warren complained, "creates an influence here which is impossible to counteract." Goodwin, also the local bank cashier, was a key figure in that "inveterate junto in this county which would long since have been extinct but for the influence of federal officers here." He too was the son of an original Pilgrim family. Like Spooner, Goodwin served as a selectman but, unlike the gauger of customs, he owned extensive property in town.

A third member of the local Federalist leadership was Thomas Matthews, an inspector of customs. Politically well placed as the local innkeeper on the town square, he was one of the few immigrants who became privy to local Federalist management in the Bay State. He had been born in England in 1725 and had settled in Plymouth by 1764. Although clearly not a placeman, Matthews's family credentials were less important to the Federalists than the fact that, in an age when taverns were the equivalent of local political clubhouses, his inn was home to Plymouth's Federalist party men.

These men worked hard at their politics. "They are all open and undisguised in their hostility to the present administration and their measures," Henry Warren wrote President Thomas Jefferson in 1802. "During the imperious circumstances of the last [Adams] administration," Warren claimed, the group repeatedly interfered in elections; in particular, polls for "a member of Congress was altogether affected by their untoward influence." A complaint frequently aired in Plymouth was that Watson's underlings were "dupe[s] to party" and favored Federalist merchants in the area; the latter, it was claimed, enjoyed an "officious servility" in their dealings with the Plymouth customshouse. Such charges provided excuse enough for Jefferson to clean out the entire Federalist cadre simply by removing Watson and appointing a Republican in his place. Watson's Plymouth Junto was from 1789 an effective local example of a professionally rooted Federalist party leadership that, closely tied to the local elite, nevertheless cut deeply and fully into the economic and social spectrum of town life.[24]

One traditional characteristic of officeholding survived the marriage of national party identification to local politics, and that was the perpetual bane of any system of public employment—nepotism. When family was involved, inferior appointments clearly cut across political as well as socioeconomic lines, as the experiences of the Portland and Newburyport customshouses illustrate. The subordinate spots in the Portland customshouse were berths of kinsmen of important Maine Federalists. Among the inspectors of customs were Collector Nathaniel Fosdick's brother Thomas, and William Hobby, a brother of John Hobby, the United States attorney for the Maine district and a notable Portland Federalist. Stephen Waite, the weigher of customs, was a brother of Thomas B. Waite, printer of the Federalist Portland *Eastern Herald and Gazette of Maine*.[25]

In Newburyport, one Republican who was not removed was Customs Inspector William Titcomb, Naval Officer Jonathan Titcomb's brother. The former was as unreconstructed and active a Jeffersonian as his brother was a Federalist. Described as "unfriendly" to the Washington administration, he had a long history of antifederalism in the 1780s. The Newburyport customshouse also sheltered Weigher John Tracy, a brother-in-law of Federalist United

States Marshal Jonathan Jackson and a relative also of United States District Court Judge John Lowell. By 1789 Tracy, himself a member of the gentry, had gone bankrupt, his counting house a victim of the economic vagaries of the Confederation years. His subordinate customs post was augmented by a paying state militia appointment. Reduced circumstances did not much hinder his commitment to the Federalist cause.[26]

Tracy's lineage was for the most part the exception and not the rule for inferior appointments in Massachusetts, if the customshouses of major ports of entry at Boston and Salem are representative. Examination of published sources for both ports in the 1790s reveals that a majority of those who could be identified were clearly middle class rather than gentry. As indicated earlier for both places, virtually all tidewaiters were Federalists before 1801.

Benjamin Lincoln's lower customs establishment suggested a healthy range of urban Federalist leadership that penetrated Boston's middle class of skilled artisans, mechanics, and tradesmen. Of the eleven (of about forty-five) Federalists in subordinate customs posts in Boston about whom biographical information was uncovered, only three could be described as gentry. Two of these latter, Ebenezer Storer and William Shattuck, customs inspector and weigher respectively, were merchants much reduced in circumstances. Nevertheless, as of 1798, Storer owned a house valued at $10,000 and Shattuck owned one assessed at $6,000, so both men still possessed significant resources as well as status at the end of the decade. The third, Thomas Kettel, lived in Charlestown, where he both owned property and was a deacon of the most fashionable Presbyterian church. Of the eight identifiable cadremen who were of middling stature in the Boston community, four had been junior officers in the Continental army. Most of the eight were inspectors, measurers, weighers, or gaugers who were able to pursue their trades as well. Five of the eight were listed in the *Boston Directory* as having other occupations: Joseph Pico and Joseph Spear were coopers, Peter Dolliver kept a small shop, Hezekiah Welch was a shipwright, and Benjamin Eaton was a distiller. Middle-class status was also confirmed either by property holdings or the absence of any. Benjamin Eaton, the Federalist distiller, owned one-third of a house in which he resided with other families and which was valued as a whole at $1,000 in 1798. John F. Barber and John Popkins, both of whose occupations are unknown, owned houses in which they lived valued at $1,100 and $500 respectively; both houses were in an unfashionable area of the city. The others probably rented inasmuch as they were not listed as owning any real estate in Boston or adjacent communities in a fairly comprehensive 1798 survey.[27]

In Salem as in Boston, most of the inferior positions were staffed by men of materially lower social status than the customs officers. Of the twenty customshouse employees who were inspectors, weighers, gaugers, or measurers, information about seven could be uncovered from published sources. Five of the seven belonged to the East Church, a distinctly middling Congregational parish, and not to one of the fashionable upper-class parishes in the city. Of these, John Berry, Thomas Dean, Andrew Preston, and Stephen Webb were (or had been) sailors. Given the slack periods common to customs business, some or all of these men may well have remained occasionally active seamen in the coasting or fishing trades even while in government employ. The fifth member of the East Church was John Webb, a shoemaker in the town. The other two subordinates who could be identified were Samuel Ropes and his brother David, representatives of an important local family whose fortune antedated the Revolution.[28]

Massachusetts, of course, was the most commerce-intensive state in the United States, so it housed a disproportionate part of the customs service. The Federalist leadership in the Bay State early on recognized its potential value to the party cause. Thus the commonwealth's customshouses became vehicles useful to the party as it developed a management structure that both assimilated the Federalist leadership within the gentry of the port towns, and penetrated deeply into the middle class as well. This organizational pattern was emulated in other New England states in the Federalist decade, as town politics in Portsmouth, Providence, and New London demonstrate.

CHAPTER THREE

Customs: Three New England Towns

Fifteen ports of entry were established in the New England states outside Massachusetts, and the customshouses in almost all of these were staffed by Federalists. Diverse political styles developed in greater New England, influenced strongly, as the examples of three of these towns demonstrate, by the nature of political formations and leadership components in the respective states of the region. Thus the local Federalist parties in Portsmouth, New Hampshire, Providence, Rhode Island, and New London, Connecticut, encountering different political challenges as they did, responded in relatively unique ways. Local Federalist parties in these tidewater towns shared a common feature, however; the nucleus of party operations in each revolved around the local customs service.

Political sentiment in the Portsmouth customshouse shifted steadily toward the Jeffersonians after ratification of the Jay Treaty in 1795, reflecting the political drift of both Customs Collector Joseph Whipple and United States Senator John Langdon. By the time John Adams became president, therefore, he faced a wholesale political rebellion in New Hampshire's only port. The story of how the Federalist state leadership at Exeter and the national leaders in Philadelphia handled the Portsmouth uprising reveals much about the ideology of the governing party, its iron will, political sophistication, and its sometimes ruthless professionalism.

Rhode Island was an exceptional state in many ways. Its politics in the Federalist decade remained faithful to the subterranean tradition of political management and ideological infighting that had characterized its colonial and Confederation history. This smallest of New England states had been a vigorous holdout against ratification. When Rhode Island was finally forced to accede to the reality of Union under the Constitution in 1790, its small, well-organized Federalist party faced an uphill fight. Local political efforts, however, as the Providence example demonstrates, were strongly supported by the Federalist administration in Philadelphia, which paid special attention to the task of "saving" Rhode Island politically.

In totally Federalist Connecticut, it was much easier for the Congregational Federalist establishment to operate without a significant challenge from the Republican minority. A sophisticated state leadership easily suppressed most political deviation. This was the pattern at the state level, and it was emulated locally in the port town of New London, where Customs Collector Jedediah Huntington presided over the local Federalist party.

Most Federalists in New Hampshire looked for leadership to a faction identified with the Exeter region and led by long-time Governor John T. Gilman, his family, and associates. Jeremiah Smith, the Livermores, and for a time the Wentworths were all connected with this elitist political fountainhead. Forced by the growing strength, appeal, and unity of the Portsmouth Republican party to compete at the polls, the conservatives after 1795 themselves developed a sophisticated party organization. Patronage aplenty, both from federal sources and the Bank of New Hampshire, lubricated the New Hampshire Federalist machine. Like its Connecticut counterpart, New Hampshire Federalist management was closely tied to the Congregational establishment. A recent study of New Hampshire's Federalists concluded that

"Gilman's supporters controlled the pulpit and the press—
the two media of New Hampshire politics." [1]

The Portsmouth customshouse, with a full complement of
Federalist officers and subordinates, was a component of the
state's Federalist establishment in the early 1790s. However,
personal animosities, the divisive impact of Jay's Treaty, and
above all the effective transitional leadership of Senator John
Langdon as he moved into the Jeffersonian camp at mid-
decade, changed all that. This combination of issues, per-
sonalities, and magnetic leadership moved virtually the entire Portsmouth customshouse out of the Federalist party between 1794 and 1798, and in turn precipitated a Federalist
reprisal in the latter year. At the instigation of Exeter
Federalists, four federal officers, three of them high customs
officials, were turned out of office by John Adams for engaging in opposition party activities. Virtually all the subordinate customs employees, more than twenty of them, quickly
went the way of their Republican superiors, and were also
turned out in 1798. The customshouse was subsequently re-
shaped to conform to New Hampshire Federalist party requirements. The episode was, in its detail, a classic if extreme example of the emotional impact of ideological two-
party politics on an early American community.

Federalist Joseph Whipple was named by Washington the
first federal collector of customs at Portsmouth. He had been
a firm and important supporter of constitutional reform in a
divided state. As late as 1792 the collector reiterated to Alexander Hamilton his "peculiar Satisfaction with . . . the effects of the Federal Government," adding that its salutary
impact "has been amply verified in the administration of the
department under which I act." Although the first secretary
of the treasury occasionally chided Whipple for his laxity in
enforcing the customs laws, by and large he extended to the
collector a discretionary local authority that was characteristic of Hamiltonian administration. Like all collectors, Whipple named his own subordinates, virtually free of any dictates
from Philadelphia. This was generally true so long as the
collector's appointments were made with an eye to their
Federalist allegiance. When Congress authorized a revenue

cutter to operate out of Portsmouth in 1790, for example, Whipple nominated its officers to the secretary, who subsequently routinely approved them and passed the names on to the president for appointment. "Those mentioned for master and first mate," the collector wrote his superior, "have many years commanded Ships and are on account of their federal Sentiments and attachments to government . . . in my opinion the best qualified of any persons in this quarter for the places to which they are respectively named." [2]

But by 1794 or 1795 Whipple's political views had changed. Always close to United States Senator John Langdon who, judging by the converts he made at Portsmouth, must have been a persuasive and magnetic figure, Whipple's politics drifted in tandem with the senator's. And as Whipple went, so in turn went his customshouse confreres, with only a few exceptions. Langdon openly broke with the Federalist party over Jay's Treaty. The political impact of both the treaty and Langdon's defection was felt locally; Whipple and most of the customshouse, as well as many other Portsmouth public men, followed Langdon into the Republican party. The senator had early in the 1790s warmly supported most of Hamilton's economic program, and had been favored in turn with the secretary's patronage. But by the end of 1794, Senator Langdon's politics were suspect to William Plumer, an increasingly important figure in the state's dominant Federalist party. Jeremiah Smith, of whom more will be said shortly, also doubted Langdon's party loyalty, and actively but unsuccessfully opposed Langdon's re-election to the United States Senate earlier in that same year. Langdon's open defection from Federalist ranks only occurred after his new six-year term had been assured, however. Only then did he lead his Portsmouth following out of the Federalist camp. [3]

Whipple after 1794 engineered almost a total conversion of the customshouse. Inasmuch as the original appointees to subordinate posts after 1789 were mostly Federalists, and since Whipple's Federalist successor in 1798 replaced twenty of twenty-three of those subordinates, we can assume that between 1795 and 1798 Whipple either politically con-

verted his underlings or replaced them with men of Jeffersonian leanings. At any rate, it was not very long before Exeter
Federalists saw the Portsmouth customshouse as a Trojan
horse in its midst. And certainly Joseph Whipple emerged as
Odysseus in the prolonged local political crisis that spanned
the years 1794–1801.

As strongly Federalist as he had been prior to 1794—that
was how zealously Republican Whipple became by 1798.
The Jay Treaty affected him deeply. "The collector observes
to merchants who complain of bad Voyages or bad Times,"
Federalist United States Attorney for New Hampshire
Jeremiah Smith complained in 1798, "that all these things
flow from the cursed British Treaty." Certainly by the middle
of 1795 there were several visible defections from Federalist
ranks in the customshouse and elsewhere in Portsmouth. "Is
it not singular," William Plumer wrote at the height of
American reaction to Jay's Treaty, "that there appeared more
men of levelling principles, real democrats, in Portsmouth,
than in all the rest of the State. But what is more extraordinary, the leading characters of this party, in that town, are
men who hold important offices under the federal
government—the very government they wish to destroy."
Among the culprits were Whipple, William Gardner, the
United States commissioner of loans for New Hampshire and
an officer who worked closely with customshouse personnel,
and two other customs officers, Hopley Yeaton, the captain of
the Portsmouth revenue cutter, and Eleazer Russell, naval
officer of customs.[4] These officials were all removed in 1798,
along with almost all the subordinates in the federal customs
service.

The moving force behind Adams's 1798 Portsmouth removals was Jeremiah Smith. An important figure in the
state's Federalist leadership cadre and an uncompromising
and sophisticated party manager, Smith served in Congress
from 1791 until 1797. In part at Governor Gilman's behest,
Smith resigned his seat in the summer of 1797 to accept a
presidential appointment as United States attorney for New
Hampshire. His return to full-time local politics helped to
tighten the state's Exeter-based Federalist organization. The

Federalists in New Hampshire came to recognize clearly by 1797 the developing threat posed by the defections of Langdon and the Portsmouth federal officers. Senator Langdon's followers, making good use of their federal positions and the popular local animosity toward the Jay Treaty, by 1797 controlled politics in Portsmouth, the state's largest city; they were making inroads elsewhere in New Hampshire as well.[5]

Smith didn't like what he saw and decided to bring the deteriorating Portsmouth political situation to the attention of the Adams administration as a first step in restoring Federalist control to the vital port area. With the advent of the Adams presidency, Smith joined Gilman as a primary force in Federalist circles in the state. After becoming United States attorney, according to his ancient biography, Smith "was consulted by the secretary of the Treasury, Mr. Wolcott, in respect to appointments in New Hampshire." Smith held strong views on patronage. He felt that the national administration was "in duty bound to appoint and continue in office, those men, and those men only, who are firmly attached to the principles of our government and the administration." Moreover, "a public officer should be removed, unless he took an active part in support of the administration." [6]

The new federal attorney acted on these premises in 1798. Smith had been needled by Fisher Ames, an old friend and colleague who, on reading of the notorious Republicanism of the Portsmouth customshouse in the Boston *Centinel*, wrote Smith expressing the "hope" that "New Hampshire keeps all its federal fires alive." [7] Within a few weeks of this prodding, Smith set about to cure the spreading Republican infection in Portsmouth. His opportunity came when Secretary of the Treasury Oliver Wolcott, Jr., sent the United States attorney a routine inquiry about the credentials of a nominee for a federal office. Smith responded with two long tirades virtually demanding that Portsmouth be swept clean of its federal officers.

A carefully orchestrated campaign to win over the secretary of the treasury and the president followed, with Whipple emerging as the main target and Yeaton, Gardner, and Russell inevitable subsidiary marks. "I can say in general terms," Smith wrote in June 1798, "that it has been a great mortification to the Friends of Government in this quarter to see the federal offices filled by the enemies of the Government. If it is true that men forfeit all claim to the protection of Government the moment they become inimical to its interests it must be equally true that they have no claim to the confidence or Bounty of Government." To gloss over a lack of hard evidence on the specific political activities of some intended victims, Smith added that "even the doubtfuls should be considered as unqualified in offices of confidence or profit." Admitting that the officers in question were "faithful and punctual in the discharge of their duties" and "free from debts and speculations," nevertheless they were also "Violent Jacobins" who "have spared no opportunity of exciting opposition to the Government and have used their official consequence and situation for that purpose." The federal officers at Portsmouth, Smith summed up, were "partizans of France and it would give me a great deal of pleasure to see them *rewarded* with offices under the latter." [8]

At the same time William Plumer, speaker of the state house of representatives, addressed a much more temperate but no less damning indictment to the secretary, alluding to the same story in the Boston *Centinel* to which Fisher Ames had referred. The *Centinel* article had described the Portsmouth customshouse as a hotbed of Jacobinism, a story that may well have been planted by Smith and Plumer to begin with, given the removal campaign that followed hard on its appearance. Plumer verified the essential truth of the article in elaborating that "Mr. Whipple is the most cautious and guarded in his opposition against the government, but tis a fact that democrats are his associates and companions." Smith had sounded the same note; Whipple was "cunning and cautious" but a "violent Jacobin" who used his "official consequence and situation" to "excite opposition to the government."

A week later Whipple was grossly slandered by Eliphalet Ladd, a Portsmouth merchant who sent Wolcott a perfectly timed letter vilifying the collector most outrageously. He expressed doubt that the government had ever received much of the customs revenue Whipple collected. No proof was offered nor was this allegation explained further. Ladd instead moved on to the main point. The Federalist merchant inquired "how it happens that a Man of his [Whipple's] Character, especially his political Character, should remain so long in the most lucrative office in the State." It was, he believed, "a wonder to *every* Merchant here, for I suppose every one esteems him one of the most inveterate Jackobins in the United States." [9] United States Commissioner of Loans Gardner and Revenue Cutter Captain Yeaton, meanwhile, were subjects of similar tirades.

William Gardner, unlike Whipple, was "open and decided" in his Republican leanings. He, like Whipple, however, had started out as an active supporter of the Constitution and later was a staunch Hamiltonian Federalist. But from 1795 onward, his politics had changed. "I have repeatedly heard," Smith wrote Wolcott, "that the loan officer would observe when applications are made to him for payment of interest [on government securities], that he is ready to pay *now*—but it is altogether uncertain whether any thing will be paid the next quarter if this or that governmental Measure should take place." William Plumer also paid his respects to the loan officer. "Mr. Gardner," Plumer wrote Wolcott, "on all occasions is indefatigable and virulent in opposing and reviling the government, its officers and measures." Characteristically, he tempered his criticism with praise: "In justice," he added, "I must say that he is well qualified to discharge the duties of his office—that is, he is accurate, attentive and even obliging; but these very qualities, however amiable in themselves, render him the more dangerous to government." [10]

At the same time Congressman Paine Wingate denounced Hopley Yeaton to the administration as a man of "antigovernmental principles." United States Attorney Smith, with whom Yeaton often had to deal officially in federal prosecutions of customs violators captured by his vessel, also had a few words for Yeaton, succinctly deriding him as intemperate and "a tool of Whipple who is the tool of Langdon."

Smith, never one to be brief, added unnecessarily that Yeaton was "an open and decided Jacobin—he is a vehement railer against the government and of course a zealous partizan of France." William Plumer wrote at the same time that "Mr. Yeaton is well known to be a violent furious democrat, and abusive in the extreme." There were hints in all of these letters that "intemperate" not only meant politically impru- dent but addicted to drink as well, an unproved allegation not dissimilar in intent to the complaint against Whipple's hon- esty.[11]

In many ways, a six-pounder was employed against the commander of the revenue cutter when, after Whipple's of- fenses against the administration had been established, a peashooter would probably have sufficed. Not knowing of the breadth of complaints lodged against him, nor given any rea- son by Wolcott or Adams for his eventual dismissal, Yeaton's view of his displacement was severely circumscribed. The only complaint he was aware of in 1801, when he petitioned Jefferson for the return of his command, was his "refusal to sign an address to Mr. Adams expressing perfect satisfaction and entire confidence in his administration." On the other hand, perhaps Yeaton's well-known revolutionary service dictated the need for a strong case against him. The master of the cutter, of middling status, had led the Portsmouth Sons of Liberty in the 1760s. Later he saw duty as a first lieutenant aboard a United States frigate during the Revolution, not only serving long and well but, he claimed, suffering economic deprivation as a result. Described by Whipple in 1790 as a Federalist, Yeaton too followed Langdon out of the party after 1794. Langdon himself in 1802 described Yeaton to Al- bert Gallatin as "a vigilant officer . . . most shamefully dis- missed by the late President [Adams] at the time that Whip- ple and Gardner were, and for the same reason." [12]

The barrage of complaints tendered in June 1798 had its desired effect. The wheels of government turned quickly and, by the end of July, Whipple, Gardner, and Yeaton were all removed from their offices, the first victims of a precedent-setting turnover. Russell, the naval officer of cus- toms and evidently a lesser offender, was either removed also or, more probably, permitted to resign under pain of dismissal. At any rate, by October he was out of office too. Some twenty employees in the customshouse were subsequently replaced by the new collector. This too was a "first" in American political history, although the expedient displacement of lower officials by new superiors quickly became a commonplace of American customshouse politics in the nineteenth century. John Adams, who had the constitutional power to act without either Senate approval or the need to supply a cause, obviously did act, on the recommendation of his secretary of the treasury.

The new collector was Thomas Martin, the incumbent surveyor of customs now promoted to Whipple's old job. He was the only remaining Federalist among the four officers of the customshouse, and was recommended for promotion both by Jeremiah Smith and United States Senator Samuel Livermore. The latter was patriarch of an important New Hampshire family and a prominent figure in the Exeter-dominated state Federalist leadership. Martin, who rather unsuccessfully kept a general store in town prior to entering the customs service in the 1780s, had supported ratification and remained active in local Federalist politics thereafter. "He suffered much" as a result of his years of political isolation, Jeremiah Smith disclosed in his recommendation. Nevertheless, "Martin preserved his loyalty entire and is universally respected as an honest man and a friend of good government." In fact, not much more could be said on Martin's behalf. He boasted neither the usually mandatory revolutionary service nor the success in a civil capacity that would normally have qualified him for the profitable post he entered upon.[13]

The same, in fact, could be said for the new second officer of the port who, however, had some other things going for him. Edward St. Loe Livermore, Senator Samuel Livermore's son, was appointed naval officer of customs. Equally disliked by both Republicans and Federalists, he was nevertheless to mature into an able lawyer and public official in his later years. The fact that in 1798 he was a bitter personal enemy of John Langdon must have sweetened his appointment for enemies of Langdon like Smith and Plumer, not to mention Edward's father. Words like "impudent," "dogmatical," "arbitrary," and "imperious" were frequently used to describe young Livermore, then embarking on a significant political career.[14]

The appointment of seaman John Adams to the command of the Portsmouth revenue cutter must have been an equally satisfying nomination. Adams had been one of Hopley Yeaton's crew who had been dismissed by Yeaton around 1795, after Yeaton had experienced his political change of heart. Adams, though a young man, boasted "respectable connections" and was "a good federalist" who took special satisfaction in replacing a man of "anti-governmental principles." [15]

A number of influential Federalists eventually questioned the precedent thus established. One of these was Benjamin Lincoln, the Federalist collector at Boston, who wrote Adams of his reservations some time after the incident. "When I came into office," the president replied early in 1800, "it was my determination to make as few removals as possible—not one from personal motives, not one from party considerations." But, Adams continued, "the representations to me of the daily language of several officers at Portsmouth, were so evincive of aversion, if not hostility, to the national Constitution and government, that I could not avoid making some changes. Mr. Whipple is represented as very artful in imputing individual misfortunes to measures of administration, and his whole influence to have been employed against the government." The beleaguered president concluded that "if the officers of government will not support it, who will?" And with the courage of his convictions so typical of John Adams, he added: "I still think his [Whipple's] removal was right." [16]

The inevitable ending to this episode comes very close to anticlimax. Soon after Thomas Jefferson's inauguration as president, three of the Republicans—Whipple, Yeaton, and Gardner—petitioned Jefferson for reinstatement; they were restored to their former offices. Thus for the second time in three years—and if one counts the 1795 shake-up, the third time in six years—the Portsmouth customshouse was cleaned out. Jefferson removed all of the Federalists designated by John Adams in 1798. Joseph Whipple subsequently turned out most of the subordinate customs employees—the second time around for him. The president and his secretary of the treasury, Albert Gallatin, read the Adams files dealing with the 1798 Portsmouth removals, for they were part of the existing archives of the State Department inherited by the new administration.

One wonders what the Republican president and secretary really thought about the Smith and Plumer letters. Jefferson, so far as can be determined, wrote nothing specific about the correspondence he read; he alluded to the incident only indirectly in his "Anas" on March 8, 1801, when he promised himself less than a week after his inauguration to remove Edward S. L. Livermore "by and by." Gallatin made only a few innocuous comments on Hopley Yeaton's file folder.[17]

What was said or written between the president and his treasury secretary notwithstanding, Portsmouth was the only major port in the United States immediately stripped of its *entire* complement of incumbent customs officers. In view of this, it might be concluded that no comment by the Republican president was necessary. What to do in Portsmouth was not a problem that Jefferson seemed to fret about. And, from the vantage point of 1801, the clear-cut Federalist operations in Providence, Rhode Island, likewise made the president's course easy to chart.

Continuity may be the key to understanding Rhode Island's complex history of political factionalism. Geographic polarization between Newport and Providence, dating to before the Revolution, was in a general sense still evident during the Confederation. In the 1780s, moreover, new ideological issues were introduced as well, namely, paper money emissions and widespread opposition to ratification. Finally, firmly rooted economic and social class distinctions that survived the Revolution also inflamed Confederation politics. Both political parties were hampered in their search for cohesive organization and political control by the stubborn survival of all these tensions beyond 1789.

Two factors made the "party of the aristocracy" competitive in a state whose circumstances were not conducive to its success. First, local Federalist organization and electoral appeal were sustained by large doses of federal patronage, sophisticated guidance, and even intervention from national leaders in Philadelphia, particularly from Alexander Hamilton. Second, strong, natural Antifederalist sentiment did not metamorphose into a stable, disciplined Jeffersonian Republican party machine, as it did elsewhere. Popular Governor Arthur Fenner was a case in point. Fenner was never a Hamiltonian and remained at odds with highly placed Rhode Island Federalists throughout the decade. In fact he had been an important opponent of the Constitution in an earlier era. In spite of these things, Fenner emerged, at least nominally, as a Federalist about mid-decade. Although some outside the state, not aware of his conversion, continued to mistake him for a Jeffersonian, the governor considered himself a Federalist and proved it by serving as an elector for John Adams in 1796. Nevertheless, he retained a complex association with the opposition. The point is that the Republican party functioned at a much less sophisticated level in Rhode Island than did its counterpart, and both party identity and discipline never really gelled in the course of the decade, its ideological links to the issues of the Revolution and Confederation notwithstanding.

So even though old Antifederalist antagonisms and ideology continued to spice the politics of the 1790s, a better-organized Federalist party helped to keep the state a keenly competitive political entity. In short, a highly articulated, modern Federalist interest surfaced in what had been an obstinately Antifederalist bastion. Given the strength of earlier opposition to the Constitution and the surviving emotional ties to past ideologies, the surprise is not that the state remained politically balanced in the 1790s, but that there was an effective Federalist party at all.[18]

Alexander Hamilton, acting for the new administration,

clearly made a special effort to succor the struggling Rhode Island Federalist interest after 1789. Painstaking care went into the procedure for making federal appointments, and particular attention was paid to the extensive customs service centering on the two major ports of Providence and Newport. As other historians have pointed out, with the growth of Providence prior to the Revolution, geographically oriented polar politics in Rhode Island became a fact of life. Commercial Newport and its agricultural-mercantile hinterland pitted its gradually waning pre-eminence against the rising commercial prosperity of Providence port and its agricultural environs.

Constitutional federalism and its antecedent, opposition to the paper money faction, totally upstaged any other considerations in handing out federal jobs in Rhode Island in 1790. The major wellspring for funneling federal positions to men of dependable political persuasion seems to have been the Rhode Island Political Club centered at Providence. The club was a primary organizational vehicle of Constitutional Federalists in the Confederation and really came into its own briefly during and immediately after the prolonged struggle for ratification in the tiny state. The prime Federalist movers in the club around 1790 were Jabez Bowen, Jeremiah Olney, and Benjamin Bourne, all of whom were themselves eventual recipients of federal appointments.[19]

Jabez Bowen, Providence's leading apothecary and in 1790 the designated United States commissioner of loans for Rhode Island, was chief among those local allies and supporters of Alexander Hamilton who oversaw the distribution of Rhode Island appointments. In every instance, federal nominations in the state were governed by the degree of the candidate's commitment to the Constitutional movement, in a state where the contest over ratification was bitter indeed. Inevitably, moveover, the Rhode Island constitutional struggle of 1789–90 recalled for contemporaries the individual's stance with regard to the earlier paper money crisis that culminated in the drastic paper money emissions of 1786. Because of the virulence of these locally ideological issues, Rhode Island was a state where political continuity with the

Confederation era was very much a fact of life. Thus, the intense struggle for federal office after ratification in 1790 forms a good microcosm for examining developing two-party conflict in a state where, not only were political loyalties about evenly divided, but where the "old politics" was not eradicated by the Constitution but, in fact, exacerbated by it.

Jabez Bowen led an insistent clique in demanding of the new federal government that it redress the political balance of the state by providing offices to Federalists. More will be said about Bowen in a later chapter, but for the moment it should be noted that the foundation of his persuasive efforts rested on allusions to the continuing strength of the Antifederalists, who still controlled the government of the state in 1790. "His zeal and abilities have been highly contributory to the accession of this state to the union," said merchant John Brown in paying tribute to Bowen's leadership shortly after ratification. The apothecary himself wrote Washington that he "most anxiously wait[ed] for the moment to arrive when infatuation and misconduct of the Rulers of this State may cease to prevent us from being partakers of the full benefits resulting from the wisdom and justice of your administration." Bowen added that he spoke "for the Federalists of this state." [20]

At the time Rhode Island entered the Union, a competition for the ear of the president in the matter of federal appointments inevitably developed between the Federalist minority and the "antis" who dominated the state government. An analysis of the nominations to office is instructive of the intense politicking and incipient party building that was taking place. Bowen sent along to Washington a list of "Friends of the general government" in the plantations who should be considered for federal appointment. "I should not have thus troubled your excellency," Bowen apologized, "but we are informed that Governor [Arthur] Fenner has and will send you the names of those persons that he and his Friends wish may be put into office, but the whole of their conduct having been uniformly opposed to the General Government I cannot think they will be anxious to promote those persons to offices as will act for the general weale." [21]

Other ranking Constitutionalists wrote the president in the same vein. The applicant for United States marshal "hath been a true Federalist," William Greene disclosed. He was "opposed to the state politicks both as to paper money laws and antifederalism," added merchant Welcome Arnold. John Brown and John Francis, partners in perhaps the most influential Rhode Island merchant house, wrote Washington at the same time to recommend "a core of Honest Faithful and Vigilent Customs House Officers for this Department [Providence]." Those, the two merchants suggested, were men who made "Grait Exertions" and were among those "Federals" who made "Very Large Sacrifices . . . to change the Policy of this Government which for this Four Years Past have been constantly opposing the adoption of this new Constitution and of course have done very great Injustice with their paper money." [22]

Figure 3. John Brown's house in Providence, about 1786.

Many other Federalists, both in and outside of Rhode Island, directed their attentions to Alexander Hamilton. Among these were Royal Flint and the future collector for Providence port, Jeremiah Olney. The latter in particular had the ear of the secretary, for the two had come to know each other well when they had served together in the Continental army. "The intimate intercourse between us," Hamilton wrote Olney, "makes us look up to you as a natural ally." Among the half dozen most important Federalists in the state, Olney found their relationship particularly advantageous. Inasmuch as the state had been under the political control of the Antifederalists for some four years, virtually all of the incumbent state-appointed customs officers, as well as others whose source of appointment would in 1790 shift from state to federal auspices, were both opponents of the Constitution and paper money men. Olney, himself a candidate for customs collector, worked through Hamilton and Royal Flint (who independently reported to Hamilton on the local political situation) to head off reappointment of Antifederalist incumbents unknowingly by Washington.

Olney's and Flint's task was complicated by the fact that Antifederalist United States Senators Theodore Foster and Joseph Stanton, Jr., were on their way to Philadelphia to influence the pending appointments. Foster in particular would try to gain the reappointment of "all the *ante* Revenue officers" in the state. What Olney and Hamilton feared the most was that, in spite of Bowen's barrage of information to Washington, "the Senator will Influence the President In the nomination of these *Bitter and Uniform* opposers of the Constitution" simply because they were incumbents.[23] As it turned out, neither Hamilton nor Olney had much to fear. The score cards show a clean sweep for the Federalist white hats.

There is no question but that the Washington administration consciously and systematically applied a political test to would-be officeholders from the first days of that administration onward. What can only be implied—"perception of pattern" as Staughton Lynd called it—for other states, was made crystal clear in Rhode Island: Antifederalists, because of their political beliefs, were denied offices, even those they already held under the state government, in favor of activists who had supported ratification.[24] Jabez Bowen, Jeremiah Olney, and Royal Flint each submitted overlapping lists of office seekers, the first-named directly to the president, the latter two to Alexander Hamilton and thence to Washington. Each list qualified or disqualified candidates for federal office on the virtually single ground of their harnessed positions vis-à-vis the Constitution and the paper money emissions. Therefore these lists, especially when compared to those submitted by the Antifederalists, are significant in determining the degree to which a political test was knowingly applied by the first president.

Jabez Bowen discussed twelve individuals under consideration by the national administration. He recommended nine strongly as supporters of ratification, and seven were subsequently appointed to the federal jobs for which they were boosted; two were not appointed, one because he would take only a United States district judgeship for which there was a better candidate, the other because he was Bowen's twenty-two-year-old son, and Washington said he found nepotism distasteful. Bowen also denounced three Antifederalists under consideration in the national capital. Two were turned down, one of them an incumbent customs officer under the state who was turned out of office. The third, the incumbent collector at Providence, was demoted to a lower customs office.

Jeremiah Olney informed Hamilton about ten candidates, eight of whom he recommended warmly. Five of the eight were named to federal offices, a sixth was elected to Congress and was thus dropped from consideration. Two more of those Olney recommended were not given jobs, but one of these was Olney's brother, who was turned down on the same grounds that applied to Bowen's son. Two more were denounced as "Antis" and were not appointed.

Royal Flint wrote Hamilton about eleven candidates: seven he recommended highly, and they were all named; four others he labeled opponents of the Constitution and of these two were not appointed, one (Theodore Foster) took a seat in the United States Senate and was thus removed from consideration, and the fourth was the above-mentioned incumbent collector at Providence who was demoted to a lower office.[25] Washington was clearly informed about and conscious of the particular issues involved in the Rhode Island appointments, and was actively involved in these decisions.

Meanwhile the powerful Antifederalist forces in the state, led in this transitional period by Governor Arthur Fenner, lobbied earnestly to protect their federal flank by securing for their supporters offices under the national government. These nominees were often men who already held the same positions under the expiring mandate of the state. Senator-elect Theodore Foster wrote the president that replacing incumbent local opponents of the Constitution with Federalists would appear to create a political test for office and thus "give occasion for Mistrust" in the state. Arthur Fenner was somewhat more subtle in dealing with Washington, pointing out that his recommendations, delivered as the governor, would "be most likely to appease and soften the spirit of Party in the state." Powerful Antifederalist merchant Moses Brown, alluding to "our present Divided and particularly unhappy Situation in this State," wrote Washington that appointment of merchant-oriented Federalists to the customs service at Providence and Newport would result in rampant "Running of Goods or Making false entries [thus] evading the payment of duties" because of the inevitable collusion between merchants and customs agents that would follow. Appointment of Antifederalist customs personnel, and Ebenezer Thompson the collector of Providence in particular, averred Brown, would lend itself to rigorous enforcement of the customs laws.[26] These pleas fell on deaf ears.

Governor Fenner, not deigning to go out on a limb for men who he anticipated would not be named anyway, conservatively submitted recommendations for four Antifederalists, three of them incumbents in their jobs. One of these was Theodore Foster, who was not a candidate. Of the remaining three, two were not appointed and Ebenezer Thompson was demoted out of his sensitive collector's berth. Senatorial courtesy did not count for much either in 1790, if it existed at all in the matter of nominations that required Senate confirmation. Senator Theodore Foster recommended six, of whom four were named to lower posts than they had held under the state, and two new men were not appointed.[27]

The result of this deliberate policy either of excluding Antifederalists or pulling their fangs by means of demotion, was
important in redressing the party balance in Rhode Island.
When President Washington visited the state in 1790, according to George C. Rogers, Jr., the Rhode Islanders who met
and entertained him "were those who had worked for union
and who were no doubt happy to use the President's prestige
to cap their recent success and to fix themselves in the seat of
power. Federal appointments had already helped in this process of consolidation." [28] While every branch of the federal
civil service in Rhode Island provided a haven for Federalist
party leadership, the customs service as usual occupied a
pivotal place in the operations of the rejuvenated Federalist
party cadre.

In the geographically and ideologically polarized politics
of the state, the rising port town of Providence anchored one
of the two major areas of party activity. Here Collector of
Customs Jeremiah Olney, with his $1,500 in federal salary
and more than twenty jobs to dole out, emerged as a nuclear
figure in the state's Federalist party. A significant long-term
limitation on his political prestige derived from his own incompetence. He chose to interpret the customs laws according to the letter, thereby involving himself and the Treasury
Department in frequent disputes and misunderstandings.
Officious and defensive, he eventually alienated friend and
foe alike among the Providence merchants and forced his
long-time friend Alexander Hamilton to spend a great deal of
time and correspondence correcting the collector's mistakes
and misjudgments.[29]

His difficulties notwithstanding, Olney wielded considerable influence in party matters. He had been a colonel in the
Continental line during the Revolution and remained active
in the Society of the Cincinnati thereafter, holding the post of
vice-president of the Rhode Island chapter for a good part of
the 1790s. The Rhode Island Cincinnati, like the Providence
Political Club, had been an important organizational vehicle
for the Constitutional movement in the state. Olney was also
a proprietor of the Ohio Company and a man of property. He

continued to act as a key liaison between party leaders in the national administration and the state organization.[30]

The naval officer of customs under Olney was Ebenezer Thompson, the man whom Olney had replaced. A source of embarrassment to the Washington administration and local Federalists alike, Thompson could neither be retained as collector nor summarily dismissed from the customs service he had headed throughout the Confederation. On the one hand, the state's Hamiltonians needed the political deference and lesser patronage the collector's job carried with it, in a state where Antifederalists held sway. On the other hand, to dismiss the popular Thompson outright would have antagonized large numbers of political moderates and passive, apolitical neutrals. The dilemma was resolved by dropping Thompson to the second slot in the customshouse; not only did this reduce Thompson's salary to one-third of its former size, more importantly it took the local appointive power over subordinates out of his hands.

To many Federalists, Ebenezer Thompson was "an austere churlish man," but even Jabez Bowen recognized that the long-time collector was "much esteemed." However, as Bowen pointed out, "he has been a friend to the late [paper money] measures of the State to the surprize of all his former acquaintances tho he has not been known in any instance to have availed himself of their paper money tender." The demoted customs officer had strongly opposed ratification of the Constitution, using all his extensive prestige on behalf of the Antifederalist cause. Thompson was a member of the upper house of the state legislature, as he had been for a quarter century. A merchant prior to the Revolution, he had occupied several significant Whig offices during the war. Thompson also acted as a county judge, was president of the Providence Town Council, and was a moving force in the considerable Rhode Island movement to abolish the slave trade during the later years of the eighteenth century. Complaints about his cut salary, his humiliating demotion, and financial need for a better office were all unavailing. As he was a Jeffersonian locked into a Federalist customshouse, the political utility of his position was severely circumscribed.[31]

In a politically competitive state, Surveyor of Customs Wil-

liam Barton must have been a real asset to the Federalist
interest, if Royal Flint's assessment was accurate. The former
Continental army officer was "popular among the lower class
of people" and "should be active," Flint disclosed to Hamilton. Barton, he added, "supports much influence in Providence." A nephew of both David Rittenhouse the astronomer
and Benjamin Barton the botanist, and cousin to the
Philadelphia Republican and botanist of the same name as
his own, Providence's William Barton was an arresting figure
in his own right. Although he had supported paper money
emissions in 1786, he ultimately emerged as a Federalist
supporter of the Constitution who pressed for ratification in
the years 1788–90, even voting for ratification in the Rhode
Island Convention. It is not hard to trace the cause of his
ideological revolution, for it was a mix of principle and the
basest pragmatism. During the Confederation, Barton, a
lawyer by profession, invested heavily and unsuccessfully in
manufacturing enterprises. He had no qualms about paying
off his extensive indebtedness in paper, and for a while before the constitutional issue took hold in Rhode Island, was a
warm advocate of paper money emissions. At the same time,
however, he published an influential tract entitled *The True
Interest*, a work encouraging manufactures and hailing that
economic enterprise as America's wave of the future. This
last conviction, among other things, caused Barton increasingly to gravitate toward the politics of Alexander Hamilton.
He eventually surfaced as a supporter of the Constitution,
one of a very few Rhode Island political figures to cross the
emotional and ideological divide separating paper money
advocates from Federalism.[32] Under the leadership of both
Olney and Barton, the Providence customshouse became an
important organizational nucleus for the local Federalist
interest.

Another former Continental army officer, General Jedediah
Huntington, was to New London, Connecticut, Federalists
what Jeremiah Olney was to party men in Providence. Politics, however, was much better ordered in neighboring Connecticut than it was in Rhode Island. Federalist authority was

so pervasive in the "land of steady habits" that Republican party opposition was at best a local factor. Hartford was the "metropolitan see" of party operations, and the "leading men in the politics of the state were also the leading men in the Congregational Establishment." [33] The Oliver Wolcotts (father and son), Oliver Ellsworth, Jeremiah Wadsworth, Jedediah Huntington, and the Hartford Wits led by the redoubtable Ezra Stiles, the high priest of Connecticut conservatism were, along with almost every other elite family, part of that Congregational establishment. The party was so deeply rooted in Connecticut life that such things as land scandals and occasional factional squabbling did not offer much advantage to the Republicans. In short, the church, commerce, and real property interests were all tied into the party leadership.

There is no doubt then, that as a result of the party's tangible connection to the Congregational hierarchy, Connecticut possessed the tightest, most close-knit, status-oriented party formation of any state in the Union. It was just this unifying force that proved to be the Connecticut Federalists' greatest strength over the long run. No town better exemplified the truth of these generalizations than did the port town of New London at the edge of Long Island Sound.

Jedediah Huntington ruled like a feudal lord over the customshouse and practically everything else in New London. He had the proper family lineage for the position and was "well qualified in point of Knowledge, Experience and *principles*" as well. Huntington was a prominent member of long-time Connecticut gentry, the son of General Jabez Huntington and a graduate of Harvard who took his place in the family mercantile business. A Congregational church activist, the New London customs collector played an important role in several national bible and missionary societies radiating outward from the state. In the early days of revolutionary ferment, Jedediah, the scion of a threatened merchant house, surfaced as a leader of the Sons of Liberty. This identification might have been incongruous in other colonies for gentry like Huntington, but it was not inconsistent given Connecticut's tight political and social order. He eventually raised a regiment and ended his service with the Continental army as a major general. In the course of the Federalist decade, he served as president of both the state and national chapters of the Society of the Cincinnati.

The general also occupied a conspicuous place in the Connecticut political hierarchy. In the Confederation he was both sheriff of New London County and treasurer of the state; he was elected intermittently to the state senate as well. All of these credits supplied him with enormous visibility and deference in New London itself, where he was the president of the Union Bank as well as the customs collector in the 1790s. Huntington's role in New London provides an excellent example of the exercise of political power that commingled traditional eighteenth-century deference leadership with the newer trappings of party organization and authority.[34]

The collector retained close ties to the national administration, bonds that rested mainly on friendships of long standing with Washington and Hamilton. These were forged in the Revolution and reinforced by Huntington's deep involvement in the movement to strengthen the central government. As a prominent member of the Society of the Cincinnati, he was an early advocate of revision of the Articles of Confederation. This commitment plus his extensive prestige led him quite naturally into a leadership role in the ratification movement in Connecticut. "The measures he took" in the ratifying convention at Hartford in 1788, Clifford Shipton has observed, "were well conceived, well planned, and executed with great certainty and effect." Huntington himself filled the role of a political moderate, conceding that "while I express my sentiments in favour of this constitution, I candidly believe that the gentlemen who oppose it, are actuated by principles of regard to the public welfare." [35] He was not nearly so tolerant of his party opponents in the ensuing decade—a comment, perhaps, on the impact that parties had in institutionalizing political enmities as well as political response.

Huntington moved quite naturally from the mainstream of the Constitutional movement in Connecticut into the forefront of the Federalist interest. He was a Connecticut elector for George Washington in 1788. While Washington had some reservations about Huntington's devotion to hard work, he judged him to be "sober, sensible and very discreet." Huntington "has never discovered much enterprise," the president observed, but in approving his appointment as customs collector, he concluded "no doubt has ever been entertained of his want of spirit, or firmness." And in 1799 when Washington died, it was Huntington who was designated to deliver one of the principal eulogies.

Huntington was also a firm Hamiltonian who, from the outset of the new government, was identified locally with Hamilton's fiscal programs. He was described by a Connecticut Republican as one of "the select Friends and Allies of the men who advocated, created and then proffited by the funding system" and among those "who have risen to affluence" as a result of advantageous speculations. Huntington was part of a "great family . . . the knot of which they are a part began by Hamilton thence to [Congressman Jeremiah] Wadsworth." The secretary of the treasury "includes them in his train all together." [36]

From the time he left his general store in Norwich and moved to New London to take up his customs post in 1789, Jedediah Huntington utterly dominated the Federalist interest in the town. His first significant act was to build a prepossessing mansion "modeled after his friend's home at Mt. Vernon." He brought with him a letter of introduction from the First Church of Norwich to New London's First Congregational Church, and thus armed quickly entered the local hierarchy as a deacon. Huntington epitomized the confluence of federalism and Congregationalism that was ubiquitously in evidence in the state. Within a few years he led the movement to organize the Union Bank of New London, of which he became the first president in 1791. This too was typical. Banks, like Congregational churches, were closely allied with Connecticut's Federalist cadre. The general naturally occupied several local offices as well from time to time during the Federalist decade. He was described by the early 1790s as "the leading citizen of the town," using

the customshouse above all other institutions at his disposal
to successfully maintain his political position.[37]

Huntington's political enemies were very certain about the
ways in which Huntington threw his weight around in the
interests of the Federalist party in town. Not only had he
made a great deal of money from the collector's post, a Jeffersonian townsman charged, he used his "official influence"
extensively to undermine the relatively weak Republican
party in New London, "particularly in cases of election."
Supervising how locals voted was an important part of the
intimidation that was one of the foundation stones of Huntington's power. The bank was another. A political opponent
left a graphic description of the role of the Union Bank in
local politics. "The Collector is President of the Bank in this
Town," Thomas Rawson reported, "and people are taught
early that kissing goes by favour; many who are in want of
Bank favours are . . . convinced that voting what the President of the Bank would call correctly is placing them in a way
to obtain discounts. This next to his agentcies [as customs
collector] is one of the most unpleasant and at the same time
powerful weapons in the hands of this collector to battle
down the republicans." Huntington's influence, in short, was
"as gigantic as any one citizens ought to be in a bad cause,
even detached from the office of collector."

But it was the collector's office that seemed to have the
greatest impact on New London politics. Huntington engaged the office politically like a surgeon's scalpel, and
missed few tricks in doing so. Dissident shopkeepers and
merchants found it very difficult, sometimes, to clear their
imports through customs. Without any apparent difficulties,
moreover, Huntington allowed the local Federalist newspaper to publish from the customshouse, making use of the
federal office's personnel and, incidentally, keeping newspaper employees close to their second jobs in the customshouse. Even by the standards of the Federalist era, this was
partisanship at its rankest. Moreover, one Republican alleged, inspectors of customs who wavered politically were
"frightened" into supporting Federalist measures despite
their "inclinations." All in all, Huntington's "office and its

appendages," as well as his wealth, "render him a most powerful adversary to the republican cause." [38] An incident in depth demonstrates the heady exercise of political power by the customs collector; it involved the building and manning of the federal revenue cutter operating out of the port of New London. Some detail surrounding the cutter's origins survives and forms an excellent example of the quality of Huntington's paraprofessional leadership.

Huntington in 1792 was authorized by Hamilton to arrange for the construction of a revenue cutter to patrol Long Island Sound. In violation of Hamilton's standing directives that federal expenditures for either supplies or labor must be contracted on the basis of competitive bidding, Huntington "had without advertising in any papers or giving it publicity in any way, contracted with John Woodward a federalist . . . to build it [the cutter]." Woodward was not a ship's carpenter, but he "possessed other valuable qualities. He was a thorough going federalist" and a member of the state legislature. By this sort of rank favoritism, a Republican petitioner later claimed, Huntington was able "to call into action hosts of voters" who were allegedly either put to work by Woodward, or friends or family of those put to work.[39]

When the cutter was completed, Jonathan Maltbie was named the first captain. He was a veteran of the Continental navy, described as "remarkable for [his] activity" as a Federalist. He needed the appointment very badly and proved a popular and able choice. Maltbie died early in 1798, and Huntington saw to it that the post went to Elisha Hinman, an aging (over seventy) retired seaman and a good party man. The latter was named over George House, the first mate of the cutter.

By 1798, House was a firm Republican although, at the time of his appointment to the cutter in 1792, he had been at least a passive supporter of the Federalist administration. Although Hinman had commanded an American naval vessel during the Revolution and was otherwise clearly qualified for his post, it was clear by 1798 that he was "incapacitated by age." Nevertheless, he was appointed on the explicit grounds, transmitted to the Adams administration by Huntington, that he was a "decided federalist and House as decided a republican." Although House admittedly was better qualified for the command, the collector wrote to the treasury secretary, "his pretensions are warmly espoused here [in New London] by certain characters who ought not to have any Influence on such appointments."

Nevertheless, House and his supporters pushed hard. A group of "violent Jacobins . . . after a grand Council" petitioned Vice-President Jefferson on House's behalf. House himself wrote Oliver Wolcott of the public's expectation that he would be promoted, alluding also to his long service in the navy during the war and concluding, without much attempt at finesse, "if any person shou'd be preferred to me it wounds me as it might convey the Idea of disqualification for the office." Neither Wolcott nor Adams were having any, and Hinman was tapped for the job, his age and consequent reputation for "inattention to his duty" notwithstanding. Jefferson in his first term remedied what he thought to be an injustice by removing Hinman, whose "politicks [was] full of Poison," and replaced him with House. Because of General Huntington's well-known military service and his undeserved reputation as a political moderate among those Republican contemporaries in Washington, D.C., after 1801 who remembered his position on the Constitution in the 1780s but had not read the State Department files on Huntington kept for the 1790s, he was never removed. He left office only in his own good time in 1815.[40]

The marriage of politics to customshouse was virtually total in the three New England port cities of Portsmouth, Providence, and New London. The same was true in other places in Federalist New England. The party clearly relied on "great men" to guide local political fortunes, but it is equally clear that the customshouses, as local federal institutions, also helped immensely to consolidate and perpetuate political and economic ties to the grass-roots middle classes as well. In these three towns, at least, as in several others in the Bay State, the "party of the aristocracy" was really not that at all; at the same time it could hardly be called a party of the people. The truth, as usual, lay in between these two linguistic extremes. The same pattern prevailed in the Middle Atlantic states, although by and large, more equally balanced two-party systems made politics via the customshouse a much less stable source of successful organization than was the case in the states to the north.

CHAPTER FOUR

Customs: Three Middle Atlantic Cities

New York, Philadelphia, and Baltimore were three of the largest ports in the new nation, and their customshouses dominated the federal civil establishment in the Middle Atlantic states. In New York, the 1797 replacement of veteran Republican collector John Lamb led to the first significant confrontation between newly inaugurated President John Adams and former Treasury Secretary Alexander Hamilton. In the City of Brotherly Love, the corruption of its first collector of customs did not at all impede the operation of a smoothly functioning, dynamic Federalist establishment. Baltimore, a bustling port, was a place of political contrasts: on the one hand, it was the only significant Republican bailiwick in a Federalist state; on the other, the customshouse formed an aggressive nucleus for Federalist party operations in a Jeffersonian enclave. In all three major ports, the Federalist customshouses sent out their tentacles to reach deep into the urban middle classes.

By the mid-1790s "evenly matched political forces" characterized New York politics.[1] In a state in which the political temperament was mercurial, a well-organized, highly ideological Federalist party emerged. That party's road to political power was smoothed by the fact that, as

Alfred Young visualizes it, "in the leadership of the Federalists, the continuities in New York politics from the Revolution through the 1790's were striking." The party in the Federalist era was led by the same men who dominated the Whig interest in the seventies and the nationalist cause of the eighties. Philip Schuyler, Hamilton, and Jay, all first among equals, were allied with placemen James Duane, Egbert Bensen, Nicholas Low, John Laurence, and William Seton among others. These men clearly represented the "landlord-mercantile aristocracy." Even though after 1789 there were notable defections from its preconstitutional ranks, the older Federalist interest remained very much intact throughout the 1790s. Leadership losses or defections (like that of the Livingston clan) were made good by the addition of new men and new interests, of whom Richard Harison and Rufus King were only two of the most prominent examples.

The talent and cohesiveness of the party's leadership, while it did not guarantee unbroken success at the polls, did provide both sophistication and organization with which to confront a rising Republican movement in a politically volatile state. The Republicans were often successful in spite of the fact that the Federalists dominated the middle ground. In a situation frequently the reverse of party battles elsewhere, it was the Federalists, according to Young, who in succeeding crises "were able to outmaneuver the Republicans, making the issue Washington or his traducers . . . ." Effective Federalist organization time after time kept the Republicans from consolidating their gains. "This extraordinary support for the Federalist party," Young concluded, "was based in large part on the widespread conviction that Federalist policies benefited the state." New York, then as always, remained one of the most important party battlegrounds of the era.

Given these circumstances, the collectorship of the port of New York was as desirable a prize in 1789 as it would be nearly a century later when Chester Alan Arthur was named to the post. The fact that General John Lamb, erstwhile Antifederalist and a distinguished veteran of the Continental

army, was the state-appointed incumbent under the auspices of Governor George Clinton presented President
Washington with a Hobson's choice. On the one hand, it was
difficult to justify the continuation in office of so conspicuous
and energetic an opponent of the Constitution, especially
given Washington's application of political criteria in making
appointments. On the other hand, the "removal" or displacement of so distinguished and close a former comrade in
arms—one, moreover, at the right hand of New York's premier politician George Clinton—was even more unthinkable.
A tacit compromise was worked out. General Lamb would
keep his profitable collector's job, but the other officers of the
port would be Federalist, and so would most of the subordinates in the customshouse. This concession by Lamb effectively drew his political fangs by severely curtailing the collector's real appointive power. Lamb also agreed to acknowledge openly his loyalty to the new president. "Washington,"
the collector was widely quoted as saying in 1789, "was the
only man [I] would entrust with the extensive powers of the
presidency." In spite of this arrangement, from the time
Lamb began to act as a federal official until his removal eight
years later, he was placed, as one historian has put it, "in a
position which kept him in continual hot water."

Alfred Young offers a reasoned explanation for Washington's appointment of Lamb over Hamilton's objections.
For one thing of course, Lamb had been a staunch Whig and a
twice-wounded general in the Continental army who was not
easily passed over. Moreover, Lamb had agreed to express
his allegiance to the president and was additionally hemmed
in by his Federalist confreres in the customshouse. Finally,
Lamb's appointment, according to Young, served several
political purposes: Washington "faintly appeased the Clinto-
nians"; he met his own stated (but often unfulfilled) criterion
to avoid arbitrary removals; "the retention of Lamb offered a
highly visible opportunity to demonstrate nonpartisanship,
reward a well known patriot, and undermine anti-Federalist
fears"; and by engaging in a kind of political tokenism, Antifederalists, in a state where that species abounded, could
find a reason to support the government.[2]

Washington's decision was not accepted gracefully either by the secretary of the treasury or the latter's local followers. "Tremendous pressure was brought to bear" by the secretary's many and influential New York City friends "to have President Washington reconsider and recall the nomination from the Senate." Less than a year after this ploy failed, Hamilton attempted to severely circumscribe Lamb's remaining freedom of action by harassing him administratively. The secretary wrote to United States Attorney for New York Richard Harison (who was also Hamilton's close friend and political ally), questioning Lamb's competence as collector and asking Harison for a legal judgment on one of Lamb's many official acts. The question involved a minor matter, the collector's standard practice of determining current exchange rates involving foreign currency in customshouse transactions with foreign vessels. Hamilton wanted specifically to deprive Lamb of that discretionary authority. Harison wrote back to Hamilton acknowledging that if he could undermine Lamb's position he would but that, if the New York collector was rendered liable on this particular count, so also would be all other collectors, creating an impossible administrative situation. Hamilton reluctantly dropped the matter.[3]

Lamb, who had been a member of the New York legislature in the 1780s as well as the head of a New York City Clintonian Club, continued to remain politically active in the 1790s. He identified openly with the budding Jeffersonian Republican party, and in 1792 scandalized local Federalists when he hosted a dinner in honor of both Citizen Genêt and the French captain of the vessel that brought the zealous minister to America. This sort of outrageous behavior, juxtaposed alongside his highly visible and totally respectable involvement in the Society of the Cincinnati, the local Episcopal church, and the Society for the Manumission of Slaves, renewed Federalist demands for his dismissal from the customshouse.[4]

While Lamb's presence in one of the most profitable federal offices in the land caused New York Federalists to see red, his tenure was really only symbolically annoying. His leadership of the customshouse did not result in its becoming

Figure 4. Harbor of New York City, East River view, about 1796.

Figure 5. New York City from the Battery, about 1793–1797.

a hotbed of Republicanism, as one normally might expect given the Portsmouth, New Hampshire, example. Only one known Jeffersonian turned up in the inferior ranks, and strong indications exist that most of the others were Federalists. Inasmuch as many customshouse positions in the large port involved only part-time obligations, we can catch a glimpse of middling Federalists operating in an urban setting. Of the seventeen subordinates who can be positively counted as locally active Federalists (of about fifty employees in all), it was possible to learn the occupations of thirteen. Nine of these were skilled artisans, including two cordwainers, a silversmith, a carpenter, a hairdresser, a staymaker, a watchmaker, a wheelwright, and a chocolatemaker; two others were tavernkeepers, an evident political occupation; one was a storekeeper and one a cartman. Inasmuch as these thirteen represented only a fourth of the subordinates, it is clear that the political arm of the local customshouse reached rather deeply into the day-to-day life of the city.[5]

Federalist stronghold or not, many Federalists wanted Lamb out of the customshouse. His visibility alone was deemed harmful to the Federalist cause. George Washington would not displace him, however. John Adams was not so squeamish, and when a pretext offered in 1797, the new president quickly removed Lamb. The dismissal touched off a major political confrontation that eventually weakened the Federalist party, for in removing Lamb the second president not only challenged New York Republicans, he threw down the gauntlet to Alexander Hamilton as well. He did both within only a few months of taking office.

The direct confrontation with Alexander Hamilton was a local harbinger of the division that ultimately split the Federalist party nationally. A deputy of Lamb's had embezzled a sizable amount of money from customs revenues. When it came to light, Lamb and several local Republicans immediately pledged themselves to make good the loss in the name of the collector. Adams, Hamilton, and the latter's New York City followers agreed, however, that the defalcation provided enough excuse to charge Lamb with laxity in office, and the Republican collector was removed. Although in other similar instances Federalist collectors' bonds were used to make good such losses and they were subsequently permitted to replenish their bonds without loss of their jobs, the incident was just good enough to justify Lamb's removal. He lost both his huge bond and his office.[6]

While Lamb's removal did not change the political character of the customshouse inasmuch as it was already Federalist, it did touch off a scramble for perhaps the most coveted second-line slot in the civil service. Initially there did not appear to be much doubt that Benjamin Walker, the naval officer of customs at the port, would get the job. He was an important Hamiltonian Federalist and a distinguished veteran of the Continental army. As the weeks passed with no word from the president, however, it became clear that Walker's chances for the appointment dimmed. John Adams knew very well that Walker was a key figure in the dominant Hamiltonian Federalist camp in New York City and, although Adams never wrote a word about the appointment, it is clear from other evidence that he had no intention, even as early as the spring of 1797, of strengthening that element of the party if he could help it.

An English immigrant, Walker emerged during the Revolution as an able staff officer both to Baron von Steuben and General Washington. He ended the war a colonel, close both to Washington and Alexander Hamilton, whose political lieutenant he became. From 1786 to 1788 Walker was employed by the Confederation government as a commissioner to settle government accounts. With the commencement of the constitutional government, he was made naval officer in the New York customshouse, from which vantage point he oversaw local Federalist concerns and engaged heavily in both land and securities speculations while collecting a very handsome salary from the federal coffers. He remained a valuable aide to both the president and the first secretary of the treasury. For example, when Washington needed a political errand carried out, as he did in January 1797, he turned to Walker. New York Republicans published some letters purportedly written by Washington during the Revolution and damaging to the retiring president's reputation. The chief executive asked Walker to quietly investigate their source and expose the letters as false. Throughout the Federalist decade, moreover, Walker remained Hamilton's chief political hatchetman and an important link for Hamilton to the fiscal activities of William Duer, the Society for Useful Manufactures (SUM) and the Scioto Land Company.[7]

Throughout this era Walker was deeply involved, both officially and unofficially, and often as Hamilton's agent, in the troubles and speculations of both SUM and Scioto. He was described also as "an intimate of Duer's in security dealings." With both Scioto and SUM in an "embarrassed" way in 1790, with William Duer's paper-laden, New York based financial empire on the verge of collapse, and with both threatening serious compromise to Hamilton himself and many other key New York Federalists, the secretary of the treasury turned to Benjamin Walker, also now threatened with ruin, to try to salvage the situation. The president tried to avoid involvement in these developments, but tangentially even he was compromised. At Hamilton's urgent request, Washington gave his treasury secretary complete discretion to grant Walker leave from the customshouse, with pay, for up to six months to go to Europe and try to avert financial disaster for Assistant Treasury Secretary Duer and his associates. Washington did this "altho it is contrary to the general sentiment and wish of the President that any officers under the general government and particularly one of such importance as the naval officer of New York, should be long absent from their trusts."

Walker apparently was told by Hamilton unofficially "that if you should stay a few months beyond your leave of absence no notice will be taken of it." All in all, the naval officer spent the better part of a year of the government's time unsuccessfully trying to retrieve the irretrievable, collecting nearly $2,000 in salary and fees from the Treasury Department for work performed in his absence entirely by deputies.

Sad to say, as an officer of SUM and a shareholder of Scioto, Walker, deeply involved himself, was in none too good shape financially. The naval officer was honest but, contemporary consensus had it, often showed bad judgment in matters financial. He justified his trip to Europe on government time on the grounds that he was going because "the honor and interest of the United States is concerned," when in fact only the honor and interest of some very important people was involved. One historian deeply immersed in the subject concluded that Walker's "chief weakness was his tendency to dabble in too many projects and to shift his attention too frequently." And his friend Robert Troup concluded that "when the madness of speculation reigned he was some degree under the influence of it." Yet Walker retained the undiminished confidence of his cohorts. As Hamilton himself put it, when questions of Walker's reliability and honesty were broached, "if Col. Walker should turn out to be a man not strictly and delicately honest I should begin to suspect myself," adding that he always conferred more authority upon Walker to act for him than he normally "prescribed for inferior officers in ordinary cases." So when the dust cleared on *l'affaire Duer*, Walker returned to the customshouse with his reputation untarnished in the eyes of those who counted, although he returned very much in need of his job.[8]

When the possibility for advancement to the first position opened in the customshouse, both Walker and his friends fully expected that, on the basis of his customshouse experience and seniority, revolutionary credentials, and Federalist ties, he would automatically be promoted. Hamiltonian Secretary of the Treasury Oliver Wolcott, Jr., solicited candidates for the post under his jurisdiction from Hamilton himself and several New York City high Federalists closely tied to Hamilton's coattails: William Seton, Robert Troup, and John Laurence were all queried for advice by the cabinet officer. Several names were submitted—Walker, Matthew Clarkson, William Seton, and Jonathan Burrall among them—but as Hamilton put it, Benjamin Walker was first among equals. If the normal procedure in these matters was followed, Wolcott turned over all the recommendations to Adams, along with his own choice among those recommended. The president would then make a selection from among those put forward. The irascible New Englander stunned everybody, probably including his own cabinet minister, when he tapped for the appointment Joshua Sands, a New York Federalist on nobody's list.

A number of important things are clarified by the incident, among them the evident fact that, from the outset of his administration, Adams doubted Wolcott's political loyalty and kept the secretary's discretionary powers to a minimum. Within six weeks of taking office, moreover, Adams challenged Hamilton's political authority in his own bailiwick, and by appointing Sands fired the opening gun in the war that raged nationally throughout his four years in office for control of the Federalist party. Adams, in short, early declared his political independence. With more than fifty subordinate posts in his grasp as well as the deference and prestige that went with the job, the new collector became overnight an important political figure in New York City. Adams clearly put a political foot in the Federalist door in the city when he made the appointment, and it is difficult not to conclude that he did it knowingly.

What Hamilton thought about the appointment was either not recorded or has not survived. Benjamin Walker, the bridesmaid, however, was irate enough to immediately resign the naval office. Sands was an important Federalist, but he was not "in," not part of Hamilton's clique. Described by DeWitt Clinton as a "decent man of moderate talents," he was a Brooklyn merchant and rope manufacturer who remained absolutely loyal to John Adams in a town where Alexander Hamilton ruled the Federalist party. In his four years as collector, he was "remarkably active" in local politics and was one of three New Yorkers singled out by Jefferson and Albert Gallatin for removal in 1801 because of the "violence of their characters and conduct." Walker vented his anger in a blistering letter to Wolcott on April 21, 1797, when it became clear that, Wolcott's efforts notwithstanding, he was not going to get the appointment. "I am extremely sorry that I have publicly held myself up as a candidate for the office of collector," Walker began. "Could I have supposed that any hesitation would have taken place I would never have subjected myself to the mortification I have already felt or risked the disgrace which must inevitably fall on me if not appointed." Foreshadowing the split in party ranks to come, Walker added that "with claims so strong [as] I believe [I] have, after they knew I was an applicant, [I never] doubted one moment of my appointment." His bitterness at John Adams spilled over when Walker heard that he had been denied. "Although I could send with it [a letter to Adams] the recommendations of seven Eights of all that is respectable in the city I should not solicit . . . for all the Treasure of the United States." [9]

Pennsylvania was another significant center of party conflict. In perhaps the most evenly matched state in the Union, the Federalists held their own in both town and country. The tentacles of Federalist organization spread outward from the eastern and western centers of Philadelphia and Pittsburgh. Despite the pacific efforts of popular Governor Thomas Mifflin, party confrontations were fierce, with the Federalist interest finding strong leadership in the likes of John Neville in the western country and William Lewis, William Bingham, George Clymer, and William Rawle in the Greater Philadelphia area. Even so, there was no more vigorous Jeffersonian party than that found in the Keystone State. The fact that the Federalists stayed abreast of their opposition, exchanging victories for the entire course of the decade, was a commentary on the depth and modernity of the Hamilton-oriented organization and the ability of that interest's management.

Despite the commonwealth's defection to the Republicans in the presidential election of 1796, the Federalists maintained their grip on the small towns and continued to hold their own in the urban centers. The party was thus able to remain very much in contention in the decade despite local setbacks. Both parties, according to Stephen Kurtz, reached "the high point of development" in 1796.[10] The Federalists did not thereafter fall apart; rather, they were overwhelmed by the same Republican tide that engulfed the parties in New York and elsewhere. For ten years, however, the Federalists constituted a vibrant and effective political organization.

In this setting, it was no surprise that, of all the major customshouses, Philadelphia's was among the most active politically. Most of the port's officers were aggressively Federalist, and this was communicated to the subordinate ranks. The scattering of customshouse employees at the bottom who even passively moved into the Republican party late in the decade were made to feel their apostasy in direct ways. The friction thus generated was resolved only after 1801, when Jefferson cleaned house. There was a great deal of political activity, all in all, in a federal agency that employed about forty men located in a city that was also the nation's capital.

After the furor over the Jay Treaty caused three defections to the Republican party among rank and file customs employees, the customs officers exerted significant pressure on their subordinates to toe the mark politically. One of the three Jefferson-leaning subordinates, Inspector of Customs Alexander Boyd, was removed in 1797. He alleged that "as soon as party spirit began to run high my known Republican principles rendered me odious to the Collector and Surveyor of the port." He stepped over the line permitted to keep his job (one that paid over $400 per year for part-time employment) when "I dared to Exercise my right openly as a freeman in an important election in this city. I was abruptly dismissed from office with no other reason assigned than that I had voted for a man Esteemed an Enemy to the Administration." Jonas Simonds, a second Republican customs inspector, hung on to his post by agreeing to refrain from all partisan activities; but his political beliefs, he claimed, "left me no room to hope or expect any preferment, and in that humble station [tidewaiter] I have been left." As Simonds so succinctly phrased it, he was led to believe that Republicanism "was a great Crime at the Customs House." [11]

The men responsible for creating this atmosphere of political tension and proscription were Collectors Sharp Delany (to 1798) and George Latimer (from 1798), Naval Officer William McPherson, and Surveyor William Jackson. All were either appointed or promoted to their posts during the mid- or late 1790s. Of Latimer's latter-day direction of the

Figure 6. An election at Philadelphia, about 1815.

customshouse it was said: "He possesses neither civility, impartiality, dignity or justice. . . . He is an insufferable tyrant." To McPherson was allotted responsibility for "the abuses of the department of the Customs to the grievous wrong of men who offended only in being republicans." And of Jackson it was charged that he was given to "regularly scolding the people for refusing to recognize the authority of their natural leaders." [12]

At the same time, nothing prevented these and other officers, as well as most of the subordinates, from actively engaging in local Federalist politics. The original customs collector had been Sharp Delany, an immigrant apothecary from Ireland who had made good prior to the Revolution. He had held various civil and militia posts during the war. Thereafter he emerged as a nationalist, an honorary member of the Cincinnati, and he served in the Pennsylvania legislature during the Confederation. He moved easily from support for the Constitution to advocacy of Hamiltonian measures; indeed, he carried out various political chores for the first secretary of the treasury while holding down the collector's office. His official tenure came to an abrupt halt in 1798, however, when it was discovered that he had over the past decade embezzled at least $86,000 in federal revenues from the customshouse. Delany, by this time broke, was let off remarkably easily, being permitted to resign. He never paid back the money nor was he ever prosecuted on either criminal or civil charges.[13] The treatment he received contrasted vividly with that meted out to John Lamb at almost the same time.

George Latimer supplanted Delany as collector. A member of the Philadelphia gentry, he was a graduate of the University of Pennsylvania, a former officer of the Continental army, and a successful merchant. After the war he served from time to time in the Pennsylvania Assembly and was twice elected speaker of that body. He was also an important Federalist member of the Pennsylvania Ratifying Convention of 1788. Like the other officers of the Philadelphia customshouse in the latter part of the decade, Latimer remained a part of the mainstream leadership of the Federalist interest in the capi-

Figure 7. Port of Philadelphia, about 1828.

Figure 8. The first U.S. Customs House at Philadelphia.

Figure 9. A McPherson Blue.

Figure 10. The executive mansion on High Street, Philadelphia, used by Presidents Washington and Adams. The building to the right, at the Sixth Street corner, was the house of Robert Morris.

tal city. As David H. Fischer has observed, Latimer enjoyed emoluments exceeding $8,000 per year and was a "regular member of the electioneering committees in Philadelphia," a city and state where party formations clearly antedated the Constitution.

Like so many other Federalist civil servants in areas where the idea of party was so well rooted, Latimer was a far cry from the ideological elitist who disdained the weapons and machinery of party. He actively and publicly supported the Jay Treaty. In 1790, 1792, and 1800 (while filling the collector's office), he chaired Philadelphia's Federalist Committee of Correspondence; in the latter year the collector was counted one of the prime movers of the party machine in the commonwealth. In short, Latimer was an important and aggressive political manager. He had been appointed collector in 1798 as a result of the efforts of Secretary of the Treasury Oliver Wolcott. Latimer's removal was a foregone conclusion when the Republicans came to power.[14]

The naval officer and surveyor of the port were cast in exactly the same mold. William McPherson, promoted from surveyor to naval officer in 1793, was a military man first and foremost. A native Philadelphian and a graduate of Princeton, he joined his parents in England, where his father was engaged in trade prior to the Revolution. He embarked on a military career when he accepted a commission in the English army. After the outbreak of war, however, he resigned that commission to accept one in the Continental army, rising to the rank of colonel. He was among the most active and conspicuous members of the Society of the Cincinnati on both the state and national levels in the 1780s. His marriage to the daughter of the Episcopal bishop of Pennsylvania, his intermittent service in the legislature, and his participation in the Pennsylvania Ratifying Convention—all served to entrench McPherson as an elite leader of Philadelphia federalism.

Things military remained his passion, however. McPherson founded and, till well after 1800, commanded the famous "McPherson Blues," perhaps the best militia cavalry unit in the nation. In the meantime, a leisurely customshouse

schedule provided more than $4,000 per annum in income
and permitted him the time to take over the active direction
of the state's Cincinnati. Moreover, McPherson's Blues, described as a "Federalist Military Organization," for reasons
both political and military was in the vanguard of the march
on western Pennsylvania in 1794 to suppress the Whisky Rebellion. It was almost automatic that McPherson should be
appointed one of John Adams's generals when the provisional army of 1798 was mandated by Congress. And it was
McPherson's Blues once again that played an important part
in squashing Fries's Rebellion in 1799. It was little wonder,
in a nation almost paranoid in its fear of the military in the
first years of its existence, that McPherson became a prime
candidate for enforced retirement from the government after
Jefferson's election.[15]

The final member of the customshouse triumvirate was
William Jackson, the surveyor of customs. Like Latimer and
McPherson, Jackson had been a Continental army officer. He
acted as secretary to the Constitutional Convention of 1787,
and later was private secretary to President Washington. His
marriage in 1795 to the daughter of Thomas Willing,
Philadelphia's first merchant, and his appointment to the customshouse at the same time, along with his elevation to the
post of secretary general of the Cincinnati, brought him into
the embrace of the tight local Federalist gentry. Jackson immersed himself deeply in politics. Though, according to
Timothy Pickering, "his manners have not been ingratiat-
ing," he was admittedly "not only a warm, but active Friend
of the Government." [16]

With such a highly politicized leadership at the top of the
customshouse, it was little wonder that an extraordinary
amount of business devolved upon subordinates. In
Philadelphia as elsewhere, the officers paid as much attention to political concerns as they did to government business.
The man who actually ran the customshouse was inspector
John Graff. Though his official station was low, it was generally understood in Philadelphia that he was in charge of the
day-to-day operation of the government installation. Indeed,
in the city directory his occupational listing was "deputy col-

lector" even though the federal government carried no such job title on its books.

Generally speaking, Graff was an excellent administrator. He was virtually apolitical, uninvolved in Philadelphia party contentions, unassuming, and clearly willing to shoulder responsibility while his betters reaped the fees deriving from his labors. "Mr. Graff has been in the Execution of his office," one Jeffersonian wrote, "free from a political or commercial partiality." Thus he served both Federalist and Republican alike as the political winds shifted after 1800. For nearly twenty years he "chiefly conducted the business of the office." In many ways, Graff's career implies much about both the political orientation and the freedom from duties of many high-level posts within the higher civil service in the Federalist decade.[17]

There were three Republicans in the lower ranks, but most of the subordinate employees were Federalists of middling status. Among the Federalists employed in the Philadelphia customshouse were four former seamen of various grades, one of whom was described as having "no settled way of Business" and financially needy—in combination a euphemism for one who hadn't held a steady job prior to his appointment. Two of the Federalists were bricklayers, others included a cartman, a fruiterer, and a silversmith. The lower echelons of the customshouse also provided a haven for at least two men of marginally elite status: a younger brother of an important Philadelphia Federalist lawyer, and a local minister. The incomes of the subordinates ranged from several hundred dollars per year for part-time inspectors to upwards of two thousand dollars for steadily employed weighers and gaugers of customs. With the exceptions of the minister and the lawyer's brother, none of the Federalist employees fit the usual stereotype of the urban Federalist political activist, either in terms of status or income.[18]

Looking backward from 1800, a recent historian exaggerated only slightly when he concluded about Maryland that a "handful of influential, wealthy, conservative aristocrats dictated the choice of a majority of the voters." The Federalist party was led by many of the state's great families, a familiar configuration for Federalist leadership everywhere. The Carrolls, Keys, Gales, Howards, and William Smith and his son-in-law Otho Holland Williams all could be found at the top of the clan-oriented Federalist managerial group. A Jeffersonian majority in Baltimore, the state's only urban center, did not prevent this strongly led Federalist interest in the remainder of the state from electing governors and dominating the legislature during the 1790s.[19]

This was so in part because of the degree of continuity with the politics of the Confederation. The Jeffersonians turned to the strong Antifederalist minority of a previous decade for much of their leadership. As Libero Renzulli has noted, "in many respects the battle [over the Constitution] was a continuation of the old paper money fight" of the postwar era. Moreover, the composition of the Federalist party under Washington, initially at least, was very close to that group that earlier supported ratification of the Constitution. The pattern of party development after 1789 is familiar. By 1792 Hamilton's nationalist programs split the major party along geographic and economic lines, into a "Potomac ticket" and a "Chesapeake ticket." Both of those Federalist groups were conservative in their own way. They divided according to economic interests, however, as these interests were perceived in terms of the secretary of the treasury's comprehensive fiscal efforts. Jeffersonian Republican strength was significantly enhanced by the Federalist division, and long-term inroads were made into an early center of constitutional strength in the northeast corner of the state—a change that augmented Republican muscle in Baltimore.

Resulting Jeffersonian gains in the congressional elections of 1792 motivated the Federalists to resolve their differences and regroup thereafter. While the newly unified Federalists recaptured the middle ground, it is fair to say that a highly structured two-party situation took hold in the state from that early date. This became clear in 1795 when, as it usually did, Jay's Treaty provided a high point of party contention. The Federalists, now united and in control of the machinery of government, generally withstood the tide of unpopularity that accompanied the ratification of the treaty. But the *détente* with England made it possible for the Republicans to mount an effective challenge in 1796. Once again, however, strong pressure by the opposition brought out the best in the "party of the aristocracy," the mark of a good political organization. The Federalists overcame the challenge and retained control of both the state government and Maryland's congressional delegation.

Both before and after 1796, the source of Federalist authority continued to be "the urban [elite] commercial interests" in alliance with "the conservative agrarian exporting sections." The outlying rural Federalist strongholds spanned much of the state, where the need for stable markets abroad dovetailed with support for the strong central government at home. So long as deference remained a vital force in the hinterlands of Maryland, and commerce thrived in the many ports of an area blessed with exceptional access to the sea throughout the entire length and breadth of the state, an elite planter-merchant Federalist coalition was able to maintain its superiority over an aggressive and growing Jeffersonian minority. It was this highly competitive party situation in the state generally, in tandem with the embattled state of federalism in Baltimore, that motivated the latter interest to press its political advantage in the Baltimore customshouse.

Following a configuration evident in most American ports, the Baltimore customs service was very much a resting place for veterans of the Continental army. The natural predilection of the Washington administration to favor those who had "proven themselves in '76" was strongly reinforced locally by the enormous influence James McHenry wielded in patronage matters. McHenry, a Revolutionary War aide-de-camp to Washington, the latter's long-time confidant, and a future secretary of war in the Adams administration, quickly emerged as the man to see to acquire a federal position in Maryland. The quick-tempered and outspoken Federalist made no bones about favoring his former brothers-in-arms and, more particularly, extending his efforts singularly on behalf of active supporters of both the Constitution and the incumbent administration. Between 1789 and 1795 McHenry successfully recommended thirty appointees to the federal service in Maryland. He was as close to Hamilton as he was to Washington. One example can suffice to demonstrate the point. When Baltimore Collector Otho Holland Williams lay near death in 1793, McHenry wrote Hamilton that, should Williams indeed die, Robert Purviance, the incumbent naval officer, should be appointed in Williams's place. He added: "and then you would have an opportunity to serve me by Mr. Salmons taking Mr. Purviance's place. . . . If neither can be appointed I request that I may hear from you before you determine a successor." [20] Not many people wrote to Hamilton that way.

The chronically ill collector was McHenry's nearest competitor for influence with the national administration, but Williams, influential as he was, remained a distant second. In the city itself, however, the customs collector was widely acknowledged to be "the Baltimore Federalist leader" and the "local fulcrum" for party management.[21]

Williams was no placeman; certainly he did not conform to the first-generation Federalist stereotype of the archetypal representative of a long-existent landed gentry. Instead, he was cast very much in an early day Horatio Alger mold. He was born in 1749 of poor parents who died while Otho was in his early teens, leaving him not only an orphan but the oldest of seven dependent children. He was apprenticed by relatives to a merchant house and served as a clerk for seven years, during which time he educated himself. In a period of relative social mobility, he was able to use his extensive native ability to work his way into the firm and make a small place for himself in Maryland society prior to the Revolution.

An early supporter of independence, he was able to land a commission in the Continental army and, again solely on the basis of ability, move up in the ranks. He eventually ended the war a general. A grateful Maryland legislature appointed Williams the customs collector at Baltimore in 1783. Soon thereafter he married a daughter of William Smith, a prominent local merchant who was tied to a wealthy political family. The general, through a combination of distinguished revolutionary service and a successful marriage, thus emerged as a force within the Maryland establishment. With one exception, however, his siblings remained illiterate and, in Williams's eyes, *déclassé;* he remained torn between acute embarrassment and a continuing sense of obligation to his brothers and sisters, succumbing to both from time to time.

He was, as James McHenry observed, of an "ambitious cast" both politically and financially. As a result of prudent investments, the aid of a well-to-do father-in-law, and his lucrative public office in a time of economic difficulty, Williams amassed some money and much land, both in Maryland and the Ohio valley, in the course of the Confederation era. By the end of the decade, the former Continental army general had been transformed into a man of both means and manners, and moved into the political mainstream of the Constitutional movement in his native state.[22]

His political activities in the waning days of the Confederation and until his death in July 1794, however, were restricted by declining health; he was a victim of consumption acquired while in the service. Nevertheless, he was a valuable local figure in the fight for ratification, particularly in his role as president of the Maryland chapter of the Society of the Cincinnati. His political leverage expanded after Washington's inauguration: his father-in-law William Smith was elected to the First Congress, he was naturally reappointed to his old customs post, this time under federal auspices, and as an old comrade-in-arms of Alexander Hamilton he acquired important ties to the new administration.

If Williams's relationship to his brothers and sisters was unusually complex, the same was true of his dealings with the new secretary of the treasury, with whom he had much in common both emotionally and by way of background. The Baltimore Federalist was an experienced and thoughtful customs officer, and the new administration sought his counsel as it drafted enabling legislation for the service in 1789. Several of Williams's suggestions found their way into the bill. At the same time Williams's advice on Maryland appointments was sought and often taken, although he was not nearly so influential on this score as McHenry.[23]

Hamilton knew Williams to be a man of prestige and good

judgment, but one extremely sensitive to the smallest snub, real or fancied. Hamilton's and Williams's relationship dated to the Revolution, their common personal backgrounds perhaps drawing them together initially. Although both men were on guard against any slight, Hamilton's greater maturity made it possible for him to deal with Williams with kid gloves. The secretary frequently had to work his way around the collector's piques, and when he did so he was rewarded with important administrative or political assistance. At Hamilton's urging, Williams advised his superior on a wide variety of matters, ranging from rescuing the military reputation of Nathaniel Greene to providing suggestions on how to handle negotiations with Indians. In this way the two enjoyed a sometimes stormy, free-wheeling relationship built on professional understanding, political convenience, and apparently a personal rapport that transcended both the first two factors.

Nevertheless, Williams harbored some resentment against the treasury secretary, and his feelings toward Hamilton were ambivalent. Even as the Baltimore collector was engaged in writing a series of newspaper essays in 1790 supporting Hamilton's economic program, he wrote privately to a friend that "Hamilton's abilities are greater than the perfection of this [funding] plan." And when Hamilton expressed dismay after receiving one of Williams's biting letters of criticism, Williams wrote his father-in-law that he was "sorry the Secretary feels hurt but I do not see the necessity of another letter to the paper [lauding Hamilton] to soothe him."

A pair of incidents underlines the complex administrative and personal relationship existing between the two men. A Freudian analyst perhaps could have a field day. In the first instance, friction developed between Williams and Robert Ballard, the surveyor of customs at Baltimore. Williams initially recommended Ballard for the post in 1789, describing him as one who "uniformly acted with the friends of order and good government." Nevertheless, by 1792, tensions between the two threatened to disrupt the customs service in Baltimore. In part, the falling out resulted from the fact that Williams's rapidly declining health left "more and more of the work of Williams' office falling on his deputies." Ballard complained to Hamilton about the extra burden this placed on his shoulders. The whole matter was rendered more complicated by the subsequent complaints coming out of Baltimore from several subordinate customs inspectors who accused Ballard of tyrannizing them although he was not properly their superior.

When Hamilton wrote Williams inquiring into the circumstances of both Ballard's complaint and those of the tidewaiters, Williams took the inquiry as a personal rebuke, blasted Hamilton in his response to the secretary, and threatened to resign. Uncharacteristically, Hamilton by return mail apologized for any offense, adding that he had no desire to place Williams "in a situation to be the instrument of rigorous measures auxiliary to such arbitrary or oppressive conduct" as that of which Ballard appeared to be guilty. The secretary added that the surveyor was "*in all cases* subject to the controul of the Collector," as of course were the inspectors. Hamilton ended his unusual placatory letter by promising to back Williams to the hilt without any further inquiry into Ballard's claims: "nothing will be wanting on my part to give energy to the representations which you shall make," and signed his letter "with undiminished consideration and esteem." Only Ballard's death shortly thereafter prevented his removal

The second confrontation also involved open disrespect on Williams's part and Hamilton's wholly uncharacteristic retreat from a showdown with a subordinate. At Otho Williams's urging, Hamilton in 1791 awarded a contract to Elie Williams to supply American troops in the West. Elie was Otho's brother and a partner in the struggling new merchant firm of Eliot and Williams. The contract was palpably never honored; deliveries were either late or never arrived, accounts were badly kept and Williams's brother proved totally unreliable and perhaps even dishonest. Although cause clearly existed, and Hamilton from time to time was occupied with the problems the younger Williams caused, the secretary did not terminate the arrangement and even refrained from too much overt criticism for nearly two years. But even the relatively little there was, justified though it was, pained Williams and caused him to sulk. The collector made clear that he felt any fault lay with Hamilton and the government and not his brother. Again with uncharacteristic forebearance, the secretary repeatedly backed away from an open clash with his subordinate and ended the costly contract only after Williams's death.[24]

The ambivalence of the collector's relationship with Hamilton did not interfere with the political character of the customshouse or its personnel. Williams himself, in so far as his health permitted, was deeply engaged in electioneering. He had been in the thick of efforts "to defeat the advocates of paper money" in the Confederation—a euphemism, of course, for active aid in behalf of ratification. At that time Williams's high office in the Cincinnati, his appointment under the state government, his family connections and military record made him a natural "fulcrum for party correspondence," a political centricity he maintained until his death. Williams was an indefatigable contributor to the newspapers on subjects ranging from endorsement of all Hamiltonian measures to election advice to the voters. He was one of the many agents of the Federalist party whose task it was to disseminate tracts and broadsides through the mails to party faithful. The collector, moreover, actively electioneered both in the congressional races of 1790 "to advance the friends of the new Constitution," and in the local election in Baltimore in 1791. Like many another party leader who tempted the fates by campaigning for candidates, Williams admitted after the 1790 canvass that his "conduct in the late election for representatives has been misconstrued by both parties." He organized poll watchers and conveyances to bring voters to the polls and perhaps even harangued a crowd. On election day 1791, maybe because of failing health, perhaps because of his difficulties the year before, he "was necessarily more engaged . . . in keeping the peace; many of the respectable part of the citizens [another euphemism for Federalists] encouraged him in this duty." [25]

The other officers of the customshouse had been chosen in 1789 explicitly because they supported ratification. Thereaf-

ter, as James McHenry said of Naval Officer Robert Purviance, all the customs officers, with one exception, "never
shrunk from the right cause." The exception was David Porter, captain of the Maryland revenue cutter, who by 1794
moved in Republican circles. At Hamilton's urging,
Washington forced Porter to resign from office on pain of
removal.

Naval Officer Robert Purviance was a member of a
formerly wealthy and still prominent Baltimore merchant
family that had suffered reverses and declared bankruptcy at
the end of the Confederation. An influential local supporter
of the Constitution, Purviance "while not of the best
abilities" was entitled to a "sinecure." When Otho Williams
died in 1794, Purviance was promoted to the top spot in the
customshouse. The new naval officer was Daniel Delozier, a
moderate and widely respected young Federalist who,
throughout the Federalist era and thereafter, actually ran the
customshouse, first as Williams's "deputy" and later as the
naval officer. All of the officers, Porter excepted, in the words
of Baltimore merchant and Congressman Samuel Smith,
"acted with the federal party." Another Jeffersonian after
1801 wrote the new president that "Federalism has long
triumphed here in that [customs] department." [26]

Party involvement characterized the entire customshouse
from top to bottom. It is possible to glimpse into the lower
ranks of officeholders and perceive something about the
backgrounds and activities of Baltimore's middle-class
Federalist managers. Information was unearthed for six
Federalist employees in the customshouse—four inspectors,
a weigher, and a measurer of customs. All were of middling
or even lower-class social and economic status. Their income
from federal employment ranged from about $150 to $1,000
per year, those in the higher figures earning that much by
working full time at their customs jobs. All six were veterans
of the Continental army, serving either as enlisted men or
junior officers. All of them were active in one way or another
in local Federalist politics in the 1790s. Three had come to
their political involvement and perhaps their jobs via local
espousal of the constitutional cause. Two of the six in particu-

lar stand out as examples of middle-class federalism in an urban setting.

Martin Eichelberger had been a foot soldier in the Maryland line during the War for Independence. After the war he returned to his native Baltimore and opened a small retail shop that barely provided him with a living. When his former superior officers, notably James McHenry and John Kilty, called on him to beat the drums for the Constitution, he responded, as he acknowledged, in a small way. Eichelberger carried some weight politically "in some quarters of town," according to McHenry. He was a "Dutchman" who "was not without influence among his countrymen" settled in Baltimore. This influence, McHenry noted in recommending him for a federal post, the shopkeeper "used like a good citizen." He was particularly adept politically, according to Kilty, at the "practice of importunity" of would-be voters. Eichelberger was appointed weigher of customs in 1789, a job he needed to supplement his income from the store. His appointment "had a good effect upon his countrymen most of which in this place are highly antifederal." This particular Dutchman remained throughout the Federalist era a "firm friend of the new government."

Alexander McCaskey was appointed an inspector of customs in 1789. Like Eichelberger, he was a veteran of the Maryland line; unlike the former, McCaskey was never able to establish himself even marginally after the Revolution. He wrote Washington that even an appointment, much as he wanted one, "will never fully compensate for the fatigues I have undergone in the War." He had been a minor supporter of ratification in the Confederation and remained devoted to the Federalist cause in the ensuing decade. This was interesting because his long-time economic difficulties—he too was a shopkeeper—resulted both in his imprisonment for debt in 1791 and again in 1792, and the loss of everything he owned as well. Otho Williams, perhaps because appearances demanded it of him, removed McCaskey from his customs post, causing the former inspector to slide even farther downhill. Even "my reputation is impeached" by the dismissal, McCaskey told Williams shortly afterward. Yet in a plaintive appeal to the president in 1793 that was never answered, McCaskey reaffirmed his Federalist "attachment" to the "Present Government of America." Other office seekers, he added, were "aided by Powerful and rich Connexions," but he and his family were "helpless" in the face of the losses he had sustained.[27]

At least in the early years of the Federalist decade, the "party of the aristocracy" exercised a remarkably deep emotional appeal to a broad range of American interests, if men like Eichelberger and McCaskey were at all indicative. For as long as deference remained an important social force in American life, the Federalist party benefited. In purely local terms, the Baltimore customshouse provided most of the basic Federalist cadre in a Republican city, and thus remained an important part of the Federalist machine in an administration-oriented state.

Regional differences and local peculiarities aside, the customshouses of three major eastern cities in the 1790s operated politically in some very uniform ways. These ports were staffed by Federalist personnel knit into strong party formations that exerted a significant impact, not only in the immediate urban areas of which they were a part, but in their states as a whole. These customshouses were in a sense targets of opportunity for an entrenched national party leadership in Philadelphia; engaged in a political game that was in some ways new to the American experience, the Federalists turned out to have played it well after all. If the customshouses provided examples, they were in a very real sense testimony to the modernity and strength of the Federalist party. This generalization was borne out with equal force in the ports of the South.

CHAPTER FIVE

Customs: Virginia and the Carolinas

Virginia was generally Republican country in the early 1790s, but a stubborn, adept Federalist party centering on Richmond occasionally moved that commonwealth into the Federalist column as the decade waned. Small and medium-sized Chesapeake area customshouses, particularly those at Norfolk and Alexandria, were significant components of the Federalist party structure in the Old Dominion. Each of several thriving ports of entry contributed its Federalist cadre to that party's professional infrastructure. A similar scattering of even more Lilliputian harbors helped to sustain the Federalist party in North Carolina, a state that had started the decade as a surviving bastion of antifederalism. As in the case of Rhode Island, where a similar problem existed, North Carolina federalism was nurtured by the national administration in Philadelphia with tender loving care. All southern ports were dwarfed in comparison to Charleston, the premier port of the original South and, as a result, customshouse politics in South Carolina differed markedly from that of its southern sister states. The Federalist cadre in the Charleston customshouse was a potent centralized source of organizational strength within a dominant, though sometimes divided, Federalist interest in the Palmetto State.

105

At the outset of the 1790s, Virginia was for the most part "politically alien territory" for Alexander Hamilton and the Federalist party.[1] Edward Carrington, the supervisor of internal revenue in the state, surfaced as the key local Federalist linking the treasury secretary to the Federalist clique centering on Richmond and headed by John Marshall and the Lees. This "junto," if the term applies, eventually gained the support of not only the urban elite in that town but also the outlying planter factions as well. This early Federalist minority demonstrated an ability to survive, mainly by paying lip service to conservative party ideology on the one hand while engaging in vigorous organizational efforts on the other. Though the Federalists confronted an entrenched, ably led Republican party, they claimed a few political bright spots. In addition to Federalist Richmond, the Marshall, Lee, and Carrington clans could count on Federalist strength in several thriving ports and "nationalist counties," particularly Norfolk and the Northern Neck counties. These commercial areas found Hamilton's commercial policies increasingly more salutary to their interests. This economic affinity was augmented by Hamilton's effective use of federal offices to shore up Federalist leadership in the commonwealth's several harbors.

Careful husbandry of political organizations in these areas and elsewhere began to bear fruit for the Federalists in 1796 when, in at least a symbolically important victory, one Adams elector was named from the Old Dominion. The Federalist situation improved thereafter, as the organization clustered more and more extensively around federal officeholders. Seven of ten congressmen elected in 1799 were Federalists, and that party picked up strength in the Virginia legislature as well. A confession of respect for mounting Federalist clout was made explicit in 1800, when the Jeffersonians prudently districted the state so as to concede three presidential electors to John Adams in order to guarantee their majority within the commonwealth's electoral delegation. Though always a minority, the Federalist interest in Virginia remained very much in the game, and must be counted among the most effective Federalist parties in the United States.

Norfolk, situated at the point where the Chesapeake Bay meets the Atlantic Ocean, was one of the two most important Virginia ports. It was an urban center characterized by fierce two-party rivalry, a town in which the Federalist interest counted heavily on its customshouse to anchor its local party organization. The degree to which this was true became evident in 1797, when a new collector was named. That story not only indicates the centricity of the customshouse to the party, it reveals a great deal about the relationship of the local to the national party in the Adams years. In this respect the conflict was not unlike the controversies involving the customshouses in Portsmouth, New Hampshire, and New York City.

The central figure in the Norfolk drama was Daniel Bedinger, a well-to-do landowner in the town. Born in 1761, he had enlisted in the Continental army at the outbreak of the Revolution and in 1778 had been breveted lieutenant, a battlefield promotion resulting from his conspicuous bravery. A product of German stock who had migrated from Pennsylvania to the Shenandoah valley before the war, he inherited some land from his family and added to it by means of prudent purchases after the war. At the same time, he was employed as the second officer in the customshouse during the Confederation, serving under his friend Josiah Parker. When the latter was elected to the First Congress (he surfaced as a Republican), he recommended that Bedinger be named to replace him. Circumstantially it would appear that Bedinger had been an Antifederalist, for Washington, despite Bedinger's war record, not only did not name him collector, he did not even appoint Bedinger to the second office, in which he was an incumbent—a rare happenstance usually reserved for Antifederalists in 1789. The former hero had to settle for the surveyor's post, the third slot in the Norfolk facility.[2]

The collector's job went to William Lindsay, a Federalist lawyer in town and also a veteran officer of the Continental army. The real signal tipping Bedinger's status with the Washington administration was his replacement as naval officer by Philemon Gatewood, Parker's former clerk. Gatewood was named despite the fact that the outgoing

Federalist collector later described him as "not qualified" and "an easy man and illiterate." [3]

Politically the president made a wise decision, for Bedinger matured into a raging critic of his administration. In a state where resistance to Jay's Treaty was especially strong, Bedinger appears to have been a most conspicuous opponent. From the promulgation of the "British Treaty" until Washington left office, moreover, the Norfolk surveyor committed the then almost unpardonable sin of heaping public odium on the president. Bedinger described Washington as "a partizan of war and confusion" and was said to have asserted that Benedict Arnold would have made a better president than the Virginian. [4] So it was that, when William Lindsay died in 1797 after a long illness during which Bedinger carried a large part of the day-to-day work-load at the customshouse, the surveyor was hardly a shoo-in to replace him. Indeed, only his visibility in the community, revolutionary service, and mastery of the customshouse kept him from being removed earlier by Washington. John Adams had been in office only a little more than a month when Lindsay died, but it was quickly understood that while it was impossible to promote Gatewood because of his official shortcomings, it was equally unwise to elevate Bedinger in view of his political posture.

Strong efforts by local Republicans to influence the new president to appoint Bedinger were more than offset by a campaign on the part of key Virginia Federalists to see that Bedinger was not named. Republican Congressman Josiah Parker strongly urged Oliver Wolcott to promote Bedinger on the strength of his undoubted ability, his assumption of almost total authority in the customshouse during Collector Lindsay's protracted illness, and on the basis of his revolutionary service. The surveyor's professional and personal claims on the job were so great that the situation required a delicate but firm effort by some of Virginia's first Federalists to prevent the yet untried president from being swayed by arguments urging merit over politics.* In this debate lies

---

* Adams and Wolcott were almost simultaneously dealing with not dissimilar situations at Portsmouth and New York City.

much of the significance of the battle over the appointment.

After succeeding in having the decision postponed for a few months, the Federalists offered a strong outside candidate for the collector's spot in the person of Otway Byrd, scion of perhaps the oldest and best-established gentry in the state. At the same time they barraged the administration with advice that followed a singularly identical pattern. Edward Carrington, supervisor of the federal internal revenue for Virginia, wrote Wolcott conceding that "as a Port Inspector I will not hesitate in saying that he [Bedinger] is not surpassed in the United States." The influential Virginia Federalist added, however, that "candor calls me to mention that he is understood to have been amongst the opposers of this administration . . . and with those connected with the appointment it must rest how far that circumstance should have weight."

William Heth, the politically important collector of customs at Bermuda Hundred, wrote the new treasury secretary that "there can be no question about Bedinger's capacity or fitness for the office. But whether what some hath said respecting his political conduct . . . ought to be a bar to his promotion is not for me to say." "Public concerns," added Heth, and not his "private inclinations" in favor of Bedinger should prevail. The strongest letter to Wolcott came from the most highly placed Virginia Federalist, United States Attorney General Charles Lee, himself a former customs collector at Alexandria. He rejected the Republican's aspirations for promotion on the grounds of his "blind and unalterable attachment to a foreign nation, which is carried to such an extremity as to make him the least proper of all the candidates."

At the same time Copeland Parker, surveyor of customs at nearby Smithfield and Federalist brother of Congressman Josiah Parker, claimed that he was quoting President Adams himself when he asked Bedinger to withdraw his candidacy on the grounds that "any man's political creed would be an insuperable bar to promotion." The remark was widely bandied about in local discussion of the appointment; William Heth, in fact, used it almost verbatim in dismissing Bedinger as a serious candidate for collector. The president a few years later quibbled a bit about the introduction of both his name and views into the Norfolk controversy but, in essentially objecting only to the use of the word *insuperable*, Adams conceded much. "Neither Mr. Parker nor any other person ever had authority from me to say, that any man's political creed would be an insuperable bar to promotion." He then went on to say, however, that "political principles and discretion will always be considered, with all other qualifications and well weighed, in all appointments."

And "political principles" clearly weighed heavily in Bedinger's case. The surveyor, contemporarily aware only of local Federalist opposition, attempted to offset it. He wrote Congressman Parker to tell Wolcott that a Norfolk petition opposing his appointment "had been handed about in the most private manner possible." The petition, moreover, derived from "a set of men, the majority of whom are strangers [Scotch merchants] or characters who were never friendly to the Revolution . . . [who] now support [Byrd] for particular reasons and to answer particular [political] purposes." [5]

Some six months after Lindsay's death, Otway Byrd was named collector at Norfolk. Byrd's father was a well-known Tory who before the Revolution had placed his son in the Royal Navy. When war broke out, the younger Byrd deserted and joined the Continental army, ultimately attaining the rank of colonel. He was disinherited by his father; but utilizing his family name, connections, and some property he already owned, he became a modestly successful merchant after the war. Carrington, Heth, and Charles Lee, an important Federalist triumvirate in Virginia, all recommended Byrd as "a firm supporter of the present government." Perhaps William Heth summarized as well as anyone Byrd's attractiveness in 1797 when he wrote to Wolcott that Byrd's "abilities, celebrity of name and character, and peculiar fitness are greater" than those of any other candidate. [6]

When news that Byrd had been appointed reached Norfolk, Daniel Bedinger resigned from the customs service. Otway Byrd, in turn, was among those removed by Jefferson shortly after he assumed the presidency in 1801. [7] Apparently

Bedinger could not be persuaded to return to the customs service, although he most certainly must have been given the opportunity by the Republican administration.

Alexandria was the other major port in Virginia. That Potomac River town was, with Richmond, one of the two major centers of federalism in a Republican state. Federalist strength in this community derived in large part from the vigor and commitment of the party leadership centered on the customshouse. Three collectors headed the federal establishment in Alexandria at different times in the decade: Charles Lee from 1789 to 1795, John Fitzgerald from 1795 to about 1797, and Charles Simms thereafter. The three were all able men, politically active, representative of the commonwealth's gentry, and possessed unusually strong personal ties to the Federalist administration in Philadelphia. The trio's collective political skills were committed in the course of the decade to a host of Federalist interests. These included efforts to establish a Virginia branch of the Bank of the United States, drumming up local support for the excise tax, aid in suppressing the Whisky Rebellion, public endorsement of the Proclamation of Neutrality and Jay's Treaty, and active participation in the national elections of 1796 and 1798.

The duties of office, on the other hand, encroached but little on the time of the Alexandria collectors. In 1792 Federalist Surveyor of Customs Samuel Hanson, the second officer of the port, complained to President Washington "that Lee is absent for most of the year" from the customshouse, leaving the day-to-day business in the hands of a deputy. Nearly a decade later, when Charles Simms was about to leave the office, it was still described as "a perfect sinecure, the duties being performed by a Deputy, while he [Simms] attends his profession as a lawyer." Yet the office retained its political importance. "It is impossible," a Virginia Republican complained to Thomas Jefferson, "to estimate the influence which may be exercised in the collection of large sums of money payable for [customs] duties in a commercial town." [8]

Charles Lee had been named collector of customs at

Alexandria during the Revolution. By 1790, after he had gained reappointment via the federal government, the office was producing an income of more than $1,000 annually and employed some fifteen subordinates. After 1789 Lee was described as one of "the second-rate followers" of Hamilton nationally and, as a member of the "Richmond faction," a local ally of his "close friend" John Marshall. One brother, Richard Bland Lee, was a Federalist member of the House of Representatives and another, Henry ("Light-Horse Harry") Lee, was for a time governor of the state. A graduate of the College of New Jersey, Charles served in the Virginia legislature and maintained a law practice in Alexandria in addition to his customs duties.[9]

Lee surfaced as a staunch supporter of ratification in the waning days of the Confederation. In the early years of the 1790s, moreover, the collector was a "popular and politically influential" leader in the Alexandria-Richmond area—a local bastion of federalism in a state that quickly moved into the Republican orbit after 1790. In the months before he entered Washington's cabinet as attorney general, Lee was a key defender of the Jay Treaty; his speeches in the House of Burgesses were especially effective in the waning days of 1795, a view grudgingly offered by James Madison, a leader of the effort to prevent United States Senate ratification. Once in the cabinet (his arrival more or less coincided with Hamilton's departure), he began to move "outside Hamilton's political orbit," emerging as an Adams Federalist in the last years of the decade. Still, Lee retained a vital and important interest in Virginia politics throughout the Federalist decade. For example, he was unquestionably a key figure— perhaps even *the* key figure—in putting together the unusually successful Federalist ticket for Congress in 1798. This was a kind of involvement not usually attributed to Federalist leaders, let alone cabinet ministers. By that date, Oliver Wolcott, Jr., reported, Lee "frequently dissents what is proposed by others [Hamiltonians in the Adams cabinet] and approves of the sentiments of the President." He was rewarded by the outgoing president in 1801 with a short-lived "midnight" appointment to the newly created United States Circuit Court.[10]

John Fitzgerald succeeded Lee to the collector's office in 1795. A member of the Virginia gentry and a close friend of the first president's nephew, he had served as one of Washington's aides during the War for Independence. Fitzgerald was a locally important Federalist supporter of Hamilton's economic program in the early years of the Federalist decade. At Hamilton's invitation, he helped to line up Virginia Federalist investors in the Bank of the United States in 1791. At the same time he urged upon Virginians the establishment of a branch of that institution in the Old Dominion. The excise tax, promulgated in 1791, "had my warmest and most active support," Fitzgerald wrote the president, even though, as the owner of a distillery himself, he knew he would be heavily taxed. Late in 1793 he chaired a Federalist meeting in Alexandria convened to endorse the Proclamation of Neutrality just issued by Washington and to denounce the Whisky insurrection then developing in Pennsylvania. Fitzgerald's political credentials when he took office, in short, were impeccable, and his party involvement did not diminish during his brief tenure as customs collector.[11]

The third collector among the trio of customs officers who headed up the federal establishment in Alexandria was Charles Simms. Like Lee, he was a local attorney who maintained his practice while occupying federal office. Simms was described as "very wealthy" with property worth an estimated $50,000 and a law practice that brought in $2,500 a year; some Republicans after 1801 would allege unfairly that he had come into office a poor man and would leave it a rich one. An officer in the Virginia line of the Continental army and an active member of the Cincinnati, he had served as a Federalist delegate to the Virginia Ratifying Convention of 1788, and was a sometime representative in the House of Burgesses during the 1790s.

Like his predecessors, he was an ardent Federalist. Contradicting completely the aloof stereotype often invoked to

describe elitist Federalist candidates, he campaigned vigor-
ously in 1796 for the office of elector for John Adams. In one
public speech he "accused Jefferson of cowardly conduct as
Governor during [Benedict] Arnold's invasion of Virginia" in
the Revolution. He was extremely active in that presidential
canvass and seemed to be an important source for the perpetuation of the discredited but lingering charge of cowardice that followed Jefferson through his political career. Little
wonder that, according to one Federalist, in 1801 Simms's
"removal was on the list of probabilities," although another
naively said that "Revenge . . . [was] beneath the Ideas of
Mr. Jefferson." [12]

The customs service in Virginia provides a good case study
of the universality of nepotism as a commonplace practice
among Federalists in that era. A problem in public life at any
time, both the relatively rigid social structure of the Old
Dominion and the plenitude of small port towns in the
Chesapeake and Potomac river basins may have made Virginia in the era of the first party system even more susceptible than other states to this official disease. Small ports
were especially subject to the affliction. Even that model of
public rectitude President George Washington could not escape the epidemic, for he suffered from that human frailty
visited on so many, in-laws who needed help. Nepotism in
the revenue service in the Old Dominion took two forms: the
passage of an office from one relative to another, and the
appointment of young sons of first families to well-paying
sinecures.
There are several examples of outgoing officers passing on
customs posts to close relatives. When Josiah Parker was
elected to the First United States Congress, he resigned his
customs posts at Norfolk and neighboring Smithfield and
succeeded in rounding up the latter appointment for his
brother Copeland, then only twenty years old. While the
elder sibling drifted into the Republican camp in the House
by 1793, Copeland remained very much a Federalist.[13] A
similar development occurred in 1795 at the tiny port of
Dumfries on the Potomac River. Richard M. Scott, both a

local merchant and the collector of customs (the two were not always necessarily deemed incompatible in small ports), having gained "fairly easy circumstances and wishing to retire," successfully recommended his brother David for the post.[14]

An equally usual form of nepotism was the transfer of office from father to son, in spite of the administration's announced fears of inherited officeholding. Federalist merchant Hudson Muse, the long-time collector at the small Potomac port of Tappahannock, continued to engage in trade during his tenure in office. When financial reverses set him back in 1793 and 1794, he used customs revenues to ease his plight, rendering the collector unable "to meet the [United States] Treasurer's drafts on him." Washington promptly removed him from office for what was termed by the administration a "misdemeanor," although the elder Muse was neither prosecuted nor forced to make good the customs losses, not even from his bond. What makes the story incredible in light of the oft-repeated stories of Washington's and Hamilton's public virtue, was that the secretary of the treasury and the president promptly appointed Hudson Muse's son Laurence to the collector's post, accepting transfer of the unencumbered bond from father to son. This happened although the younger Muse had for several years served as his father's deputy in the federal service and was a junior partner in the family's merchant firm, and could hardly have been unaware of what had been happening to the federal revenue collected at Tappahannock. The only logic that fits is that Laurence Muse was a member of the Virginia House of Burgesses in 1794, had been for many years, and the father and son were both highly respected local Federalist cadremen.[15]

Two other Virginia fathers passed on offices to their sons during the years of Federalist rule. When Jacob Wray resigned as customs collector at Hampton, opposite Norfolk at the mouth of Chesapeake Bay, George Wray succeeded to the post. Zachariah Rowland, a prominent Federalist merchant in Richmond, was named collector of customs in that town in 1790. He had been a Loyalist during the war and had even been arrested as such just prior to the battle of Yorktown, but he had clearly lived down that stigma very well. When he resigned in 1796, he still retained enough leverage to influence the incoming Adams administration to name his son James to the collector's job in spite of the fact that the offspring was only twenty-one.[16]

Relatives of highly placed Virginia gentry did well also. President Washington especially compromised himself repeatedly; his appointments too frequently did violence to his oft-stated injunctions against nepotism and favoritism in granting office. A few examples will suffice. "My political conduct in nominations," Washington wrote in July 1789, "even if I was uninfluenced by principle, must be exceedingly circumspect and proof against just criticism, for the eyes of Argus are upon me, and no slip will pass unnoticed that can be improved into a supposed partiality for friends or relatives." Indeed, within a week of assuming the presidency, he had written that "I will, to the best of my judgment, discharge the duties of that office with that impartiality and zeal for the public good, which ought never to suffer connections of blood or friendship to intermingle, so as to have the least sway on decisions of a public nature." And two weeks later, on March 21, 1789, he added: "I know in my own heart, I would not be in the remotest degree influenced in making nominations by motives arising from ties of amity or blood." [17]

Within months of making these statements, George Washington appointed William Lewis the surveyor of customs at Fredricksburg. Lewis, a brother of Fielding Lewis, the president's brother-in-law, was ill and infirm in 1789, and not really able to conduct the business of the office. He was also in financial need, in part because the Lewis brothers' land speculations had proven conspicuously unsuccessful. As if to ensure that this was not a singular occurrence, Washington appointed several more of Martha's relatives to federal posts shortly before he left office. In rapid succession in 1796, he named Martha's nephew Thomas Peter the postmaster at Cabin Point, Virginia, another nephew, John Lewis, collector of the internal revenue in the Old Dominion, and two of Martha's cousins, Francis and Miles Lewis, federal auxiliary officers of the internal revenue. No contemporary, Republican or Federalist, seems to have picked up the significance of these appointments, Washington's early fears about the eyes of Argus notwithstanding. In fact, Tench Coxe, in his tract *A View of the United States of America*, noted that Washington "has not, during so long a term, appointed a single relation to any office of honour or emolument." [18]

A well-chronicled radical tradition dating back to before the Revolution continued to exert its influence on North Carolina politics in the 1790s.[19] Most of the antirevolutionary radicals were centered in the mountain areas, and so political differences usually could be fixed on an East-West axis. Both Republicans and Federalists in the Tarheel State suffered from this historic and emotional geographic schism, with western elements who opposed the Revolution in the 1770s also against the Constitution in the 1780s and carrying over their hostility to national government in the 1790s. These historic differences not only ensured that the Federalist party was born a minority party in North Carolina, they also contributed to deep leadership differences within Federalist ranks.

Two distinct Federalist leadership groups formed in the 1790s. One faction was composed of leading members of the bar and was dominated by James Iredell, William R. Davie, Archibald McLaine, and Samuel Johnston. A somewhat less orthodox merchant-oriented faction grew up around the Blount family, and especially the magnetic John Gray Blount. The first-named interest remained tied to the Federalists throughout the 1790s. The latter faction gravitated toward the Jeffersonian orbit around the time of Jay's Treaty. The political power and involvement of the Iredell-Davie group was subject to attrition at about the same time, however, through death, retirement or, in Iredell's case, appointment to high judicial office. Moreover, North Carolina Federalists remained a distinct minority in a state where a still viable radical Antifederalist tradition contributed to the vitality, staying power, and able leadership of a Jeffersonian majority. The latter never completely shook off a strong, stubborn Federalist opposition though, so North Carolina did retain its competitive two-party character throughout the Federalist decade. The safest statement to make about two-party combat among the Tarheels was that it always revolved around peculiarly "unresolved issues that continued to pit section against section and, within the eastern interest, town against town."

So it was that North Carolina shared with Rhode Island an intense antifederalism that survived the waning days of the Confederation. Opposition to the Constitution survived even ratification and the installation of the new national government. The Tarheel State did not ratify until the end of 1789, and then only reluctantly, bowing to the futility of further resistance. Washington's administration pursued much the same appointments policy in this southern state as it did in Rhode Island. That is to say, Washington explicitly involved himself in local appointments, compiling careful information before making any. This practice was evident in dealing with the whole range of United States openings in North Carolina, the relatively large customs service included.

The Federalists in Philadelphia solicited political data from a congressional triumvirate that became almost totally responsible for arranging a strongly Federalist customs service. The three were Congressman Hugh Williamson and Senators Benjamin Hawkins and Samuel Johnston, all active proponents of the Constitution in this Antifederalist state. These three submitted detailed lists to Washington in 1789 and 1790, identical in form to those submitted by Rhode Island's Federalist leaders Jabez Bowen, Jeremiah Olney, and John Brown among others.

With its rippled coastline, North Carolina was geographically reminiscent of Massachusetts, but in miniature. There were an unusually large number of ports, though none handled the kind of volume found in harbors to the north. Nevertheless, the sheer number of anchorages created important local jobs for nineteen customs officers in 1790, with at least as many more subordinate positions created as well.[20] The most important of the thirteen North Carolina ports were Edenton and Camden on Albemarle Sound, Washington and New Bern off Pamlico Sound, and Wil-

Figure 11. Map of North Carolina coastline, about 1779.

mington, the largest port in the state, in the Cape Fear region. Senators Hawkins and Johnston submitted a list to President Washington early in February 1790 containing nineteen recommendations for appointments to the customs. Tobias Lear, the president's secretary, in a conversation with Hugh Williamson, then asked the Congressman, on behalf of the president, to also submit a list at the same time. This early political involvement by the president belies anew most of the stereotypes of the apolitical George Washington in office.

Williamson was well known to Washington, and the latter probably came to trust Williamson's judgment when they served together as delegates to the Philadelphia Convention of 1787. The North Carolinian was a strong, involved supporter of the Constitution. He reinforced this commitment by working long and hard for ratification. During the First Congress, at least, he was perhaps the key North Carolina liaison to the national administration.[21]

Williamson alone, and the two senators jointly, submitted lists of nineteen nominees each to the president. There must have been consultation, for sixteen of the nineteen names appear on both rosters. Clearly these Federalist representatives, almost certainly at the oral request of the administration, made support of the Constitution an important qualification for office in the customs service. All sixteen who were recommended by both the senators and the congressman were nominated by the president. Of the sixteen, at least ten had been spirited supporters of the Constitution in a staunchly Antifederalist state. The only known opponent of the Constitution on either list was Michael Payne, who was recommended only by Williamson and who was appointed, only to be removed later by John Adams.

This strong evidence that a political test was applied to North Carolina by the first Federalist administration is reinforced by the fact that Governor Alexander Martin, the Antifederalist chieftain in Tarheel country, also made five recommendations to the president. None were nominated. The fact that Martin's letter to Washington followed those of the three members of Congress by some three weeks indicates that he wasn't asked for his suggestions and sent them only when word came back from Philadelphia that local Federalists were naming names for the chief executive.[22] The North Carolina customs appointments were made with the same precision in Philadelphia that governed nominations in Rhode Island.

The Albemarle Sound area at the northern end of North Carolina's erratic coastline formed one of the three distinct customs districts in the state. The region was dotted with several small ports, for the most part satellites of the central harbor at Edenton, where a customs collector presided. He directed the service for almost the entire region, with surveyors of customs under him responsible for several smaller anchorages, including Hertford, Plymouth, Winton, and Murfreesboro. Another collector directed the customs service in the harbor at Camden, and oversaw other tiny ports in the immediate area as well.

The geographic oddity in the Albemarle area that resulted in the wide dispersal of customs personnel created a difficult administrative situation that helped breed an almost unbelievable degree of nepotism. The only element that did not suffer administratively as a result was the Federalist party.

The ensuing laxity rendered Albemarle a managerial horror. Surveyors of customs administering offices by themselves in isolated backwaters were often slow in reporting and transmitting the money they collected. Absenteeism, if two extreme examples bear witness, was widely tolerated in an area where kinship and personal ties prevailed over official responsibility. Thomas D. Freeman, the surveyor at Plymouth, ruled in such solitary splendor that it took six months for Thomas Benbury, the Edenton collector and Freeman's immediate superior, to learn that the latter had moved away, leaving the port unattended. Although Freeman had departed in February 1792, it was not until July that the collector reported that just-learned fact to Philadelphia. It took another two months for the administration to anticlimactically dismiss Freeman because of his "prolonged absence." [23] The odyssey of Laurence Mooney, the surveyor of Winton in 1795, was even more improbable. The Irish-born Mooney apparently became homesick shortly after his appointment in 1795 and returned to Ireland for five years. Nobody officially missed him, and he returned in 1800 to resume his duties as if he had never been away. The story was so fantastic that some years later Treasury Secretary Albert Gallatin went to the trouble to verify it as a vintage example of Federalist maladministration.[24]

Nepotism was as much a problem in the Albemarle area as was administrative dereliction; the two were probably closely related. In 1793 Samuel Tredwell was appointed customs collector at Edenton, the central administrative position in the area. He replaced the deceased Thomas Benbury. Although Tredwell was extremely young and inexperienced at the time of his nomination and a scion of a well-known formerly Loyalist family in the area, he was also a nephew of Federalist United States Senator Samuel Johnston. The latter was the fact that most accounted for his appointment.[25]

The Tredwell nomination was in keeping with the dominant motif of the area. The surveyor of customs at Hertford was Joshua Skinner, Jr., a nephew of William Skinner, the treasurer of the state in the 1780s, United States commissioner of loans for North Carolina in the nineties, and a ranking Federalist in the state. Joshua's cousin John Skinner served at the same time as North Carolina's United States marshal, and the former's brother Stephen was the surveyor of customs at Edenton as well as the area's collector of internal revenue. All the Skinners were Federalist cadremen.[26]

The Blount family, an integral part of the Federalist leadership in the early years of the 1790s, was also represented in the Albemarle area customs service. Levi Blount was promoted from customs inspector to surveyor of customs at Plymouth in 1792. He represented a tightly knit clan headed by William, Thomas, and John Gray Blount. At that time, according to Lisle Rose, the family led an important faction in the state's Federalist party: the Blounts "represented the dominant native merchant and speculative interests in the state. As merchants, these men wanted all restrictions on trade with the British West Indies lifted," a goal that only a strong central government could attain. The Blounts only renounced their federalism after 1796, in reaction to Jay's Treaty and after a realistic appraisal of the dim future of federalism in the state. Levi Blount was apparently only a poor relation, but one of the Blount brothers in the early 1790s was in the House of Representatives, a second was moving toward the top of the political heap in the Tennessee area of North Carolina, and a third controlled a chain of federal post offices in the state.[27]

The only customs officer in the Edenton complex unrelated to anyone of importance in the Federalist party in the Tarheel State was Hardy Murfree. But then the surveyor at Murfreesboro seemed to own most of that port, a factor that perhaps left him less in need of kinfolk to help him gain an appointment for himself than others in the region. Murfree, a Federalist who had earlier worked for ratification of the Constitution, possessed both "personal popularity" and a great deal of land in the area.[28]

The ubiquitous Sawyer clan, involved deeply in local Federalist politics and tied closely to Senator Johnston, dominated the customs service in and around Camden, a port town also off Albemarle Sound. Enoch Sawyer, a "gentleman planter," was the collector of customs at Camden and the premier officer for the customs district. The family owned a schooner collectively and engaged in the West Indies trade from these ports. Enoch himself possessed a "considerable inheritance" and voted "with the plantation aristocracy" of eastern North Carolina. His father-in-law was the county's state senator and served as a customs inspector in his spare time. Enoch Sawyer's three brothers, M.E., Frederick, and Edmund, in turn were all surveyors of customs at Camden, Newbiggen Creek, and the Pasquotank River respectively. It cannot be assumed that all these Sawyers held customs offices because there were no other takers for the jobs; Frederick Sawyer, for example, lived "at least Thirty Miles from the Port." Jefferson relieved them of their offices after 1801, admittedly because of their party activities, and found no dearth of takers for the posts.[29]

Neither close ties to the Federalist party nor extended nepotism were characteristics of the customs service peculiar only to the Albemarle region. At the port of Washington in the Pamlico Sound area, a single family monopolized the federal offices. In this case it was the Keais clan, tied very closely to the political apron strings of the Blounts. Nathan Keais and his sons were merchants and storekeepers in the port town, often acting as agents for the Blounts in both mercantile dealings and land speculations. The elder Keais was designated collector in 1790 at the urging of Congressman Thomas Blount and in spite of the fact that, as collector of customs under state auspices during the Confederation, he was still in arrears to the state treasurer for customshouse receipts. When Nathan died in 1795, his son William Keais was named to succeed to the collector's job, again after the vigorous intercession of the Blount brothers. John L. Keais, William's brother, was the port's weigher and gauger of customs. Although they maintained their commercial relationships with the Blounts, the Keaises did not follow that powerful family out of the Federalist party in the waning years of the decade.[30]

While the Cape Fear area's customs service was not shot through with the rampant nepotism evident elsewhere in the state, it suffered more than its share of slack administration. Benjamin Cheney, the collector at Beaufort, occupied a "mere sinecure," according to a local critic. "The duties will be performed by deputy while Mr. Cheney continues to reside as he has for many years past and during the whole of his continuance in office at a distance from Town." In truth, however, the job paid only about $50 a year in fees and so, even though Jefferson in 1803 did not want to reappoint Cheney because of his Federalist activities, Treasury Secretary Gallatin reminded the president that he had no choice: "there is no other applicant." [31]

A much more serious administrative situation developed at Wilmington, the state's largest port, located near the mouth of the Cape Fear River. President Adams in 1798 was forced to remove James Read, the Federalist collector at the port because of the pervasive mismanagement evident in the collection of customs. Read left his official business almost entirely to a deputy and thus did not provide "that kind of security" the service required. The president admitted that he did not know whether the resulting large embezzlements were the result of a "lack of vigilance" or a lack of "integrity," but in either event the collector was responsible, hence his removal.

This was a difficult situation for the Adams administration, for Read was both an important Federalist and a man of consequence. He had been a colonel in the Continental army and in later years was very close both to the prominent Federalist Haywood family and John Steele. The latter had been a United States senator from North Carolina until he was appointed by Adams to the post of comptroller of the treasury. Read himself was active politically, moreover, serving continuously in the state Assembly. Although Adams refused to prosecute the collector, it is clear that he was guilty. By 1796 he was deeply in debt to the Haywoods and imploring them not to sue him lest he lose his federal post as a result. In the meantime, returns of customs monies to the federal government were made ever more slowly, until the collector found himself more than a year in arrears. The overt act that finally caused a reluctant Adams to move on the case occurred in 1798; Read appropriated for himself the entire cargo of a prize French brigantine brought into his port during the undeclared war with France. When Read claimed he no longer had the money realized from the sale of that cargo, Adams turned Read out. The latter hinted that his allegiance to Hamilton was more at issue than his financial difficulties. When Jefferson became president, the new administration successfully sued Read for forfeit of his $10,000 bond, which the Adams administration inexplicably had neither seized nor returned. The former collector remained in Wilmington until 1803, when, with his local debts at last paid off, he settled in the Louisiana Territory.[32]

Unlike its northern neighbor, South Carolina boasted a single major port that ranked among the busiest in the nation. There was no dispersal of customs personnel throughout the state as there was in North Carolina. Fifty officers and subordinates were employed in Charleston, the largest port in the

South. Parallels between the ports of North Carolina and that
of Charleston did exist, however, in that the customs service
at Charleston was both dominated by Federalists and victimized by corruption.

In post-revolutionary South Carolina, the political interests
that governed Charleston also exerted control over the rest of
the state.[33] But in Charleston itself in the 1790s, though the
Federalists held the upper hand in the early part of the decade, no single clearly dominant faction within that party
managed to rule without help. Moreover, the allegiance
Charleston Federalists paid to Philadelphia had its limitations. At the outset of the Federalist era, Alexander Hamilton
ardently and successfully courted the Pinckney-Rutledge
faction, then the premier component within Charleston's
Federalist party. Successful manipulation of patronage
among other things contributed to early Federalist successes
and made it possible for Vice-President John Adams to look
to South Carolina as the best Federalist hope in the Deep
South. This hope was dealt a major blow in 1795, however,
when much-respected Edward Rutledge defected to the Jeffersonians. The overt reason was that ever-troublesome issue, Jay's Treaty. This turn of events set in motion forces that
eventually undermined the state's Federalist party.

Up until 1795, the Palmetto State was usually counted in
the Federalist camp chiefly because of the weight of the elite
leadership it could bring to bear. Rutledge's defection dam-
aged the administration cause. Not only did the Rutledge
name provide significant symbolic value to the opposition,
the Jeffersonians capitalized as well on the unpopularity of
the treaty in 1795. The pressures created by these two factors
increased the factionalism within the Federalist interest
even as it inspired the Republicans to greater efforts.
Nevertheless, the Federalists were able to draw on a wide
range of elite support, divided though it was, at a time when
there was no other real source of political leadership in the
state.

While none of the other Charleston factions equaled the
authority of the Rutledge-Pinckney axis in the early years of
the Federalist era, the smaller Federalist components could

hardly be dismissed as insignificant. Indeed, after the changes in alignment triggered by the Jay Treaty, these other Charleston factions took on increasing importance in the Federalist spectrum. Even as Rutledge moved into the Jeffersonian camp, his former ally Charles Cotesworth Pinckney emerged as a key supporter of the Adams wing of the Federalist party. At the same time, the William Loughton Smith-Ralph Izard group and the Jacob Read-James Simons faction increasingly indentified with the Hamilton arm of the party. Both the defection of Rutledge and the local Federalist schism that mirrored national differences notwithstanding then, these Federalist groups offered a continuing party presence in the state. As a result, the administration party sustained its position in Charleston and thus the state almost to the end of the Federalist era. And if Charleston was the hub of South Carolina politics, the town's customshouse formed the critical mass for the local Federalist organization.

George Abbott Hall was named the first federal collector at Charleston by President Washington in 1789. An aging but important merchant, he was allied politically with the Federalist Pinckneys, the Rutledges, and William Moultrie, all of whom were instrumental in gaining the appointment for him. Although he had been a supporter of ratification, his age and declining health effectively kept him out of active politics in the two years he acted as customs officer prior to his death in 1791.[34] Hall's passing opened the way for the nomination of Isaac Holmes, an appointment that eventually proved most unfortunate for the United States.

In a state where a relatively small number of closely entwined first families exercised enormous political power from their seats at Charleston, Holmes was a significant figure. He had held many offices dating back to the Revolution and in 1791 was lieutenant governor of the state. This Charleston merchant was recommended to Washington as an influential Federalist of "tried attachment" to the Washington administration, and he was duly designated collector shortly after Hall's death. He was removed in 1797 by President Adams, who on taking office discovered that Hall had failed to remit customs duties for nearly three years; his delinquency

amounted to a staggering three-quarters of a million dollars.
Not only was the money never collected, Holmes was never
prosecuted. His only penalties were the stigma of removal
from office and the forfeiture of his bond, a nominal $10,000
in light of the losses the United States Treasury sustained.
Either Oliver Wolcott, Jr., Hamilton's successor, had never
informed Presiden Washington of the delinquency or the latter on learning of it decided not to act, leaving the political
and financial mess to be cleaned up by his successor.[35]

The naval office, the second spot in the Charleston customs
service, was reserved, it appears, for relatives of Charleston's
Federalist leaders. The first naval officer at the port was Isaac
Motte, brother-in-law both to William Moultrie, a wealthy
South Carolina party manager, and Federalist United States
Senator William Loughton Smith. Motte, like the collectors
under whom he officiated, was himself an influential
Charleston merchant and part of the upper crust of that
town's society. He had served as a colonel in the Continental
army and later was one of South Carolina's representatives to
the Continental Congress. A key figure in the political circle
surrounding William Loughton Smith, he had actively supported the Constitution at the South Carolina Ratifying Convention.

The naval officer in 1791, along with his brother-in-law
serving in the Senate, held a potentially valuable piece of the
national debt, the funding of which Congress debated vigor-
ously even as Senator Smith instructed Naval Officer Motte
in the buying and selling of the securities that constituted
that debt. In 1789 Motte himself owned almost 1,300 acres of
cotton land, 40 slaves, and nearly $13,000 in government
securities. His death in 1795 opened the way to the appointment of another well-connected Federalist.[36]

Motte's successor in the naval office in 1795, and the man
who was promoted to collector to succeed the dismissed
Isaac Holmes two years later, was James Simons. The latter
was the son-in-law of Jacob Read, the head man of an important South Carolina Federalist faction and from mid-decade a
United States senator. What Motte was to Senator William

Loughton Smith, Simons became to Senator Read. Utilizing the political weight of his customs office to immense advantage, Simons built a powerful Federalist organization within faction-ridden Charleston. His customshouse served as a politically central force in the city and was a potent factor in the consolidation of Jacob Read's Federalist leadership in South Carolina in the waning years of the decade. And "the fortunes of James Simons rose with those of Jacob Read," as George C. Rogers has put it.[37]

Simons was an able and engaging figure. He fought with the Continental army through the whole of the Revolution, rising through the ranks to major. Even a staunch Republican like Pierce Butler was willing to recommend his appointment to the naval office in 1795, noting that "when they [the other applicants] were writing in Mercantile Houses, he [Simons] was fighting for his Country and freely shedding his blood for her." After the war and his marriage to Jacob Read's daughter, Simons opened a mercantile establishment in Charleston, one that was never very successful. In his world of notable wealth, Simons just managed to keep his head above water, and that only because of the continuing help provided by his father-in-law. Consequently, his appointment to the naval office in 1795, and his promotion to collector by John Adams two years later, were most welcome to the financially embattled merchant. Friend and foe alike agreed that he was an excellent federal officer. He put the Charleston customshouse back in shape after the demoralizing peculations of his predecessor had nearly wrecked it. He was honest, fair, and a hard worker.

But Simons was also deeply involved in South Carolina politics and had no compunctions about using the customshouse for all it was worth politically. When, after the change of administration in 1801, he was accused of compelling his customshouse employees to work for John Adams's election, Simons as much as admitted the truth of the allegation to Comptroller of the Treasury and good friend John Steele: "I did not know of any officer in the Customs appointed by me who was adverse to Mr. Adams election and consequently no occasion presented itself to use compulsory measures." In short, under Simons, the customshouse at Charleston housed "a little army" of Federalists.

From its outset, the Jefferson administration was in a quandary about how to handle Simons. Acting Secretary of the Navy Samuel Smith acknowledged to John Rutledge in May 1801 that the collector was "an officer of great Value." Nevertheless, the cabinet minister added, Simons "made use of his official situation in an unwarrantable Manner to compell others to vote contrary to their sentiments." Albert Gallatin, who was Simons's superior, described him in 1801 as a "violent federalist" who "commands a great interest." At virtually the same time, Gallatin disclosed in another context that Simons was "an excellent officer much afraid of being removed." The collector's fears were well grounded in reality. Jeffersonian Charles Pinckney, who stood high in the regard of the first Republican president, was among those who "strongly urged his removal." After all, "the Read-Simons combination became the most powerful in the state" by 1797, and Simons, it was said, "ran the customshouse in the interests of the Federalist party."

Simons admitted that the accusations made by Republicans about his role in the 1800 presidential election were true. He had openly "support[ed] Mr. Adams election which I did as well from a just sense of Services as from personal gratitude for the benefit he conferred on me and my large family by the beneficent office to which he Appointed me." However, like the Boston collector Benjamin Lincoln, in 1802 Simons pledged that he would disassociate himself from all politics if allowed to keep his post. However much he may have refrained from politics after 1801 as a matter of self-interest, it was clear that the same force motivated Simon to mobilize the Charleston customshouse before that date. By Simons's own admission, subordinates were expected to exert their influence politically, and most especially on Adams's behalf in the election of 1800.[38]

Thomas Waring's experience personified the difficulties inherent in this situation. He was one who engaged in politics reluctantly and, apparently, only to the degree necessary to avoid compromising his position in the customs service. Waring was appointed to the naval office by Adams in 1797 to replace the promoted Simons. He had been a much more devoted Federalist in the early years of the decade than he was after the ratification of Jay's Treaty. A planter and a man of substance and local reputation, he had supported the Constitution at the South Carolina Ratifying Convention in 1788. But by the time of his nomination in the early days of the Adams administration, his zeal had worn thin. Albert Gallatin, perusing the patronage lists in 1801, described Waring as a "good man" who "never meddles" in politics; he was "no more federalist," according to the Treasury Secretary, "than would keep his office." [39]

Robert Cochran's experience formed a different kind of example of the pitfalls inherent in politicizing the civil service. Cochran was at once a much better Federalist and a much poorer federal officer than Waring. The captain of the Charleston revenue cutter, Cochran was a man of influence in Federalist ranks, primarily as a result of the clout of his more important brother Charles, who was United States marshal for the state. Robert, who had served in the infant Continental navy during the war, was a shipbuilder in Charleston and politically a lieutenant of James Simons. He was removed from his command in 1798, however, when in seeking to avoid a confrontation with a lightly armed British merchantman, he ran the revenue cutter aground. Even a Federalist like Thomas Pinckney was forced to admit that the action "agrees with the character I have lately heard of the commander."

Secretary of the Navy Benjamin Stoddert, who had just gained administrative control over the federal revenue cutters, told John Rutledge that he had "to suspend Cochran from his Command of the armed vessel at Charleston and to give the command to [one] . . . I hope will better know how to defend it and the honor of the Country." Stoddert acted even in the face of many letters from South Carolina Federalists who pointed out that the removal for cowardice of a well-known local Federalist would embarrass the party and "give pain to some honorable men." Significantly, pressing questions about Cochran's original fitness for his office were never raised; it was widely understood that his was manifestly a political appointment. After his removal, a loyal and politically harried Simons found a minor place for Cochran in the customs service as a tidewaiter. It was perhaps the only instance in the Federalist era where a removed officer in the civil service immediately found his way back into office, even a lowly office, under the same administration. It may well have resulted from a compromise between administration officials' demands for his scalp and local supporters' concern for the reputation of the party. The publicly known political texture of the Charleston customshouse clearly made it a natural solution.[40]

A host of subordinates of middling social and economic status in the city were all Federalist operatives, according to both the collector himself and his Republican critics. In a customshouse whose employees numbered fifty or more by 1801, this was a sizable contingent. That Simons knew of not a single opponent of John Adams in that installation in 1800 was a unique commentary on one of the best organized official cadres of the Federalist party in the United States.[41]

The customs service in the South was no less politically inspired than its counterpart in the North. In fact, cultural and social differences generally notwithstanding, the similarities were indeed striking. Political practices and considerations in Charleston differed very little from major northern ports of entry, and it was very much politics as usual in both southern and northern minor customshouses in the Federalist decade. These similarities of both practices and personnel reached into other areas of the federal civil service, as a study of America's first internal revenue service will demonstrate.

CHAPTER SIX

The Internal Revenue Service: The Upper Echelons

The internal revenue service was established in 1791 and placed under the supervision of the Treasury Department. It was mandated to collect the excise tax on distilled liquors levied by Congress, after a great deal of well-known political contention over the kind of broad-based tax the nation needed. The agency employed 450 men by the end of the Federalist era. Of these, 59 supervisors and inspectors of the revenue in the several states were incorporated into the higher civil service, holding elite positions both in terms of deference and income. There were below them 296 collectors and 95 auxiliary officers in the service at one time or another during the Federalist decade. These held less visible, less prestigious appointments in the Treasury Department.

Two other separate but significant agencies indirectly linked to the internal revenue service also dealt with internal revenues. There were United States commissioners of loans in each of the thirteen original states, appointed initially in 1790 to administer Hamilton's complex funding program. They were responsible in their respective states for validating United States indebtedness to individuals on the one hand, and paying out the interest and principal when it was due on various government securities that formed the backbone of Hamilton's economic program on the other. This small group of higher civil servants differed from other elements of the treasury establishment in that it employed a significant proportion of Jeffersonian Republicans.

The second allied group, the land commissioners, were appointed by President Adams in 1798 to collect the land taxes imposed by Congress. The tax was levied to pay for the new provisional army and the expanded naval building program, both conceived primarily in response to the confrontation with France. The high significance of this agency of seventy-nine commissioners functioning in the states lay in the fact that it was the only sizable, coherent group of federal civil officers appointed by John Adams. Thus its composition provides some unique insights into the Adams Federalists. Inasmuch as the land commissioners formed a part of the lower civil service, I will defer discussion of them until the next chapter.

The internal revenue service was not only as politically oriented as the customs branch, it was in a way better positioned to spread the Federalist gospel in the sixteen states. In several states where supervisors were especially political, virtually the entire service was employed in the Federalist cause at election time. The supervisors in some states chose their subordinates on the basis of their political talents as much as on their ability to collect the revenues. The subordinate employees, unlike those in customs, were not limited to tidewater areas; in fact, they were highly mobile because of the travel requirement inherent in their jobs. This circumstance enhanced their political utility manyfold.

Daniel Stevens of South Carolina was one supervisor of the internal revenue service who quickly grasped the possibilities of this situation. Encouraged in the early 1790s by the Pinckneys and the Rutledges, who felt that "their political enemies should not be strengthened by gaining government positions," the internal revenue service in the state was founded as a mobile, activist squadron of the Federalist party. Senator Pierce Butler informed President Jefferson in

1801 that Stevens "has been represented to me as having previous to the late [presidential and legislative] election written circular letters through the State, propagating the grossest falsehoods of the present Chief Magistrate of the U.S., [and] as having sent all the petty Excise officers posting through the State to try to prevent the Election of such men as were of Republican principles." Stevens "himself and his Satellites," Butler added, "influenced one hundred Votes in Charleston only." [1]

In Virginia, the supervisor of the revenue was Edward Carrington, a particularly close confidant of Secretary of the Treasury Hamilton. Within two weeks of Jefferson's inauguration, Republicans in the Old Dominion importuned the new president to remove "the Supervisor of this State and the Inspectors under his direction." As he differed with the Federalists in the early 1790s on some issues, Carrington's appointment was specifically designed to keep him "in the administration camp after 1790." Washington's former aide in the Continental army responded directly to the twin lures of office and money, according to Lisle Rose. Despite his earlier criticisms of Hamilton's programs, after his 1791 appointment Carrington became "immediately useful as an agent between Hamilton and the Richmond financial community." [2]

The same pervasive political involvement of supervisor and service was evident in northern states as well. The 1801 removal of Connecticut Supervisor John Chester and all his collectors caused "an intire revolution in that Department." Chester's termination along with "all those who acted under Chester" elicited a "God be thanked" from one Republican. The newly elected Republican governor of New Jersey alleged a month after Jefferson's inauguration that Internal Revenue Supervisor Aaron Dunham was "subordinate to the will of the aristocratic Junto." He had "gone all lengths to support the late election [in 1800] of our political opponents, More by the characters and electioneering abilities of his Deputys in the several countys than by his own influence." It was a "well known fact in New Jersey," Governor Joseph Bloomfield charged, "that Dunham threatened his deputys with removal if they presumed to favor the Democratic interest." When one subordinate in the internal revenue service refused to electioneer for the Federalists in 1800, telling Dunham "to take his damned [job], that he and his [job] might go to the Devil," the collector was replaced by one more amenable.[3]

The politicization of the new internal revenue service in Pennsylvania contributed significantly to the political polarization that resulted in the Whisky Rebellion. With arch-Federalist Supervisor George Clymer at the head of the Pennsylvania revenue service in its early years, charges of political interference between 1792 and 1794 were virtually inevitable. A former congressman and a Pennsylvania notable with important Federalist family ties, Clymer clearly exacerbated the developing confrontation, one result of his obtuse partisan dealings with the rebels.

He had much to say about the moral and personal weaknesses of the lesser folk. The supervisor, the chief government agent on the spot in the early stages of the uprising, used his position to try to frighten leading Antifederalists like John Cannon. Clymer made it widely known that he was consulting several "gentlemen friends to the government"—a clear euphemism for Federalists in 1792 and 1793—about the appropriate means of breaking the rebels' resistance. Clymer's partisanship by his own admission firmed up the resolve of the rebels, who believed initially and later that they were shabbily treated by the government. He personalized and inflamed an already combustible situation and convinced the rebels that they were victims of a partisan, elite Federalist administration. Clymer thus almost singlehandedly transformed the Whisky Rebellion into an ideological confrontation from its earliest stages. Even Federalist Judge Alexander Addison, a friend of Clymer's and a supporter of administration policy with regard to the rebellion, told the supervisor the same thing, but with no effect.

Clymer's reports to Hamilton, meanwhile, were not only bitter, they also revealed his unerring ability to alienate the government's supporters in the trans-Allegheny west. A moderate Pittsburgh committee of Federalists, seeking to negotiate an agreement between government and rebels and thus avoid a confrontation, was organized after the most painstaking efforts by Revenue Inspector John Neville. This committee was roundly denounced by Clymer, Neville's immediate superior, on the former's arrival in Pittsburgh. "They [committee members] greatly want sincerity or spirit or both, [while] still professing friendship to the federal government," Clymer reported to the treasury secretary. His public references, during his stay in Pittsburgh, to the "sordid shopkeepers" who wielded political influence in the western counties and who encouraged rebellion, did little to inspire a sense of compromise. Other utterances denouncing "the greatly depraved," whose "moral sense" was undermined "by the intemperate use of the favourite drink," moreover, rendered the saving of face by the rebels virtually impossible.

Clymer's resignation from the supervisor's post was almost certainly forced by Hamilton at the end of 1794. Politically oriented though the treasury secretary wanted the internal revenue to be, Clymer was clearly a little too much, given the tensions that were building. He was exiled to the federal territories for two years to help negotiate two Indian treaties, but not before his official contributions had greatly escalated the whisky confrontation.[4]

Henry Miller, Clymer's replacement, saw to it that the internal revenue's political function did not suffer. Republican Congressman William Findley, referring specifically to Miller in his official capacity, reported to Jefferson in 1801 that "he has been active against us to the last degree." Indeed, the congressman disclosed, a consensus among Pennsylvania Republicans clearly existed on the need for "a thorough change . . . in all the offices of the internal revenue" in the Keystone State. He added "that the opposition to the Excise Law chiefly if not solely originated from the contempt in which the character of the persons appointed to fill these offices had always been held and from their indiscretions in office." Miller, like Clymer, had "encouraged the most obnoxious and improper characters to push themselves into office." As supervisor, Findley concluded, Henry Miller was nothing more than one of Pennsylvania's foremost "political agents." [5]

In Pennsylvania and all the larger states, the inspectors of the internal revenue, functioning directly under the supervisor in the chain of command, acted as influential political lieutenants. Because the Keystone State was large and enforcement of the excise law threatened, several inspectors were necessary to help oversee the collectors and act as liaisons to the supervisors. These inspectors held responsible jobs; they were well paid and usually highly placed local party men.

Three key Federalist cadremen served as internal revenue inspectors in central and western Pennsylvania in the 1790s. John Neville, Edward Hand, and John Boyd, in fact, were the highest local federal officers on the spot during the whisky uprising. Neville was responsible for the transmontane survey (the term *survey* applied to the collection territories mandated by Congress), Hand the south central survey, and Boyd the north central survey. Each of these men, both during the rebellion and after, reinforced by their presence and activities the firm belief of the rebels that they were victimized by a partisan administration. The three lieutenants, in sum, were no less politically oriented than were Clymer and his successor.

Neville was an able man who, according to Harry Tinkcom, "headed a powerful little group that exerted great influence throughout the western country." Continuously harassed by rebels during the early 1790s because he was the chief United States governmental presence in the Pittsburgh region, John Neville for the most part remained reasonable. His son Presley and his son-in-law Isaac Craig, both involved federal civil officers themselves during the rebellion, were not nearly so temperate and sometimes undid the placatory missionary efforts of the family head. Even after his estate at Bower Hill was set afire in the course of a rebel assault, however, Neville's circumspection, firmness, and the general respect accorded him kept the uprising from becoming worse than it was.

The esteem he commanded locally derived from his general's commission in the Continental army during the war, his enormous wealth and landholdings, and his long-time personal friendship with Alexander Hamilton. Even though he personally opposed its passage, once the excise tax became law his deep commitment to "Federalist men and measures" flowing out of Philadelphia caused him to seek its enforcement. It was his bad luck that his survey became the eye of the storm developing in the nation as the tax was collected.

Neville sometimes bypassed Clymer and reported directly to the treasury secretary in an attempt to maintain a semblance of communication between the farmers and distillers and the Federalist hierarchy in the nation's capital. Inevitably, however, his moderation was eroded by the violence he both witnessed and suffered. Perhaps in part because he thrust himself between government and rebels, by 1793 he and his family emerged as lightning rods for all the bitterness attached to the government's policy. In the end, Neville's centricity in the rebellion seemed to fix in the public mind the idea that the official establishment collecting the tax in the region and the Federalist establishment exercising political leadership in the western country were one and the same. Neville remained, after all, both the chief tax gatherer and the chief Federalist in the transmontane counties.[6]

Central Pennsylvania Inspectors John Boyd and Edward Hand were Federalists whose partisanship was also made apparent during the uprising. Of the two, Hand was clearly the more important. He administered his office from Carlisle, an office he needed "to relieve [him] from [financial] Embarrassments." Like Neville a former Continental army general, Hand had enjoyed several high appointments conferred by the commonwealth of Pennsylvania before his elevation to the handsome federal post. He repaid the appointment with extensive party activity. The former general led a militia force against the whisky insurgents in 1794, in the face of the fact that he was also a civilian enforcement official. In all the analyses of the Whisky Rebellion offered by historians, none have effectively taken into account the significant role of the Pennsylvania federal officials on the spot in bringing the uprising to the point of crisis. Only Neville was something of an exception, and even he was locally identified as a Federalist cadreman as well as a federal civil servant.

Hand generated an even more partisan image. Motivated by "a conventional prejudice for a strong government and a structured society, and a hatred of Jeffersonian forms," Hand continuously thrust himself into Federalist politics. In 1800, for example, he was the chairman of his county Federalist committee as well as a chief lobbyist for the Federalist cause as the Pennsylvania legislature deliberated over the casting of the commonwealth's electoral votes. The county group which he headed was guilty of "extreme violence" during the elections of 1800, an involvement that, according to a Republican petition, helped to maintain a Federalist majority "for several years back." Congressman William Findley supported this allegation in 1801 when he wrote Jefferson that Hand "behaved very improperly" in 1800 when he "openly took a lead in endeavoring to starve the Mechanics . . . who would not vote as he directed." For an "old school" Federalist, Hand certainly engaged in new school tactics in his electioneering.[7]

New York was another large state in which the officers of the internal revenue service were also prominent members of the Federalist party hierarchy. The most visible appointees were William Stephens Smith, John Adams's son-in-law and the supervisor from 1792 to 1793, and Nicholas Fish, who headed the New York internal revenue service from 1793 to 1801. Richard Morris, the elderly brother of Gouverneur Morris, was the state's first supervisor. A prominent member of an elite family, Morris, forced by an age limit to retire as chief justice of the New York Supreme Court and nearly broke by 1790, badly needed the federal appointment. Advanced age and consequent laxity in office forced his resignation in the middle of 1792.[8]

William S. Smith succeeded him. The former Continental army colonel was a stormy petrel in the Federalist era. Smith over the long run was an effective trimmer, but while the

Federalists were on top he publicly counted himself among their number.

The last conclusion is drawn in the face of contradictory evidence. Years later Smith would make much of his public opposition to Jay's Treaty in 1795. On the face of it, the evidence indicates that Smith chaired a public meeting that ended by opposing its ratification. It is this fact that historians fix on when discussing the checkered political career of John Adams's son-in-law. A closer examination of the real circumstances of that meeting reveals, however, that Smith presided over the meeting at the behest of Alexander Hamilton, who was also present. Hamilton feared that the gathering would get out of hand politically (as it did anyway) did not a "leading character" take over. Smith took the chair, a person agreeable both to the retired treasury secretary and the aroused, politically mixed crowd. Although Smith remained firm and fairly impartial, the meeting finally divided into hostile camps. Over his objections, a majority passed a resolution opposing the treaty. The most that could be said for Smith was that he publicly neither endorsed nor denounced that resolution. Privately, however, he made his support of the administration very clear.[9]

The second confusing bit of evidence, involving almost a classic example of eighteenth-century trimming, had to do with Smith's private political assurances delivered at different times in the Federalist era. Washington's former aide-de-camp wrote to the president early in 1794 that he had resigned as United States marshal for New York two years before because, as a State Department employee, he was uncomfortable working under "the then administration" of Thomas Jefferson. However, by January 1794, "the late change in administration [Jefferson's resignation] removes all my personal objections to public stations." He said nothing about his having resigned the supervisor's post in 1793. Smith's known contacts with Citizen Genêt may have been a factor in his departure from the supervisor's office, although nothing firm can be said. At any rate, by early 1794, he acknowledged himself back in the Federalist camp and applied to George Washington for yet another office. While Jefferson thought of Smith as a firm Republican, Smith not only claimed an unwillingness to work under the Republican leader, he assured Washington that "I am firmly attached to the Constitution and government of my Country," as well as "attached to [its] measures."

His efforts to seek military office from his father-in-law, the president, in 1797 and 1798 did not prevent Smith from successfully trimming his sails in order to gain a federal job in 1801. He wrote Jefferson that if any part of his official involvement during the 1790s appeared to benefit the Federalist party, it was a result of the fact that he was "interfered with" by men more highly placed than he and with more authority; he could only be counted a victim of circumstance. Smith assured Jefferson that he had neither supported Federalist views nor benefited from Federalist favor. Indeed, to charges by men of both parties that he frequently changed his politics, he told the incoming president, he could only respond that despite what his enemies might say, he adhered only to "the pure preservation of Principles of the earliest part of our revolution." If Smith had, as one historian has written, "accumulated a host of enemies" over the years, clearly few had worked harder to earn them.[10]

Nicholas Fish started out in 1791 as the inspector of the internal revenue for the survey encompassing New York City. He was promoted to supervisor for all New York State in 1793, remaining in that slot until the end of the Federalist decade. The son of a wealthy city merchant and a graduate of Princeton, Fish served as a lieutenant colonel in the Continental army during the war. He was trained to the law and engaged in some banking activities, but some contemporary descriptions simply refer to him as a "gentleman." He wrote Washington in 1791 that he wanted to be "employed under an administration which you preside over," and was rewarded with the inspector's job.

He was a deeply dedicated, somewhat pompous Federalist. Fish was one of those, according to Dixon Ryan Fox, who "did not think themselves discharged from public duty when they had set their names to an address." He believed the Jeffersonians to be tainted with a polyglot political theory consisting of "modern philosophy, of French Jacobinism, and local prejudice." The supervisor was prominent enough to be one of three Federalists in the civil service in 1801 to be singled out for removal by Jefferson "for the violence of their characters and conduct." [11] Unlike his predecessor in the supervisor's job, Fish was reliable politically, stolidly looking after Federalist interests as well as ably carrying out his official responsibilities.

The same could be said for Fish's counterpart in Massachusetts. Nathaniel Gorham, the supervisor from 1791 until his death in 1796, was appointed specifically because he was supposed to be a popular leader. A member of the Massachusetts delegation to the Constitutional Convention at Philadelphia, Gorham had run unsuccessfully for both Congress and the lieutenant governor's office in the early 1790s. Despite his setbacks at the polls, some Massachusetts Federalists believed that "he had quite a personal following." Moreover, a bankruptcy soon after ratification left Gorham in dire need of an office. Although he was considered only a "moderate" Federalist by many, and was described as "lukewarm" by others, he responded with gratitude to the strongly entrenched Hamiltonian "high Federalists" in the Bay State who were responsible for his nomination. Though not one of them, he used his influence in their behalf. In a way he was like Customs Collector Benjamin Lincoln, a bridge to moderates, useful to the party as such, and a visible notable who could cultivate moderate support even from those who "had little in common with the Federalist party." Gorham's successor after his death in 1796 was Jonathan Jackson, a high Federalist who was much more a part of the existing party establishment. [12]

Shortly after Jackson replaced the deceased Gorham, he was party to a removal by President Adams that perhaps the more moderate Gorham would not have gone along with. Leonard Jarvis, an internal revenue inspector who presided over the Boston survey, was a Republican. The president dismissed Jarvis in November 1797—at Abigail Adams's insistence—to make room for an old friend. Jarvis was a fairly prominent political figure in Massachusetts until his antifederalism first and later his Jeffersonian Republicanism got in the way. Already, in becoming an inspector of the revenue in 1791, he had taken a demotion. Jarvis had supervised the collection of internal taxes in the Bay State during the 1780s when the post was a state position. In 1797, when the axe fell, he paid his second installment on his political debt.

Jarvis's replacement was Ebenezer Storer, born into a prominent merchant family that had seen better days. Whether because of his own mismanagement or simple hard times in the 1780s (both versions of the cause of his financial difficulty survive), he lost the family fortune and, like Nathaniel Gorham, experienced bankruptcy. At any rate he was clearly rescued from further impoverishment by the intercession of the Adams family; Jarvis was explicitly removed, in sum, to make room for a friend and a Federalist.[13]

The pattern of political leadership in the internal revenue service in the South was identical to that of the North. Prominent Federalists held both the supervisors and inspectors posts in Maryland, Virginia, and the Carolinas. In Maryland, both supervisors in the Federalist era, and the two inspectors as well, were closely tied to the Federalist leadership. George Gale, the first supervisor, and his successor John Kilty were prominent members of the Maryland establishment.

Gale, who served from 1791 until he resigned at the end of 1795, was a member of the Maryland upper house during the Confederation years. Descirbed as of the "planter aristocracy," Gale was outspoken in favor of the Constitution as a delegate to the Maryland Ratifying Convention. He was elected to the First Congress, where he earned a reputation as a "steadfast supporter of Hamilton's measures from beginning to end" and was rewarded with his federal appointment at the end of his term. Gale remained politically involved in the ensuing years and in particular gained a reputation during election campaigns as an effective "adversary" of Republican candidates.[14]

John Kilty, Gale's successor, had also been a long-time member of the Maryland upper house as well as an officer in the Continental army. His "attachment to the general government," in his own words in 1794, was "unquestioned," and it remained so. In 1801, as he waited for the axe to fall, he wrote to an applicant for federal office that the best recommendation he could offer at the moment was to remain silent, for "reasons sufficiently obvious." He wrote for Jefferson's eyes that, although he had always been and remained a Federalist, Republican "pretensions . . . never was at any period a bar to my accepting the services of a candidate" for the revenue establishment. The claim, not founded in fact, did not save his position.[15]

The two inspectors of the revenue in Maryland were also Federalists. Philip Thomas was an Annapolis physician and a son-in-law of John Hanson, and was thus connected to one of the first families of the state. He had been both an earnest supporter of ratification and an elector for George Washington. Thomas was also a close friend and business associate of Baltimore Customs Collector Otho Holland Williams. The other inspector was William Richardson, a "decided character" connected to a notable Baltimore family who, it was promised at the time of this appointment in 1791, could "act with a very decided influence" as the inspector of the Baltimore survey. A colonel in the Continental army, Richardson too was a presidential elector in 1789 as well as a Federalist member of the Maryland Ratifying Convention. Both inspectors were extraordinarily well placed and politically oriented.[16]

In neighboring Virginia, Edward Carrington presided over a large, well-dispersed cadre of Federalist revenue inspectors. Carrington, a brother-in-law of John Marshall, was a major figure in Virginia in his own right. He was one of a prominent political family and a close associate of George Washington and many other Old Dominion notables for many years prior to his appointment. He surfaced as an equally trusted advisor to Alexander Hamilton in the Federalist decade. Carrington worked hard and effectively to maintain a Federalist presence in the commonwealth. The supervisor's frequently sought advice to Hamilton and others was unusually candid and often critical of Federalist policies but, on the major public issues, he went down the line with the party. He openly supported neutrality in 1793, for example, and two years later somewhat regretfully publicly supported Jay's Treaty. Carrington identified himself closely with the treasury secretary until Hamilton's retirement from office. He circulated Federalist literature via the revenue service in the state, wrote newspaper essays and engaged in electioneering as a matter of course. Moreover, the supervisor of the revenue presided over a partisan force of higher civil servants who did much to cement the minority Federalist interest in this large and pivotal state.[17]

Nine of the ten revenue inspectors in the commonwealth were also Federalists. One of these was Mayo Carrington, Edward's brother and, like most of the other revenue officers, a veteran officer of the Continental line and a member of the Cincinnati. Another of the inspectors was Edward Stevens of Culpeper, a former Continental army colonel and a long-time member of the Virginia upper house. Stevens was deeply engaged in local politics, both as a supporter of the Constitution in the late 1780s and as a presidential elector for Washington. He continued politically active after his appointment. For example, in 1793 he chaired a Federalist meeting in Culpeper that denounced France and endorsed Hamilton's economic measures. Another inspector, James Gibbon of Petersburg, was described by Federalist Customs Collector William Heth as "barely literate" and "prying and inquisitive." At the same time, Heth admitted, he was a man of "good principles" with a deserved reputation as a war hero for his conduct in the storming of Stony Point. What he lacked in official capacity, it is clear, he compensated for by his political activity. Other Virginia inspectors more or less fit the same mold.[18]

Under the close tutelage of supervisor Daniel Stevens, so did the revenue inspectors in South Carolina. Stevens's role in politicizing the entire revenue service in the state has already been described. He himself, like Maryland's Otho Williams, was the epitome of the eighteenth-century self-made American. Orphaned at an early age and apprenticed to a merchant, he made his own way in the firm. When the Revolution broke out, Stevens joined the Continentals as an enlisted man and saw extensive combat in the South. As a result, he was commissioned a lieutenant in 1781 and ended the war an officer. In the years that followed, he accumulated little property but, nevertheless, rose to prominence. Stevens was both the sheriff of Charleston in the Confederation and a member of the South Carolina Assembly. He was influential in securing that state's ratification of the Constitution. What he lacked in private means was supplied by office. In addition to the supervisor's post and some state perquisites, Stevens was also superintendent of the Charleston lighthouse and in 1798 was granted the contract to supply the South Carolina brigade of the newly established and short-lived federal army called forth by the French crisis.

In a state where factional divisions among Federalists were almost institutionalized, Stevens for many years was a political agent of Senator William Loughton Smith. When Smith retired from politics in 1797, Stevens took his following into the equally Federalist camp of Senator Jacob Read, who soon came to work "through Daniel Stevens." Interestingly, Stevens's political followers were drawn from "the interest of the mechanics" in Charleston, although he was also "generally esteemed by the gentlemen." Albert Gallatin was reluctant to remove him in 1801, even though the treasury secretary was amply informed of the provocative electioneering both Stevens and other revenue officers engaged in over the years. The supervisor, Gallatin acknowledged, "commands a great interest" among potential Republicans like the mechanics, and he did not want to damage the still fragile Republican movement in the city by carrying out a removal unpopular with the middling elements there.[19]

North Carolina's William Polk was a committed Federalist presiding over the collection of the federal excise tax in an Antifederalist state. Tench Coxe, the United States commissioner of the revenue in Philadelphia, told his superior, Treasury Secretary Hamilton, in 1792: "I consider that [North Carolina's] Survey as the most opposed of any in the

United States except . . . in Pennsylvania." He added that the supervisor "appears to have great firmness and considerable weight and popularity," a fact that made collection of the tax at least possible. In general, the accolade was merited. Polk was closely tied to Senator John Steele, one of the most respected men in the state. He was also a confidant of the Haywood clan, among the most powerful political families in North Carolina. He was, finally, on good terms with the Blounts, committed Federalists in the early 1790s, when collections would prove most difficult. Among other connections, Polk speculated extensively with the Blounts in Tennessee lands.

Like Stevens and Williams, Polk was a self-made man. Originally a surveyor by trade, he made shrewd land purchases that eventually elevated him to the planter class by the outbreak of the Revolution. He served in the Continental line during the war, eventually reaching the rank of lieutenant colonel. In the 1780s he was a highly esteemed figure in North Carolina, serving continuously in the state legislature. He remained passive on the question of ratification of the Constitution in this Antifederalist bastion, but he very early surfaced as a strong supporter of Alexander Hamilton. Polk remained an outspoken Federalist throughout the era, denouncing the Republicans' "demonic rage" and their "jacobinism." Polk immersed himself in state politics, attending the polls at elections and writing letters widely in support of Federalist candidates during political campaigns. In a state where party feelings ran high and Republican sentiment was strong, Polk pulled few punches. He denounced the new Republican legislature in 1800 as one where "there never was so much ignorance collected in a legislative capacity since the days when Laws were enacted prohibiting the frying of Pancakes on Sundays."

The five revenue inspectors serving under him were an unlikely mix of former Constitutional Federalists and Antifederalists. Some were politically active thereafter in the Federalist cause; others were not involved politically. None, however, were overtly Republican after 1791. Polk clearly set the tone of the revenue service in North Carolina, the strength of the Republicans in the state notwithstanding.[20]

Perhaps not surprisingly in light of the foregoing description of the internal revenue service, the chief officers of that service in the new, Republican-oriented states of Kentucky and Tennessee were also Federalists. James Morrison supervised the revenue in Kentucky. He was a Lexington merchant and, though related to the landed Republican Nicholas family of Virginia and Kentucky, was himself a Federalist. The one revenue inspector in the new state was Thomas Marshall, John's father. He was, in the words of one recent historian of Kentucky politics, "the center of Federalism in the state." He "pursued his tax collections tirelessly" as well. The elder Marshall was perhaps the single most important liaison to the Washington administration in the new state. In Tennessee, John Overton, later a significant figure in the heyday of Andrew Jackson, was named supervisor of the revenue at the time the state was admitted to the Union in 1796. He too was a Federalist with close ties to the administration in Philadelphia, as well as a land speculator of gargantuan appetite.[21]

The commissioners of loans in the thirteen original states together formed an independent agency, but one closely allied by function with the internal revenue service. The commissioners all held lucrative, prestigious appointments in the higher civil service. They acted as local, direct agents of the Treasury Department; their primary functions were to pay out the quarterly interest on the new bond issues, dispense federal war-invalid pensions and frequently, as an implementation of Hamilton's funding program, to examine and validate claims against the government that antedated the Constitution. Theirs was a complicated and time-consuming job that required prudence and discretion, extensive bookkeeping knowledge, and skilled judgment.

While these positions were not entirely immune from the politics that pervaded the first civil service, the loan offices were more free than all others from the usual political test.

Thus here and there Republicans found the door open. Probably the exacting nature of the work and the skill required rendered political allegiance a secondary consideration; a moderate man was allowed to keep his post even if his politics took him into the enemy camp. Perhaps too the office was itself so complicated that a change was too much trouble to contemplate unless absolutely necessary. In any event, Republican loan commissioners turned up in every part of the Union.

In South Carolina and Maryland, Republicans held their offices for the entire Federalist era. John Neufville of Charleston, a member of the South Carolina gentry and already in his seventies in the 1790s, remained a firm Jeffersonian for the whole decade. "No man in the state was ever more respected," Wade Hampton disclosed in 1804. Clearly even the state's Federalist factions found this Huguenot descendent an acceptable civil servant. The same could be said for the Harwood brothers of Maryland. Thomas, a friend of President Washington's, held the post from 1790 to 1792, when he resigned in favor of his brother Benjamin in order to become treasurer of the state. In 1801, Jefferson reappointed Thomas to his old position. Both the Harwoods, members of the merchant elite of Annapolis, were "undeviatingly republican through all the revolutions in the public sentiment which have so rapidly taken place under the Federal Government." [22]

Dr. James Tilton, an eminent physician and a former Continental army surgeon, was named commissioner of loans for Delaware in 1790. President Washington clearly thought he was naming a political supporter. Tilton was an advocate of constitutional reform in the 1780s and an active member of the Society of the Cincinnati. Nevertheless, in the early 1790s Tilton surfaced as a Jeffersonian Republican. He kept his office until July 1795, when he resigned, with no indication that the resignation was forced.[23]

The cause of the demise of Republican Loan Commissioner William Gardner of New Hampshire in 1798, however, was very clear. He was removed by President Adams for overtly political reasons as part of a clean sweep of Repub-

lican officeholders in Portsmouth, a town that had become a
hotbed of Jeffersonian Republicanism in the years following
the Jay Treaty.* Gardner was a state legislator in the 1780s
and rose to prominence as a devoted supporter of the Constitution. As late as 1792, when he wanted to resign his complex federal office, Hamilton discouraged him from doing so,
pointing out the value to the government of his experience,
ability, and character. His drift to Republicanism, in common
with many other federal officers in town, began after that date
and was certainly completed well before 1798. It was as a
result of that political odyssey that Gardner found himself
the target of United States Attorney for New Hampshire
Jeremiah Smith, who in 1798 wrote the administration in
Philadelphia that he wanted Gardner out.

Although Gardner, according to Smith, had been "faithful
and punctual in the discharge of the duties of [his] office," his
"political conduct has been disrespectful to the Government
and offensive to good men in the extreme." Moreover, according to the federal attorney, the loan commissioner used
his "official consequence and situation" to undermine the
Adams administration. William Plumer very neatly summarized for Treasury Secretary Oliver Wolcott, Jr., the prevailing Federalist attitude toward the obligation of political
conformity incumbent on any officeholder. "Singular indeed
must be the views and motives of that government," Plumer
observed, "that finds its account in appointing and continuing men in office who employ their talents in weakening and
destroying the confidence of the people in that very government." To continue Republicans in their snug berths, Plumer
concluded, "is [to give] aid to Jacobinism—disgusting and
discouraging the friends of government and encouraging
officers in reviling the authority under which they act."
Given the mood of New Hampshire Federalist leaders,
Gardner had to go, and Adams removed him. His reappointment in 1801 was one of Jefferson's first acts of office.[24]

* See chapter 3 for the events of 1798 in Portsmouth, and especially its customshouse, that led to the wholesale removal of several
Republican federal officers, of whom Gardner was one.

Though a minority of the loan commissioners were Republicans, most were Federalists. Moreover, both the prestige and income were high, so in the nature of things the post usually fell to high-ranking party men. Massachusetts was a good example. Nathaniel Appleton of Boston occupied the post from 1790 until his death in 1798. He was close to the Essex Junto, in particular to United States District Judge John Lowell and Navy Agent Stephen Higginson. The commissioner was very active in Boston party circles and sometimes acted as liaison for Alexander Hamilton.

On Appleton's death in 1798, the loan office passed to his son-in-law Thomas H. Perkins, a rising star in the Massachusetts Federalist firmament. Perkins was a ship's master who had made a fortune in the China trade, completing a successful voyage to the Orient as a young man. On his return to the Bay State in the early 1790s, he was absorbed into Federalist political circles. He was well connected to begin with: in addition to his kinship to Appleton, he was a brother-in-law of Stephen Higginson. His no-holds-barred involvement with the majority party was clearly in the Higginson high Federalist mold. Within months of his return to Boston in 1794, he was named a member of the city's Federalist "electioneering" committee, designed to secure Fisher Ames's re-election to the House. The young merchant, more interested in the mobilization of the party than in elective office for himself (he turned down several opportunities to run for office in the decade), next threw his energies into popularizing Jay's Treaty. He helped to organize and manage the 1796 Boston town meeting that voted its support for the Anglo-American accord.

Perkins's appointment to the loan office was enthusiastically supported in 1798 by both the Adams and Hamilton wings of the Massachusetts party. His kinship to Higginson, a Hamiltonian, was balanced by a warm, enduring friendship with Congressman Harrison Gray Otis, an Adams Federalist. Judge John Lowell effectively summarized the case for appointing the deceased loan commissioner's son-in-law. Perkins's "Federalism has been constant unshaken and avowed," Judge Lowell wrote Oliver Wolcott, Jr., in 1798.

"No appointment as I conceive would be more universally satisfactory to the Friends of government here."

Official station did not dim either Perkins's activities or his enthusiasm for cadre politics. In 1798 the new loan commissioner first organized a committee and then a public meeting in Boston to endorse the Adams administration's foreign policy. A member of the gentry with a natural disinclination for this kind of popular politicking, Perkins engaged in it reluctantly and because it was the only way to counter the rising ability of Massachusetts Republicans to get their message across to the voters. "It is a melancholy concession to make that our government has need of this sort of aid," the high Federalist wrote Otis, but "it is a duty in us to give it." Perkins continued to give unstintingly. In 1800 he chaired a nominating meeting that designated Josiah Quincy the Federalist candidate for Congress, and he served as well on a Massachusetts electioneering committee organized to coordinate efforts for all party candidates for Congress running in the Bay State. Thomas Perkins's early career, not untypical of other Federalists young and old, is another example that undermines David Fischer's contention that somehow important Federalists did not generally engage in popular party activities. Perkins was neither an isolated case in Massachusetts nor in the rest of the nation before 1801.[25]

Loan Commissioner Jabez Bowen of Providence, Rhode Island, was another example of the same type of cadreman. Although "aristocratic in his bearing" and kin to such families as the Browns and the Fenners, he had "a healthy respect for popular opinions." Moreover, he had no compunctions about employing his office to the advantage of the party. A shrewd politico with fingers in many pies, he was also a wealthy man with every conceivable type of investment in hand. Bowen was a devoted supporter of the Constitution in an Antifederalist state and as such emerged, along with Customs Collector Jeremiah Olney, as a key party contact with the Federalist leadership in Philadelphia. His patronage recommendations and tactical political suggestions for dealing with the delicate Rhode Island situation were given respectful and usually fruitful hearings by both George

Washington and Alexander Hamilton. He boasted wide-spread associations in both town and state. The loan officer was a member of the Providence Political Club, a director of the Providence Bank, an officer of the Rhode Island Cincinnati, a deacon of the Congregational church, and grand master of the Rhose Island Masonic Lodge. Not much got by Bowen.

The commissioner of loans had no compunctions about using his office for partisan purposes. By 1790, in the crucible of Rhode Island politics, he already distinguished between Hamiltonian Federalists as a current, distinct entity as compared with their predecessors, the "wiggs" who "equally" supported the Constitution, but prior to its ratification. He recognized a clear political link between the two groups, but understood that a new political era had dawned, creating new situations and new responses, but not particularly new alignments.

One issue, however, remained extant. The most emotional state issue after ratification remained the paper money emission of 1786, a *casus belli* that had divided Rhode Island into bitter, competing factions in the late 1780s. These factions, in turn and with some changes, formed the nuclei for party divisions in the nineties. Bowen, probably uniquely among United States loan commissioners, ruled at the outset of his tenure in 1790 that "no securities which had already been reclaimed in eventually worthless paper currency [in the 1780s] would be acceptable in exchange for federal stock [new United States bond issues]."

The practical result of this arbitrary ruling was that "only those individuals who had fought the paper money system [the Federalists of the eighties] and refused to surrender their securities in accordance with the [state's paper emission] law [of 1786] were to be compensated." Given Rhode Island's debtor-creditor combat in the Confederation, it is clear, Bowen occupied the most sensitive federal office in the state. What remains unclear is how he got away with such a partisan interpretation of federal law. It was true that both his local and national connections were superb, and this might provide a partial explanation. At any rate, his administration of the loan office was, in the words of Irwin Polishook, "a hard blow to harmony in state politics and undeniably provided important vindication for the minority Federalist forces in the state." [26]

The personnel of the loan office in New York reflects some interesting insights into Alexander Hamilton's complicated commitments to his local allies. The first loan officer was Dr. John Cochran, a physician married to Philip Schuyler's sister and thus kin through marriage to the secretary of the treasury. By the admission of important New York Federalists, he was clearly not up to the task; after accepting the protection of his nephew by marriage, Cochran resigned at the end of 1794—only months before Hamilton himself did the same. Cochran's health was bad enough so that his political partisanship was limited, although he is frequently described as having acted as a kind of political broker for the Schuylers. As a loan officer, he certainly accorded the Schuylers privileged treatment. They manipulated their United States securities with a great deal more impunity and assurance than others with similar holdings. Hamilton was obligated to the commissioner of loans for more than family reasons, however. Cochran had been among the hardest hit by the 1791 failure of William Duer, and he badly needed the income from the office. The secretary of the treasury evidently felt a degree of personal responsibility to Duer's victims anyway, and Cochran's treatment at his hands may be a significant case in point. Frequent complaints about Cochran from important Federalists like William Seton notwithstanding, Hamilton kept Cochran on under his protection for as long as he could.

Although Matthew Clarkson, Cochran's successor, shared many characteristics with the doctor, the former more clearly earned his keep politically. Like Cochran, Clarkson (not to be confused with a Philadelphia cousin of the same name) was connected to one of the premier families in the Empire State, had held field rank in the Continental army, and was an active proponent of ratification at the close of the 1780s. Moreover, while Clarkson was a relative improvement in the office, he shared with Cochran a "weakness" as an accountant that the position could ill afford, an impairment that Clarkson's Federalist confreres readily admitted in the years following his 1794 nomination. Nevertheless, unlike Cochran, "Clarkson was a man of consequence within the circle of Hamilton and King and Morris." Described as a "gentleman" by profession, he was not adverse to plumbing the depths of popular politics. In 1793, for example, he formed a public committee to defend George Washington against the abuses of a local Republican newspaper, and then took the initiative in suing that paper for libel. Republicans thereafter considered Clarkson one of their ranking tormentors, and a "constant friend of national . . . government."[27]

In circumstances briefly analogous to New York, kinship also had something to do with the appointment of the first loan commissioners of Pennsylvania and Delaware. Thomas Smith, who held the office in the Keystone State from 1790 until his death in 1793, was a brother-in-law of United States District Court Judge Richard Peters, one of the state's eminent Federalists. Smith's successor, Stephen Moylan, had been a colonel in the Continental army and an aide to General Washington. After the war he was both active in Pennsylvania politics and a ranking member of the Society of the Cincinnati, so he brought a certain amount of political leadership to the office.

John Stockton, the loan commissioner in neighboring Delaware, was also a significant political force. He had been the long-time sheriff of New Castle County during the Confederation and was part of a notable New Jersey and Delaware Federalist family. During the Adams years, Stockton's accounts turned up short by nearly $2,500, and he was accused by the Philadelphia *Aurora* of tapping the public till, a charge for which substantial evidence existed, despite the partisan nature of its source. Jefferson ultimately removed Stockton on these grounds, although he was never prosecuted.[28]

The level of competence among southern loan commissioners was very much higher than among those in the middle states, although they were no less party oriented. John Hopkins, the Virginia loan officer, was one of the most respected Federalists in the commonwealth. The illegitimate son of a tenant farmer, he had made his own way to a fortune as a merchant in revolutionary America. In the 1790s he was allied politically with John Marshall in the Federalist stronghold of Richmond. Using the connections of his office well, Hopkins "exhibited detailed knowledge of political affairs and sources of Federalist loyalty in most of the counties east of the Blue Ridge and north of the James." In 1798, for example, he put his knowledge to practical use, electioneering extensively during the successful Federalist congressional campaign. He predicted accurately to Treasury Secretary Wolcott that the results "will be better for talents, virtue and federalism than heretofore." [29]

In Antifederalist North Carolina, establishment Federalists who were clan-oriented retained a tight grip on the loan office. The commissioner of loans for most of the decade until his death in 1798 was William Skinner, uncle of John Skinner, the Federalist United States marshal for the state. The elder Skinner was a member of a family that "have long been influential and much respected in this state." Sherwood Haywood, who succeeded to the loan office upon Skinner's death, was of an even more eminent family. Sherwood's brother John, the state treasurer, was often acknowledged as North Carolina's ranking Federalist. His appointment, John Steele advised Wolcott, would be salutary for the state's Federalist minority. The Haywoods were "influential" and "generally known in the state." Steele's recommendation to the Adams administration was frankly political. John Haywood's "opinions would I believe go farther to promote a public measure than that of any other man in the state, and this is among my reasons for wishing that one of the brothers might receive the appointment." [30]

Even more than the customs department, the upper levels of the internal revenue service were almost totally dominated by "family interest" offspring of major American clans. This is very much in line with the existing stereotype of the Federalist party, a party led by close-knit American gentry.

However, as a group, the Federalists were deeply active

politically, in the same ways as the Jeffersonians. Moreover, Federalist politicking was by no means either selective or belated, as most students of the party have heretofore thought. Finally, while the elite dominated the top of the internal revenue service, the men who filled the middle and lower echelons, with the exception of the Adams-appointed land commissioners, represented a much broader spectrum of the nation's society than did their superiors. The subordinates, it is true, were frequently party leaders of the first or second rank politically themselves. But they held their official stations more as a consequence of their party commitment than as a result of their exalted places in the local social structure.

An examination of the lower levels of the internal revenue service will thus unearth the existence of a broad social and economic spectrum of local political leadership, a managerial group upon which the Federalists in the states were as dependent for their political success as they were reliant on the oft-stereotyped Federalist "aristocracy."

CHAPTER SEVEN

Internal Revenue:
The Lower Civil Service

The collectors and auxiliary officers of the internal revenue service were men on the move, government agents who visited the distillers and collected the taxes. In general these subordinates can be profiled as Federalist middle-class cadre in terms of occupation, status, education, and property. Some were gentry, of course, particularly in those towns and regions where there were many party men and few government jobs. A third group were tangentially connected to elite families, men with marginal or reflected status but in need of both position and income.

These generalizations must be scrapped when dealing with the Adams-appointed land tax commissioners of 1798, however, for while their function and place in the federal service were akin to that of the collectors, they formed a singular group. The 1798 commissioners comprised the only coherent body of appointees Adams ever named, and he used his unique opportunity both to recognize some very important Federalist supporters and to strengthen those party elements that sustained him in the states. Thus, the status level of the 1798 group was closer to that of the higher civil service than the lower, the classification of the position notwithstanding.

While they remain the hardest to identify, the middle-class nominees in the states in some ways form the most interesting group of Federalist leaders. They were local cadremen who bore little resemblance to the elitist portrait of party leadership often painted by historians. These Federalists were middling townsmen or yeomen who were neither rich nor particularly successful, men of limited backgrounds and attainment. Yet for them the Federalist party induced a clear ideological commitment, and even offered a way up. In many ways their life styles had little in common with the high-powered, well-born men who were their superiors in the federal service.

There were a few collectors who fit the above description who held politically sensitive occupations. While they were not nearly so prevalent in the revenue department as they were in the post office, there were enough tavernkeepers in the ranks to make them noticeable. The fact that they were large-volume purchasers of the distilled beverages they were to tax did not prevent their nominations, a self-evident conflict of interest even by eighteenth-century standards.

Perhaps because of the open clash over the collection of the tax in western Pennsylvania, and to a lesser extent in Antifederalist North Carolina, two extant examples survive in these states. John Webster owned a tavern at Stony Creek in trans-Allegheny Pennsylvania. A group of whisky rebels complained that Webster, wearing his tax collector's hat, overtaxed the poorer farmer-distillers, played favorites, and "avoided troubling the distillers who had influence or money." The latter were the men from whom he bought his whisky. Although his biases and conflict of interest were made abundantly clear during the post-rebellion investigations, he held on to his job right to the end of the Federalist era. In North Carolina, where collections were only a little less difficult, Auxiliary Revenue Officer Edward Yarborough operated an inn at Salisbury that was also a popular Federalist meeting place.[1]

In both Pennsylvania and North Carolina, farmers also occupied federal positions rendered significant by the local tensions over collections. James Brice, a Washington County,

Pennsylvania, farmer later removed by Jefferson, was one Federalist collector thrust into the center of the Whisky Rebellion. In seeking a federal post he described himself as poor and humble, but pointed out that "sometimes a gem may be found among the ready mass of matter. I hope you will not despise [me] . . . on account of my obscurity." The Federalists in Philadelphia didn't, and the new tax gatherer was unexpectedly thrust into the center of the rebellion.

Another pair of yeomen who found themselves in the same position were Benjamin and John Wells, father and son, of Connellsville. The two collected the excise tax in Fayette and Westmoreland counties. The father, an ardent party man, was labeled "despicable and untrustworthy" by the rebels. Many in rebellion believed that the elder Wells exercised his political grievances against them in assessing and collecting the revenue and "proposed that they would submit to the law if Wells were displaced and an honest and reputable collector put in his stead." His "offensive personality" was not noticeably modified after the rebels burned his farmhouse to the ground; neither the father nor the son resigned his federal post thereafter, duress notwithstanding. Federalist western Pennsylvania farmers and Collectors John Hughes, Jacob Humphreys, and Robert Johnson were also singled out as partisans by the rebels as they pursued their tax-gathering duties.[2]

In restive North Carolina, Alexander Hamilton appointed two former regulators, back-country farmers in the 1790s as they had been in the 1760s. Regulators had often become Loyalists during the war, largely because of their grievances against the local North Carolina colonial authorities. Perhaps that had something to do with these two collectors' identification with the Federalist national government rather than with the generally Republican state administration in the Federalist decade. James Hunter and George Sims, the former regulator leaders and Loyalists, remained respected figures in the North Carolina piedmont. Theirs were, as someone noted, "artful" Hamiltonian appointments, and they helped to avoid the depths of unrest plumbed in Pennsylvania, where most subordinate appointees were not nearly so respected personally. Federalist Jacob Blume, a revenue collector from Salem, was equally useful in dealing with another special North Carolina constituency, for he was a prominent Moravian farmer and elder in that town.[3]

Yeoman Federalist collectors appeared elsewhere in the rural South. John Wright, a farmer in the Ninety Six district of South Carolina, was reprimanded by Hamilton in 1793 for employing "rough and menacing conduct" in the collection of the revenue in an area "violently opposed to the Excise." Concentrating on Pennsylvania, the treasury secretary did not want to stir up unnecessary trouble elsewhere, so Wright's partisan bias in this instance found no support in Philadelphia. Thomas Carter of Russell County, Virginia, fancied himself gentry but did not quite make it. The owner of one slave, he was clearly a farmer rather than a "planter," as he described himself. As he was a vigorous Antifederalist in the 1780s, his sympathies increasingly went to the national government in the nineties, and for his efforts he was named an auxiliary officer of the revenue in 1796.[4]

A significant array of shopkeepers, small commission merchants, and mercantile employees were rewarded with minor federal offices in the revenue department for their political labors. Kendle Batson, a young shopkeeper in Georgetown, Delaware, was a Federalist follower of Senator Outerbridge Horsey, and a self-styled "friend to party. I shall always feal myself bound to stand to what my party shall do," he vowed during the election campaign of 1796, just three months after his nomination as collector of the revenue. He pledged to "push the Tickett" in Sussex County. By 1798 he identified with the high Federalists, but as one who did not shun electioneering. "I expect to see you at Geo. Town Tomorrow," Batson wrote a friend, "as that is a day appointed by our friends to have some consultation respecting our Election etc." "Anything" that could be done should be done, he agreed in 1799, "to disappoint and Shagrin the Jacobins."[5]

Benjamin Cheney was another shopkeeper, owner of a country store outside of Beaufort, North Carolina. Cheney, a local Republican wrote Albert Gallatin in 1802, held his office as a "mere sinecure," a deputy performing all duties while Cheney minded his store. When Cheney's job was abolished in 1802, he applied to President Jefferson for a customs post which he did not get. "Not one of the recommendations say a word about Mr. Cheney's politics," Jefferson wrote Gallatin, "an omission which in application to this administration I have observed to be almost invariably a proof of federalism." Collectors Duncan McRae, a Scotsman from Fayetteville, North Carolina, and Jacob Elmendorf of Esopus, New York, both kept general stores and were local party activists. The latter was singled out for removal by Aaron Burr in 1801 as a particularly obnoxious Federalist. The former was a visible party man among his fellow Scottish settlers in the area. George Sears of Providence, Rhode Island, was a local shopkeeper and an ally of Loan Commissioner Jabez Bowen in the town.[6]

Occasional clerks also found their way to leadership positions in the Federalist hierarchy. Collector George Price of Baltimore was described as a man of "low standing" in society, "Mr. Price never having had a station in life higher than that of a clerk." In Price's case, when the Republicans accused him of being "violently opposed to us," they were not, for a change, speaking euphemistically. He had led "the mob that cut down a liberty pole" erected by Jeffersonians at a Fourth of July celebration. Despite his "low station" in the community, he was a major figure in the congressional campaign of Thomas Sprigg in 1794. Six months after that campaign, he received his federal appointment. Another collector, Thomas Clarke of Boston, a clerk in a merchant house, served on a Federalist electioneering committee in 1800, formed to co-ordinate election efforts for a whole range of party candidates. His presence on the committee signified his responsibility for getting out the vote in one small part of the city. [7]

Some artisans were also found among the party's local cadre. The collector of internal revenue on Nantucket Island, Massachusetts, was William Coffin, a barber. He was also one of the most important party men on that Federalist island. Comfort Tyler of Manlius, New York, a former private in the Continental army, was a surveyor in the upstate area, combining his tax-collecting travels with his surveying commissions. He too was something of a local party notable, singled out for his opposition to Jefferson's election in 1800. John Armistead of Plymouth, North Carolina, was a retired sailor, and James Patterson of Chatham in the same state was a carpenter.[8]

The presence of some farmers, clerks, shopkeepers, and artisans in the second rank of the official Federalist hierarchy makes it probable that they were a fairly significant force in the party, not merely as followers or believers but as local leaders. Because of the difficulty in ascertaining information about these middling types, the fact that a variety of examples can be turned up should demonstrate the importance of middle-class elements within the Federalist leadership.

Collectors close to the top of the middle class included some small merchants and commission brokers who were active in the Federalist party. Two New Jersey Federalists, merchants in small towns and dealing with local trade, were good examples. Elisha Clark of Gloucester was a Quaker who engaged in the local commerce common to the Delaware River basin. A party manager in town who during the 1790s held a number of state and local positions in addition to his federal post, he was stripped of both his collector's appointment and a state position in 1801. Without the income and perquisites his offices provided, he couldn't maintain his small business and was forced to sell out at public auction. Clark moved to Philadelphia to take a job with a relative. John Bray of New Brunswick engaged as a commission broker in the local trade of the Raritan River. He was among the revenue collectors who, like Elisha Clark, were singled out by the incoming administration in 1801 for mixing politics with official conduct. The Republican governor and United States senator, both just elected, wrote the national administration demanding his removal. Not only had he actively campaigned for Adams in 1800, the two Jeffersonians disclosed, he had as early as 1796 used his internal revenue service position to persecute and intimidate Republican merchants and distillers.[9]

A significant proportion of the inferior positions in the internal revenue was filled by middling relatives of important Federalists. The service, at the level of collector and auxiliary officer, provided a home for needy or "deserving" kin of Federalist placemen. Another group of Federalist collectors were themselves placemen of declining status who had lost their wealth and perhaps their local stature as well and simply needed the appointment to earn a living. Still others were local gentry in relatively remote areas of the nation. There were often no positions in the higher civil service for Federalist notables in these areas, so these men accepted what was available—usually a nomination as collector or postmaster. Probably the only unifying characteristic of these three groups of collectors was their devotion to the Federalist cause.

Federalists in New England could always find room for the stray relative. New Hampshire Supervisor Joshua Wentworth found berths in the revenue service for both his brother and brother-in-law. Brother George was an unsuccessful shipmaster in Portsmouth before he was named collector. Both siblings were caught up in the wave of Republicanism that swept the port town when Senator John Langdon broke with the Federalists about the time the Jay Treaty became an issue. The Wentworths followed Langdon into the Jeffersonian camp and eventually the two lost their federal posts. The cause of the removals involved an indeterminate mixture of politics and corruption, for Joshua in 1798 was accused of embezzling government funds and some of the tar rubbed off on George. At least the latter was caught in the backwash of the allegations, and he lost his job too.

Brother-in-law Daniel Warner of Concord, meanwhile, was more fortunate and perhaps more cunning. At about the same time his kin by marriage were putting their federal jobs on the line by changing their politics, Warner, who possessed a well-deserved reputation as a trimmer up to 1795, was promoted from auxiliary officer of the revenue to collector. Perhaps as a direct consequence, even as his in-laws moved away from Federalism, Warner committed himself more and more unreservedly to that party's efforts. He was a Federalist elector for John Adams in 1796, and was described in the local press during the campaign as a man whose "Federalism [was] uniform and established." [10]

Collector Jesse Root, Jr., of Coventry, Connecticut, was the son of the chief justice of the Connecticut Superior Court. The elder Root, very much a part of the Congregational Federalist establishment, was an elector for John Adams in 1796. Reverend David Austin of New Haven was another well-connected Federalist collector. His daughters were married to Congressman Roger Sherman and United States District Court Clerk Simeon Baldwin, two of the more important establishment Federalists in the state. Austin's reputation for eccentricity hindered and eventually undermined his ministerial function, and he badly needed the federal job. He became mentally ill in 1795, maybe as a result of scarlet fever, although one contemporary Federalist blamed his malady on the "evils of the French Revolution," anxiety from which caused the clergyman to become "distraught in his wits." [11]

Kinship was a prominent factor in internal revenue service nominations in Vermont and Rhode Island. Collector Elijah Brush was brother to Vermont Revenue Supervisor Nathaniel Brush, and Collector Daniel S. Dexter of Rhode Island was the brother of Supervisor John S. Dexter. Another Rhode Island collector, Paul Allen, was the father of a prominent Federalist printer as well as kin to a notable Rhode Island Federalist banking and commercial family. The elder Allen, an active supporter of the Constitution in an Antifederalist state, like George Wentworth was an unsuccessful shipmaster who very much relied on his federal appointment for the livelihood it produced. [12]

Family connections also turn up in the lower ranks of the internal revenue service in the middle states. Collector John Ewing of western Pennsylvania, a Federalist who was prevented from measuring stills by a mob in Daregall Township in 1793, was the half brother of his inspector in the service, Edward Hand. In New Jersey Federalist Collector Thomas Lawrence of the rural hamlet of Hamburg was the son-in-law of Lewis Morris and a nephew of United States District Court Judge Robert Morris. He was thus connected to one of the first families of the state.[13]

Abraham Low of New York City, son of ranking upstate gentry and the son-in-law of Abraham S. Bancker, a wealthy New York City Federalist, proved to be a very unfortunate nomination. Young Low lived far beyond his means. Frequently delinquent in his remittances to Philadelphia over a period of years, Low defaulted altogether on his 1798 tax collections. Federalist Supervisor Nicholas Fish was forced to cover for him and then ease him out of the service. Low's father and father-in-law made good the loss, and the whole affair was hushed up. "No proceedings will have taken place" against Low, Fish reported to Abraham Bancker in 1798, "from the friendship which I had for him and his connections. . . . In the adjustment of Mr. Low's affairs with the United States," the supervisor continued, "he shall experience all the lenity and liberality consistent with the duties which I have to myself and to the Public." Low was sent home to his father, and the whole scandal was kept from the Republican press. Officially, Low resigned, and the Lows, the Banckers, and Nicholas Fish all remained politically unembarrassed.[14]

Significant instances of nepotism appear in the South as well. President Washington, his admonitions about the dangers of favoritism notwithstanding, found the internal revenue a haven for some collateral relations. John Lewis of Virginia, the president's nephew, was named an auxiliary officer late in Washington's second term. Two more Lewises, Francis and Miles, also found their way into the service at about the same time. In North Carolina, John Gilchrist, a brother-in-law of Supervisor William Polk, was a collector. Benjamin and Levi Blount, members of an important Tarheel clan, were named collectors during that family's Federalist period. Archibald Murphey's father-in-law and Daniel Hunt's brother were also collectors; both Murphey and Hunt were important North Carolina Federalists.[15]

The lower ranks of the internal revenue service also sheltered a considerable number of well-connected gentry who had suffered financial reverses in the economically tumultuous Confederation era. These collectors, virtually broke and very much in need of their federal jobs, were almost always merchants who had lost their businesses. Abel Whitney of Westfield, Massachusetts, was one such victim who, as collector, did not let his "scanty and inadequate" circumstances hinder his "spirited exertions" for the Federalists in the elections of 1796. Joseph Storer of Maine had started out life as the son of the "richest man in Wells." The inheritance was dissipated by the son in various ways during the 1780s, and by the dawn of the Federalist decade he was virtually broke. Continuing financial problems did not prevent Storer from playing an important role in Federalist politics in Kennebunk, a town adjacent to Wells to which he had moved. Storer was one of the chief proponents of Jay's Treaty in a town that formed a Republican stronghold. In 1796 he actively campaigned for John Adams. George Phillips of Connecticut was another Federalist merchant who lost virtually everything he had in the Confederation. He could not survive, however, even on a collector's income, and in 1797 he resigned and moved to Georgia to start again.[16]

John Berrien, originally of New Jersey, was also a merchant who migrated to Georgia as a result of financial difficulties during the Confederation. A minor member of the early Federalist establishment of that frontier state in 1789, he received the small office gladly. George F. Norton, a collector in Winchester, Virginia, had been rich. His father's merchant house was among the largest and most prosperous Scottish firms in revolutionary Virginia. A combination of economic and social changes brought the house to ruin by 1795. Norton, a Federalist, had little choice but to accept the low office tendered him a year later.[17]

A third group of collectors comprised men who were clearly well-heeled gentry, but who were residents of rural or frontier areas where there simply were no high federal civil service jobs for the government to hand out. The post office and the internal revenue department offered acceptable berths for these notables in outlying areas of the nation where, in general, Republicanism was assumed to be strongest. These back-country Federalist gentry, literally less urbane, certainly more provincial, than their tidewater counterparts, proved as a group to be the most unreconstructed and irreconcilable of party men after 1800.

Henry W. Dwight of Stockbridge in Berkshire County, Massachusetts, was a good example. This revenue collector headed one of the first families in Stockbridge. Related by marriage to the Sedgwicks and other western Massachusetts gentry, the Dwights were "intertwined in one extended cousinage, 'one union of political influence' which allowed no alternative to rule by the wise and good." Dwight's home town was at the heart of the existing Massachusetts frontier, an area that had spawned Shays's Rebellion and was in the 1790s honeycombed with pockets of Republican strength. An ally of Theodore Sedgwick, Dwight was very close to the top of the "Federalist dynasty" of Berkshire County. He was the primary founder in 1794, and the chief financial supporter thereafter, of the outspokenly Federalist Stockbridge *Western Star*. It was Dwight's influence that was responsible for the *Star*'s editor Loring Andrews becoming postmaster of the town. On the eve of the Republican victory in 1800 an implacable, puritanical Dwight wrote Sedgwick that "if the United States are not . . . Politically, Physically, and Morally damned" by the looming changes, "it will not be because they do not deserve it. Individually and in Church and State, I am more than ever convinced of the Doctrine of Total Depravity." [18]

Stephen Hussey, internal revenue collector as well as collector of customs at Nantucket, was equally well connected and irreconcilable. Like Dwight, he too headed an extended and powerful family, one with roots deep in the island. As late as 1804, a Republican complained, "his politics are Federal [and] he always has done all in his power to oppose the Republican Ticket." Shubael Breed of Norwich, Connecticut, was carved out of the same mold. This collector was a Yale graduate, a merchant, and the son of the mayor of Norwich; Breed was also a major lay figure in the town's Congre-

gational church. When local Republicans called for his removal in the summer of 1801, he defiantly told them that he
would remain an ardent opponent of Republicans office or
no office, and he "wished to be ranked among the high
Federalists." [19]

As part of the American response to the crisis with France,
President John Adams convinced Congress to appropriate
considerable sums of money to raise a new army and begin
building a fleet of large fighting ships. The money to pay for
these military expenditures was to be raised by a new
broad-based federal tax on all improved lands. The "land
tax," as it quickly became known, was to be collected immediately. To ensure this, a new tax collection agency was
established, designed to work independently of the internal
revenue service. The latter was too burdened already by the
excise tax to handle a major new assignment. At least that was
the conventional wisdom offered. Perhaps the president understood as well that the internal revenue service was almost
entirely Hamilton-appointed and, at least at its upper levels,
oriented toward the high Federalists. To expand it in 1798 to
fill this new need really meant to permit Hamiltonian revenue supervisors to name still more of the kind of subordinate Federalists about whom Adams already had doubts.

In any event, the political opportunity opened up by the
power to appoint seventy-nine new land tax commissioners
in sixteen states was not lost on the president. Adams had
inherited almost all of his civil service from Washington and
Hamilton; these 1798 nominations formed the only opportunity he would have to systematically reward his supporters
and strengthen those organized elements in the states clearly
committed to him. The determined chief executive named
moderate Federalists in a party already beginning to divide
into "war" and "peace" factions.

In some ways the tax collectors, class of '98, comprised the
most thoroughly partisan body of civil servants yet named to
a federal service already saturated with the politically involved. Not more than a handful of the new appointees could
be considered of middling status. Virtually the entire new

department, as it existed in the states, was composed of elite—men who were influential, politically active, successful, and well to do. Less than a handful, moreover, were Hamilton-oriented. If the land commissioners' particular official function was relatively mundane, nevertheless many of them considered themselves, and were looked upon by others, as agents appointed to carry out an important patriotic mission in a time of crisis. Few who were involved in politics, moreover, could avoid the perception that Adams had strengthened his hold of the Federalist party. Only in New York and Massachusetts, the two states where Federalists were most inclined toward Hamiltonian views, did Adams follow a path of accommodation.

In the Bay State the most prestigious figure to accept Adams's nomination was Nathan Dane of Beverly, Essex County. Dane was a wealthy charter member of the Essex Junto. The junto, or its remnants, by 1798 formed the core of high federalism in the state, so Dane's appointment took on a particularly symbolic relevance. As he was a former delegate to the Continental Congress and a late but influential convert to the cause of ratification, his federalism was never in doubt after 1788. Dane was repeatedly elected to the Massachusetts upper house in the 1790s and remained a major supporter of "firmness and order" throughout the decade. But he was never closely identified with the high Federalists' views on war and peace, so his identification with Hamiltonian elements of the party really remained only symbolic.[20]

Several other Massachusetts senators were named by Adams as well, including Beza Hayward of Bridgewater, Thomas Davis of Plymouth, Eleazer Brooks of Lincoln, and Nathaniel Wells of Wells, Maine. The last three had been Federalist members of the Massachusetts Ratifying Convention. All were Federalists who willingly engaged in popular politics, defying most existing stereotypes. Davis, for example, was described by a Massachusetts party leader in 1798 as "extremely useful" to the party. He had at a 1793 public meeting demanded Citizen Genêt's expulsion from the United States, and was never reluctant to engage in electioneering. Nathaniel Wells, an Adams elector in 1796, was widely "regarded as one of the leading Federalists of Maine" and the most clearly Adams-oriented party man among the new nominees. A popular Fourth of July orator, he had headed some other Maine public meetings as well, supporting Jay's Treaty in 1796 and, two years later, shortly after his appointment, organizing and chairing two public gatherings defending Adams's foreign policies. For western Massachusetts, Adams named William Bacon, a local lieutenant of Theodore Sedgwick. The president touched most of the political bases in his home state with his six appointments.[21]

One of Adams's four appointees in Vermont was Moses Robinson, Jr., son of Vermont's leading Jeffersonian, but the other three were ranking Federalists. Jonathan Spafford of Williston was a close friend and political ally of Federalist Governor Thomas Chittendon. Despite his increasingly shaky financial position in the late 1790s, Spafford remained very much a notable in the frontier state. The other two nominees were Federalist legislators Jonathan Hunt of Kinsdale and Ebenezer Crafts of Craftsbury. The latter had founded his town after the Revolution and dominated it politically and socially ever since. He was described variously as a "firm and active" Federalist and a "strong" party man. Jonathan Hunt, like Crafts, owned vast tracts of land and was rich, and like both Spafford and Crafts, he was one of Vermont's founders. A candidate for Adams elector in 1800, he was a man of "decided Federalism." [22]

John Adams paid special attention to New Hampshire, a state in which a Republican tide was beginning to run by 1798. Nathaniel Gilman, brother to the Federalist governor and an influential party man in his own right, was named one of the land tax commissioners. Nathaniel himself was showing signs of wavering in his commitment to the party, although he had "supported the Constitution and most of Hamilton's early financial measures." His appointment, apart from placating his brother and Exeter area Federalists generally, helped to postpone till after 1801 Nathaniel Gilman's defection to the Jeffersonians; at least it appeared that way.

Other elements of the New Hampshire party were encouraged as well. David Hough, the brother of the printer and publisher of the Federalist Concord *Courier,* was also named a commissioner. Another Adams appointee was John Bellows, Federalist state senator from Walpole and a member of that town's first family. Joseph Badger of Gilmantown, also a Federalist legislator and a former opponent of the Constitution, was another who accepted a land tax commission. Badger was openly active on Adams's behalf from 1798 through 1800. One more convert from antifederalism rounded out the New Hampshire appointments.

Joshua Atherton was the father-in-law of rising young Federalist official William Gordon, and a highly visible appointee in rural New Hampshire in his own right. He had had a remarkably checkered political career, managing to live down both his unwavering loyalism during the Revolution and an implacable opposition to the Constitution in the 1780s, only to become an influential Federalist in the ensuing decade. Atherton was named the state attorney general in 1793 and resigned that post in 1798, in favor of his son-in-law, in order to accept Adams's nomination.

Even in an essentially conservative state, one recent historian has written, Atherton's "political ideas became as out of date as his tie wig, which was one of the last in the county." Capable of magisterial, not to say emotional, commitment to political causes, usually of the unpopular variety, he was an indefatigable Federalist campaigner. There was nothing "tie wig" about his political involvement: "Because of his admiration for England and his fear of France he strongly supported the Jay Treaty and was hanged in effigy." As land tax commissioner, it was alleged, he taxed Republicans excessively. The elitist Atherton said, in a final political testament, that he hated "Jacobins, the Irish-brotherhood [and] the Jeffersonians." As he was already an old man by the end of the Federalist decade, his ardent support of John Adams was in the nature of the former Loyalist's and Antifederalist's last hurrah.[23]

All three nominations mandated for Rhode Island went to Adams men in a state where, because of earlier federal patronage, a Hamilton-oriented faction was deeply ensconced. Elisha Potter of South Kingston, a highly visible politician, had served in the 1790s first as speaker of the Rhode Island Assembly and, until his appointment by the president, a member of the United States House of Representatives. The source of his appeal as a Federalist leader was in itself significant because he did not at all fit the elitist image usually drawn of Federalist managers. A former private in the Continental army and a blacksmith, he struggled to read law and become an attorney, eventually succeeding without either family connections or initial high status. Thus he "seemed to carry about with him a certain homespun certificate of authority." At the same time he was described as an "uncompromising" and "bombastic" Federalist whose "devotion to the Federalist party was nearly complete." He was recommended to the Adams administration as a man who "had much influence" with the middling ranks in the Kingston area. After his return to Rhode Island from Philadelphia to accept his federal appointment in 1798, this reputation was borne out by his prompt election to the state legislature.

John Dorrance, the second Rhode Island commissioner, was no less influential politically. He edited and published the Providence *United States Chronicle,* the leading Federalist sheet in the state. He also sat in the state senate, was president of the Providence Town Council, a trustee of Brown College from 1798, and a justice on the county court of common pleas. Dorrance was known to Republicans as an "aggressive opponent" and was obviously in a position to do Adams a great deal of good. The third nomination also went to an Adams-oriented Federalist legislator. Commissioner John L. Boss was a fairly influential Newport merchant who, like Dorrance, was involved in a variety of local political activities.[24]

In keeping with the character of the Federalist interest in Connecticut, only gentry were appointed by Adams in 1798. Andrew Kingsbury, the long-time state treasurer, was described as one of the "Federalist bosses" of the state, a label Richard Purcell applied to the entire coterie comprising the Congregational establishment that dominated the "land of steady habits." Three Federalist state legislators were also commissioned: William Heron of Reading, Shubael Abbee on Windham, and Epaphroditus Champion of East Haddam, all of whom spoke for important party constituencies. The final office went to Julius Deming of Litchfield, an affluent merchant and close political associate of Federalist leader Benjamin Talmadge. Deming, who held a variety of local offices, was known among Litchfield Republicans as the "crowbar justice" because, according to the Republican press, he exerted his leverage on the bench against Republicans who came up before him. Repeated Jeffersonian attacks of this nature in the local party newspaper finally caused Deming to sue for libel, but even in partisan Connecticut the suit was thrown out.[25]

In sum, it is clear that Adams's 1798 appointments in New England were astonishingly political in nature, in the main going to those Federalists who could bring their influence to bear on the president's behalf, both within the already riven Federalist party and at the polls in 1800.

The same was true in the middle states. In New Jersey two of the four identifiable appointees had been Adams electors in 1796. One was John Blackwood of Gloucester in South Jersey; the other was Jonathan Rhea of Trenton. The latter, a lawyer and a former Continental army officer, was fairly well to do and deeply immersed in the Federalist politics of New Jersey's capital city. John Black of Burlington was Adams's third New Jersey commissioner. He was a wealthy farmer and a locally renowned breeder of livestock. Black became deeply involved in the campaign of 1800, among other things delivering an address at a public meeting calling on West Jersey voters to repudiate "Jacobinical disorganizers" and Republican chairmen who were "resolved in the overthrow of public order." The fourth Adams nominee was David Ford, who headed Morristown's first family. A lawyer and iron manufacturer, he had gained local notoriety in 1794 when the cavalry troop of militia he commanded was employed to help suppress the Whisky Rebellion. A year later the Federalist governor of New Jersey described Ford to President Washington as "very well known in Jersey, and universally acknowledged as a gentleman of strictly Federal Principles and Conduct." [26]

Political power in New York, the "graduate school" of American political behavior as Roy F. Nichols has called it, rested almost exclusively on elite family connections in the eighteenth century. A survey of Adams's land tax appointments in 1798 reveals that the president adhered faithfully and astutely to that premise in filling vacancies. A variety of well-connected Federalist notables, with family tentacles collectively reaching in every direction from the political center at New York City, were neatly wooed with the siren song of office.

Jacob Radcliff, the commissioner in the city itself, was a young, widely esteemed Federalist representing old-line New York City gentry. A future mayor of New York, he served on the city's Federalist Committee of Correspondence in the waning years of the 1790s. His credentials, for Adams's purposes, were impeccable: Radcliff had attended Princeton, read law with forner Federalist Congressman Egbert Benson, and was closely allied with the Bancker and Low families, as well as with Revenue Supervisor Nicholas Fish. Surprisingly, at virtually the same time as he accepted his federal job, he also accepted an appointment to the New York State Supreme Court. [27]

Selah Strong, the commissioner for Long Island, was also closely tied to the New York City Federalist leadership. Strong in fact lived in the city, where he was an "eminent merchant" in the 1790s, but he also owned St. George's Manor, an estate at Brookhaven which provided the labored justification for Adams to pass on the Long Island nomination to him. A state senator, both Selah Strong and his son Benjamin, like Radcliff, had no compunctions about engaging in election politics. [28]

Moss Kent, one of the new Adams land commissioners upstate, lived in Cooperstown. He was the fledgling brother of New York Chancellor James Kent and, of course, was not only a member of one of the first families of the city but closely tied to the dominant elements of New York City federalism as well. The Kents, like many of the city's patricians, owned vast tracts in the wilderness of New York State, where they were secondarily a part of the landlord aristocracy. Moss, while still in his early twenties, settled upstate to both read law and oversee the family's land; he made his home for many years in the 1790s with William Cooper, the squire of Cooperstown and the county's premier Federalist. In fact, only her death prevented the younger Kent from marrying "The Bashaw of Otsego County's" daughter.

Kent, very much in the active tradition that Cooper had established in the area, plunged deeply into Federalist politics. "I very early embarked myself warmly in the Interest of Mr. [John] Jay," he wrote James Kent in describing his baptism in the art of electioneering during the exciting 1792 New York gubernatorial contest. "Had not the wicked and corrupt [Clintonian] majority of Canvassers rejected the Ballotts of this County I have the vanity to believe that my exertions and Influence would have added a considerable number to the large Majority which would undoubtedly have been in favor of Mr. Jay." Moss thereafter attended Federalist caucuses from time to time in New York City as Cooper's representative, and continued politically active upstate. In 1795 he was "warmly engaged" once again in Jay's bid for the governorship, even campaigning in neighboring Herkimer County "in order to animate those to turn out who were favorable" to the Federalist candidate.

He early became enamored of Alexander Hamilton, "a Man of the most accomplished Manners, most agreeable and sociable that I was ever in company with in my Life." Admiration for Hamilton notwithstanding, Moss Kent matured into an Adams Federalist. He campaigned hard for the New Englander in upstate New York in 1796; his appointment followed two years later. By 1798 Kent was a candidate for the state senate, a frequent contributor to various upstate Federalist newspapers, usually writing in support of Adams's foreign policies, and a spokesman at several Adams-oriented county Federalist meetings. He was at the time of his nomination, in the words of Alfred Young, "a force to be reckoned with" in Otsego County Federalist circles.[29]

John Adams's other collectors of the land tax in the virtually limitless wilds of upstate New York were equally
politicized. Former Federalist Congressman James Gordon
of Ballstown near Saratoga was one. He had served in the
House from 1791 to 1795, and at the time of his appointment
was a state senator. Gordon owed his early political prefer-
ment "to the influence of Philip Schuyler and the growing
power of Federalist land proprietors on the frontier," according to Young. Indirectly at least, the powerful Hamilton faction in New York was not entirely ignored. However, Charles
Newkirk of Palatine and Peter Cantine, Jr., of Rhinebeck
both had been Adams electors in 1796, and were important
upstate Adams Federalists at the time of their nominations.
Wealthy young Stephen N. Bayard of Schenectady, scion of
an elite political family with large upstate landholdings,
rounded out the New York State contingent of tax commissioners. Bayard's connections reached into New Jersey inasmuch as his two sisters were married to the Boudinot
brothers, heads of the most important Federalist family in
that state. Bayard was involved in the election of 1800, and
for years thereafter remained unreconciled to the fact of Republican ascendency. "The aura of Federalism," he claimed
vainly, would once again brighten the "political horizon." [30]

Geographically complex Pennsylvania also required a sizable corps of land tax commissioners. The coveted Philadelphia appointment went to Israel Whelen, a Quaker merchant
who had seen better days financially and needed the job, but
whose political influence remained unimpaired in the
Federalist decade. A member of the Philadelphia Federalist
Committee of Correspondence since 1792, a candidate for
state senator in 1798, and an Adams elector in 1800, he had
ranked high in Philadelphia Federalist circles ever since
1789. "From the commencement of the Federal Constitution
to the present moment [1798]," several Federalists
petitioned President Adams, "he has given uniform zealous
and active support to the government of his Country." Robert
Morris endorsed this view, describing Whelen as a "Warm
Friend of the Government" in a letter to Oliver Wolcott, Jr.
His nomination, another party man added, "would give gen-

eral satisfaction to the Federal inhabitants of the State at Large." Whelen's brother Dennis, also a state senator, candidly conceded that one of Adams's attractions for him in 1800 was that, if Adams won, Israel would remain on the federal pad, whereas, if he lost, Jefferson would certainly remove him. Dennis Whelen was correct, of course, in predicting that particular result of Jefferson's success.[31]

Well-placed Federalists were also nominated in the interior of the state. Paul Zantzinger, the Federalist mayor of Lancaster and an important Lutheran layman in that center of German settlement, was one of these. He had started out life as a tailor but had made money selling supplies to the Continental army during the war and in land speculations thereafter. He was able to rise to the first rank among the Pennsylvania Dutch population by these means. Propertied as he was by 1798, with eighteen children he needed any appointment he could get. Seth Chapman, both a lawyer and son of the Federalist congressman for the region centering on Montgomery County, was also named a land commissioner. Perhaps it was a reward for the father's support, perhaps it was simply an effective way of harnessing the congressman's influence to the Adams camp. Collinson Read, Reading's leading attorney and the young head of the most prominent family in town rounded out Adams's known appointments in the Keystone State.[32]

John Adams made his nominations with an eye to political realities in the South and Southwest also. In Maryland the president shored up the wavering loyalties of two of the state's most influential moderate Federalists by naming close relatives to office. Cornelius Howard, father of the incumbent Federalist Governor John Eager Howard, and John Gale, a Somerset County physician and the brother of Federalist Congressman George Gale, were named land commissioners. Other nominations also went to well-placed party men. State legislator Upton Sheredine, a Federalist congressman in the early 1790s, was a large landholder and a major political figure in Frederick County. Jacob Graybell, the recipient of the Baltimore commission, was described as one whose "connections . . . are very respectable and numerous." His Federalist credentials were good. Graybell had "marched against the [Whisky] Insurgents" and "was firmly attached to our Government and Laws," a standard euphemism for federalism.[33]

Adams courted several prominent Federalist factions in conferring his commissions in Republican North Carolina. State Senator James Murphey's appointment not only gave "pleasure to the people of Candour in this District [Burke County]," it provided needed recognition to Archibald Murphey, a party leader who was related to James. United States Senator Benjamin Hawkins prevailed on Adams to appoint Thomas Henderson, a close friend from Rockingham. A third Tarheel nomination went to Joseph Dickson of Lincoln, a major party figure in the state who won a seat in the United States House of Representatives six months after accepting his commission. At the time of his nomination by Adams, Dickson was a state senator and close friend of both John Steele and William R. Davie. Throughout the 1790s, in fact, he had been Davies's manager in the latter's several bids for elective office. It is conspicuously evident that Adams, in North Carolina as in other states, prudently mollified and rewarded both major figures and important factions when he passed out the relatively few jobs he had to offer.[34]

In Republican Kentucky, former Federalist United States Senator John Edwards was designated one of the new land commissioners. He was a mover in the "Country Party," the local version of the Federalist party. A frequent target of the Lexington Democratic Society, Edwards had remained a "staunch Federalist" even after his bid for re-election to the Senate failed in 1794. Another nomination fell to John Caldwell of Christian County, in some respects a strange appointment. Caldwell was the needy brother-in-law of high Federalist Secretary of War James McHenry, and was described as a local Federalist of "character, Talents and influence." Perhaps Adams and his local advisers felt the office would cement Caldwell's loyalty, even if the president could not count on the fidelity of the Secretary of War. Other nominations went to Federalist James French, a surveyor in frontier western Kentucky, and Robert Breckenridge, brother of John Breckenridge, Kentucky's premier Jeffersonian Republican in 1798. An early supporter of the Constitution and a firm Federalist in 1798 in spite of his brother's connections and Jeffersonian commitment, Robert Breckenridge's appointment was a sophisticated and visible local political thrust by the president.[35]

The single Tennessee appointment went to James White, one of the state's best-known Federalists. He was the speaker of the Tennessee Assembly in 1798, and the father-in-law of John Overton, supervisor of the federal revenue in the state. White, after distinguished service in the American Revolution, became one of a minority of champions of the Constitution in Antifederalist western North Carolina (later that area became Tennessee) during the late 1780s. He virtually founded the town of Knoxville in the early 1790s, just a few years prior to Tennessee's admission into the Union. White went on to hold a variety of state positions during the remainder of the decade. Adams's recognition of him helped to solidify what little Adams support there was in this Republican state.[36]

At least some political information was found for fifty-four of Adams's land commissioners, or more than two-thirds of the whole corps of seventy-nine. Although the numbers are necessarily small, the quantitative data are significant for what they tell about both Adams's political leadership as a whole and the direction he was already taking within his own party. At least forty-seven (87 percent) were involved Federalist political figures in their respective states. Only one Republican was named. Of the fifty-four, at least forty-one (76 percent) were placemen, gentry of high status.

Both the quality of the officeholders' political commitment and the level of the Federalist involvement of the commissioners can be discerned from the following: eighteen or one-third of the known party men were either serving in the upper houses of their state legislatures in 1798, or had served within the two-year period prior to their appointments. Another nine (17 percent) were sitting or recently had sat in the lower houses. Five more (9 percent) held an assortment of other high offices (e.g., sheriff, state treasurer, state supreme court justice, etc.) in 1798. Thus more than half (59 percent) of the known appointees held significant statewide elective or appointive offices circa 1798. The distinction is significant, for the figure does not even take into account the plenitude of county or local positions almost all the nominees occupied. These men were, in short, important, influential Federalists in what still must be counted a deferential society. Indeed, eleven (20 percent) of the Adams appointees in 1798 are clearly identifiable as Federalists of the first rank in their states.

The quality of the appointees as well as the evident attention the president paid to the uses of patronage within a divided party are also implicit in the application of other data. Fifteen (28 percent) were related to first-rank Federalists. Six (11 percent) stood as candidates for Adams electors in either 1796 or 1800. Only four (7 percent) were identifiable Hamilton-oriented high Federalists in 1798, and all of these were from centers of Hamilton strength in Massachusetts and New York. The rest were, or quickly became, Adams Federalists. There were few demonstrable flaws or errors in judgment in this significant demonstration of Adams's political awareness and ability. By 1798, if these figures offer any proof, Adams not only was not particularly trying any longer to placate those in his own party who opposed his policies, he was already thinking about his prospects in 1800, with or without high Federalist support.

The preponderantly middle-class character of the lower echelons of the internal revenue service brings to light many local Federalist leaders who do not fit the usual Federalist stereotype. Perhaps too the shrewd, commanding character of the Adams appointments to the land tax commission also defies the existing stereotype of a president who was largely ineffective as a party leader.

CHAPTER EIGHT

Postmasters and Politics:
The More Articulate

The United States post office was particularly vulnerable to the importunities of the Federalist party.[1] Its dynamic growth rate alone, from little more than 100 postmasters in 1789 to well over 800 in 1800, made it a natural shelter for party men. It offered political advantages not even found in the customs service, the only department larger than the post office within the first United States civil service. Every town and village, no matter how small or off the beaten track, soon boasted of local postal service, so it was possible for the Federalist administrations in theory (and, to a remarkable degree, in practice) to find a job for one deserving party man in almost every community in the nation.

Unlike the customs department, multiple local appointments were not possible, but there was an offsetting flexibility in that there was no need for the proximity to the sea that was a requisite of occupancy of customs offices. Moreover, continuing business activities and affiliations were neither an embarrassment nor a liability in holding down a postmastership; rather, it was a virtue, for the more accessible and central to the life of the town the business establishment, the more serviceable the post office. Within the postal service, finally, an occupational connection with politics developed so quickly and pervasively that politicization was virtually inevitable under the Federalists. For reasons that will be

183

made clear, the department often uniquely accommodated itself to certain politically related occupations: Federalist printers in significant numbers maintained post offices throughout the nation; innkeepers whose establishments frequently served as informal party headquarters formed another cadre occupation; aspiring and ambitious young lawyers found a postmastership a useful springboard early in their careers.

Above all other departments, the post office was a haven for middle-class Federalists. The visibility the local post office provided to these middling types diluted and perhaps even countered the sometimes harsh, exclusive and aristocratic Federalist image projected by the party's opponents. This was especially true in the small inland towns and villages where there were no other federal civil servants, and the postmaster represented the most visible presence of both national government and Federalist officialdom. While many of high status were Federalist postmasters, an absolute majority of the party men in the service were middling men who held important positions within the local party interest. Their presence in numbers among Federalist party cadre belied the stereotype almost always applied to that party. While busy merchants, rising lawyers, and a sprinkling of manufacturers, clergymen, and physicians held down postmasterships, there were significantly more men who were small shopkeepers, printers, tavern keepers, surveyors, teachers, or yeomen.*

The post office for a variety of reasons was more directly drawn into politics than any other branch of the early civil service. This is saying a great deal, for the highly political nature of the service in general is a major theme of this study.

* Occupations are not the only criterion used in this study to ascribe middling status to individuals. See chapter 11 for the definitions that apply in this work. The use of occupation as an ascription of status here is illustrative only. In general, I accept the guidelines laid down by Stuart Blumin, as well as the limitations he imposes on occupation as a mark of status. See Blumin, "The Historical Study of Vertical Mobility," *Historical Methods Newsletter*, I (1968), 1–13.

Much of the responsibility for this politicization may be laid at the door of Timothy Pickering, the second postmaster general, who filled that spot in the critical, expansive years from 1791 through 1794. He hedged not at all in establishing political criteria for appointment, and he openly discriminated against Antifederalists and Republicans. A few examples will suffice to make the point.

In a claim accompanied by an impressive petition, William Clarke, the former postmaster at Cannonsburg, Pennsylvania, asserted that he had been removed by Pickering "for no other reason than holding certain political sentiments obnoxious to men in power." Pickering himself, early in his tenure, generally justified this course of action. Writing to an applicant for the postmastership at Marblehead, Massachusetts, the postmaster general wrote early in 1792: "I should not think it expedient for you to receive it [the post office] on account of [your] political sentiments . . . it would subject me to *censure*." He added that "as a *private* man, I should defy reproach for my attachment to an upright fellow citizen, of whatever opinions in politics or religion, [yet] as vested with a *public* trust, I think myself bound" to introduce to public office only "honest men *who have claims on the public* for their services in effecting the establishment of a government."

At the same time, as will become clear, Timothy Pickering, sometimes willingly, other times reluctantly, but always knowingly, kept incompetents in office if they were good party men. In short, Pickering bowed repeatedly to powerful Federalist interests in molding post office practices and interpreting postal laws to the advantage of the party.[2]

Joseph Habersham, the postmaster general from 1795 until his forced resignation shortly after Thomas Jefferson's inauguration, subtly followed the political line drawn by Pickering. In view of the deluge of complaints of party abuse in the post office that Jefferson encountered (indeed he himself had been an early, ardent complainant), the president-elect asked Abraham Baldwin of Georgia, a Republican senator from Habersham's home state, to investigate Habersham's administration of the post office. Baldwin, who was obviously no friend politically to the postmaster general, reported to Jefferson that the department's rapid growth and increasing complexity made it one of the most difficult government establishments to administer. Nevertheless, Baldwin reported, Habersham had presided expertly over a doubling of its size in six years, reduced illegal postal banking, maintained the integrity of the post office against Treasury Department encroachments and, above all, kept the mail moving in better and better fashion by his industrious attention to detail.

However, Baldwin concluded, the many complaints about politics in the post office were accurate enough, and most were in particular "industriously circulated against that officer [Habersham]." The latter permitted the "most partisan discrimination" in post offices in "several of the eastern towns" and generally around the nation. The grievances about Habersham were frequently both specific and personal. For example, when Federalist Banjamin Tallmadge of Litchfield, Connecticut, was elected to Congress in 1800, a leading Connecticut Republican wrote Jefferson that Habersham acted with undue haste in appointing an equally Federalist postmaster as Tallmadge's replacement before Jefferson's inauguration. The Georgian's action was rendered visible in this instance because the new postmaster at Litchfield was Frederick Wolcott, Federalist brother of outgoing Treasury Secretary Oliver Wolcott, Jr. Habersham was kept on by Jefferson for six months, only long enough to find a successor and effect an orderly transfer of the complex office.[3]

The complaints that inundated the Republican administration catalogued most of the abuses of which the post office had been guilty. These jeremiads resurrected earlier fears expressed by Republicans about the potential for mischief in the postal service. One congressman soon after ratification pressed the First Congress for legislative control over the establishment of post roads, arguing that that power in the hands of the president could well become "an engine destructive to the liberties" of the United States. New post roads, after all, meant also new post offices, and social and economic advantages then accrued to one town's inhabitants, perhaps at the expense of neighbors. That power must at least be shared with Congress, the representative argued, so that fair play would be more perfectly guaranteed. Secretary of State Jefferson concurred for different reasons, noting that he viewed the post office "as a source of boundless patronage to the executive."

By 1800, Republicans felt, most of these older fears had metamorphosed into fact. "The Post Offices in this part of the United States have for years past been almost universally in the hands of violent political partisans," Connecticut Republican Ephraim Kirby informed Jefferson. "This engine [a wonderfully descriptive and ubiquitous political term of the 1790s] of private abuse and public deception" was responsible for many of the disadvantages under which the Republican party had long labored.

The most common complaint was that "Republican Newspapers [and literature] conveyed by mail have either been suppressed or redirected at the office of delivery." Kirby claimed more or less accurately that this was done "in such a manner as to deter many from receiving them." Federalist newspapers, on the other hand, "calculated to poison the public mind, such as the New England Paladium &c have been circulated free of postage . . . in every corner." Another Republican waxed wry on the subject after the fact, recounting the miscarriage of an important political pamphlet. "This has been my loss," John Armstrong wrote in 1801, "and I owe it, I suppose, to that laudable curiosity which was made to pervade the whole post office Department during the old order of things."

That Republicans experienced a "failure of regular communications" at the hands of Federalist postmasters was a widely held belief. "The loss of letters and papers &c," new Postmaster General Gideon Granger disclosed in 1801, "has extended itself so far that confidence is at an end." The Republicans, he concluded, have "suffered many embarrassments." The "abuses in that department have been general and scandalous," Republican Congressman William Findley agreed. "All the changes since [Adams's election] within my knowledge have been for the worse," he declared, and

Findley concurred in Granger's assessment "of the necessity of a thorough change in the post office department." The powerful voice of Senator John Langdon, a former Federalist himself, was added to the rising symphony of complaints. Regular communication "is impossible to effect without Republican postmasters," he wrote Granger, neatly summarizing both the complaint and the remedy for the new administration.[4]

Although only a minority of the nation's Federalist postmasters were drawn from the gentry, the well-connected ones filled the most visible positions in the larger cities. These powerful urban partisans were in excellent positions to put their offices to work for both the party and themselves. The responsibilities and incomes they enjoyed were great, so that, contrary to the practice of postmasters in less urban areas, these big city officeholders did not engage directly either in a business or a profession but instead devoted most of their attention to the office. The pay was high, even taking into account unreimbursed expenses, and the informal fringe benefits could be enormous. The postmasters in the four largest cities of the nation were all Federalists who earned well over $2,000; that figure could reach as high as $4,500 in some years. They well understood the political obligations the office imposed.

Sebastian Bauman was nominated postmaster of New York City in 1789, at a low point financially for him. An immigrant from Germany who came to America before the Revolution, he served as a field officer of artillery in the Continental army for the duration of the war. After the Revolution, he set up as a merchant. Suffering serious financial reverses, he went out of business and, virtually broke, turned for relief to prominent former comrades. As he was "A friend of Washington, as well as an intimate friend of Hamilton," they responded handsomely, and he was given the most lucrative post office in the nation. On more than one occasion he was reprimanded both for laxity in office and taking undue pecuniary advantage of his position. Even Timothy Pickering, who also counted Bauman a friend and whom Bauman revered, was forced to bring the former artillery officer to account for repeated instances of slackness in office. Warnings and evidence of continuing derelictions notwithstanding, Bauman was never removed by the Federalists.

The New York postmaster had actively supported ratification and continued a devoted Federalist thereafter. He was not above combining business and politics, even to the point of compromising his office. From 1791 onward, he actively sought subscriptions to British and Federalist publications, receiving commissions on every sale. He advertised that the advantage of dealing with him was that there would be none of the usual postal delays in delivery and, better yet, the periodicals would be sent through the mails free to his subscribers. Even though he did not publish a newspaper himself, Bauman claimed the same right to free postage for his "subscribers" that printer-postmasters did for theirs. Three successive Federalist postmasters-general looked the other way when Bauman's side line was called to their attention. But when the Republicans won in 1800, Bauman, justifiably fearful of being removed, asked outgoing Postmaster General Habersham to put in a good word to Gideon Granger about his efficiency. Even Habersham couldn't really do that.[5]

The weighing of official incompetence against political utility was even more cogently at issue in the case of Jonathan Hastings, the postmaster at Boston. The Boston appointee, like Bauman a former Continental army officer and an early adherent of ratification, was a well-connected and influential Federalist. Nevertheless, "continued blunders in his accounts" as well as other deficiencies caused Pickering to decide to remove him in 1791. The postmaster general expressed the hope to a friend of Hastings "that your particular influential friends will offer the requisite vindication to any who may not know the reasons" for the removal. Pickering had concluded, on the basis of many complaints and a personal investigation, "that the business of the office have not been duly attended to by Mr. Hastings as must be apparent from the circumstance of his living four miles from it." His returns, moreover, "also have been inaccurate as to manifest either carelessness or incapacity."

But important Massachusetts party men chose not to understand Pickering's concern for the service. He was immediately subjected to tremendous pressure to retain Hastings from first-rank Federalists like Nathaniel Appleton, Stephen Higginson, and Fisher Ames, among others. Forceful and strong-willed though he was, Pickering was compelled to back off: "I am now embarrassed with some contrarity of opinions," the postmaster general lamely concluded. "For the present therefore I shall suspend my determination." The politically astute but officially incompetent Hastings continued in office until Jefferson finally removed him for all the wrong reasons.[6]

Robert Patton and Thomas Bacot, postmasters at Philadelphia and Charleston respectively, were much more able, competent types than their New York City and Boston counterparts. They were no less Federalist in their politics, however. Patton, also a former Continental army officer, was flagrantly discriminatory in administering the particularly sensitive office located in the nation's capital. "The situation of our post office is a great evil," Philadelphian Tench Coxe wrote Jefferson. Letters from Republicans were delayed and passed on to political enemies, or were opened, read, and then sent on. Senator Baldwin reported in 1801 that while Habersham had long known about these abuses and admitted that Republicans had repeatedly asked him to remove Patton, the postmaster general could do nothing. Patton, Habersham claimed, was technically good at his job, and was among the few postmasters who "were so necessary to his department that he could not dispense with their services or supply their places," whatever their political activities and however flagrantly they favored the Federalist interest. It was not the kind of defense that endeared the outgoing postmaster general to the new administration, whatever the latter's qualities as an administrator.[7]

Thomas Bacot, postmaster at Charleston, was a moderate Federalist who ranked high in the local party faction headed by William Loughton Smith. Bacot, of an influential Huguenot family, was of the "first eminence" among the

Charleston gentry. All political elements agreed that he was an attentive and efficient officer, but whether or not he was partisan in official matters as well was disputed. Republican Senator James Jackson reported to Jefferson in 1801 that Bacot "is a good officer," and, unlike many postmasters elsewhere in the South, he did not interfere with or delay Republican correspondence and newspapers. Another Republican at about the same time, however, sent Jefferson a letter by private conveyance, noting that "there are strong reasons for believing that a letter addressed to yourself would be opened at the Charleston post office by Mr. Bacoat." [8]

The postmasters in the smaller cities were stamped more or less out of the same mold. They earned fees averaging a thousand dollars a year and devoted most of their attention to their offices in return. Jacob Richardson at Newport, Rhode Island, Elias Beers at New Haven, Connecticut, George Mancius at Albany, New York, and George Craik at Alexandria, Virginia, were examples of postmasters functioning in relatively small urban settings. Collectively they were accused by Republicans either of abusing their official trust by tampering with Republican mail or holding their offices only by virtue of close ties to important Federalists.

Richardson, Mancius, and Beers were all charged with the former political crime. Beers in particular, from Granger's home state of Connecticut, was singled out personally and with feeling by the new postmaster general for his partisan handling of the mail. Postmaster Mancius of Albany, by all accounts an able official, nevertheless had to go on the dual grounds that he tampered with Republican mail and held his office as a result of his kinship to New York City Federalist bigwig Abraham Bancker. George Craik, a moderate Federalist, was nevertheless flawed politically in the eyes of local Republicans by his kinship to Charles Simms, the high Federalist customs collector at Alexandria. Craik, moreover, had gained his office through President Washington's personal intercession; he had done the favor for young George's father James Craik, Washington's physician and long-time friend.[9]

It was in the small towns and villages of America that the post office really came into its own as a highly personalized, highly visible adjunct to the Federalist party organization. It was in these small communities that a kind of occupational propinquity prevailed in making appointments, an eligibility that went hand in hand with the more familiar political test often applied to other branches of the civil service. That occupational preference sometimes directed itself toward livelihoods that naturally lent themselves to politics, a phenomenon found mainly but not exclusively among middle-class Federalists discussed in the next chapter. Among the more prestigious careers, politically ambitious lawyers, just starting their practices, formed the major exception to this otherwise middle-class Federalist domination of the postal service. Also merchants, if the town was large enough to support one of their number, and physicians and clergymen to a lesser extent, were readily eligible for postmasterships in smaller towns on the basis of their availability to local residents and their eminence in the community.

Merchants were the most ubiquitous among the minority of elite postmasters. Probably this reflected both the importance the Federalist administration in Philadelphia attached to the political support derived from merchants, and a recognition that the postal service was vital to the economic viability of the commercial arm of the economy. Ranking administration Federalists clearly felt that, in matters touching on the delivery of the mail, merchant needs must be honored above all others. One way of assuring the confidence of the mercantile community was to appoint some of their number; another was to honor their choices for office.

Timothy Pickering summed up the reigning administration attitude. In passing on the bad news of his removal to a Salem, Massachusetts, postmaster, the postmaster general reminded that "you cannot be uninformed of the prevailing wishes of the merchants in Salem to have a person appointed to succeed you in the P Office. The *merchants* support the Department," he emphasized, "because all correspondence yielding postage is chiefly amongst them. The merchants therefore must be accommodated." Nor was this uniquely a

Pickering attitude. His predecessor Samuel Osgood, responding to a Newport, Rhode Island, petition in 1790, acknowledged that "the Letter and representation of the Merchants of Newport is before me—It will always give me pleasure to afford them all the Assistance in my Power."

But when Pickering took over the office, he brought that principle of "merchants first" to a new eminence. "The general accommodation of the public, especially of the mercantile interest," he acknowledged, "is my sole object." And to a postmaster about to change locations: "In choosing a place for your office, you will be governed by the convenience of the mercantile interest, by which chiefly the office is supported." In acknowledging receipt of a petition from Charleston merchants recommending Thomas Bacot for the postmastership, Pickering responded that he needed "no further proof of his merits." In the larger towns where there were available merchants centrally located in business, the postmaster general preferred them for the post office.[10] That these expressions and views buttressed a distinctly Hamiltonian conception of American economic priorities should be so apparent as to need no further comment.

John Gray Blount of Washington, North Carolina, was perhaps the most enterprising politician among all the merchant-postmasters. His avoidance of high office for himself notwithstanding, John Gray was clearly the leader of a clan that included his two more highly placed brothers: William Blount was at different times in the 1790s governor of the Tennessee Territory and United States senator from that state; Thomas was a congressman from North Carolina through most of the decade. Several North Carolina postmasters believed correctly that they owed their federal jobs to John Gray Blount, and were connected to him either commercially or through kinship. Besides his extensive West Indian mercantile trade, he was thought to be the "largest landholder in the state" as of 1789, with acreage both in eastern North Carolina and the transmontane area that became Tennessee. The Blount clan collectively was one of those ubiquitous families with feet planted in the course of time in both political camps. Both John Gray Blount and the local postmasters in his train were devoted Federalists until the Jay Treaty in 1795 made it too uncomfortable for them to remain in that party in North Carolina.[11]

Thereafter JG adopted an increasingly independent stance, eventually allying himself with Republican elements in North Carolina sometime before 1800. His satellites did the same. JG, at least, nevertheless remained on good terms with North Carolina Federalist leaders Hugh Williamson, John Steele, and William Polk. Even before 1795, John Gray Blount had played the same game only vice versa. Thomas Blount was a Republican congressman when John Gray was a Federalist, but this did not prevent the latter from supporting his brother's successful elections to the House. The eldest brother was content to sit in the North Carolina legislature, where he clearly carried great weight as a Federalist leader. William Blount was also a Federalist early in the 1790s, moving over to the Republicans only after the ratification of Jay's Treaty. He looked after the clan's interests in the western country, and family interests formed the major motivating force among the Blounts generally throughout the decade.

The Blounts' independent political power, moreover, in a state where party lines only partly explained political differences even in the late 1790s, permitted them to abuse mercilessly the integrity of the developing two-party system. Even in his best days as a Federalist, JG picked and chose those Federalist policies and candidates he would support. Even more so than in most states, local issues, affiliations, and considerations counted for more than national factors and alliances.

The firm of "John Gray and Thomas Blount, Merchants" was founded in 1783 and prospered from its inception. Specializing in the West Indian trade, the firm also trafficked extensively with European and the large northeastern American ports. Thomas oversaw this latter commerce from his vantage point in Congress at Philadelphia, just as William paid attention to the firm's significant southwestern interior trade. John Gray looked after the West Indies exchange and supervised the landed interests of the family from his seat at

Washington, North Carolina. There he also operated under one roof both a large general store and the area's post office.

The Blounts first appeared prominently in national politics as proponents of the Constitution in 1789, in an Antifederalist state. Lisle Rose explained that position as deriving from the fact that the family "represented the dominant native merchant and speculative interests in the state. As merchants, these men wanted all restrictions with the British West Indies lifted," Rose concluded, "a goal beyond the power of the individual states or the Continental Congress." Western land holdings also played its part in determining the Blounts' political position, for the inability of the state of North Carolina alone to meet the Indian menace jeopardized the value of that wilderness west of the mountains of which the Blounts owned a part and which would become the state of Tennessee. The family, with JG calling the signals, continued to endorse most Federalist measures after 1789, although its unanimous opposition to the assumption of state debts (again for personal financial reasons) formed a single early exception that betokened, in retrospect, more to come.[12]

Until Jay's Treaty finally tore the fabric of his allegiance, however, by and large John Gray Blount remained a good Federalist. In 1792, for example, he led the effort to forge a "coalition of Eastern and Western" North Carolina interests behind Federalist leader John Steele. His unique virtual domination of the North Carolina postal system (discussed in the next chapter) made John Gray indispensable in the early 1790s in effecting and facilitating political communication in a state where communication was not easy. With his connections, he could guarantee the delivery and distribution of Federalist newspapers and pamphlets, perhaps even free of charge, and delay the missives of his opponents. Such political ill-usage was common in the 1790s. At the same time, at the behest of Congressman Hugh Williamson, Blount helped to maintain unity in the Federalist legislative contingent to prevent disunion among "some disappointed factional incindiar[ies] . . . among the new Members who are incautious . . . ." JG electioneered openly for himself and most other Federalist candidates in the early 1790s, as well as for his Republican brother.

Blount's ties to federalism were based wholly on self-interest and not ideology. Lisle Rose's explanation of Blount's opposition to Jay's Treaty is anchored to the Blounts' mercantile interests, and is good as far as it goes, but it does not go far enough. "An increase in British seizures and impressments" did produce some anglophobia among the Blounts, whose own goods were occasionally victimized. However, this did not abruptly precipitate a clan departure from the Federalist party; Thomas had always been a Republican, but William remained a Federalist until 1797. For his part, JG assumed that the Federalist interest in North Carolina, never particularly strong to begin with, had a bleak future. Nevertheless, important North Carolinians remained committed ideologically to that interest, so Blount planted himself and his family firmly in the middle with ties, not only to each camp, but to the several factions in each party as well. He remained on good terms politically, personally, and commercially with virtually every important North Carolina Federalist right down to 1800, even though he was a Republican by that time. His business tentacles, wide family interests, and the press of local issues that really determined political alignments in the Tarheel State all made this possible.[13]

James Winchester, the postmaster at Craig Font, Tennessee, was as important a figure in the area west of the mountains as John Gray Blount was east of them. A Continental army officer in the Revolution and virtually an adventurer thereafter, he acquired a great deal of wilderness land in the Mero district and moved into the forefront of developing Tennessee politics. When the territory became a state in 1796, Winchester, already a militia general, was elected speaker of the state senate. By that date, he had developed a thriving counting house that specialized in trade through the Spanish port at New Orleans, newly opened to Americans. This merchant had surfaced as one of the few important Federalists in transmontane North Carolina in 1789, and he continued a Federalist thereafter, allying himself with William Blount. Winchester remained a Federalist after Blount broke with that party.[14]

Other high-status merchants elsewhere also found small post offices useful adjuncts to their extensive trade (most notably the use of the postal frank for commercial correspondence, a practice that may have been widespread). Perhaps Federalist merchants also found the post office a fitting and visible reward for their political involvement. Nathaniel Rochester and Lord Butler both exemplify this last generalization. Rochester, the postmaster at Elizabethtown in rural Washington County, Maryland, earned a reputation early in the 1790s as a moderate Federalist who "stood high in the judgment . . . of all parties." He was one of the "most respectable inhabitants" in the area, having founded a merchant house in 1783 that, bucking the economic tide of the Confederation years, prospered and expanded. In addition to his extensive trade in the American Southwest and the West Indies, he invested in land. By the 1790s, moreover, he operated a nail manufactory, rope walk, and gristmill as well.

Foreign policy developments, beginning with the Jay Treaty, had a much different effect on Rochester than it apparently had on John Gray Blount. The treaty appears to have erased the former's aloofness and propelled him actively into Federalist electioneering politics and, eventually, the Adams camp. An antitreaty "mob" gathered in Washington County, as Republicans were beginning to do everywhere in the United States, to denounce the negotiation. Typically, it erected a liberty pole. This apparently infuriated Rochester, who came out to counterdemonstrate in support of the pact. He was drawn into the ensuing altercation between Republicans and Federalists.

The experience must have touched a nerve. He had already shown signs of deepening commitment, and after the liberty pole incident his involvement increased significantly. His name appeared as one of the electioneering committee organizing Federalist Thomas Spriggs's campaign for Congress at the end of 1794. In 1798 he was one of the instigators and public spokesmen for a Federalist meeting that vowed its support for the president and denounced the avarice and hostility of France. Later that year Rochester led a second meeting designed to affirm publicly presidential leadership and to rally local Federalists to Adams's cause. This gathering not only applauded the creation of the new federal army, it asked by resolution that Rochester run for Congress as an Adams Federalist. While he declined, he "applaud[ed] the course of the President and pledg[ed] support" for his policies.[15]

Lord Butler, the postmaster at Wilkes-Barre, Pennsylvania, was another small-town Federalist merchant cut from the same mold. "One of the early and most prominent men in the Wyoming Valley," he got in on the ground floor of emerging central and western Pennsylvania commerce in the 1780s, acquiring goods imported into Philadelphia and selling them throughout the interior of the commonwealth. By the 1790s he was comfortable financially and deeply engaged in Federalist politics. Butler sat in the assembly and later the executive council of the commonwealth, and served as sheriff of Luzerne County as well. His counting house became the seat of both the Wilkes-Barre post office and the sheriff's office. Butler proved to be a zealous, almost fierce party man, "decided in his political opinions and free in expressing them." His offices did not deter him from electioneering extensively for Federalist candidates.

The Wilkes-Barre postmaster's activities and outspokenness made him one of Gideon Granger's earliest targets for removal. The measure of Butler's political emotions is perhaps best revealed by his response to his ouster from an office he really no longer needed. Butler informed the Republican postmaster general that he would relinquish neither his commission nor the office property in his possession, asserting that his removal was illegal. He also had some fun at Granger's expense, writing him that, though admittedly his position was unusual, the real reason he was keeping his post office was that it "encouraged my happiness whilst in no way affected the happiness of any other being," and that this was reason "sufficient enough" for his rejection of Granger's orders. As it was meant to, this Aristotelian response infuriated the postmaster general, who responded by "commanding you to deliver over . . . all the post office property in your possession." Only a final threat of federal prosecution brought the charade to an end, and ended as well Butler's stormy tenure in federal office.[16]

Two other Federalist postmaster-merchants demonstrate anew another dimension of the first civil service. The appointments of John W. Gilman and Thomas Peter point up the casual acceptance of nepotism as a fact of life in the postal service. Gilman was named postmaster at the newly expanded post office at Exeter, New Hampshire, in 1792, following a bitter struggle in the House of Representatives over the location of a local post road. The victory went to Exeter as a result of the strenuous efforts in Congress of Representative Nicholas Gilman, whose brother thus gained a post office the emoluments of which were significantly enhanced by the congressman's political labors. Thomas Peter, a merchant and a nephew of Martha Washington, was named postmaster of Cabin Point, Virginia, during her husband's administration. He was one of five relations of Martha's to pick up a civil service appointment, a number that precludes any possible explanation for the nominations other than the passive or active influence of the president, his repeated railings against "nepotism" and "connections of blood and friendship" notwithstanding.

Other examples of post office nepotism abound. Among the more gross examples were Timothy Pickering's nomination of two relatives to office during his tenure as postmaster general; the appointment of the brother of Treasury Secretary Oliver Wolcott, Jr., to the Litchfield, Connecticut, post office; the nominations of relatives of Senator William Richardson Davie and Congressman Joseph McDowell to North Carolina post offices after the legislators' intercession in Congress in the matter of establishing the local offices.[17]

A significant collection of neophyte Federalist lawyers in small towns found the post office an attractive vehicle that enabled them both to establish local contacts and gain visibility at the beginning of their careers. These attorneys found the professional perquisites of office far more attractive than the money the government paid in fees, for that often was little enough in a small community. But the Federalist cadre generally gained enormously from the attorneys' presence in party ranks. They were as a group enthusiastic and articulate local political leaders, young men who gained some status in their towns through a combination of profession and office. There were enough men found who possessed this particular combination of age and profession to conclude that the Federalist administration in Philadelphia used the local post office wherever possible to aid and encourage politically sympathetic young lawyers almost as a matter of standing policy. Some of them in time matured into relatively important public figures. Uniquely for the first civil service, a small but surprising contingent of Republican lawyers, at the same point in their careers as their Federalist counterparts, also found their way to post office appointments.

Many of those Federalist attorneys born after 1760 who became postmasters in the 1790s derived from New England. Ezekiel Williams, Jr., was a very well connected postmaster at Hartford, Connecticut. His father was the sheriff of Hartford County, and his father-in-law was United States Supreme Court Justice Oliver Elsworth. Under thirty years of age at the time of his appointment and a relatively recent graduate of Yale, he could only have owed his appointment to these connections.[18]

Two Massachusetts postmasters also fitted this model. Solomon Vose of Northfield, a graduate of Harvard, settled in the town in 1796, but quickly moved into its mainstream. He ran the post office from his law offices and was soon elected to the Massachusetts legislature. Josiah Stebbins settled in New Milford, a rough frontier town in the Maine district in 1797, the only attorney in that town then and for nearly two decades thereafter. An unregenerate Federalist till the 1820s, he was a Yale graduate who had read law with highly placed Federalist Elizur Goodrich of New Haven until 1796. It was probably Goodrich's recommendation that gained Stebbins his appointment. The latter rose to some prominence in Maine after the turn of the century, becoming a ranking local Federalist in a Republican area.[19]

Thomas W. Thompson, the postmaster at tiny Salisbury,

New Hampshire, was also an aspiring young attorney. By the time Jefferson was inaugurated for the first time, Thompson was, according to William Plumer, "the leader of Federalism in the Merrimack Valley." After the turn of the century, he went on to the House of Representatives and eventually the United States Senate. Prior to that, however, in 1798 when he was given the post office, Thompson was a young lawyer who had only recently settled in New Hampshire. Born to Massachusetts gentry, he had graduated from Harvard in 1786 and, after a hiatus, had read law with Theophilus Parsons at Newburyport. He used that break after graduation to serve as an aide to Benjamin Lincoln when the latter was commissioned to head the troops raised to suppress Shays's Rebellion. As he was a "party wheelhorse" and well connected to important Federalists as well, the post office was, along with successive town offices in the 1790s, a source of both professional and political advancement for Thompson early in his career.[20]

In the middle states, James W. Wilken's early career followed the same pattern. The postmaster of Goshen, New York, where his law office also served as the post office, he was described as an "influential" Federalist party captain in Orange County. Like Thompson of New Hampshire, he was born to an elite family and established his political credentials as a Federalist while still in his twenties. Wilken graduated from the College of New Jersey (Princeton) in 1788, passed the bar, and opened offices in Goshen in the early 1790s. He was quickly elected to the New York lower house, where he emerged as an able defender of the Jay Treaty in particular and Washington's administration in general.

Two Pennsylvania postmasters were also young Federalist lawyers. Thomas B. Dick of Easton was named to the post office in 1798 but lasted only until Gideon Granger removed him in 1801, in order, as the new postmaster general said, "to promote the public interest." David McKeehan of Greensburg, the other known Federalist attorney in the Keystone State, was also quickly dispatched by Granger. According to a Republican congressman, McKeehan "had nothing to recommend him but a talent for low invective," a talent "which he unceasingly exercised against the Republicans." William Findley, the congressman in question, went on to document the allegation that his letters from Philadelphia were "burned in the [post] office during one session of Congress. Every letter of mine sent by that McKeehan's office was lost except those to my wife and to a Federalist friend." Findley complained at the time to Postmaster General Habersham, who acknowledged that there had been similar complaints from others about the Greensburg postmaster. Instead of removing McKeehan, however, the congressman added, the former postmaster general encouraged him to submit a list of the letters allegedly sent and lost. These, Habersham ascertained, were sent illegally under a congressional frank, and the old postmaster general promptly billed the Republican member for the postage due, while ignoring the congressman's charges leveled at McKeehan.[21]

There were some young Federalist postmasters in the South and Southwest who were also rising young attorneys. Samuel Wilds of South Carolina, born in 1775, was a struggling neophyte lawyer of poor origins when he was given the post office at Cheraw Court House in the late 1790s. Benjamin Shackleford, the postmaster at Culpeper, Virginia, was well born, but also new to the bar at the time of his appointment. Haden Edwards, who kept the post office at his Middlebury, Kentucky, law office, was the son of former Federalist United States Senator John Edwards. The postmaster at Greensville, Tennessee, was William Dickson, a relatively young attorney allied with Federalist manager John Overton. Dickson started out politically as an opponent of the Constitution in Antifederalist North Carolina. By 1790, however, having moved farther west, he concluded that "a better plan of federal government could not be formed in the United States. . . . It laid the foundations," he asserted, "of one of the great empires in the world." Shortly thereafter Dickson was both elected to the Tennessee legislature as a Federalist and named postmaster at Greensville.[22]

Several Jeffersonian attorneys, the only identifiable and significant bloc of Republican civil servants in the United

States in the 1790s, were found in the postal department. They were mainly from New England, particularly Massachusetts and Vermont, and were nominated to local post offices even though their politics were known to local Federalists.

Inasmuch as this was an exceptional situation with the post office, and certainly in the first civil service in general, it is possible to conclude that these men gained and, more significantly, kept their jobs because they were in the best positions in their respective towns to handle the official duties. None were removed nor were their political activities masked in any way, so no other explanation for this unusual Federalist political toleration is likely. It was simply easier administratively for Habersham to keep them than to dismiss and replace them; he was no Federalist zealot and, as we have seen, tended politically to follow the line of least resistance. It was not a practice that either Alexander Hamilton or Oliver Wolcott, Jr., followed, for there is no sign of such political leniency in any branch of the much larger Treasury Department. Moreover, none of these Republican lawyers, it appears, gained office until after Timothy Pickering departed the postmaster general's position.

There were four Republican attorneys among the postmasters in Massachusetts. The best-known of these was Jonathan Grout of Belcherton, a supporter of Shays's Rebellion, staunch Antifederalist and one-term antiadministration representative in the First Congress. Defeated for re-election, he practiced law in Belcherton and sometime after mid-decade was made postmaster by Habersham. Samuel Dana, the postmaster at Groton, Massachusetts, was almost as well known as Grout. Although Dana was deeply and steadily involved in Republican politics, he kept his post office, pursuing his law practice from the same establishment.

Two much younger Republican members of the bar held post offices under the Federalist regime while actively engaging in opposition politics. Both were named by Postmaster General Habersham during the Adams administration. Eliab Brewer of Lenox was a brother-in-law of western Massachusetts Republican manager Barnabas Bidwell, with whom he had read law after graduating from Yale in 1793. Benjamin Whitman, postmaster at Hanover, graduated from Brown College in 1788 and was admitted to the bar in 1791. He thereafter authored "various orations and addresses" that espoused the Republican cause. After Habersham named him to the post office, he became even more prominent as the able defender of Abijah Adams and the Republican Boston *Independent Chonicle* against Federalist prosecution for sedition in 1799.

Habersham's strange combination of administrative intolerance tempered with occasional lapses into tolerance toward Republicans can be explained logically only in the most human of perspectives. He cheerfully tolerated Federalist partisan abuses of post offices all over the nation because to do anything about them would have jeopardized both his position and the efficiency of the department. The vast majority of his postal appointments, moreover, went to Federalists. Yet, if few or none complained about an occasional postmaster who engaged in Republican political activities, Habersham equally cheerfully let him be.[23]

Two more youthful attorneys, both of notable families and graduates of Yale, found their way into the postal service in Vermont. Horatio Seymour, who went on to a long political career, graduated from Yale in 1797, settled in Middlebury two years later to establish his practice, and was named to the post office at the end of 1800. He clearly started out as a trimmer, "always more swayed by principles than by party ties" in the politest of phrases, and his eventually evident Jeffersonianism may not have been so obvious to a harried outgoing Federalist administration anxious to fill any open civil service slot before the Republicans should inherit it.

The other appointee's politics could not have been unknown. John Fay, the postmaster at Burlington, graduated from Yale in 1790. He was related to Republican Governor Moses Robinson, who had enjoyed another political favor from the Adams administration (Robinson's son had been named land tax commissioner by Adams in 1798). Fay's politics were well known locally, but apparently there was some rapport between the Republican governor and the Federalist administration. Fay, moreover, was a notable in his own right, not only respected at the bar but a "large holder of and dealer in lands" as well.[24]

Other elite occupations were also represented significantly in the serried ranks of the Federalist postmasters. There were some important local manufacturers and physicians who kept their post offices at their establishments, and a few clergymen who maintained post offices in their rectories. Among these gentry, there were no deviations from political orthodoxy; all were Federalists.

Samuel Smith, the postmaster at Peterborough, New Hampshire, was the younger brother of Jeremiah Smith, a member of Congress and, by the time Adams became president, probably the undisputed leader of New Hampshire Federalists. In 1793, the younger Smith built a paper factory, sawmill, and textile factory (he called it a "clothing shop") under one roof at Peterborough. The post office was located there too, and from it flowed Federalist propaganda to every corner of the state.

The Peterborough post office became the vehicle by which Jeremiah Smith distributed THE WORD in his rural state. Copies of Washington's denunciation of democratic societies in 1794, for example, were passed on from Jeremiah to Samuel for distribution. Dozens of speeches and pamphlets defending Jay's Treaty also were routed through the postmaster's hands in 1795. Many copies of a speech by Fisher Ames were circulated by Smith a year later, prior to the presidential canvass. There are indications, but no proof, that much or all of this material, and more like it, was sent under frank from Philadelphia by the congressman. His brother's post office became a useful adjunct to the state's Federalist party organization.[25]

Among the Federalist postmaster-physicians were John Rogers and Ezra Green, both also from New Hampshire. Rogers was a notable in Plymouth, holding down many local offices as well as serving as the local postmaster. He was "continually rebuked for his zeal," even by Federalist moderates apparently, but, we are assured by the local antiquarian, his enemies were "all political ones." Green was the postmaster at Dover, where he not only conducted a medical practice but kept a general store under the same roof. He moved from staunch support of the Constitution in the New Hampshire Ratifying Convention to active federalism in the 1790s, like Rogers occupying several town offices in the course of the decade.[26]

A small but significant group of clergymen, mainly New England Congregational ministers, held down post offices under the Federalists. Charles Turner, Jr., of Scituate, Massachusetts, was clearly the most open about his politics. This Congregationalist cleric had become deeply involved in the debate over the Constitution in the 1780s. He emerged as a leader of the Antifederalist bloc at the Massachusetts Ratifying Convention, "unquestionably the ablest and most dignified, as well as the most sincere, opponent of the new government." He shifted suddenly to become a champion of ratification at the very end of the convention, however, finally voting with the Federalists. In a divided state, his change of heart was crucial, and he claimed it hinged on the promise to amend the Constitution to protect civil liberties after ratification.

Turner, a graduate of Harvard and born to a prominent Scituate family, was no stranger to politics. He was a liberal Congregationalist who had strongly endorsed the Revolution; he served in both houses of the Massachusetts legislature as well in the succeeding two decades. In the 1790s Turner openly sided with the Federalists, even from the pulpit. "At the time of the Jay Treaty he was an outspoken Federalist" and was rewarded as such with the post office during Adams's presidency.[27]

Turner was not a singular example. Paul Coffin, the Congregational minister and postmaster at Buxton, Maine, had also graduated from Harvard and derived from an elite Essex County family. Unlike Turner, however, he was a declared neutral during the Revolution. He continued to avoid politics in the ensuing years, ducking both the turbulence of Shays's Rebellion and the struggle over the Constitution in the Bay State. The French Revolution, and particularly the activities and writings of the "godless" Thomas Paine got to him, however, and did what none of the events of more immediate moment in Massachusetts over the previous quarter century could do: aroused his indignation enough to propel him into politics. He openly sided with the Federalists in the late 1790s, in particular preaching a ringing denunciation of Paine to the Massachusetts General Court. It was at about this time that the Adams administration rewarded Coffin, as it did Turner, with a post office. Nathan Stone of Dennis on Cape Cod, and Ebenezer R. White of Danbury, Connecticut, were two more Congregationalist clergymen who were also Federalist postmasters.

John Croes of New Jersey, the Federalist postmaster at Swedesboro, was the young Episcopal minister in that town from 1790. He would much later become a bishop of the church. Gottlieb Shober of North Carolina was a Lutheran minister and postmaster at Salem. Also a Federalist, among his other connections he engaged heavily in Tennessee land speculations with Postmaster General Timothy Pickering, to whom he owed his 1792 appointment.[28]

Federalist politics very deeply involved the gentry, as one might suspect. More surprising, however, was the degree to which the "party of the aristocracy" reached down to the middle class for its leadership. The post office, more so than the customs and internal revenue services, provides the clearest insight into the sources of Federalist followings and leadership within the middling elements of small town and rural America.

CHAPTER NINE

Postmasters and Politics:
The Less Articulate

In the small towns and villages of America the local post office matured into a vital center for Federalist party cadre. This was a significant product of the postconstitutional expansion of the federal government, for it permitted it to exert a growing influence over the history-shadowed world of small-town politics at the end of the eighteenth century. As a result of expanding post office involvement, new sources of political authority were encouraged, thus transforming the local political landscape.

While notables were present in significant numbers in the postal service, they were outnumbered by those whose backgrounds were clearly middle class. Among the most prominent of the middling postmasters were some whose occupations naturally led them into politics. In particular, these included printers (less articulate in the sense of property, place, and overall status within the community) and innkeepers. There were also many other small-town Federalist postmasters who were shopkeepers, farmers, and artisans. Collectively they add a new perspective to the real sources of Federalist management, popular strength and local party structure in a changing political environment.

Printers formed the most significant political bloc among America's postmasters: twenty of the twenty-one printer-postmasters from eleven states edited Federalist newspapers.[1] South Carolina Senator Aedanus Burke's 1790 allegation that the Federalists were in the process of establishing a "Court Press" turns out to be very close to the truth. By means of office and other perquisites, the Federalist party directly supported a score or more of party newspapers in every section of the nation, sheets that the administration in Philadelphia clearly recognized as indispensable adjuncts of Federalist—if not federal—authority. The degree of official support these printers received was totally inconsistent with hostile administration attitudes toward "party," attitudes bitterly expressed by a whole range of Federalist leaders. These newspapers, underwritten extensively with federal money and services, were uniformly the vehicles for local party organization and propaganda.

In general, postal salaries and fees were not the major consideration for a printer, although Augustine Davis of Richmond, Virginia, clearly would not have dismissed lightly the nearly $2,000 per year he earned in post office fees; nor would Timothy Green of Fredricksburg in the same state, William Hobbey of Augusta, Georgia, or William Wilkinson of Providence, Rhode Island, have sniffed at the $800 in fees they averaged each year. But these were exceptional sums, restricted to postmasters in larger towns and small cities. Most of the newspaper-publishing postmasters were "country printers" rarely earning more than $250 a year in fees, and often much less than that.

The most significant advantage for the printer-postmaster was the free and certain delivery of his papers to subscribers, even those difficult to reach or far removed from the printing office. Other vital perquisites included: the certainty of receiving the first communications of news via the mails, on which intelligence early American printers depended so heavily; the economic centricity the post office accorded the printing establishment (which invariably housed a book and stationer's shop as well); the unsubtly exercised authority the sheet exerted locally as a result of the identification of its editor as a federal officer, a representative of the national government. Moreover, not only every printer-postmaster

Figure 12. Reconstruction of an eighteenth-century print shop and post office.

discussed here, but most other Federalist editors as well, were recipients of administration largess in the form of sizable sums (usually several hundred dollars a year) to print the session laws of Congress as required by federal statute.[2] Republican Postmaster General Granger retrospectively noted a final fringe benefit Federalist postmaster-printers derived from their office: "Printers of newspapers ought not to be employed as postmasters," he observed, "because they have a special interest in suppressing for a time the intelligence forwarded to rival printers." Granger, for all his piety, nevertheless followed the path rough cut by Timothy Pickering, who observed that "it is true diverse postmasters are printers of newspapers." [3]

The most important benefit accorded printer-postmasters was the right to free postage for the delivery of their papers and sundry other business-related items. Very often it came down to an arrangement whereby post riders, in order to get the contract to convey the mail between two points, would agree to deliver newspapers along the way for nothing. In other cases it involved the printer's use of the franking "privilege" pure and simple, mailing out newspapers to subscribers with no fee paid at either end. If the practice was not illegal, it certainly was extralegal, but it was a perquisite dear to the heart of an editor.

Federalist printers used "the right of franking to an extent never contemplated by law," and demanded it in lieu of the usually small income the office provided. John Wyeth, printer of a Federalist newspaper in Harrisburg, Pennsylvania, for example, would only take the postmastership if a clause was inserted in his agreement giving him "the privilege of carrying newspapers [free of postage] for your own emolument." Isaiah Thomas, the dean of early American printers, agreed to accept the postmastership at Worcester, Massachusetts, because "one great advantage which Thomas enjoyed," his biographer has written, "was that as postmaster he could frank at least part of the heavy mail which these [printing] businesses involved." The combination of franking privileges, federal printing, and high post office fees, one

Republican observed in referring to Richmond printer Augustine Davis, "made him rich."

Franking of newspapers was not part of some tradition the Federalist administration in Philadelphia inherited, It was a deliberate policy it invoked to aid in the creation of a virtually national Court Gazette to disseminate Federalist instruction. Deputy Postmaster General Jonathan Burrall summarized the new administration's position on the matter to an inquirer in 1791. "The Ordinance of Congress does not require that newspapers should be carried free," he wrote, but the "Postmaster General has a discretionary power of regulating that business." The first Federalist Postmaster General, utilizing this discretionary power, directed that printer-postmasters be "permitted to send them [their newspapers] by post, free of postage, when it could be done free of inconvenience." The last Federalist postmaster general, writing to one of his postmasters in 1801, warned him to expect the axe to fall shortly, for "there have been several applications for your removal . . . on the grounds of your being the Editor of a newspaper." For a decade, however, a score of Federalist printer-postmasters were among the most damaging and feared foes the Republicans encountered among the army of Federalist civil servants.[4]

The most-renowned Federalist printer-postmaster was Isaiah Thomas. His reputation as perhaps the best American printer of his generation was far reaching, both professionally and politically. An ardent Federalist himself, he also launched the careers of many other New England Federalist printers, four of whom he helped to obtain postmasterships in the course of the decade. Thomas published and edited the Worcester *Massachusetts Spy* and operated a large, high-quality publishing and bookselling establishment as well. He had a virtually national reputation as both a singularly talented printer and publisher and a dedicated political figure dating back to well before the Revolution, when he first surfaced as a supportive chronicler of the Whig cause. He was a printer in the most catholic sense of that eighteenth-century trade. From his press flowed a steady stream of influential books and tracts.

Isaiah Thomas's value to the Federalist cause, because of the uniqueness of his contributions, was beyond calculation. His own newspaper, of course, was an influential party sheet, the more so because it was issued under his imprimatur. His press also turned out many party imprints in the course of the decade. Most importantly, perhaps, there emerged from his printing house in the late 1780s and 90s a steady stream of talented young Federalist apprentices, seasoned into potential editors and publishers by the master. His role went beyond their training. On completion of their apprenticeship, Thomas invested his own money to found Federalist newspapers in several New England and New York State towns, printing establishments in which he became an absent partner to his young protégés. Invariably he employed his influence to have these fledgling printers named postmasters, knowing as he did the advantage that office provided a newspaper. Thomas Jefferson, his respect for Isaiah Thomas personally notwithstanding, removed the latter from his federal office in 1802. This indignity, according to Clifford Shipton, weighed heavily in Thomas's decision to retire from active printing.[5]

Among the apprentices who established Federalist newspapers with Thomas's help were Thomas Dickman, David Carlisle, Alexander Thomas, and Loring Andrews; all of them were named postmasters in their respective towns. Dickman left Worcester in 1792 to found the Greenfield [Massachusetts] *Gazette*, a Federalist paper that was deemed necessary to the party's success in the region. The town's most important Federalist was William Coleman, who combined with Thomas to "aid" in establishing the press, a euphemism for providing the initial bankroll. Within a year or so, Dickman was also sustained by his appointment as the local postmaster, an office which he maintained in the same quarters as his press and bookstore. In one way, at least, he was not one of Isaiah Thomas's better efforts. Although he was "zealously federal," in Harrison Gray Otis's words, he

was also "destitute of talent." Dickman's paper, nevertheless, filled an important void for the Massachusetts Federalist
party.[6]

David Carlisle was destitute of neither talent at his craft
nor Federalist commitment, but he proved a hopelessly inept
businessman. In 1793, after his apprenticeship, he was dispatched by Thomas to Walpole, New Hampshire, where in
partnership with his mentor he published first the *New
Hampshire Journal* and later the *Farmer's Weekly Museum.*
In the course of the decade, Thomas sent out successively
two more apprentices, Joseph Dennie and Alexander
Thomas, a relative, to take over the publishing chores from
Carlisle, who remained as editor. It was necessary, for as able
a printer as he was, Carlisle showed little aptitude for the
business end of things. He was a native of Walpole, the son of
a local artisan and farmer who returned to the town as a
young man of twenty-three after his apprenticeship at Worcester. Despite the fact that he was both backed financially
by Thomas and instantly named postmaster at Walpole, and
even though he "soon gained a respectable circulation" for
the *Museum,* he went broke about 1797.

His lack of commercial acumen notwithstanding, he possessed an acid pen and real political sophistication, and was
indispensable to the local Federalist organization. "Since the
Editor has been splashed with the mud of the [Republican
Boston] *Chronicle,*" Carlisle wrote in 1798, "he has gained
upwards of seven hundred subscribers. . . . He therefore
requests . . . the honour of future abuse." His financial
difficulties were fair game for Republican printers, but he
turned liability to asset in his reponse: "he [Carlisle wrote
about himself] even thinks he can afford them a small reward. . . . Divided among hungry and shivering Jacobins, it
might occasionally afford each forlorn patriot a hot loaf." By
1800 Carlisle, always a high Federalist, had turned against
John Adams, castigating the president for removing Secretary
of State Pickering. But Carlisle, for all his acerbity, clearly
needed help.

Joseph Dennie arrived in 1795 and apparently did no better with the business end than had his predecessor. After the

bankruptcy, the paper was reorganized, its name was changed, and twenty-four-year-old apprentice Alexander Thomas was dispatched to put things right. Carlisle continued as editor, but was dropped from the masthead as publisher. Moreover, taking no chances with this reorganization, the Federalists in the area were somehow able to replace Carlisle with Thomas in the local post office; apparently the former hadn't done too well there either. The elder Thomas was cajoled into putting more money into the rejuvenated printing establishment at Walpole, and the newspaper struggled on into the nineteeth century.[7]

In many ways, Loring Andrews was the most interesting of Isaiah Thomas's apprentices. A real partisan, he both expressed and exemplified exceptionally well the deference and even subservience the middle-class Federalist often accorded his social and political superiors in the 1790s. Andrews arrived in Stockbridge, Massachusetts, in the Berkshire Mountains in 1789 after a post-apprenticeship stint on a Boston paper. At Stockbridge he founded and edited the *Western Star,* a sheet which quickly became known as the mouthpiece of Congressman Theodore Sedgwick. The latter was the Berkshires' leading Federalist and a member of the western Massachusetts gentry who took both his politics and status very seriously. Sedgwick was described by his biographer as Andrews's "patron," and it is virtually certain that the congressman put up the money—or at least raised it—to found the *Star.* Thomas and Sedgwick, moreover, combined to help make the newly arrived Andrews the postmaster of the town. The young printer was talented, politically astute, and energetic, and knew his place, judging by his actions. The paper was both a financial and political success, becoming the most important means of Federalist communication in western Massachusetts. Its editor has been described by Sedgwick's biographer as a "virtual echo" of the congressman.

In 1797, however, the success of the newspaper notwithstanding, a personal problem disturbed the relationship between the two men. It was a difficulty that perhaps was not unrelated to the political attitudes of Sedgwick, Andrews, and Federalists generally, attitudes that enhanced class distinctions and smacked of deeply ingrained deference. For all of his political contributions and his close working relationship with Sedgwick, Loring Andrews, like all of Thomas's former apprentices discussed here, remained merely an artisan printer, a factotum, to the "patron" of the press. For his part, Andrews, like Dickman or Carlisle, clearly accepted his inferior status, maybe as part of his inbred Federalist ideology, and thus acquiesced in his role. In 1797 Andrews, after "having served him [Sedgwick] faithfully with pen and type about seven years," was denied the apparently willing hand of Sedgwick's daughter, the western gentryman perhaps feeling that the printer was beneath her station. Proud, but nonetheless bending to the decision, Andrews left the woman, the post office, and the paper behind and removed to Albany, New York, where an equally long-suffering Isaiah Thomas set him up with still another Federalist gazette under the masthead of Thomas and Andrews.

That Andrews could, Candide-like, experience these things passively, accepting that everything was for the best in this best of all possible worlds if his betters told him so, was a result of his own clear sense of personal insecurity combined in tension with his Federalist ideology. Baldly put, Andrews was given to fawning on Sedgwick. It was the result of more than simply a personality trait, however, for it derived as much from a sense of station which in turn carried over from Andrews's Federalist ideology. On one occasion he described himself as "a feeble . . . individual," who "can only express my ideas and feelings to those whose Situation in Life [e.g., Sedgwick] gives them the privilege to commune with the guardians of our country." Here was a middle-class mentality with brains and some education who echoed the class bias common to a significant portion of the gentry of the Federalist era. "Those who are not led by the *voci seva-tions*[?] of empty-headed Demagogues and Sounds of self conceited and ignorant declaimers," the Stockbridge printer once wrote, "to believe *that the people* in this country are a *race of gods* . . . would [urge] the necessity of firm laws and energetic restraints." "Republicanism and despotism," he averred on another occasion, "were synonymous terms. . . . Why, Sir, if this Doctrine [Republicanism] is *orthodox*, we may as well emigrate to Turkey . . . as to remain in America, and have our understandings insulted with sounds of Democratick privileges."

Among the first things to be checked in this overly free land, the Stockbridge postmaster contended, were "those infernal engines of deception, the antifederal papers." So much for constitutional protection of freedom of the press. This printer advocated that those "papers ought to be quelled . . . those vile vehicles . . . ought to experience the Silencing *veto* of Government." At the same time, the natural aristocracy must educate and uplift those below. In a classic deferential expression of *noblesse oblige* American style, Andrews urged that "influential characters must be active—they must throw off all reserve—they must speak to the people in terms, and in a tone, which the apparently all-important approaching crisis requires. . . . They must go forth among the multitude and personally discuss with them the things which appertain to their existence as an independent nation." Accepting conservative eighteenth-century political theory even as he imbibed the methods of a new politics, Andrews agreed that the "mass of mankind" do not "think deliberately, and act from the dictates of reason," therefore they must be ruled by "a small minority." And accepting a stake-in-society doctrine, Andrews counted himself out of that minority. As the printer not so elegantly put it in establishing his political priorities, "Viva la Consistency."

Neither Andrews's deference nor his elite political theory, however, kept him from energetically engaging in the new politics of the postconstitutional period. The young postmaster's activism derived from an instinctive awareness of "the importance of the press" in an area where primitive conditions of travel largely precluded mass meetings or electioneering devices. Over several years he wrote ringing editorials glorifying Washington's foreign policy, endorsing Jay's Treaty, or defending the constitutionality of Adams's conduct of the executive branch. Andrews, moreover, wrote and distributed a host of Federalist broadsides in both western Massachusetts and New York State. One throwaway, for example, outlined the legal arguments in favor of John Jay's thwarted bid for election as governor of New York in 1792. On another occasion he wrote, printed, and distributed through his post office a broadside assaulting "the abettors of French intrigue."

The Federalist printer was all over the Berkshires in the presidential canvass of 1796. He started out by personally circulating and collating petitions supporting Jay's Treaty. His post office became the western Massachusetts Federalist party headquarters, from which emanated political correspondence, broadsides, and pamphlets far and wide through the mountain area. He kept Congressman Sedgwick abreast of political developments by means of an extensive correspondence, and laid the groundwork for a pre-election public rally endorsing Adams. He combined a modern grasp of the organizational requirements of the new political structure and the evident need for elite involvement in electioneering with a more traditional acceptance of his own low place in the real scheme of things and a pronounced humility toward his betters. He might well be taken as an outspoken but typical example of the middle-class Federalist party cadreman.[8]

Isaiah Thomas's apprentices were not the only printers who were aided by post office appointments in New England. Samuel Trumbull, the postmaster at Stonington, Connecticut, for example, was neither trained by Thomas nor did he have much in common ideologically with those who were. A very young man in the 1790s and of middling background, he was at an early age most worldly in the ways of politics. He settled in Stonington in 1798, after taking his apprenticeship with his father, a printer in Norwich. At Stonington, the younger Trumbull founded the *Journal of the Times* and was almost immediately rewarded with the local post office even though he was a newcomer in town. In the next year his paper carried ringing defenses of the Adams administration's foreign policy, denunciations of American "Jacobins," and several strong endorsements of the Sedition Act. On the last day of 1799, however, when it may have become clear to him that the Federalists were vulnerable in the forthcoming elections, Trumbull changed the name of his paper to the *Impartial Register,* and in a month's time opened it to Republican as well as Federalist views.

At first the weight of the material greatly favored the Federalists, but about the time that the Republicans carried the legislative elections in New York in May 1800, guaranteeing that they would win the Empire State's electoral votes, the *Register* became truly impartial. By 1802 Trumbull was passing himself off an as old-line Jeffersonian (his paper was by then thoroughly Republican) in correspondence with the new national administration. He not only kept his postmastership, but the Republicans at Washington, still hungry for Jeffersonian support in the solidly Federalist "land of steady habits," gave him the area's contract for printing the session laws as well. It was, all in all, a virtuoso performance that set Trumbull dramatically apart from one so wholly ideological and committed as Loring Andrews or others among Isaiah Thomas's apprentices.[9]

George Hough's trek through the political thicket offers still another variation on the Federalist theme. Hough was the printer of the Concord *Herald* in New Hampshire. During the first years of the Federalist decade, the paper was clearly neutral, almost apolitical in fact. Hough was nominated postmaster of Concord around June 1793, and from that time on not only the paper but the printer personally drifted into the Federalist camp. The character of the *Herald* changed markedly over the next few years, culminating in a change of name to the *Courier of New Hampshire* in 1796. Under its new masthead, Hough's paper was unveiled as thoroughly partisan. Jay's Treaty was the political issue that midwifed the transformation. Within only a few months of taking over the post office, moreover, Treasury Secretary Alexander Hamilton asked Hough to undertake a political errand in Concord, and Hough obliged. One can conclude that politically the Federalist administration was as expert as any later counterpart in playing the game of carrot and stick with its spoils.[10]

In New York, both Nicholas Power and T. O. H. Crosswell,

the postmasters at Poughkeepsie and Catskill respectively, were Federalist printers. The latter was a very young man who established his press at the very end of the decade. Crosswell's paper, the *Balance and Columbian Respository*, ran under the masthead "We are federalists, but not monarchists," and, as its slogan suggested, it was a moderate sheet. Not so Power's Poughkeepsie *Journal*. Power himself, unlike Crosswell, was a veteran of the political wars and could never be described as a political moderate. The Poughkeepsie postmaster established his press during the Confederation era and emerged as a key upstate proponent of the Constitution. Always adept at getting his slice of the pie, he was named printer to the New York Ratifying Convention in 1788. He moved naturally thereafter into the Federalist camp, and in particular was a disciple of Alexander Hamilton. When the opening became available in 1792, Postmaster General Pickering named Power postmaster at Poughkeepsie. After the Republicans came to power, Aaron Burr strongly recommended Power's removal, a recommendation quickly acted upon by Gideon Granger.[11]

The postmasters of three key Pennsylvania towns—Reading, Harrisburg, and Pittsburgh—were all Federalist printers whose papers serviced important rural hinterlands. Gottlob Jungmann, the postmaster at Reading, edited the Federalist German-language *Readinger Zeitung* for the extensive German population of eastern Pennsylvania. John Wyeth, printer of the Harrisburg *Oracle of Dauphin* fed the entirely rural expanse of central Pennsylvania east of the Alleghenies. The Pittsburgh *Gazette,* the only Federalist paper on Pennsylvania's transmontane frontier, was published by John Scull.

Jungmann first joined the *Zeitung* in 1789, and by 1794 had become a partner. It was he who gave that weekly its prepossessingly political character. Jungmann performed a unique and invaluable service for the Pennsylvania party; his paper provided perhaps the only source of continuous political information about issues, news of meetings, and electioneering exhortations to which the exclusively German-reading population had access. His press, moreover, printed "Federalist propaganda" rather extensively, in the form of German-language political tracts—for example, a translation of "Peter Porcupine," William Cobbett's acid Federalist commentary.[12]

John Wyeth, publisher of the *Oracle*, was the postmaster at Harrisburg. Only twenty-two when he founded the paper in 1792, and fresh from his apprenticeship in Philadelphia, Wyeth soon made a success of the Federalist gazette. So much so, in fact, that his "conduct and principles" made him "odious" to the area's Republicans. The printer clearly carried his federalism beyond the immediate requirements imposed by the press, and he was among the earliest victims of the Republican victory in 1800. The importance of the post office to the profitable operation of the *Oracle*, serving a geographically extensive rural constituency as it did, was made clear by Wyeth's repeated requests to the postmaster general for assurance that he could deliver his paper free of postal charges if he accepted his appointment. He was one of the few to receive such a guarantee in writing. Numerous and continuing Republican complaints followed his nomination, culminating in "several applications . . . for [his] removal" in 1801, complaints that soon cost him his federal office.[13]

The third printer-postmaster in Pennsylvania was John Scull, editor of the Pittsburgh *Gazette*. Pittsburgh was at the eye of the political hurricane brought on by the Whisky Rebellion, and throughout that "insurrection, John Scull held his paper unswervingly with the government." The visibility this drama brought Scull, plus his deep personal involvement in the western country's Federalist organization, made the printer a prime target for Washington County Republicans. Political tension in the area escalated in 1798, moreover, when a Republican paper edited by John Israel, a Jewish printer, was established in Pittsburgh specifically to counter the *Gazette*'s far-reaching influence.

Scull persistently injected anti-Semitic matter into his paper, along with the usual political barbs directed at the area's growing Republican party. Coincidently or by design, it was at about the time these diatribes against Israel reached their peak that Scull lost his post office. It remains impossible to establish any cause-effect relationship between Scull's loss of the federal office and the outbreak of anti-Semitism in western Pennsylvania politics. However, it is clear that Scull did not lose his office because of any political backsliding in 1798, for he remained a "steadfast Federalist, and his unvarying and undiminished support was always given to that party." Even after Jefferson's election, the "Anglo printer" continued "to throw as much odium on the President as he can, and misses no opportunity of Scandalizing him and Republicanism." [14]

The postmasters in several southern towns, including Richmond, Virginia, Annapolis, Maryland and Augusta, Georgia were likewise Federalist printers. These three quasi-urban centers were, with Baltimore, Maryland and Charleston, South Carolina, the most important centers of Federalist organization in the South. Augustine Davis, printer of Richmond's *Virginia Gazette and General Advertiser,* was an important figure in a Federalist organization that emanated from Richmond and was headed by John Marshall, Edward Carrington, and Richard Lee. Davis had been a Loyalist during the Revolution and later an energetic proponent of ratification in a deeply divided state. From 1790 on, the Federalist postmasters general received several complaints alleging that Davis was often tardy in forwarding the mail from his post office, which served as a kind of gateway for mail deliveries heading south. The importance of the *Gazette* to the Federalist party in Virginia and his own high place in the party combined to protect him from any threat to his federal office, however. In 1800 the Richmond printer gained national prominence when he helped to bring Republican printer James Callender to book via the federal sedition law.

Shortly after Jefferson's election, Gideon Granger both removed Davis from the post office and deprived him of his contract to print the congressional session laws. The postmaster general reminded Davis "that you are in easy circumstances in life" and added tartly: "You have enjoyed the public patronage so far within the last ten years as to earn for your service in the department the sum of seventeen thousand three hundred eighty dollars." In a final ironic twist of the knife, Granger pointed out that a factor in the decision to cut Davis off from the public teat was his recent employment of the same James Callender who by 1802 had turned against Jefferson and was in the process of being exploited politically by the Federalists. The major reason for his removal, however, lay in "the tendency of his paper" which was "calculated to obstruct the progress of these principles, which we have at length so happily established." [15]

Postmasters Samuel and Timothy Green, almost certainly father and son, were printers of the Federalist Annapolis *Maryland Gazette* and the Fredricksburg *Virginia Herald* respectively. The Annapolis Green, by the dawn of the first party system, was a venerable and widely respected printer. His newspaper had equally supported the Whig cause during the Revolution and the movement for constitutional reform a decade later. While he opened his press to high Federalists in the 1790s, moreover, his editorial policy and the tone of his political news were both moderate. The younger Green established the *Virginia Herald* in 1786, at the age of twenty-one, on completing his apprenticeship, perhaps with his father. Like the *Maryland Gazette,* the *Herald* came out strongly in support of the Constitution and moved on later to espouse the causes of the new Federalist administration. The two Greens were rewarded with post offices which, apart from their advantages for the printer, in these instances paid well also. Timothy Green's Virginia paper was as moderate as the elder Green's journal. [16]

The same adjective could not be applied either to the Augusta *Herald,* the most important party gazette in Georgia, or to its printer William Hobbey. The editor, who was postmaster in that town from 1789, was one of the oligarchy of five who absolutely controlled the destinies of Georgia politics until the Yazoo land scandals, initially exposed in Georgia in 1797, wrecked the state's Federalist party. Senator James Jackson described Hobbey in 1801 as the long-time "Orator the Writer and the Almost Bully of the pretended Federal administration." As to his management of his post office, Jackson wrote Jefferson, "this [letter] will therefore be longer delay'd." Augusta, he added, "needs a change."

In fact, it appears that Hobbey was guilty of every possible breach of ethics that could be laid at the door of a printer-postmaster. In removing him, Gideon Granger enumerated candidly the list of his sins. Hobbey used the post office "as well on politics as on business." He evinced a "special interest in suppressing for a time the intelligence forwarded to rival printers," and finally he showed "an uncommon interest in using the right of franking to an extent never contemplated by law." [17]

In a geographical sense, Hobbey's post office and newspaper both represented the last links in a chain of officially connected Federalist way stations stretching from Maine to Georgia. These stations constituted together a kind of Court Gazette, a professional network of party communications media that served up issue-oriented propaganda vital to the effective functioning of a national Federalist party machine. Some of the printer-postmasters who anchored the system were men of rank and consequence in their areas. More usually, though, they were young, energetic subordinates who willingly followed the party leadership and bore the brunt of the political fallout. These latter, for all their political ability and centricity within the party, remained distinctly within the middling status assigned them by postconstitutional eighteenth-century society. As such, the printer-postmasters as a whole formed an important, visible middle-class spearhead of the elite party's cadre.

Innkeepers formed another small but highly conspicuous group that was drawn into the party vortex by occupational gravity. Like the printers, these publicans were usually—though not always—men of middling status, men who gained economically in significant ways by aligning their establishments with the Federalist party.

In the daily life of the postrevolutionary era, inns and taverns were very nearly institutionalized centers for political communication. It is generally accepted that in eighteenth-century towns the tavern was as much a social center as it was a watering place. Men gravitated to an inn frequented by others of like political views, and so in most towns in the 1790s there might be a Federalist tavern and a Republican inn. These pubs subscribed to sympathetic partisan newspapers that could either be read there firsthand by men who could not afford to subscribe themselves or be read (or transliterated) to those party followers who read poorly or not at all. In any event, political communication was as common in the inn of the 1790s as it was in any other era. The tavernkeeper in many towns and villages was thus easily tabbed politically by his townsmen by the leanings of the public house he kept.

This identification was inevitably strengthened by the possibility of direct material benefit. Post offices drew patrons to taverns just as they did to stationery establishments and book stores, and returned at least a small, easily come-by income through postal fees. The partisan innkeeper, moreover, as a result of widespread practice, profited enormously from letting his public rooms and kitchen and bar facilities for party meetings and celebrations. A glance at random newspapers in the 1790s will reveal that most public party meetings, private caucuses, rallies, July Fourth celebrations, and Washington Birthday dinners took place at pubs. All of this involvement in politics made the inn a virtual party headquarters in many towns, and its host a fairly notable figure in the community's political life, his less than elite social position notwithstanding. The potential immorality of joining the local post office to the town watering place caused a still naive Joseph Habersham, who had just taken over as postmaster general from Timothy Pickering, to conclude in 1795: "I do not think Tavern keepers are proper persons to be postmasters." His predecessor hadn't so concluded, and had appointed several publicans as postmasters; to his credit, Habersham learned fast, for in the course of the next few years he named at least a half dozen innkeepers to post offices himself.[18]

One of these was John Lenox, the postmaster at Lenox Castle, North Carolina. He was named to the office in 1799, one of a small minority of innkeepers who were part of a local elite. He owned Lenox Castle, a mineral springs resort, as well as a tavern. He had emigrated from England in the 1780s and did very well in the ensuing decade. Apart from his inn and resort, by 1795 he also owned a general store and a large plantation. Described as "witty and eccentric," Lenox was also a firm Federalist. For the sake of his regular patrons, he subscribed to most of the important Federalist publications, making them available to his out-of-the-way corner of the South. The *Gazette of the United States* and Cobbett's *Porcupine Gazette* were two examples. In 1799 he boasted to John Steele that he was ready to take up arms against the French "whenever General Washington sounds the trumpet of War." Lenox was one innkeeper Postmaster General Habersham named to a post office who never even applied for the job. "I have never fish'd for any Post either civil or military," he wrote Steele in 1799, "the present commission being sent to me without my application." [19]

Three New England postmasters were also innkeepers of local consequence. Joseph Bliss of Haverhill, New Hampshire, was kin by marriage to the notable Livermore family and a Federalist "of influence" in his own right. His tavern was the "aristocratic headquarters . . . for the judges and lawyers," a common combination of euphemisms employed to describe the Federalist party. Benjamin Fearing, the postmaster at Wareham, Massachusetts, graduated from Yale in 1776, and returned home to succeed his father as the local Federalist innkeeper. The postmaster at Wiscasset, Maine, was Ebenezer Whittier, whose tavern, like Bliss's, was described as a center of Federalist activity. A man of affairs who had started out as an apprentice carpenter, he eventually served in the Massachusetts General Court (legislature) in the Confederation era, filled many town offices, and became treasurer of the local Presbyterian church in the Federalist decade. [20]

Most publicans did not reach this eminence, however. Several New Jersey innkeeper-postmasters were men of middling status deeply involved in local Federalist politics. These men were closer socially to the norm for occupants of the post office generally. Archibald Campbell, for example, the postmaster at Hackensack, was light years removed socially and economically from the Dutch-descended Federalist elite in the town. Yet he too was a committed Federalist in the 1790s even as he had been a Loyalist a score of years before. His tavern was the acknowledged center for the middling English-derivative portion of the Federalist interest in the town. Tavernkeepers John Branson and Reuben Tucker, respectively postmasters at Haddonfield and Tuckerton in southern New Jersey, were also men of middling status whose inns occupied important places in the local Federalist organizations.

Certainly the most notorious of the New Jersey Federalist hostlers was John Burnet, the postmaster at Newark. His was a particularly rewarding appointment financially. Not only did his post office draw patrons to his premises, it paid between $300 and $400 annually. Republicans were clearly made to feel conspicuous in his "dram shop" as local Jeffersonians derisively referred to it, and they bitterly resented having to stop there; but, if they wanted their mail, that's where it was. On at least one occasion a local Republican sympathizer paid dearly for his visit to Burnet's Tavern, a visit that transformed both himself and his obscure Federalist host into nationally known celebrities. It was in this tavern that Luther Baldwin uttered a blasphemy that became infamous to Federalists all over America.

As a local militia unit fired its two-pounders in salute to welcome President Adams to town in 1798, Baldwin, a self-described "captain" of a garbage scow plying the Passaic River, muttered, as he sat at Burnet's bar, that he hoped that the president would be "shot through the arse" by one of the cannon balls. The infuriated postmaster, then tending bar, stormed out and fetched the sheriff, who eventually arrested Baldwin for sedition under the recently passed federal law. The Newark tavernkeeper emerged only a slightly less luminous star in the nation's press than did Baldwin. Burnet was the government's chief witness against the transgressor in the successful prosecution that followed. If Baldwin was transformed into a Republican martyr for Jeffersonians everywhere to capitalize on, Burnet was made over rather improbably into a courageous Federalist hero, a notoriety

Figure 13. The original nineteenth-century country store and post office at Headsville, now in West Virginia.

that contributed to his removal from his postmastership after Jefferson was elected president.[21]

Shopkeepers formed the most prosaic occupational grouping among Federalist postmasters. As in the case of printers and innkeepers, the combination of occupation, limited in-

Figure 14. General store, about 1790, restored at Old Sturbridge Village, Massachusetts.

come, and meager education consigned a large majority of these storekeepers to middling status in their respective towns. Their politics, therefore, provide a good entrée into both the attitudes and posture of the less articulate Federalist party advocates. At least a hundred of the nation's postmasters owned retail stores of one kind or another, and this accounts only for those who could be identified with certainty; clearly there must have been many more who pursued the same livelihood. These men, with their stores on the main streets of towns and hamlets in all parts of the nation, were natural choices for postmasterships, for they were regularly accessible and centrally located. A significant proportion of these shopkeepers, lack of status notwithstanding, were locally important Federalists; enough so that it is possible to conclude that politics was a decisive factor in determining which shop on Main Street or Broad Street would be blessed with the significant economic advantage the post-office designation conferred.

Examples illustrating this particular Federalist profile are plentiful, but the pattern becomes familiar even via a short examination. The postmasters at both Brattleboro and Bennington, Vermont, are cases in point. John Holbrook was thirty-five when he moved to Brattleboro on the Vermont frontier from his native Boston in 1795. A year later he opened a general store that by 1800 had become a local landmark—in part because Holbrook was named postmaster shortly after opening his doors. The postmaster brought in his goods by flatboat up the Connecticut River from Hartford. Already an important local Federalist, about 1800 Holbrook increased his involvement by setting up his son-in-law William Fessenden as the Federalist printer in town. The paper was given space in the same building that housed the store and post office, a building which had long since become the acknowledged Federalist headquarters for the town.

Micah Lyman of Bennington kept his post office in his apothecary shop. He had settled in Bennington in 1790, having moved to the small town from Connecticut at the age of twenty-three. By 1800 his establishment had become a "flourishing business." As in Holbrook's case, the post office was a significant factor in his early success. For Lyman, the last was punctuated by the fact that, some time after he was removed from office by the Republican administration, he had to close his doors, the shop having failed. He moved on to settle in a frontier town in Canada.

Perhaps the character of his federalism explains the economic difficulties Lyman latterly had encountered in a town where, by the time Jefferson won the presidency, the strength of the local Federalist party had waned. In the 1790s, Lyman's political activity and economic success were of a piece. His use of the post office for political ends, however, "was extremely disgusting" to local Republicans. One Jeffersonian claimed that he and his compatriots were "frequently oblidged to send their Letters and communications to the next or distant post offices fearing least they should be either opened or wholly suppressed." Lyman was, according to one Republican notable, "a man Most Intollerant in his political sentiments," a man who was "very officious in distributing Newspapers teaming with abuse of the best men and Measures of our country." It was little wonder that, as the political character of Bennington changed, Lyman's apothecary shop, so closely tied to the post office in the local public's mind anyway, suffered an acknowledged loss of patronage. His economic success proved as ephemeral as his claim on a federal office.[22]

The pattern was common elsewhere in New England as well. Samuel Batchelder, the postmaster at New Ipswich, New Hampshire, migrated from Massachusetts and settled in the town in 1785, opening a bake shop. Like Lyman the baker was a high Federalist, unswerving in his views and, the evidence reveals, intolerant of those who disagreed with him. Very shortly after Jefferson's victory, several townsmen petitioned the president for the still-outspoken Batchelder's removal; and, before the year was out, Gideon Granger did remove him, admittedly for political reasons.

John Stoddard's tenure as postmaster at Pittsfield, Massachusetts, was also layered in controversy. He kept a general store in the western Massachusetts town. As a result of his political activity, attested to by influential Federalists in Pittsfield, he was given the local post office in 1797. The appointment "excited the warmest indignation of the Republicans" in the town because the situation recapitulated in real life the Jeffersonian propaganda they had been fed for five years. Stoddard had been a Loyalist during the Revolution; and to create the vacancy Postmaster General Habersham, probably only at Adams's instigation, had to remove from office a rival storekeeper who was not only a Republican but a veteran of the Continental army as well.

The contrast in revolutionary participation rankled Jeffersonian townsmen as much as the dismissal of a Republican. A factor in Habersham's decision was the efforts of Stoddard's brother-in-law Ashbael Strong, a local Federalist notable and state legislator who both owned the building in which Stoddard's store was located and was a silent partner in the operation. Clearly economic wheels were turning within political ones in this western town, with the post office as a prize that occupied the central place in the sometimes complex machinations.

Apothecary Thomas Thaxter of Hingham was another beneficiary of John Adams's frank political approach to appointive office. Less than two weeks after Adams's inauguration the Republican postmaster was removed and Thaxter's drug store was made the new post office. "Many influential friends and connections" had supplied the pressure. In the ensuing years, town legend recalls, the apothecary shop on Main Street was the place "where the Federalists used to assemble to discuss the affairs of the town." [23]

Many similar stories can be told for other quarters of the nation, but a few examples will suffice. Elizur Mosely was a young man who settled in the raw Oneida County, New York, frontier community of Whitesboro in 1791. His general store was the first emporium of any kind in the town. Operating the only post office for miles around out of that store, he made a quick success of it. In 1798 Mosely was the victorious Federalist candidate for sheriff in the county but, unlike some of his more zealous New England counterparts in the postal service, he apparently remained a moderate party man who aroused little personal antagonism among his political opponents.

James Wilson, postmaster at Presqu'Isle on the western Pennsylvania frontier, was a man of similar moderation. Like Mosely, he too kept a general store in a relatively unsettled area. Shortly after Jefferson's inauguration and after the president had removed the Federalist customs collector at Presqu'Isle, Wilson wrote to Gideon Granger inquiring whether he too could expect to be removed for political reasons. If that was the case, he concluded, he was submitting his resignation first. Granger assured Wilson somewhat less than candidly that he never removed anyone for political reasons alone. Even though Wilson was a Federalist, the postmaster general wrote, there had been no local complaints lodged against him. "I should not wantonly wound the feelings of any one," Granger wrote, "or assume unnecessary labours and the evils of party calumny" by deposing a good postmaster. What was left only half said in light of other situations elsewhere was that Granger would have been hard put to replace him in that sparsely settled area. A short time before Granger wrote to Wilson, however, he had shown no compunctions about removing John P. Thompson, another Federalist storekeeper, from the post office at Carlisle, Pennsylvania, on the grounds, according to Republican Congressman William Findley, that Thompson used his office to aid the Federalist cause in the area.[24]

John F. Verdier, a Beaufort, South Carolina postmaster, can serve as a final example. He managed a general store owned by Federalist United States Senator William Loughton Smith. The senator had secured the postmastership for his employee to enhance the store's utility to the community—and thus increase his own profits. Verdier, like his employer, was a Federalist ("a steady friend of government"). Quite clearly, Smith had no moments of uneasiness about having Verdier named in the commission for, if the latter should have left the senator's employ, Smith could quickly have the store manager stripped of his federal office. There seemed to have been no trouble either about Smith's direct intercession in obtaining an office, the indirect profits from which would accrue to himself.[25]

Among the United States postmasters were several skilled artisans, some farmers, and even, curiously enough, three men who were unemployed when they were named to federal office. The most interesting and least representative of the artisans was undoubtedly Richard Cranch. In most ways it is difficult to describe Cranch as middle class. There was nothing ordinary about his mind, his education, or his connections. Yet he remained poor and not particularly devoted either to improving himself materially and getting ahead, or leaving his artisan status behind to rise to the station eighteenth-century America clearly held open for him.

It is not easy, after all, to describe a Harvard graduate and

John Adams's brother-in-law and "best friend" as part of the mass. Yet the Quincy, Massachusetts, postmaster was content to pursue his trade as clockmaker and repairer from his small shop, wherein he also kept the post office, eking out a poor living between the two. Cranch was already in his mid-sixties when he was given the postmastership in 1793 at Abigail Adams's intercession. The clockmaker, an *émigré* from England, had gone to Harvard with John Adams and later married Abigail's sister. He had served for long periods through the 1780s in both houses of the Massachusetts legislature, been active in a number of humane and dissenting religious organizations, and was a vigorous supporter of the Constitution at the Massachusetts Ratifying Convention. In the 1790s he was a strong Federalist who "naturally had no use at all for the French Revolution, and after the defeat of John Adams in the election of 1800, he began to doubt democracy and to remember statements in the classics about the failings of popular governments." Several times Cranch had attempted to start manufactories, but for one reason or another he always failed, becoming dependent in his old age on his considerable mechanical skills and the largess and influence of relatives.[26]

But Cranch was a most unusual artisan. The others who were Federalist postmasters more clearly fit the stereotype of the eighteenth-century laboring man, free and independent but at the same time deferential and looked down upon by those considered his betters in a tiered society. The postmasters at York, Maine, Peru, New York and Catawissee, Pennsylvania were all Federalist surveyors in frontierlike areas. Joseph Horsefield, the postmaster at Bethlehem, Pennsylvania, was a saddler. He was a Moravian, born to German immigrants, who had done well enough in his saddlery shop to enter politics in middle age. Horsefield supported ratification at the Pennsylvania Constitutional Convention in 1788, and went on from there to become involved in the local Federalist party in the next decade. He was made postmaster in 1792 and kept the office in his saddlery, although it had to be less than comfortable for the public because of the oft-described, pervasive smell. The office remained in these fragrant quarters until Gideon Granger, finally tempering politics with an unusual display of mercy, removed Horsefield in 1802. Rosewell Billows, a carpenter in Rockingham, Vermont, kept his post office at home until Granger removed him too in the same year for purely political reasons. Dummer Sewell, the postmaster at Bath, Maine, was a miller who followed the natural path from active support of the Constitution at the Massachusetts Ratifying Convention to service as a Federalist cadreman in the 1790s.[27]

A few farmers served as postmasters in wholly rural areas and, although the total is too small to reveal any significant trend, more of these yeomen were Republicans than were Federalists. Perhaps it only demonstrates that post offices were badly needed in these rural spots, and the choice of possible postmasters was necessarily small, so the Federalist administration had to subordinate political considerations to practical needs. In Massachusetts, for example, John Chandler and Moses Ames, postmasters at Monmouth and Fryburg respectively, were both Republican farmers. William Wilson, postmaster at Clermont, New York, and Thomas Lewis, the Georgetown, Kentucky, postmaster, were both husbandmen who can best be described politically as trimmers.

Wilson was the overseer of Republican Chancellor Robert R. Livingston's lower manor at Clermont. Like virtually all hirelings and tenants of manor lords in late eighteenth-century New York, Wilson took on the coloration of his better, professing to be a Republican when the latter did. Yet he managed to find a way to actively work for the local Federalist candidate for Congress in 1794. Lewis, a frontier farmer, claimed to be a Federalist and, reversing the situation just described, was able to find cause to sometimes help Republican candidates in a Republican state.

Hugh White, postmaster at Pinckneyville, South Carolina, and William Richardson, postmaster at Elizabethtown, North Carolina, were both owners of small plantations who could as easily have been designated farmers as planters had they lived in the North or West. White was an Antifederalist and later a Republican, and Richardson, stepfather of Federalist

United States Senator William Richardson Davie, was a
Federalist proponent of the Constitution and thereafter a
Federalist party follower.[28]

In some ways, only the most blatant political considerations accounted for the appointments of Alexander Gilbert,
John Bradley, and Joseph Wales during the administration of
John Adams. The three, unemployed prior to their appointments, could offer but little in the way of proof of responsibility, although each claimed the friendship and intercession of
an important political figure as well as acceptable party credentials in his own right. Gilbert, named postmaster at
Rutherford Town, North Carolina, in 1798, was described
delicately in a recommendation on his behalf as "At Leasure"
at the time of his nomination. He spent "much time in literary pursuits," Comptroller of the United States Treasury
John Steele reported, but at the age of twenty-six could claim
no earlier steady employment nor any literary productivity.
Nevertheless, he was apparently one of the few Federalists
in the town, and he got the appointment. Gilbert's indolence
thereafter apparently extended to his official duties for his
first official report to the postmaster general was at least two
years late.

John Bradley was another North Carolinian who claimed
Steele's help. At the time of his appointment as postmaster at
Wilmington, he had just gone bankrupt, and immediately
thereafter the warehouses and buildings he owned burned to
the ground. He had not yet acquired a place to house the post
office at the time of his appointment, but it was felt the nomination would help Bradley get back on his feet. The Wilmington post office was well-paying, averaging about $400 a
year; and Bradley, another political friend pointed out, was
"a firm federalist and advocate for the measures of our government."

The most interesting appointee in this respect was Joseph
Wales, the postmaster at Lancaster, Massachusetts. Given the
eighteenth-century American view of idleness of the fit, the
personal stigma attached to bankruptcy, and the cloud that
hovered over individuals with debts long unpaid, there was
little to recommend Wales appointment except his political

connections and involvement. He had been long unemployed at the time of his 1797 appointment and deeply in
debt as well, both by his own admission.

Wales asked a compassionate Richard Cranch to intercede
with his brother-in-law, the newly inaugurated president of
the United States; and Cranch, who himself knew a lifetime
of economic reverses, obliged. "Present me most respectfully
to the President of the United States," Wales implored.
"Should he wish to know anything relative to my political
sentiments—my friends will assure him that . . . I am a firm
friend to the *Constitution, Government* and *Administration.*" On this basis—and in this case it could only have been
on the basis either of charity or politics, or both—Wales was
commissioned. It may well have been the humane thing to
do, but it is difficult to visualize it happening to a Republican
in the same circumstances. The stronger possibility remains
that it was simply an expedient and politic nomination. In
any event, three unemployed men could not by any stretch of
the imagination, given eighteenth-century attitudes, have
qualified as the best men available for the responsibility of
federal office had they not been Federalists.[29]

While most postmasters were of middling status, virtually
all the appointees in the judiciary were of elite backgrounds.
The federal officeholders in the judiciary fit much better the
stereotypical view of Federalists, as the next chapter demonstrates. But if judicial nominees differed economically and
socially from federal employees in the post office service, the
two groups of appointees shared a common perception of
their political responsibilities.

CHAPTER TEN

The Judiciary Compromised

The Constitution, after spelling out the provision for the Supreme Court, simply left the remainder of the federal judicial establishment to the enabling legislation of Congress. As part of the Judiciary Act of 1789, Congress established two inferior federal courts to complement the Supreme Court: the Unites States District Court and the United States Circuit Court. The remainder of the federal legal establishment consisted of a United States district attorney in each state, a United States marshal, and a district court clerk. The first two officers were entitled to appoint impermanent staffs of varying sizes depending on the needs of the state, paid by fees as services were required rather than by salary. The entire federal judiciary, judges included, were under the nominal jurisdiction of the State Department, although in practice during the Federalist decade Alexander Hamilton exerted much greater influence with the federal judiciary than did Jefferson; later in the decade, moreover, Adams exercised a relatively direct control, often bypassing his secretaries of state.

The men who filled the inferior judicial establishment, the most prestigious and best-paying federal appointments in the states, were notables of ability and power. It was to be expected that the inferior judicial establishment would, by the very nature of its functions, fall gracefully into politics. It took a supreme wrenching of ethics, however, for the federal judges to fall into the same trap.

The operative provisions of the Judiciary Act of 1789, with respect to the federal courts, mandated that there be a United States District Court, the districts of which were to be coterminus with existing state lines (Maine, a subdivision of Massachusetts in the 1790s, formed the only exception in that it quickly became a district of itself). This plan for the drawing of district lines derived from a proposal made in the *Federalist Papers* by Alexander Hamilton. The district judge by law had to be a resident of the district (state) in which he was appointed. The court was required to hold four sessions annually, with some district courts in the larger states to convene in different cities within the state.

The 1789 enabling legislation also grouped the districts into three circuits—eastern, middle, and southern—for purposes of merging with the Supreme Court to create a United States Circuit Court. In each of the three circuits, two sittings of the circuit court were to be held annually, consisting of two Supreme Court justices and the district judge for the district which was the seat for that particular sitting of the circuit court. The district judge exercised a significantly strong role in the circuit court despite his judicial inferiority to the Supreme Court justices. For one thing, by statute the district court judge was the resident local authority, "privy" to local judicial practices which, by law and de facto understanding, would prevail in each circuit court sitting. For another, in practice the circuit court usually consisted of only one Supreme Court justice, not two, plus the resident district judge.*

Thus, in the circuit courts, according to Julius Goebel, Jr., "there flourished . . . divergencies from English common

* In 1793 Congress regularized the practice, by law reducing the number of Supreme Court justices who need hear a circuit court case from two to one.

law procedures and native inventions in every state peculiar to its jurisprudence." These "divergencies" were tacitly accepted as operative in the circuit courts via the silence or vagueness of the Judiciary Act of 1789. This practical solution, what Goebel calls the "localization of the Federal inferior courts," was designed to quiet the fears of Antifederalists and others who were apprehensive about the usurpation of local law by a newly dominant federal legal system.

In sum, the district court judge would meet twice a year with one or two Supreme Court justices to form a federal circuit court. Additionally, the district judge would hold district court four times a year, acting alone as the agent of an inferior federal court. The competence of the court under each arrangement would vary. "The real meat of the District Court's [exclusive] jurisdiction [was] . . . the cognizance of 'all civil causes of admiralty and maritime jurisdiction.'" Thus the district judge tried "all seizures under laws of impost, navigation or trade of the United States where the seizures were made within the district on waters navigable by sea by vessels of ten or more tons burden, as well as upon the high seas." This exclusive jurisdiction formed the basis of authority for district court actions regarding the neutrality issues that faced the nation between 1793 and 1796.

If, as Goebel asserts, "the District Courts were viewed primarily as courts of special jurisdiction, the Circuit Courts were created as courts of general original jurisdiction." It was responsible, within the confines of a federal jury system and among other civil and equity responsibilities, (a) for original civil jurisdiction "where the United States was a plaintiff or petitioner or where a 'foreigner' " was a party to the action; and (b) for cognizance of all cases where "crimes and offenses against the United States" were involved. The circuit courts, in fact, became the federal judicial bodies with authority to deal with all cases prosecuted under the federal alien and sedition laws between 1798 and 1800.[1]

The independence and impartiality of the federal judiciary has always been a cardinal article of faith in American jurisprudence. The provision that all federal judges from the Supreme Court down are appointed on good behavior and not for specific terms of office is a revered American principle that, it is usually argued, shields federal judicial decisions from political pressures and eliminates the judges' involvement in politics. In this sense, the concept of an independent judiciary has assumed the proportions over time as a cornerstone of American liberties. Recently, however, historians of the early Supreme Court have called this general view into question.[2]

We know now, for example, that John Marshall, the most famous American jurist, perpetuated Federalist principles in a larger sense and at the same time, while chief justice, allowed his decisions to be affected significantly by expedient political considerations. In *Marbury* v. *Madison*, for instance, Marshall's opinion both strengthened the Supreme Court's power and independence and augmented the staying power of the existing Federalist party organization. In accomplishing this pragmatic political goal, he fit very well into the pattern established by his Federalist associates on the Supreme Court in the 1790s, for others among the original justices of the Supreme Court were deeply committed political partisans; Justice Samuel Chase was only the best-known example among the Federalist Supreme Court jurists.

Very little has been written about the functioning of the first federal inferior courts, however. At a time when every action of a federal judge set a political as well as a legal precedent, these jurists too, by and large, were openly involved in partisan politics, even more so, in fact, than their brethren on the Supreme Court.

From its inception in 1789, the first federal judiciary was deeply compromised, both responsive and submissive to the needs and demands of the ruling Federalist party. The decisions of its jurists were tainted in important ways by relatively crass political concerns. These jurists, moreover, yet unfettered by the nicety of an ethical precept that demanded disengagement, participated freely in the budding national politics of the Federalist era. The thoroughgoing politicization of the United States district judges was particularly evi-

dent, and this was a condition that endured for at least the
first dozen years of the national experience under the Constitution. Thus the 1790s formed a judicial era that, on balance, was the worst and most dangerous in American history.
It established highly personalized partisan judicial prece-
dents that, if they had not been corrected subsequently,
would have soon sapped the vital integrity of the court system and with it an important anchor of freedom in the emerging republic.

The district judges were prominent men. Some collective
insights into their backgrounds, therefore, suggest some
causal motivation for their continuing political commitment
while on the bench. The judges matured in an era of revolutionary political turmoil and manifest national development. In fact, escape from political responsibility for men of
their stature in a still deferential society was nearly impossible prior to 1789. More than any other generation of American jurists, this one was a product of a shared political experience. For nearly a quarter century, the district judges had
taken political involvement as an obligation, and they naturally carried that attitude into the period after ratification. In
1793 a Federalist civil servant in a position to know com-
mented that the federal judiciary had "assumed a party com-
plexion." "It has . . . become a regular practice of the federal
judges to make political discourses to the grand jurors
throughout the United States," another critic noted in 1797.
"They have become a band of political preachers." [3] This last
observation was not far off the mark. The political
backgrounds of these early jurists indicate that as a group
they were politically committed at the time they accepted
judicial office.

The twenty-eight men [4] who sat on the United States district court in the 1790s had been deeply a part of the process
of nation-making. Nine had been officers in the Continental
army, and another eleven had held notable civil positions in
their states during the War for Independence. Only three had
been at all equivocal about the Revolution, and none of these
were Loyalists. During the Confederation, twelve had served
in the Continental Congress while another eight held high

judicial office in their states. Most importantly, fourteen were delegates either to the Constitutional Convention at Philadelphia or to state ratifying conventions, all as supporters of the Federalist cause. Another seven had been politically active in favor of the Constitution outside the conventions.

In short, in a political process that comprehended only a tiny part of the entire American population, fully three-quarters of the new federal judges had been strongly identified with the nationalist movement. Only three were initially equivocal about the Constitution, and all three—Harry Innes of Kentucky, John Laurence of New York, and William Paca of Maryland—had come to favor ratification before the event, and vowed themselves in favor of the new government prior to their appointments to the federal bench.

Several of the judges-designate, in accepting their nominations, claimed a political theory that committed them judicially to the Federalist cause. Nominee John Lowell of Massachusetts wrote President Washington, in accepting his commission in 1789, that he was "impressed with the strongest Ideas of the Necessity of the firm Establishment of the national Government to the Peace and Happiness of every Member of the Union." Richard Law, newly named judge for the district of Connecticut, recalled in his letter of acceptance to the president his earlier political adherence to the Constitution and professed himself eager to consolidate it as the supreme law of the land.

The views of several others, moreover, were never tempered by their judicial experiences in the Federalist decade. In seeking the district judgeship for New York, James Duane wrote Alexander Hamilton in 1789 that he was "warmly attached to the Constitution." In resigning in 1794, he told George Washington that he was proud to have served as a "steadfast friend of the general government." Similarly, in accepting his commission in 1789, District Judge Nathaniel Pendleton of Georgia expressed "all the zeal a citizen ought to have" to provide "stability and dignity to the National Government." On resigning from the bench in 1796, Pendleton hoped he would be remembered as an "enthusiast always" of the Constitution. Perhaps this sense of participation in the ongoing political process was best summed up by District Judge Robert Morris of New Jersey, who in 1800 conceived it was his "duty to promote welfare and honour of our country and make every possible exertion to maintain them. Public good and our own [are] closely united therefore [we] must do everything to enrich our country and prevent its disgraces." Significantly, there were literally no expressions of the value of impartiality, obligation to see justice done, or detachment from the affairs of state in all the sources touching on the judicial careers of these men.[5]

This nearly collective and almost emotional involvement with the implementation of the Constitution can be viewed as a starting point for the process that drew many of the twenty-eight inexorably into politics. Indeed, more than half of them remained party men and political leaders even while on the bench. John Lowell of Massachusetts, for instance, was variously described during the 1790s as "a warm Federalist" and "a leading man of the [Essex] Junto." David Sewell of Maine was known as a "firm Federalist" and a "firm supporter of Washington." Judge Benjamin Bourne of Rhode Island remained a leader of Providence's "political club," the "headquarters of national principles in Rhode Island in the 1790's." Jurist Nathaniel Chipman of Vermont also sustained a highly partisan reputation as a "Hamiltonian nationalist" and an "effective and unscrupulous practitioner of magnate politics." He was one of the top three or four "major political strategists" in Vermont in the Federalist decade.

James Duane of New York was a "leading figure in the Federalist ranks," while for Pennsylvania's William Lewis there was no perceptible break in open party activity during his brief tenure as United States district judge: "Pope Lewis," one historian has noted, "participated actively in party affairs." Richard Peters, Lewis's successor, described himself as "of the old school." He continued to clear most Federalist patronage in the Delaware valley on behalf of the administration in Philadelphia even as he sat on the bench. Judge Thomas Bee of South Carolina was described as one of the seven most influential Federalists in Charleston while Judge Nathaniel Pendleton of Georgia was one of five "influential political leaders" who "energetically represented the rising partisan spirit of Federalism in the state." [6]

By and large, moreover, the party activity of these sitting judges was not limited simply to private political manipulation. A significant number of them openly headed public party meetings, participated in election campaigns, and spoke freely on the emotional issues that dominated the politics of the decade. Public identification with the Federalist party organization, regardless of the damage to the judicial integrity of the court as a whole, was far from a random occurrence.

Judge Lowell regularly participated in Federalist caucuses and nominating meetings in his native Essex County and in Boston during the election campaign of 1800. He was the featured speaker, for example, at a Federalist Fourth of July rally in Roxbury that signaled the opening of the presidential campaign, where he delivered a highly partisan oration denouncing the Jeffersonian Republicans. John Laurence of New York, whose tenure as a United States district judge from 1794 to 1796 was sandwiched between service in the United States House of Representatives and Senate, never shed his partisan commitment. Always deeply into Federalist party functions in New York City before 1794, he continued to involve himself while on the bench, "serving as chairman of federal nominating meetings" and, in 1794, chairing a public meeting called to protest alleged French encroachments on United States sovereignty. Similarly, Georgia Judge Nathaniel Pendleton at about the same time chaired a Savannah Federalist meeting that denounced France and sent a "commendatory address" to the president signed by the jurist lauding Washington's foreign policies. Judge Richard Peters was prominently on display at a 1795 Federalist rally in Philadelphia called to defend and endorse Jay's Treaty. [7]

At least some of the other district judges openly campaigned for Federalist candidates. "I shall endeavor to assist the Doctor's Election as I uniformly have been doing since I knew he offered," North Carolina's John Sitgreaves reported, disclosing his participation in Federalist Hugh Williamson's effort to win a seat in the House in 1790. "Shall I dare say [I will] secure all the votes of this County for him, that are given at all?" Pennsylvania Judge William Lewis provoked Republican derision as a result of his open participation in the congressional elections of 1792, first as a member of Philadelphia's Federalist Committee of Correspondence and later as a city representative to a statewide Federalist convention at Lancaster.

Federal Judge James Duane maintained a residence in New York City, but he was also a manor lord who owned vast tracts of upstate land peopled by tenant farmers. Following the prevailing custom in the Empire State in spite of his judicial responsibility, Duane was one "powerful landlord" who did not hesitate to "exert undue pressures on [his] tenants at election time." Thus, in the bitterly contested New York gubernatorial poll of 1792, Duane herded "about two hundred [tenant] votes into the fold" for Federalist John Jay. In 1796 Judge David Sewell of Maine helped disseminate Federalist literature and otherwise involved himself in the "Electioneering Campaign [which] begins to open for governor." [8]

The highly ideological and emotional issues that characterized national party politics in the 1790s drew many of the Federalist judges into the political mainstream. John Lowell of Massachusetts, Nathaniel Chipman of Vermont, and Henry Marchant of Rhode Island all expressed partisan public support for Hamilton's hard-medicine fiscal measures in 1790 and 1791. Chipman and Judge Thomas Bee of South Carolina both openly condemned the excesses of the French Revolution in 1793, and what they took to be a manifestation of the American counterpart to these excesses—the newly fashionable, party-oriented democratic societies blossoming around the nation. Judges Sewell, Peters, and Bee all publicly endorsed the Jay Treaty in 1795, certainly one of the more contentious party issues of that decade. Judges John Sloss Hobart of New York and Chipman at different times denounced the political leadership of Thomas Jefferson.

Chipman's well-disseminated views, contained in the

widely quoted pamphlet *Sketches of the Principles of Government* published in 1793, can serve as an example in depth of the degree to which sitting federal judges were uninhibited about expressing their political views for the enlightenment of the public. In the interest of the "general education . . . of the people," the jurist condemned in print the Democratic Society of Chittendon County, Vermont, in particular and all democratic societies in general as Republican political vehicles attempting "to govern the majority by a minority faction." He thus embroiled himself in a public political controversy from which he never entirely extricated himself prior to his retirement from the bench to take a seat in the United States Senate. Taken as a whole, the jurists of the United States district court really dissipated any public claims they might have had to judicial objectivity and invulnerability to political pressures.[9]

The most critical result of this ubiquitous slide into politics was that the United States district judges' biases spilled over alarmingly into decision-making on the bench. This dangerous willingness to undermine the integrity and independence of the third branch of government fell into two distinct periods. The first cycle manifested itself between 1793 and 1796, as an accompaniment to the maturation of an opposition party. It was characterized by attempts in the district court, which possessed original and sole jurisdiction, to force on the political opposition and the public at large a general acquiescence in American foreign policy. The second round revolved around the federal sedition laws of 1798: it involved the United States circuit court (one Supreme Court justice sitting with the resident United States district judge) in efforts to stifle dissent in the last two years of the Adams administration. It wasn't merely Justice Samuel Chase, the Supreme Court justice who was later impeached but not convicted, who was guilty of judicial politics; it included a significant number of district court jurists as well, men who jeopardized both the independence of the federal judiciary and the scaffolding of the newly created system of checks and balances.

The early round of judicial politics had its inception in 1793, when Citizen Genêt appeared on the scene, according to Federalist litany, to threaten the sovereignty and well-being of the nation. He was guilty in particular, according to the Federalists, of both activating American political opposition to the Washington administration and subsequently attempting to enlist American vessels illegally as French privateers to plunder English shipping. New York District Judge James Duane, the Federalist landlord who had brought his tenants to the polls some months before, was moved to respond to Genêt's successes by initiating anti-French policy through his court. The French consul in New York, on instructions from the French government, lodged an official protest with the State Department at the end of 1793, charging Duane specifically "with an abuse of power and acting in opposition to the friendly disposition which the political treaties [of 1778] ought to establish." Duane honed federal jurisprudence into a fine-edged Federalist tool. He had seized and condemned several French vessels (*not* American privateers) in New York harbor in violation of existing treaty rights. At the same time, his "philosophical jurisprudence," according to his biographer, was "spiced with Federalist propaganda" aimed at discrediting local Republican francophiles.

As a result of the furor Duane created, Secretary of State Edmund Randolph informed the judge that he had gone too far. Duane in turn complained to Randolph that the French consul was taking advantage of his (Duane's) ill health in pressing his "complaint to government" and threatened to resign if he was not vindicated by the Washington administration. Randolph's State Department, which had administrative jurisdiction over the federal district courts, was still committed to maintaining a strict neutrality early in 1794; given the opening by Duane, the secretary of state suggested not very delicately that a resignation due to ill health might be in order to placate the French government. The New York district judge was, according to New York Federalist leader Robert Troup, made victim to local "partizans of the French Sans Culottes." Judge Richard Peters, one of the most parti-

san of the district court jurists, commiserated with his colleague on the strength of French influence. Counterpres-
sures were unavailing, however, and Duane, having earlier
committed himself, soon resigned from the bench.[10]

Further south, in Charleston, District Judge Thomas Bee
was more successful in pressing Federalist interests. As
Judge Bee was widely known as one of the local leaders of
the "government party" in 1794, one observer noted that "it
is difficult to conceive of a man with deeper distaste for the
French revolutionary principles being trumpeted through
Charleston." Bee invoked his federalism from the bench in
disposing of privateering cases at Charleston port. His partisanship was evident in several condemnations of French vessels that may or may not have been acting as privateers that
found their way to Charleston. Of these condemnations carried out in Bee's court, the most blatantly political was that
resolved in the case of *Costello* v. *Bouteille,* in which the
jurist challenged and summarily rejected "points essential"
to the defense. He meant to and did embarrass local Republican supporters of the French Revolution in the course of his
disposition of the case. Moreover, after the ratification of
Jay's Treaty in 1795, Bee consistently defended it ex
cathedra, lashing out from the bench at the "French faction"
in the city and nation.[11]

An even more distinct example of judicial federalism in
defense of Jay's Treaty occurred in Maine. Stung by the an-
gry, widespread, and very effective Republican reaction to
the Anglo-American accord, District Judge David Sewell departed from strict enforcement of the law itself in order to
attack its attackers from the bench. Hearing a case early in
1796 in which the defendant was charged with violating the
treaty's commercial regulations, Sewell instructed the jury to
find him guilty. In his charge to the jurors, he pointed out that
both the defendant and his defense attorney were political
opponents of the government and Constitution, the "supreme law of the land" which sanctioned the legality of the
treaty. While in retrospect the sophistry involved in labeling
opponents of the administration opponents of the government and Constitution as well is clear, it was a common and

effective judicial device. Even rudimentary jurisprudence, moreover, would forbid a judge in any era to relate the commercial violation in question to the politics of both the defendant and the defendant's attorney.

Before ending his instructions to the jurors, Sewell, who at the same time was involved openly in the election campaign of 1796, told the court that "the specious and fine spun objections that have been made to the treaty . . . it is highly probable time and experience will discover to be as futile and erroneous, as those made to the acceptance and introduction of the federal constitution." The Maine judge ended with a widely disseminated peroration generally chastising Republican newspapers that propagated objections to the treaty to the detriment of national unity; for it was the Republican newspapers, according to the judge, that encouraged would-be violators of the treaty's provisions.[12]

A few specific examples of the even more rampant judicial partisanship involving the implementation of the Sedition Act will suffice, although fully half of the sitting district court judges at the end of the decade were glad enforcers.[13]

District Judge Richard Peters of Pennsylvania took it as a personal obligation between 1798 and 1800 to ferret out "Seditious scoundrels." There were "some Rascals," Peters wrote Timothy Pickering, "whom he wanted to handle if he could do it legally." Peters got several opportunities, most particularly in the prosecutions of Republican editors Benjamin Franklin Bache and Thomas Cooper. In the Bache case, James M. Smith concluded, Peters was clearly biased against the defendant in the crucial preliminary hearing held before Peters, who sat alone. The same was true in the Cooper case, where Peters sat in circuit court with Supreme Court Justice Samuel Chase. In a style reminiscent of Judge Sewell in 1796, Chase and Peters permitted the United States attorney to urge on the jury "the necessity of making an example of Cooper in order to deter others from misleading the people by false and defamatory publications."[14]

Richard Peters took the high ground in punishing sedition, compared to John Lowell in Massachusetts. By 1798 Lowell was actively and openly enmeshed in the Massachusetts

Federalist organization, and allowed his bias to find expression in a number of ways. In a novel enforcement of the new law, he ordered that a liberty pole erected in Dedham be taken down "to demolish" that "Symbol of Sedition."

Lowell later handed down a warrant for Nathaniel Ames, a Republican who was arrested for contempt in failing to appear as a prosecution witness in a sedition trial. Convicted and fined in a circuit court action with Supreme Court Justice William Cushing and Lowell presiding, Ames requested and was denied copies of the proceedings because, the jurist declared, Ames "should make bad use of them." But the worst indignity to which gentryman Ames was subjected at a trial in which he was "spunged of 8 dollars" was that he was deliberately "set among pickpocks at the Bar." Ames thought this last was a partisan nicety added unnecessarily by the judges.

Far more serious, and much more typical of Federalist jurisprudence generally, was Lowell's permissiveness in selecting jurors. He was made specifically responsible, within the structure of the circuit court, for selecting juries for Massachusetts cases falling under its jurisdiction. He allowed his marshal in one sedition trial to send "Venires for 30 jurors to federal towns, and by a second selection of twelve from these 30, could obtain one panel of full blooded filtrated federalists, and from them the political verdict." [15]

Other Federalist district judges were equally permissive in filling juries hearing sedition cases. Thomas Bee's district court in South Carolina "unremittingly checked the free course of justice" by allowing "a partial selection of jurymen." In the circuit court trial of James Callender for sedition in 1800, Judge Cyrus Griffin was the district court's representative, sitting with Supreme Court Justice Chase. The mechanical problem of putting together a jury was, as usual, left to the inferior judge; Griffin, like Lowell and Bee, painstakingly constructed an entirely Federalist jury. In Vermont, Samuel Hitchcock had succeeded Nathaniel Chipman to the district court bench at the end of 1793, the latter taking a seat in the United States Senate. In the course of the decade, Chipman had become "one of [Matthew] Lyon's . . . bitterest enemies." When Lyon, the militant Jeffersonian journalist, was tried for sedition in 1798, Hitchcock (one of two judges comprising the circuit court hearing the case) nevertheless called on Senator Chipman to draft at least part of the indictment, a violation of the constitutional separation of powers. In order to enhance the chance for conviction, Lyon was hastily brought to trial after being refused several reasonable requests for postponement in order to prepare his defense. The two judges finally permitted the trial to open even though Lyon's lawyers were not present. The same pattern emerged in subsequent Vermont sedition trials over which Hitchcock presided alone.[16]

It is clear that what happened in the district and circuit courts in the 1790s cannot simply be written off as the bias of a few partisan judges involved in a handful of isolated cases. Political prejudice in the courts appears to have been pervasive and deeply rooted in ongoing political involvement on and off the bench. Political activism helped to loosen political emotions and corrupt the objectivity of otherwise distinguished, highly qualified jurists in every part of the nation. Thus, it may be said, if an independent federal judiciary did emerge as a basic building block of American liberties, it was a lodgment that took place only *after* the generation of the Founding Fathers. Neither the "good Behaviour" clause of the Constitution nor the integrity and perspicacity of the Founding Fathers, nor even the eminence and abilities of the judges themselves, assured the creation of an independent federal judiciary.

It is clear, on the contrary, that both the first United States district and circuit courts were among the most thoroughly politicized federal judicial institutions in American history. They posed a major threat to American civil liberties, the moderate application of American law, and the concept of the jury system—all at perhaps the most vulnerable and sensitive period in American judicial history. The Federalist judges believed that talented, superior men like themselves, by virtue of their inherent stature, could stretch and dilute their judicial mandate with impunity in the best interests of the nation and its people as they saw those interests.

The Federalist judges were very dangerously wrong. Their greater ability and influence only created a greater threat to the constitutional liberties of the nation. This was one elite, its judgments clouded by partisan involvement, that really didn't know what was best for the mass after all. In their zeal to protect the Constitution, these jurists ironically took a step toward undermining its virtues.

The United States attorneys in the several states, working closely with the federal judges as they did, were also very much a part of the Federalist organization. These men exercised a great deal of discretion in determining what alleged violations of federal law were to be investigated. They determined the scope of the investigation, moreover, presented the case to the grand jury, and prosecuted it before the federal bench. Working with an ill-defined fee system, the attorneys were able to farm out cases for investigation and even prosecution, expanding their staffs as the need arose. The patronage inherent in such a system augmented the already weighty political power accruing to the position. It is not surprising, therefore, that most United States attorneys were both placemen and highly placed party leaders. Men like Harrison Gray Otis and Christopher Gore of Massachusetts, Jeremiah Smith of New Hampshire, William Rawle of Pennsylvania, Richard Harison of New York, and John Julius Pringle and Benjamin Woods of South and North Carolina were all at the apex of the social structure in their respective states. Many of the others were only marginally less notable; most were deeply involved in Federalist party affairs.

If we take into account the prevailing historical view of Federalist aloofness from electioneering, the deep involvement of several United States attorneys is astonishing. These men were upper class and supposed to possess all the usual biases against descending into the arena to garner votes. Yet many federal attorneys belied this stereotype, frequently engaging in political campaigns with a zest that defied both their social status and the impartial exercise of their official duties. United States Attorney Christopher Gore, for instance, a member of the Essex Junto, publicly campaigned for his close friend Fisher Ames, who was running for Congress in 1790. Gore dwelt on the salutary effects of Alexander Hamilton's fiscal program in this and several other canvasses in the early years of the Federalist decade. Richard Potts, Maryland's federal attorney, stood as a candidate for elector for George Washington in 1792. In Georgia, United States Attorney Matthew McAllister, one of the five most "influential political leaders" in the state, worked very hard for Anthony Wayne, who ran for a House seat as a Federalist in 1791.

Later in the decade Daniel Davis, the self-made federal attorney for the Maine district whom Thomas Jefferson described in 1801 as a "violent" Fed, so deeply immersed himself in a congressional campaign that he was, he claimed, "threatened with personal injury" by Portland Republicans. In another poll he was a principal contributor to the local Federalist newspaper. Harrison Gray Otis agreed to serve as acting United States attorney for Massachusetts in 1796, and did so for about nine months before he was elected to Congress. During this period he campaigned hard for the Adams-Pinckney ticket, even as he himself ran for election to the lower house. This activity came on the heels of his famous "second shirt" speech defending Jay's Treaty, so he had already established himself as a notable party campaigner.

New Jersey's Lucius Stockton, brother to United States Senator Richard Stockton, was the state's federal attorney from 1798 through 1800. Although he possessed a reputation, according to no less a Federalist authority than Treasury Secretary Wolcott, as a "crazy, fanatical young man of Trenton," another party man paid tribute to his ability on the stump. He was "not a water-gruel wellwisher, but has always been a decided and *active* Friend of the present government." Stockton threw himself into the presidential election of 1800. The federal attorney spent almost a month in the autumn of that year traveling on horseback through the state, in "fearful suspense," he wrote, about the outcome of "this awful crisis." He "rode . . . with Parson Linn's poisonous pamphlets, preaching that Religion was in danger, etc., if Jefferson was elected." According to the Republican governor,

"Stockton did more injury [to Jefferson] with his pen and tongue, than any man in N. Jersey." [17]

When it came to popular politics, certainly the most ubiquitous and enterprising Federalist attorneys were Richard Harison of New York, Jeremiah Smith of New Hampshire, and William Rawle of Pennsylvania. Harison, a former Loyalist and after 1789 a close friend and lieutenant of Alexander Hamilton, occupied his office with ability, if not impartiality, for the whole of the Federalist era. He was a highly placed New York City Federalist manager and a seasoned campaigner. To Harison, the Jeffersonians were "disorganized Banditti" who sewed "Confusion to all Order" and sought only "the Humiliation of the government." It was the United States attorney who "was often called upon to make the statement of the party faith in public meeting." Harison was openly involved in the 1792 campaign to elect John Jay governor; thereafter the federal attorney used his office to attempt to establish federal jurisdiction over the disputed election returns from Otsego County that would have made Jay the winner, although clearly that conflict was a matter for adjudication in the state courts. In that same year, Harison was the key figure in lining up the Federalist ticket for the state senate in the downstate area. His activities in 1792 provide a guide to his involvement in subsequent New York polls as well.[18]

Jeremiah Smith, the New Hampshire attorney for the Adams administration, was openly contemptuous of his Republican opponents. He had spent several years in the House of Representatives prior to his nomination to federal office; there he had become an important figure within the majority bloc and a growing power in New Hampshire politics. With his ties to the administration, it was natural that he surfaced as a key liaison between the Adams leadership in Philadelphia and New Hampshire Federalists. Among other things, he was the guiding force in stripping several prominent Portsmouth Republican followers of Senator John Langdon of their federal offices in 1798.*

---

* See chapter 3 for Smith's role in purging Portsmouth Republicans from the civil service.

Smith's "contempt and revulsion" for the opposition party was both deep and widely acknowledged, and he proved an indefatigable organizer and campaigner in New Hampshire canvasses after he retired from Congress. In 1800, for example, the federal attorney used the first anniversary of George Washington's death to deliver a highly partisan public attack on the Jeffersonians, an oration denouncing them in virtually Calvinist terms. One recent historian has described Smith as among the most aggressive campaigners in the state's Federalist party. A contemporary labeled him a "most violent" party man. These are credible views of a man who professed "that a public officer should be removed, unless he took an active part in support of the administration." [19]

William Rawle, the United States attorney for Pennsylvania for most of the Federalist decade, was also an elite political figure "who participated openly in party affairs." The scion of a Quaker family and a graduate of the Middle Temple, like Harison he had been a Loyalist during the Revolution. In 1792 the federal attorney was listed as a member of the Federalist Philadelphia Committee of Correspondence, which had responsibility for co-ordinating the party campaign for Congress. He surfaced again in 1798, when he unsuccessfully attempted to heal a breach in the local Federalist organization that ultimately resulted in Federalist candidates competing against each other for the state senate. In 1800 Rawle once again appeared as a member of the Philadelphia committee, first directing Federalist publicity for the presidential election and later, after the Pennsylvania legislature agreed to bar a popular poll and name a slate of electors itself, working to assist the Federalist legislators in drafting an acceptable ticket. Despite his wealth and conservatism, there was nothing to indicate that he ever held himself aloof from popular contests at the polls. In fact, like many of his cohorts, Rawle seemed to enjoy that part of the political process and evinced both enterprise and ability in its execution.[20]

In an issue oriented decade the United States attorneys responded with ideological devotion to party positions. As often as not, they mixed their official and political responses in ways that threatened the integrity of the judiciary no less alarmingly than the activities of the district judges with whom the attorneys worked. The domestic issues that most lent themselves to politics during the Washington administrations were the fiscal policies of Alexander Hamilton. In foreign policy, allegations of violations of American neutrality, and later the furor over the Jay Treaty, attracted the commitment of the most political of the federal attorneys.

Christopher Gore, the Massachusetts United States attorney from 1789 to 1796, was one who was most deeply committed to Hamilton's banking and funding plans. He was known by reputation to the treasury secretary in 1790, but an introduction from Fisher Ames brought the two men together in 1791, when the political fate of the proposed Bank of the United States hung in the balance. Gore traveled to Philadelphia to speak to Hamilton in the autumn of 1791, in order to bring back assurances to the uneasy Boston merchant hierarchy that their "apprehension" respecting the Bank of the United States was unfounded. This Boston interest, whose support was essential if the BUS was to succeed, was concerned lest the national bank limit the potential profit and power of the merchants' Massachusetts Bank. "Tho a great stockholder" in the Massachusetts Bank, Congressman Ames wrote Hamilton about Gore, "you will find him *national*." Ames added that "party schemes will be nursed in the city [Boston]" that could jeopardize the BUS, but Hamilton could count on Gore's "steady opposition to them. . . . I think it will be useful and almost necessary that you should *know* him."

At the same time, as one of the United States attorney's foes put it, Gore was a "funding Federalist." He owned more than $30,000 in United States securities in 1789, and stood to profit enormously from Hamilton's plan for funding. Gore was so deeply involved, in fact, that President Washington reluctantly dropped him from consideration as United States attorney general in 1795. "Gore's handsome talents were countered by the fact that he had amassed a large fortune not as a lawyer but as a speculator in paper securities," so he was not named even though he was the president's first choice.[21]

Other United States attorneys also aligned themselves behind the treasury secretary's economic undertakings. Richard
Harison was a close friend and long-time political ally of both
Hamilton and sometime Assistant Secretary of the Treasury
William Duer. It was known to only a very few in 1789, at the
time Duer was given the subcabinet post, that his accounts as
secretary to the Treasury Board of the Continental Congress
in the 1780s were "short" a quarter of a million dollars.
Hamilton knew, but chose to ignore the shortage and its possible origins. But when Duer's failure in 1792, triggering a
major New York City financial panic, threatened public expo-
sure of the financier's earlier peculations of Treasury Board
funds, Hamilton finally ordered a treasury audit—much too
late to retrieve the government's money from the then bankrupt speculator. At the same time, under the pressure of the
events surrounding Duer's failure, Harison was reluctantly
instructed by the federal administration to investigate Duer
for possible violations of federal law. Harison's examination
was so uncharacteristically perfunctory and his efforts so
drawn out that, although Duer went to debtor's prison as a
bankrupt, he was never brought to justice as an embezzler.
Deeply involved with Duer himself, and a Hamilton "satel-
lite," Harison was hardly the disinterested person to implement an investigation of Duer.[22]

At virtually the same time as Duer's failure was becoming
public knowledge, United States Attorney William Rawle of
Pennsylvania, another proponent of Hamiltonian measures,
agreed to act privately as counsel to the newly chartered
BUS, accepting an annual retainer as part of the agreement.
The contract between the public official and the Phila-
delphia-based public corporation would seem to have
guaranteed the fledgling institution an investigation-free
start at a time when its constitutionality had just been questioned. Pierpont Edwards, United States attorney in Connecticut and kin to Republican Aaron Burr, emerged as an important if quiet advocate of Hamilton's fiscal proposals even
though he was supposed to have been a Republican. In fact,
his politics during the decade are almost impossible to un-
ravel; he was one of those most adept at playing both sides of
the political street in the Federalist decade.[23]

In another area of ideological confrontation, several United States attorneys were able participants in efforts to suppress French influence. Via their offices, they enforced an unneutral brand of the "neutrality" that was the stated policy of the Washington administration. The question of the legality of American vessels acting as French privateers in particular became an issue in 1793. Secretary of State Jefferson had prevailed over Hamilton in convincing the president not to suspend the Franco-American treaties of 1778, and thus the way was left open for American privateers to raid English shipping quasi-legally under the protection of the tricolor and French letters of marque. Subsequent captures thus involved the United States attorneys directly in the prosecution of these well-known cases.[24] The arrival of Citizen Genêt, and his subsequent unilateral instruction to French consuls in American ports to act as agents in condemning captured English shipping further heated up this already warm controversy. A few examples of the extended role the United States attorneys corporately played will suffice to illustrate their partisan involvement, well beyond the bounds of clear-cut law enforcement, in 1793. The ideological-political conflict is well known; the role of the federal attorneys is not.

After Jefferson convinced Washington not to repudiate the treaties of 1778, Hamilton wrote urgently to Richard Harison that he was to ignore Secretary of State Jefferson (Harison's immediate superior in the administrative structure of the federal government in the 1790s). In particular, Harison was told to bypass the state secretary's liberal instructions in dealing with alleged French violations of American neutrality. United States Attorney Harison, Hamilton suggested, was instead to "resort to principles." This meant that the attorney was to seize and condemn privateering vessels putting into New York harbor regardless of what Jefferson said. Harison complied, taking his orders from Hamilton—who clearly went over Jefferson's head. It is morally certain that this little-known confrontation was a contributing factor in hastening Jefferson's departure from the cabinet.

It is fairly obvious that Gore in Boston and Rawle in Philadelphia accepted similar instructions from Hamilton. Boston was another prominent privateers' port of call, and

Gore zealously prosecuted what he considered were violations of neutrality. In fact, the Bay State federal attorney was
responsible for the revocation of accreditation of the French
consul in Massachusetts on the grounds that the latter acted
as an agent for privateers. Gore thus earned Stephen Higginson's compliment that he had "behaved well certainly." In
Philadelphia, a third important privateering port, United
States Attorney Rawle clearly not only prosecuted but insti-
gated the famous *Henfield* case in May 1793, a landmark
prosecution of an alleged French violation of American neutrality.[25]

Later in the decade still other United States attorneys were
drawn into active political conflict by John Adams's forceful
foreign policies. Benjamin Woods, the federal attorney for
North Carolina, organized and chaired a public meeting to
marshal public opinion behind Adams in 1798. That gathering forwarded to the president an address delivered and
signed by Woods that was "very flattering and otherwise
pleasing" to the chief executive. On another occasion, Woods
recommended an applicant for federal office mainly on the
strength of that individual's sympathy for Adams's foreign
policy. One high Federalist, disgusted with the president's
unwillingness to go to war with France, identified the North
Carolina United States Attorney as one of those Adams
Federalists "who loudly and publicly proclaim that the
Executive neither has done nor can do wrong."

Both John Davis and Frederick Frelinghuysen, United
States attorneys for Massachusetts and New Jersey respectively at the end of the decade, circulated petitions endorsing
the president's foreign policies. Other federal attorneys were
equally partisan. Charles Marsh of Vermont was described as
a "valiant partisan" of Adams. Jeremiah Smith, denouncing
those Jeffersonians whose removal from federal office in New
Hampshire he had engineered in 1798, assured the national
administration that these Republicans were "open bitter
enemies of the Government and partisans of France and it
would give me a great deal of pleasure to see them *rewarded*
with office under the *latter*." Richard Harison was outraged
that a "gentleman" like Republican Robert R. Livingston

"should prostitute his genius, forget his Station, prefer the glory and Interests of a foreign nation to his own." The New York federal attorney, "trimming his sails to the wind" as the contemporary political cliché went, endorsed "cautiously adhering to Adams' policies" in counseling an upstate Federalist about how to handle the developing schism in the Federalist party.[26]

The Federalist United States attorneys, like the district judges with whom they collaborated, were unable to deal objectively with the sedition laws. While the prosecution of the cases as a collective assault on civil liberties has been described by several historians, the range of hostility toward dissent on the part of many Federalist officials is worth examining briefly. Their animosities were often deeply personal, sometimes motivated by class antagonisms, and occasionally evidenced a deep-seated fear of both freedom of speech and the press. There were times in 1798 when sedition prosecutions deliberately used the judicial process to inflict indignity rather than achieve justice. Nathaniel Ames of Massachusetts, for example, subjected to what he considered degrading treatment in a sedition-related trial, believed that much of his trouble was "by instigation of John Davis," the federal attorney. There can be little doubt, moreover, that United States Attorney Charles Marsh's handling of Matthew Lyon's sedition trial was designed to heap maximum humiliation on his political enemy.[27]

More serious were the class hostility and related fears of too much representative government the sedition trials sometimes evoked from prosecuting attorneys. William Rawle really believed in 1798 that there was a conspiracy of rabble, in the form of the "United Irishmen," that was engaged in "secret projects" against the United States. By his own admission, he was hipped on prosecuting "Irishmen" whom, he said, were among the most "discontented characters which infest our country." Rawle described one sedition trial "as akin to a personal libel suit of a ruler against the ruled." Richard Harison in New York considered his Republican opponents "Banditti." [28]

The most common prevailing attitude of the attorneys

prosecuting the sedition cases was their collective lingering doubt about the wisdom of open government, an attitude that in the final reckoning was a cornerstone of Federalist ideology. Pierpont Edwards, United States attorney for Connecticut and presumably a Republican, prosecuted his fellow party men (?) with no less zeal than his Federalist colleagues. Edwards successfully convicted Charles Holt, editor of the New London *Bee,* for example, and his attitude, if a later expression can suffice, constituted "astonishing doctrine" for a Jeffersonian. In a post-1800 case, Edwards told a grand jury that publications defamatory of the government "will more effectually undermine and sap the foundations of our Constitution and Government than any kind of Treason that can be named." William Rawle expressed a similar view in the 1798 sedition trial of Thomas Cooper when he "stressed the necessity of making an example of Cooper in order to deter others from misleading the people by false and defamatory publications." [29]

Charles Marsh and Thomas Nelson, the United States attorneys in Vermont and Virginia respectively, went even further. Marsh, according to one historian, favored a "paternalist government." He feared "the spasmodic and zealous demonstrations of partisan popular sentiment," according to another study, and "regarded the vote of majorities as a very uncertain and unstable test in politics." As Marsh made clear in the trial of Matthew Lyon and others, disrespect, sedition, and instability were the bitter fruits of too much democracy.[30]

Thomas Nelson was the man who put together and prosecuted the case against James Callender in Virginia. In doing so, he introduced "the closest statement of presumptive guilt made by any district attorney prosecuting a case under the Sedition Law." By his writings alone, Nelson told the court, Callender must be "presumed guilty unless proven innocent." The defense, in other words, "had to disprove the charges" instead of the "government having to prove falsehood." In making the case, moreover, Nelson "used the words 'administration' and 'government' interchangeably," according to James M. Smith, and was one of the first architects in American history of a judicial process that rested on "guilt by accusation." [31] These federal attorneys were fitting advocates of Federalist ideology, and suitable alter egos to the federal district judges in whose courts they labored.

Of all the incumbent Federalist officeholders whose official fates Thomas Jefferson pondered before his inauguration, he reacted most vehemently to the incumbent marshals. In the privacy of his "Anas," it appears that these enforcers of federal law were, for the president-elect anyway, the most visible abusers of Republicans. Jefferson's antipathy was based on the marshals' collective political exploitation of the office. In particular, as Manning Dauer has put it, "the practice of the marshals in empanelling Federalists for jury service converted the law into an engine of the Federalist political machine." [32]

Jefferson singled out seven of the seventeen incumbent marshals by name, promising himself the removal of five as soon as possible: John Hall of Pennsylvania, Samuel Bradford of Massachusetts, Robert Hamilton of Delaware, Jabez Fitch of Vermont, and David M. Randolph of Virginia. The dismissal of Randolph was complicated for the president by the fact that the marshal was his son-in-law's brother-in-law; he was replaced anyway. In fact, of the seven that Jefferson mentioned specifically, only Federalist marshal for New Hampshire Bradbury Cilley was spared, and he only "because of his [Republican] connections," according to the president-designate. Jefferson described Isaac Parker of Maine as "a very violent and influential and industrious fed," slated for removal "by & by." [33] The marshals' abuse of the power to deputize assistants wholly at their own discretion and their control over the jury selection process were what rankled most deeply.

Deputies of Marshal Ambrose Gordon of Georgia, Republican Senator James Jackson complained, were all Tories who "harass the innocent and old republican characters of this country." Gordon was "open and unrestrained" in his contempt for Jeffersonians. The senator concluded "all the world this way expects" his removal. "He will fall . . . unpitied," wrote another Georgian. According to Matthew Lyon, who claimed to have been victimized by the Vermont marshal, Jabez Fitch had "no title to the good opinion of any honest man." He was a "hard hearted savage" who could "satiate his barbarity on the misery of his victims." Fitch was as severe with other Republicans, James M. Smith has written, as he was with Lyon. Samuel Bradford's deputies in Massachusetts "openly revile and calumniate" Republicans, a Bay State Jeffersonian alleged late in the decade so, even though Bradford remained aloof, he could not be counted an impartial enforcer of the law. The Whisky Rebels in western Pennsylvania considered Marshal David Lenox a personal enemy and singled him out for some very rough treatment in 1793.

Other marshals rigged juries during the wave of sedition trials in 1798–99. David M. Randolph, United States marshal for Virginia, was "alleged to have packed juries," and certainly cooperated with the presiding judges in the Callender trial in empaneling a wholly Federalist jury. Pennsylvania Marshal John Hall in 1801 reminded President Jefferson of his moderate inaugural address, but to no avail. He was displaced after several complaints that he lacked "impartiality in the selection of juries." Charles B. Cochran of South Carolina was described to Jefferson as "a factious and wrong-headed youngster" who "unremittingly checked the free course of justice by his partial selection of jurymen." [34]

Marshals were paid fees for each task, not salaries per annum, and indications are that it led to a significant degree of slackness, if not quite corruption, in the office. Scrupulous marshals like Federalists Allen McLane of Delaware and Jonathan Jackson of Massachusetts found the office "unproductive and troublesome" and successfully petitioned the administration to find them something "more lucrative." [35]

Others, however, found ways to improve the take. Samuel McDowell certainly compromised himself when he made his two brothers deputies. The subordinate McDowells, in turn, allegedly "exacted large Sums of money for the performance of those duties which they alone could execute." Samuel McDowell, the correspondent added, "has not been wholly

ignorant of the profitable game which his Brothers are playing."

It had always been true, former Treasury Secretary Alexander Hamilton wrote to his successor early in 1797, that
Aquila Giles of New York had been guilty of long "delays in
bringing forward monies which came into his hands as Marshal." Although his official income rarely exceeded $100 per
year, Giles himself claimed the office to be all important in
supporting his large family in style. One Republican newspaper was guilty of exaggeration but not fabrication in claim-
ing for Giles in 1800 "a snug little [government] income of
15,000 dollars per annum." True or not, there was patently a
degree of hypocrisy in the administration's response to "delays" in settling accounts involving the collection of fees.
Giles was an ardent and important Federalist, so his remiss-
ness was acknowledged but tolerated for years.

But United States Marshal Michael Payne of North
Carolina, who had gravitated into the Republican party as a
result of his antipathy for the Jay Treaty, was dismissed "for
delinquency" in 1798 when his account was settled a few
months late. Republicans claimed, in restoring Payne to
office three years later, that "his Manly Resistance [to the
treaty] and Independent Mind caused his Dismission."
Whatever the truth of this particular charge, it is patent that
the national administration applied a double standard in
judging "delinquency" in settling marshals' accounts.[36]

The United States marshals, as law enforcement officers,
were in positions visible enough to aid the Federalist interest, both by influencing voters at elections and in other more
subtle ways. Allen McLane of Delaware was marshal during
the presidential election of 1796 when, Richard Peters asserted, "his exertions alone turned the Scale" and produced
a Federalist victory in that state. New York's Aquila Giles
was described in 1800 as "strutting about [the polls] with his
sword and cockade, preaching against the profligacy and
Deism of Jefferson." John Huger, United States marshal for
South Carolina, openly campaigned for John Adams in 1800.
He had succeeded his brother Isaac in that office earlier in

the decade. "The position of federal marshal was awarded to a Huger," George Rogers has written, "to keep that important family group in the Georgetown area allied to the federal cause."

Both Jonathan Jackson of Massachusetts and Thomas Lowrie of New Jersey were closely identified with Alexander Hamilton early in the decade. Both men were state senators as well as marshals. Jackson's "political opinions were those of Hamilton." Lowrie, a director and shareholder of the Society For Useful Manufactures, was perhaps Hamilton's leading advocate in the New Jersey legislature early in the 1790s. Other marshals later in the decade were well-known Adams Federalists. Bradbury Cilley of New Hampshire was identified in 1798 "as firm a federalist as the state affords." John S. West was successfully recommended for the office in 1798 on the basis of "his activity, faithfulness . . . and attachment" in a "particular manner" to the moderate wing of the Federalist party.[37]

The potential for political abuse of the office of United States district court clerk was almost nil, yet it too served a very real political function. It was, to be sure, the lowliest line appointment in the federal judicial establishment, so the clerk's position was used as a dumping ground for relatives of important party men with families they wanted to provide for. The post possessed features that made it compatible with nepotism: it required very little work or skill; it did not pay enough to make it really valuable and, therefore, it was not a widely sought after position; and it was sufficiently powerless, innocuous, and invisible so that it was never singled out for either the attention of the public at large or the opposition party. Enterprising administration leaders in Philadelphia took advantage of the job's very weaknesses to put it to good use.

Two of the clerks were sons-in-law of the district judges in whose courts they served. Robert Boggs, clerk of the United States district court of New Jersey, and Jonathan Steele in New Hampshire, moreover, were both involved Federalists. The former was married to Judge Robert Morris's daughter, the latter to the daughter of Judge John Sullivan. Several others were related to highly placed administration Federalists or kin to important Federalist families in the states. The long-time clerk of the district court in Virginia was William Marshall, John Marshall's brother. Samuel Caldwell, who was court clerk for Pennsylvania's district court, was a nephew of James McHenry, secretary of war to both Washington and Adams. Court Clerk Simeon Baldwin of Connecticut was a highly placed Federalist in his own right and part of the Congregationalist elite that dominated politics in the "land of steady habits." He was also Federalist Congressman Roger Sherman's son-in-law. Abner Neale, clerk of the North Carolina district court, and Matthew Pearce, who occupied the same slot in Delaware, were married into the Blount and Read clans respectively. These two families were highly placed within the Federalist parties of their respective states.[38]

The federal judiciary established in 1789 was politicized from top to bottom, George Washington's "independence" and "integrity" and the obvious threat to constitutional liberties inherent in the situation notwithstanding. Of all the branches of the civil service, the compromising of the judiciary perhaps posed the greatest travesty the Federalists perpetrated in constructing their political organization by means of staffing the federal civil service with party followers. Jurists and law enforcement officers accepted a sensitive and critical responsibility in the new nation, a responsibility they did not always meet impartially and honestly. On the other hand, given the pervasive political atmosphere that governed the entire federal service in the 1790s, little else reasonably could have been expected.

CHAPTER ELEVEN

Party Formation and the Civil Service:
A Quantitative Overview

The following quantitative analysis attempts for the sake of comparison to provide another dimension to this examination of the first United States civil service. The five tables that form the scaffolding for this chapter appear in the appendix. They attempt, with the interpretations here, to place that civil service in a historical perspective that has been necessarily fragmented by the need to deal with it piecemeal up to now. Table 1 analyzes political affiliations in the civil service; Table 2 relates the service to the American Revolution and its political aftermath; Table 3 provides some insight into the relationships of Federalists and Antifederalists in the 1780s to party formations in the 1790s; Table 4 compares the appointees of George Washington to those of John Adams; Table 5 deals with the class and status of the Federalists in the civil service. Together they may provide a useful overview of what actually happened politically to the first civil service under the Federalists.

Most of the rank and file of that first civil service in the 1790s left no historical information behind, beyond some stark vital data in various federal, state, and local records. Nevertheless, enough data were uncovered from sources described elsewhere to analyze more than one-third of that group. Table 1, *Political Affiliations in the First Civil Ser-*

vice, indicates that about 2,435 men at one time or another appeared on the roster of federal employees in the states between 1789 and 1801. The political affiliation of 885 (36.3 percent) was uncovered. Of these, 559 (63.1 percent of those known, 22.9 percent of the entire service) were Federalists.[1] Of those identified, 58 (6.5 percent of those known, 2.3 percent of the entire service) were Jeffersonian Republicans. The remainder, so far as is known, eschewed politics. These figures indicate beyond doubt the significant degree to which the first civil service was politicized by the Federalist party.

Tables 2 and 3 lend support to those recent interpretations that conclude the early national period cannot be understood only as a separate historical entity beginning with the ratification of the Constitution, but as part of the revolutionary era as well.[2] The Constitution, if the composition of the first civil service is an indicator, was a much less profound catalyst of political change than historians have traditionally believed. If we suspend for a moment the concept of the year 1789 as forming a political watershed year, and think of the era 1763–1801 (and perhaps beyond) as an era in itself, then Table 2 will suggest the extensive degree to which the politics of the 1790s was conditioned on both the political loyalties developed during the American Revolution and the political conflicts engendered by the Confederation.

The continuing impact of the American Revolution on the "new" politics of the 1790s is made clear in Table 2, *Federalists in the First Civil Service and the American Revolution*. It is well known, of course, that revolutionary rhetoric formed a significant part of the verbiage of party hostilities in the Federalist decade; Table 2 indicates that the association went well beyond words. To a significant degree, revolutionary credentials were necessary, along with Federalist political leanings, for a place in the civil service. Some 487 known Federalists in the civil service were old enough to have taken part in the Revolution. Of these, 225 (46.2 percent) were active in the Whig cause: 134 (27.5 percent) were officers of the Continental army; 11 (2.2 percent) were enlisted men in that army; 56 (11.4 percent) saw active militia service; and another 24 (4.9 percent) held visible

Whig civil positions. On the other hand, only 17 (3.4 percent) were identifiable Loyalists. This small representation from among a significant element of revolutionary society, according to credible studies of loyalism, indicates that, even by the 1790s, former Loyalists were still fiercely discriminated against in politics. Significantly, some 74 former officers in the Continental army (55.2 percent of the Federalists who were Continental army officers) were members of the Society of the Cincinnati.

All in all then, if the composition of the civil service in the 1790s may be taken as an indicator, there were strong links, not only between the politics of the Revolution and that of the 1790s, but some relationship in particular between service in the Continental army and visible positions with the Federalist party cadre. The data do not indicate that Federalists were Whigs to a greater extent than were Republicans; they do demonstrate the close political ties to the revolutionary past.[3]

This last conclusion is borne out more directly by the findings summarized in Table 3, *Constitutional Federalists and Antifederalists, 1780s/Federalists and Republicans, 1790s: The First Civil Service*. The degree of political continuity between the politics of the Confederation and that of the Federalist decade runs fairly high.[4] There were 559 known Federalists in the first civil service. Some 198 appointees in the 1790s can be identified as active Constitutional Federalists in the 1780s. That is to say they supported the Constitution at the Philadelphia Convention, at a state ratifying convention, or openly in their communities. If we remember that the Constitutional movement, by all accounts, attracted few activists and was not particularly a popularly oriented movement, that number seems fairly high in and of itself.[5] More to the point though, is the degree of continuity evident within these figures. Of the 885 whose politics and backgrounds can be determined, the 198 (22.3 percent) represent nearly a quarter of the known civil service appointees. Moreover, 173 (87.3 percent) of the 198 known Constitutional Federalists on the civil list surfaced as Federalist party activists in the 1790s. If the latter may be assumed to be party

cadre in the states, political continuity with the preconstitutional past within secondary leadership ranks of the
Federalist party ran very high, perhaps as high or higher than
it did at the national leadership level.

This continuity is borne out by other data. Only ten (5.0
percent) of the Constitutional Federalists in the civil service
became Republicans in the 1790s. Attrition in Antifederalist
ranks the other way was much higher, however, indicating
the degree to which the success of the movement for constitutional reform undermined the passing political opposition of the 1780s. Some thirty-one (3.5 percent of the identifiable politicos in the civil service) were Antifederalists in
the 1780s. Of these, only nine (29.0 percent of the Antifederalists) became Republicans in the 1790s, while fifteen
(48.3 percent of the Antifederalists) ended up in the
Federalist party.* From these data we can draw some sugges-
tive inferences, pending other studies: (1) there were, in fact,
strong ties, based on hard evidence, between active support
for constitutional reform in the Confederation and leadership
in Federalist ranks in the 1790s; (2) the success of the Constitutional movement may have decimated the ranks of the
potential opposition for at least part of the ensuing decade;
(3) known unrepentant Antifederalists were systematically
excluded from appointment to the first civil service.

Table 4, *Party Appointments in the Civil Service: George
Washington and John Adams,* carries the story into the 1790s
by taking into account and comparing the appointment and
removal records of the two Federalist presidents. The most
salient fact to bear in mind in comparing the political pre-
dilections of the two Federalist presidents is that George
Washington made more than three-quarters (78.4 percent) of
the known appointments to the federal civil service. Of his
appointees for whom biographical and political data can be
found, 371 of the 576 (64.4 percent) were Federalists. John

---

* The significance of the numbers here will be distorted by the
fact that the individuals tallied were *all* in the civil service, and
federal appointments may well have been an important factor con-
ditioning latter-day political affiliations.

Adams inherited a functioning federal bureaucracy and, succeeding the idolized Washington as he did, and with no bracing removals precedent to sustain him, found that his ability to clean house was severely circumscribed. Thus Adams nominated only 158 (21.5 percent) of those for whom data could be found. Of these, 124 (78.4 percent) were Federalists, indicating that the New Englander brought to office with him a somewhat greater political awareness than his predecessor. Within this context, of course, both presidents clearly took political affiliation into account in shaping the federal service and, given the cycle of increasingly intense party politics in the Federalist decade, Adams's relatively greater awareness of political realities was, after all, to be expected. George Washington, however, was clearly the first partisan Federalist president.

Perhaps the divergence of political attitudes between the two Federalist presidents can best be demonstrated by taking note of their respective nominations of Jeffersonian Republicans and their policy with regard to removals. In the eight years of his presidency, Washington named some thirty-five Republicans to office, or 6 percent of all his appointees about whom information could be found. John Adams named just two Republicans, or 1.2 percent of all those appointed in his administration. In eight years in office, moreover, Washington removed just ten federal officers, of whom four were Federalists, two Republicans, and the remainder possessed of no discernible political leanings. Adams, on the other hand, in one term removed sixteen, of whom six were Federalists and nine Republicans. Perhaps the growing consciousness of party is as evident in this last statistic as it is in the first grouping of data introduced on the overall prevalence of Federalist party men in the first civil service.

Who were these party men? Table 5, *Class and Status of Federalists in the Civil Service,* attempts to confront this question. Perceptions of class and status factors vis-à-vis occupation, education, officer rank in the Continental army, or other criteria may differ, so I have introduced both several complementary indexes and a summary category dividing this microcosm of Federalist society into "More Articulate" and "Less Articulate." The latter designations are based on evaluation of known factors suggesting class and status taken in combination. These include several factors also evaluated individually in this chapter. Altogether, the combined class/ status factors include property ownership and financial condition, occupation, nature of revolutionary service, place in community, kinship ties, education, and officeholding outside the civil service.

Much overlapping and a good deal of conflicting evidence crop up, as one must expect in an eighteenth-century American society that was at least somewhat mobile. In this case, my rule of thumb was not to finally categorize any Federalist as "Less" or "More" Articulate unless I had hard information for six of the eight enumerated categories. Once this qualification was met, to be placed in either category there had to be a preponderance of evidence on one side or the other by at least a four-to-two ratio. For example, if an individual postmaster was a college graduate, clergyman, tied by marriage to gentry, and clearly held a high place in his community but was just as clearly possessed of a modest income and property, he would be considered "More Articulate." On the other hand, if a customs officer was a small shopkeeper with a fair amount of property but with a grade-school education and had never held office in his town, he would be considered "Less Articulate."

The 559 known Federalists in the first civil service form the basis for this appraisal. Of these, 260 (46.5 percent) held elite occupations while 148 (26.4 percent) did not. No decisive information could be found for 151 (27.0 percent). With regard to wealth and property, 192 (34.3 percent) were clearly rich or well to do, while 83 each (14.8 percent), or 166 in all (29.6 percent), were either just solvent or in some kind of financial difficulty. The financial condition of 201 (35.9 percent) remains obscure or indeterminate. In sum, following the previously outlined guidelines, 284 (50.8 percent) of the Federalist leaders in the civil service can be described as "More Articulate" while 126 (22.5 percent) were clearly "Less Articulate." Either no information could be found for 149 (26.6 percent), or they defied facile pigeonholing. These data on class and status rest on hard information for nearly three-quarters of the known Federalists in the first civil service; it is worth adding that only half of those about whom judgments can be made can be described as gentry, elite, or upper class. On the other hand, about one-quarter of the men were clearly in and of the American middle class.[6]

If we accept the premise that all of these men may fairly be characterized as part of the local party leadership cadre, then it becomes clear that the Federalist political base has been misrepresented in the past. The "party of the aristocracy" really had strong local ties to the middle class, ties that were both personal and quasi-professional and not merely ideological in nature. It explains more logically, perhaps, why that party held virtually full power for more than a decade and survived as a major political force for more than a quarter century.

APPENDIX

Quantitative Data
Tables 1–5

TABLE 1

Political Affiliations in the First Civil Service, 1789–1801

DEPART-MENT	tot. men in CS	# pol. & biog. data avail.	% data avail.	# of F	% of F: total CS	% of F: known only	# of R	% of R: total CS	% of R: known only
CUSTOMS	944	295	31.2	178	18.8	60.3	17	1.8	5.7
INTERNAL REVENUE	533	262	49.1	178	33.3	67.9	14	2.6	5.3
POST OFFICE	824	220	26.6	112	13.5	50.9	20	2.4	9.0
JUDI-CIARY	134	108	80.5	91	67.9	84.2	7	5.2	6.4
TOTALS	2,435	885	36.3	559	22.9	63.1	58	2.3	6.5

Key to abbreviations: CS = civil service. F = Federalists. R = Republicans. tot. = total. pol. = political. biog. = biographical. avail. = available.

275

TABLE 2

Federalists in the First Civil Service and the American Revolution

DEPT.	total known F	too young for Rev.[1]	CS F adults: Rev. Era #[2]	CS F adults: Rev. Era %	# Off. CA	% Ad. F	# non-com. CA	% Ad. F	# militia
CUST.	178	19	159	89.3	70	44.0	6	3.7	20
INT. REV.	178	15	163	91.5	32	19.6	2	1.2	18
POST OFF.	112	19	93	83.0	11	11.8	1	1.0	6
JUD.	91	19	72	79.1	21	29.1	2	2.7	12
TOT.	559	72	487	87.1	134	27.5	11	2.2	56

DEPT.	% Ad. F	# sig. Whig civ. act.	% Ad. F	tot. # active Whigs	% Ad. F	# L	% Ad. F	# SC	% CA Off.
CUST.	12.5	3	1.8	99	62.2	7	4.4	37	52.8
INT. REV.	11.0	5	3.0	57	34.9	2	1.2	17	53.1
POST OFF.	6.4	3	3.2	21	22.5	5	5.3	7	63.6
JUD.	16.6	13	18.0	48	66.6	3	4.1	13	61.9
TOT.	11.4	24	4.9	225	46.2	17	3.4	74	55.2

[1] Born after 1759.
[2] Born before 1760.

Key to abbreviations: CS = civil service. F = Federalists. Rev. = Revolution. Off. = officers. CA = Continental army. Ad. = adult. noncom. = enlisted men and noncommissioned officers. civ. = civilian. act. = activity. tot. = total. L = Loyalists. SC = Society of the Cincinnati. sig. = significant.

TABLE 3

Constitutional Federalists and Antifederalists, 1780s/ Federalists and Republicans, 1790s: The First Civil Service

DEPT.	# pol. & biog. data avail.	tot. F in CS	# known CF 1780s in CS	% of F	% of CS	# CF to F	% CF/F of F in CS	% of CF only in CS	CF can't trace to 90s	% of CF only
CUST.	295	178	66	37.0	22.3	56	31.4	84.8	8	12.1
INT. REV.	262	178	50	28.0	19.0	44	24.7	88.0	3	6.0
POST OFF.	220	112	28	25.0	12.7	26	23.2	92.8	2	7.1
JUD.	108	91	54	59.3	50.0	47	51.6	87.0	2	3.7
TOT.	885	559	198	35.4	22.3	173	30.9	87.3	15	7.5

DEPT.	CF to R	% R of CF only	# AF 80s in CS	% AF in CS	# AF 80s to R 90s	% AF to R	# AF 80s to F 90s	% AF to F	# no info. on AF	% no info. on AF
CUST.	2	3.0	11	3.7	5	45.4	5	45.4	1	9.0
INT. REV.	3	6.0	9	3.4	2	22.2	5	55.5	2	22.2
POST OFF.	0	——	6	2.7	2	33.3	1	16.6	3	50.0
JUD.	5	9.2	5	4.6	——	——	4	80.0	1	20.0
TOT.	10	5.0	31	3.5	9	29.0	15	48.3	7	22.5

Key to abbreviations: CS = civil service. F = Federalists. R = Republicans. pol. = political. biog. = biographical. avail. = available. CF = Constitutional Federalists. AF = Antifederalists. info. = information.

TABLE 4

Party Appointments in the Civil Service: George Washington and John Adams

DEPT.	# pol. & biog. data avail.	# app. by GW	% app. by GW	# app. by JA	% app. by JA	F app. GW	% F of whole GW	% F of apps.	# F app. JA	% F of whole JA	% F of apps.
CUST.	295	263	89.1	32	10.8	153	51.8	58.1	25	8.4	78.1
INT. REV.	262	186	70.9	76	29.0	118	45.0	63.4	60	22.9	78.9
POST OFF.	69 *	41	59.4	28	40.5	29	42.0	70.7	19	27.5	67.8
JUD.	108	86	79.6	22	20.3	71	65.7	82.5	20	18.5	90.9
TOT.	734 †	576	78.4	158	21.5	371	50.5	64.4	124	16.8	78.4

DEPT.	# R app. GW	% R of whole GW	% R of apps.	# R app. JA	% R of whole JA	% R of apps.	# rem. GW	# F rem. GW	# R rem. GW	# rem. JA	# F rem. JA	# R rem. JA
CUST.	18	6.1	6.8	1	0.3	3.1	8	4	2	9	4	5
INT. REV.	13	4.9	6.9	1	0.3	1.3	1	0	0	5	1	3
POST OFF.	1	1.4	2.4	—	—	—	0	0	0	0	0	0
JUD.	3	2.7	3.4	—	—	—	1	0	0	2	1	1
TOT.	35	4.7	6.0	2	0.02	1.2	10	4	2	16	6	9

* Date of appointments based on partial information only (69 of 220 or 31.3 percent). Published post office records do not list dates of appointment for postmasters. Those whose dates of appointment are known were garnered from a variety of sources.

† Total diminished by gaps in information on dates of post office appointments. Data represent 734 of 885 (82.9 percent).

Key to abbreviations: F = Federalists. R = Republicans. pol. = political. biog. = biographical. avail. = available. app. = appointed. GW = George Washington. JA = John Adams. apps. = appointments. rem. = removed.

TABLE 5

Class and Status of Federalists in the Civil Service

DEPT.	# F in CS	El. Occ. F*	% of F	Mid. Occ. F†	% of F	# not known	% not known	# Rich	% Rich	# Mid.	% Mid.
CUST.	178	89	50.0	51	28.6	38	21.3	60	33.7	36	20.2
INT. REV.	178	58	32.5	37	20.7	83	46.6	56	31.4	26	14.6
POST OFF.	112	36	32.1	58	51.7	18	16.0	26	23.2	12	10.7
JUD.	91	77	84.6	2	2.1	12	13.1	50	54.9	9	9.8
TOT.	559	260	46.5	148	26.4	151	27.0	192	34.3	83	14.8

DEPT.	# ins. b.r.	% ins. b.r.	# not known	% not known	# More Artic.‡	%	# Less Artic.‡	%	# not known	%
CUST.	38	21.3	44	24.7	85	47.7	52	29.2	41	23.0
INT. REV.	27	15.1	69	38.7	88	49.4	30	16.8	60	33.7
POST OFF.	7	6.2	67	59.8	42	37.5	41	36.6	29	25.8
JUD.	11	12.0	21	23.0	69	75.8	3	3.2	19	20.8
TOT.	83	14.8	201	35.9	284	50.8	126	22.5	149	26.6

* Lawyers, physicians, manufacturers or shipbuilders, clergy, bankers, international merchants, shipmasters, gentleman farmers, or planters.

† Storekeepers, printers, artisans, seamen, clerks, civil servants, innkeepers, teachers, fishermen, farmers, unemployed.

‡ Designation of "Less" or "More" Articulate is based on an individual evaluation of known factors in combination: occupation, officeholding, property ownership, financial situation, kinship ties, nature of revolutionary service, education, and place in the community. The term "More" or "Less" Articulate is unsatisfactory in some ways, but it does convey the relative status differences I am trying to establish here.

Key to abbreviations: F = Federalists. CS = civil service. El. = elite. Occ. = occupation. Mid. = middling. ins. = insolvent. b.r. = bankrupt. Artic. = articulate.

Notes

CHAPTER ONE

1. George Washington to James McHenry, November 30, 1789, *The Writings of George Washington*, John C. Fitzpatrick, ed. (39 vols., Washington, D.C., 1931–44), XXX, 471.

2. James McHenry to George Washington, April 17, 1789, Applications For Office Under President Washington, Series VII, George Washington Papers (Manuscript Division, Library of Congress), vol. XIX; McHenry to Washington, January 1 and 6, 1791, ibid., vol. VII.

3. William Paterson to Philemon Dickerson, February 2, 1791, ibid., vol. IX.

4. Alexander Hamilton to James McHenry, April 15, 1793, *The Papers of Alexander Hamilton*, Harold C. Syrett, ed. (24 vols., New York, 1961–76), XIV, 287–89.

5. Alfred F. Young, *The Democratic-Republicans of New York: The Origins, 1763–1797* (Chapel Hill, 1967), 159–61.

6. Memo titled "Substance of conversations," undated [1791], from Jeremiah Wadsworth to George Washington, Applications For Office Under President Washington, Series VII, George Washington Papers, vol. XXVIII; Wadsworth to ——— [Washington], February 22, 1791, ibid.

7. Jabez Bowen to George Washington, June 13, 1790, Applications For Office Under President Washington, Series VII, George Washington Papers, vol. III; Bowen to ——— [Washington, undated, 1790], titled "Information from Mr. Bowen respecting characters in the state of Rhode Island," ibid.; Theodore Foster to

281

Washington, February 18, 1790, ibid., vol. XI and passim; George
C. Rogers, Jr., *Evolution of a Federalist: William Loughton Smith
of Charleston, 1758–1812* (Columbia, S.C., 1962), 212–13. The Applications For Office Under President Washington contain extensive information on the president's involvement in the Rhode Island political situation.

8. Carl Russell Fish, *The Civil Service and the Patronage* (New
York, 1905), 8–9.

9. Leonard D. White, *The Federalists: A Study in Administrative History, 1789–1801* (New York, 1948), 237–38.

10. George Washington to Richard Potts, July 20, 1794, *Writings
of Washington*, Fitzpatrick, ed., XXXIII, 436.

11. Stephen Higginson to Alexander Hamilton, November 11,
1789, *Papers of Hamilton*, Syrett, ed., V, 507–11.

12. Jeremiah Olney to Alexander Hamilton, June 7, 1790, ibid.,
VI, 458–59.

13. Alexander Hamilton, *Continentalist VI*, 1782, cited in Lisle
A. Rose, *Prologue to Democracy: The Federalists in the South
1789–1801* (Lexington, 1968), 1.

14. Alexander Hamilton to Jeremiah Olney, April 2, 1793, *Papers
of Hamilton*, Syrett, ed., XIV, 276–77.

15. White, *The Federalists*, 116–18.

16. For this particular exchange, see George Washington to
Alexander Hamilton, September 27, 1790, *Papers of Hamilton*,
Syrett, ed., VII, 75–76. Abundant documentation exists to reveal the
relationship between the two men on the matter of appointments.
See ibid., passim; *Writings of Washington*, Fitzpatrick, ed., XXX,
passim; Applications For Office Under President Washington,
Series VII, George Washington Papers, passim.

17. Alexander Hamilton to Simon Gross, April 20, 1791, *Papers
of Hamilton*, Syrett, ed., VIII, 301–2.

18. This is an important story recounted in chapter 10, dealing
with the judicial establishment. See William Ellery to Alexander
Hamilton, December 16, 1793, Applications For Office Under President Washington, Series VII, George Washington Papers, XV.

19. Alexander Hamilton to Richard Harison, June 12, 1793,
Papers of Hamilton, Syrett, ed., XIV, 539–40.

20. Alexander Hamilton to George Washington, May 4, 1793,
ibid., 412–14n. The editors provide an excellent note on the matter.

21. White, *The Federalists*, 273.

22. Ibid., 93.

23. Fish, *The Civil Service and the Patronage*, 24–25; Page

Smith, *John Adams* (2 vols., New York, 1962), II, 922. Adams's fear of congressional, and especially Senate, involvement in nominations to office went very deep. Manning Dauer believed it stemmed from fear of "aristocratic influence" from an elite body. Dauer, *The Adams Federalists* (Baltimore, 1953), 51–52. Fish suggested that Adams felt especially vulnerable to Senate influence because he knew far fewer important people than did Washington. Even as vice-president, Dauer points out, it was Adams who cast the deciding vote in the Senate to maintain the removal power of the president without the consent of the Senate. Ibid., 84.

24. Smith, *John Adams*, II, 942–43. Abigail Adams pointedly described Adams's propensity for asserting political criteria in the matter of patronage. Her husband "would appoint to office merit, virtue, and talents, and when Jacobins possess these, they will stand a chance, but it will ever be an additional recommendation that they are friends to order and government." Ibid.

25. John Adams to Oliver Wolcott, Jr., October 4, 1800, *Memoirs of the Administrations of Washington and John Adams, edited from the Papers of Oliver Wolcott, Secretary of the Treasury* (2 vols., New York, 1846), George Gibbs, ed., II, 431–32; Adams to Timothy Pickering, August 1, 1799, *The Works of John Adams* (10 vols., Boston, 1850–56), Charles Francis Adams, ed., IX, 5.

26. This episode is recounted in chapter 3. See John Adams to Benjamin Lincoln, March 10, 1800, Mellen Chamberlain Collection (Boston Public Library); Paine Wingate to ———, June 18, 1798, John Adams entry, Letters of Application and Recommendation During the Administration of John Adams, General Records of the Department of State, Record Group 59 (National Archives); Fisher Ames to Christopher Gore, July 28, 1798, *The Works of Fisher Ames* (2 vols., Boston, 1854), Seth Ames, ed., I, 237.

27. John Habersham to Oliver Wolcott, Jr., April 13, 1797, Edward White entry, Letters of Application and Recommendation During the Administration of John Adams.

28. John Adams to Elbridge Gerry, December 30, 1800, *Works of Adams*, Charles F. Adams, ed., IX, 577.

29. This incident is dealt with in chapter 5. Daniel Bedinger to Josiah Parker, April 25, 1797, and passim, Daniel Bedinger entry, Letters of Application and Recommendation During the Administration of John Adams; John Adams to Oliver Wolcott, Jr., October 4, 1800, *Works of Adams*, Charles F. Adams, ed., IX, 87.

30. Dauer, *Adams Federalists*, 215–19.

31. John Haskell to Thomas Jefferson, October 29, 1804, John

Haskell entry, Letters of Application and Recommendation During the Administration of Thomas Jefferson, General Records of the Department of State, Record Group 59 (National Archives). The "midnight appointments" were made for political reasons as much as anything else. See Carl E. Prince, "The Passing of the Aristocracy: Jefferson's Removal of the Federalists, 1801–1805," *Journal of American History*, LVII (December 1970), 563–75.

32. Stephen Higginson to Timothy Pickering, April 16, 1800, "Letters of S. Higginson," John Franklin Jameson, ed., *American Historical Association Annual Report*, 1896 (Washington, D.C., 1896), 836.

33. Allen Jones to Alexander Martin, November 27, 1798, Robert Fenner entry, Letters of Application and Recommendation During the Administration of John Adams.

34. Frederick Muhlenberg to John Adams, June 5, 1798, Frederick Muhlenberg entry, ibid.

35. Dauer, *Adams Federalists*, 137–38; Robert Troup to Oliver Wolcott, Jr., April 22, 1797, William Seton to Wolcott, April 21, 1797, William Seton entry, Letters of Application and Recommendation During the Administration of John Adams. My view of Adams on appointments differs markedly from that of Leonard White, *The Federalists*.

36. "List of Civil Officers of the United States . . . October 1, 1792," and "Roll of the Officers, Civil, Military, and Naval of the United States [1801]," *American State Papers, Miscellaneous: Documents, Legislative and Executive of the Congress of the United States*, Walter Lowrie and Walter S. Franklin, eds. (2 vols., Washington, D.C., 1834), I, 57–68, 260–319.

37. James McHenry to Alexander Hamilton, September 30, 1792, *Papers of Hamilton*, Syrett, ed., XII, 510.

38. ———— [petition torn] to James Madison [1801–3], Benjamin Lincoln entry, Letters of Application and Recommendation During the Administration of Thomas Jefferson.

39. Thomas Cooper et al. to Thomas Jefferson, May 23, 1801, William Henderson entry, ibid.

40. Nathaniel Morton, Jr., and Josiah Dean to Albert Gallatin, November 6, 1805, Josiah Wardell entry, ibid. See Leonard White, *The Federalists*, passim, on the creation and operation of the customs service. However, one should read White on this subject in conjunction with Donald H. Stewart, "The Press and Political Corruption During the Federalist Administrations," *Political Science Quarterly*, LXVII (1952), 437.

41. "Roll of the Officers, Civil, Military, and Naval [1801]," and "A List of the Officers Employed in the Collection of the Internal Revenues of the United States . . . July, 1796," *American State Papers, Miscellaneous*, I, 260–319, 568–73.

42. Alexander Hamilton to John Armstrong, Jr., April 1, 1793, *Papers of Hamilton*, Syrett, ed., XIV, 269–70.

43. James Jackson to Thomas Jefferson, July 18, 1801, William Stephens entry, Letters of Application and Recommendation During the Administration of Thomas Jefferson.

44. William Findley to Thomas Jefferson, February 26, 1801, Samuel Bryan entry, ibid.

45. Joseph Bloomfield to Aaron Burr, April 8, 1801, William Rossell entry, ibid.

46. Pierce Butler to Thomas Jefferson, September 3, 1801, Daniel Stevens entry, ibid.

47. Volumes A–K, Letters Sent by the Postmaster General, 1789–1836, Records of the Post Office Department, Record Group 28 (National Archives); "Roll of the Officers, Civil, Military, and Naval [1801]," *American State Papers, Miscellaneous*, I, 260–319.

48. This will be discussed in some detail in chapter 8.

49. Wesley E. Rich, *The History of the United States Post Office to the Year 1829* (Cambridge, 1924), 75, 115.

50. Ibid., 128.

51. Timothy Pickering to Thomas Robie, March 31, 1792, Vol. VI, Timothy Pickering Papers (Massachusetts Historical Society).

52. John Armstrong to Ephraim Kirby, June 2, 1801, Ephraim Kirby Papers (Perkins Library, Duke University); Ephraim Kirby to Thomas Jefferson, November 10, 1801, Ephraim Kirby entry, Abraham Baldwin to Thomas Jefferson, March 6, 1801, Joseph Habersham entry, Letters of Application and Recommendation During the Administration of Thomas Jefferson.

53. For the last, see William Findley to Thomas Jefferson, February 26, 1801, Samuel Bryan entry, Letters of Application and Recommendation During the Administration of Thomas Jefferson. For representative examples of other allegations, see Gideon Granger to Thomas Jefferson, April 15, 1801, Elisa [Elizur] Goodrich entry, John Langdon to Gideon Granger, December 4, 1801, Elisha Hinman entry, ibid.

54. See "List of Civil Officers of the United States . . . October 1, 1792," *American State Papers, Miscellaneous*, I, 57–68.

55. Prince, "Passing of the Aristocracy," *Journal of American History*, LVII (December, 1970), 567–69.

CHAPTER TWO

1. For background information on Massachusetts Federalism, I have relied on James M. Banner, Jr., *To the Hartford Convention: The Federalists and the Origins of Party Politics in Massachusetts, 1789–1815* (New York, 1969); David H. Fischer, "The Myth of the Essex Junto," *William and Mary Quarterly*, 3rd series, XXI (1964), 191–235; Fischer, *The Revolution of American Conservatism: The Federalist Party in the Era of Jeffersonian Democracy* (New York, 1965).

2. For Hodijah Baylies, see ———— [illegible] to ———— Bishop, December 25, 1804, Nathaniel Williams entry, Letters of Application and Recommendation During the Administration of Thomas Jefferson, General Records of the Department of State, Record Group 59 (National Archives); Nathaniel Morton, Jr., and Josiah Dean to Albert Gallatin, November 6, 1805, Josiah Wardwell entry, ibid.; Abraham Wardwell et al. to Thomas Jefferson, December 19, 1804, Anonymous entry, ibid.; Clifford K. Shipton, *Sibley's Harvard Graduates: Biographical Sketches of Those Who Attended Harvard College* (16 vols., Boston, 1873–1972), XIV, 553; *George Washington's Correspondence Concerning the Society of the Cincinnati*, Edgar Erskine Hume, ed. (Baltimore, 1941), 201; Samuel E. Morison, *The Life and Letters of Harrison Gray Otis, Federalist, 1765–1848* (2 vols., Boston, 1913), II, 133, 133n.

3. Only some of the petitions demanding Edward Pope's removal and describing his political activities survive. See Josiah Dean to Samuel Bishop, January 18, 1804, Dean et al. to Albert Gallatin, August 27, 1805, and Dean to Thomas Jefferson, July 7, 1808, Isaiah Weston entry, John Nye to Jefferson, November 28, 1804, Abraham Wardwell et al. to Jefferson, December 19, 1804, Anonymous entry, Jacob Hafford's Deposition, July 4, 1808, Nathaniel Howland entry, Letters of Application and Recommendation During the Administration of Thomas Jefferson; Daniel Ricketson, *The History of New Bedford, Massachusetts* (New Bedford, 1858), 206–7, 293, 332.

4. Other examples of Federalist customshouse officers in the Cape area include collectors Joseph Otis (Harrison Gray Otis's uncle) at Barnstable on Cape Cod, and Stephen Hussey, a representative of another powerful Federalist family, on Nantucket Island.

5. Samuel E. Morison, *The Maritime History of Massachusetts* (Sentry Edition, Boston, 1961), 144–45.

6. Both for Plymouth politics in general and William Watson, see

George Partridge to George Washington, July 27, 1789, Applications for Office Under President Washington, Series VII, George Washington Papers (Manuscript Division, Library of Congress), vol. XXII; Henry Warren to Thomas Jefferson, September 5, 1801, and November 10, 1802, Henry Warren entry, Nathaniel Niles to Jefferson, September 20, 1802, William Watson entry, Albert Gallatin's note, c. June 20, 1804, Calvin Chaddock Croswell entry, Letters of Application and Recommendation During the Administration of Thomas Jefferson; Shipton, *Sibley's Harvard Graduates*, XIII, 149–53; William T. Davis, *History of the Town of Plymouth* (Philadelphia, 1885), 102, 170, 171; Davis, *Ancient Landmarks of Plymouth* (Boston, 1883), 82, 231, 253, 278.

7. There are many secondary accounts of Benjamin Lincoln's career, but the best by far is that contained in Shipton, *Sibley's Harvard Graduates*, XII, 416–38. See also the Benjamin Lincoln-Theodore Sedgwick correspondence, passim, 1789–1800, Jonathan Jackson to Lincoln, August 1, 1789, April 3, 1791, Tobias Lear to Lincoln, April 8, 1791, and passim, William Jackson to Lincoln, March 15, 1799, and passim, Benjamin Lincoln Papers (Massachusetts Historical Society); Lincoln to George Washington, August 13, 1789, Applications For Office Under President Washington, Series VII, George Washington Papers, vol. IV, and vols. IV, XVIII, XXV, passim; George Washington to Lincoln, August 14, 1791, *The Writings of George Washington*, John C. Fitzpatrick, ed. (39 vols., Washington, D.C., 1931–34), XXXI, 335–36 and passim; Lincoln to Alexander Hamilton, February 16, December 4, 1790, Stephen Higginson to Hamilton, August 24, 1793, *The Papers of Alexander Hamilton*, Harold C. Syrett, ed. (24 vols., New York, 1961–76), VI, 268–69, VII, 196–98, XV, 273–76 respectively, and passim; Stephen Higginson to Timothy Pickering, January 12, 1800, "Letters of S. Higginson," John Franklin Jameson, ed., *American Historical Association Annual Report*, 1896 (Washington, D.C., 1896), 835; Leonard D. White, *The Federalists: A Study in Administrative History, 1789–1801* (New York, 1948), 304, 312, 315–16; Winfred Bernhard, *Fisher Ames, Federalist and Statesman 1758–1808* (Chapel Hill, 1965), 67, 73; John Carroll and Mary Ashworth, *George Washington: First in Peace* (New York, 1957), 532n; Fischer, *Revolution of American Conservatism*, 251; Page Smith, *John Adams* (2 vols., New York, 1962), II, 739, 762–63, 941–42, 982. The other customs officers at Boston—naval officer James Lovell, surveyor Thomas Melville, and revenue cutter captain John Foster Williams—were also Federalists.

8. Petition to James Madison [undated, 1801], and passim, Ben-

jamin Lincoln entry, Letters of Application and Recommendation During the Administration of Thomas Jefferson; Shipton, *Sibley's Harvard Graduates*, XII, 437.

9. Fischer, "Myth of the Essex Junto," *William and Mary Quarterly*, XXI (1964), 191–235, particularly pp. 217, 225. Benjamin Goodhue to George Washington, July 22, 1789, Benjamin Goodhue to Oliver Wolcott, Jr., March 31, 1795, Applications For Office Under President Washington, Series VII, George Washington Papers, vols. XII, XXVII respectively. Similar lists submitted to Washington from other places in the Union will be discussed at appropriate points in the book. Henry Warren to Thomas Jefferson, November 10, 1802, Henry Warren entry, Letters of Application and Recommendation During the Administration of Thomas Jefferson; Hartford, Connecticut *American Mercury*, August 7, September 4, 800; Boston *Independent Chronicle*, July–September 1800, passim.

10. For Joseph Hiller, see Henry Warren to Thomas Jefferson, November 10, 1802, Henry Warren entry, Letters of Application and Recommendation During the Administration of Thomas Jefferson; ibid., William R. Lee entry, passim; Jacob Crowninshield to Jefferson, December 15, 1801, John Gibaut entry, ibid., Albert Gallatin to Jefferson, December 10, 1802, Albert Gallatin Papers (Manuscript Division, Library of Congress); Stephen Higginson to John Adams, July 4, 1789, "Letters of Higginson," *American Historical Association Annual Report*, 1896, Jameson, ed., 767; James D. Phillips, *Salem and the Indies* (Boston, 1947), 215, 254.

11. For Pickman, see Benjamin Goodhue to George Washington, June 30, 1789, Applications For Office Under President Washington, Series VII, George Washington Papers, vol. XII; —— to ——, November 26, 1802, Joseph Story entry, Letters of Application and Recommendation During the Administration of Thomas Jefferson; James D. Phillips, *Salem in the Eighteenth Century* (Boston, 1937), 409; James H. Stark, *The Loyalist of Massachusetts* (Boston, 1910), 126–31; Morison, *Maritime History of Massachusetts*, 25.

12. For Putnam, see Benjamin Goodhue to George Washington, July 22, 1789, Applications For Office Under President Washington, Series VII, George Washington Papers, vol. XII; Samuel Ward to Thomas Jefferson, November 10, 1802, Samuel Ward entry, Letters of Application and Recommendation During the Administration of Thomas Jefferson; Phillips, *Salem in the Eighteenth Century*, 232, 398, 408; Phillips, "Political Fights and

Local Squabbles in Salem, 1800–1806," *Essex Institute Historical Collections*, LXXXII (1946), 7.

13. The ports of Gloucester, Marblehead, and Ipswich were all in the hands of important Essex Federalists. Epes Sargeant (to 1795) and William Tuck (from 1795) were the collectors, and Samuel Whittemore served as surveyor at Gloucester. Several officers and subordinates at the customshouse were members of the Cincinnati; Joseph Allen, a gauger of customs, was a presidential elector for John Adams in 1796. At Marblehead, Samuel Gerry, Elbridge's brother, was collector. Appointed in 1790 as a result of the strong intercession of Elbridge at a time when he was an important Massachusetts Federalist, Samuel was removed in 1802 by Jefferson in the face of vigorous but unavailing protests by his brother. This in spite of Elbridge Gerry's importance to the Republican party in New England. Asa Andrews and Jeremiah Staniford guided the Ipswich customshouse.

For Sargeant, see Phillips, *Salem in the Eighteenth Century*, 386. For Tuck, see William Tuck's deposition, July 3, 1795, Box 4, Harrison Gray Otis Papers (Massachusetts Historical Society); Henry Warren to Jefferson, November 10, 1802, Henry Warren entry, Letters of Application and Recommendation During the Administration of Thomas Jefferson.

For Whittemore, see Levi Lincoln to Jefferson, December 13, 1802, Samuel Bradford entry, Letters of Application and Recommendation During the Administration of Thomas Jefferson; Shipton, *Sibley's Harvard Graduates*, XIII, 156–57.

For Allen, see Stephen G. Kurtz, *The Presidency of John Adams: The Collapse of Federalism 1795–1800* (Philadelphia, 1957), 410.

For Samuel Gerry, see Marvin R. Zahniser, *Charles Cotesworth Pinckney, Founding Father* (Chapel Hill, 1967), 154n; undated note, Samuel Gerry entry, Letters of Application and Recommendation During the Administration of John Adams, General Records of the Department of State, Record Group 59 (National Archives); Isaac Story to Thomas Jefferson, August 20, 1802, Isaac Story entry, Letters of Application and Recommendation During the Administration of Thomas Jefferson.

For Andrews and Staniford, see T. F. Waters, *Ipswich in the Massachusetts Bay Colony* (2 vols., Ipswich, 1905–17), I, 246, 317, 399–400.

14. For the Cross family in the life of Newburyport, the views of the local Federalist party and the national administration in dealing with Stephen Cross, and the politics, background, and claims of

Cross, see Leonard Labaree, *Patriots and Partisans: the Merchants of Newburyport, 1764–1815* (Cambridge, 1962), 140–42, 210; George Cabot to Oliver Wolcott, Jr., October 21, 1802, *Life and Letters of George Cabot*, Henry Cabot Lodge, ed. (Boston, 1877), 328; Alexander Hamilton to George Washington, April 23, 1792, *The Papers of Hamilton*, Syrett, ed., XI, 331; Benjamin Goodhue to Washington, June 30, July 22, 1789, Applications For Office Under President Washington, Series VII, George Washington Papers, vol. XII; Theophilus Parsons to John Adams, July 8, 1794, ibid., vol. XXII; Stephen Cross to Levi Lincoln, September 20, 1802, Stephen Cross entry, Letters of Application and Recommendation During the Administration of Thomas Jefferson.

15. For Ralph Cross, see George Cabot to Oliver Wolcott, Jr., October 21, 1801, *Life and Letters of George Cabot*, Lodge, ed., 328.

For Edward Wigglesworth, see Shipton, *Sibley's Harvard Graduates*, XV, 129–33.

16. For Tyng, see "S.H." [Stephen Higginson] to George Cabot, June 19, 1795, Applications For Office Under President Washington, Series VII, George Washington Papers, vol. XXVII; Henry Warren to Thomas Jefferson, November 10, 1802, Henry Warren entry, Letters of Application and Recommendation During the Administration of Thomas Jefferson; Phillips, "Political Fights and Local Squabbles in Salem, 1800–1806," *Essex Institute Historical Collections*, LXXXII, 5.

17. For Hodge and Titcomb, see Benjamin Goodhue to George Washington, July 22, 1789, Michael Hodge to Washington, July 8, 1789, Jonathan Titcomb to Washington, June 19, 1789, Applications For Office Under President Washington, Series VII, George Washington Papers, vols. XII, XV, XXVII respectively; *The Diaries of George Washington, 1748–1799*, John C. Fitzpatrick, ed. (4 vols., Boston, 1925), IV, 39, 42; Forrest McDonald, *We, The People: The Economic Origins of the Constitution* (Chicago, 1958), 194.

18. Benjamin Goodhue to George Washington, June 30, July 22, 1789, Michael Hodge to Washington, July 8, 1793, Theophilus Parsons to John Adams, July 8, 1794, Applications For Office Under President Washington, Series VII, George Washington Papers, vols. XII, XV, XXII respectively; —— to ——, November 26, 1802, Joseph Story entry, Letters of Application and Recommendation During the Administration of Thomas Jefferson; William Wingate to Thomas Jefferson, February 15, 1804, William Wingate entry, ibid., Jacob Crowninshield et al. to Jefferson, March 23, 1804, Francis Carr entry, ibid., Josiah Smith to ——, December —,

1804, Robert Murray entry, ibid.; Michael Hodge to Albert Gallatin, January 28, 1809, Resignations and Declinations Among the Records of the Department of State, General Records of the Department of State, Record Group 59 (National Archives); Labaree, *Patriots and Partisans*, 75, 78.

19. George Thaxter to George Washington, undated [1789], Applications For Office Under President Washington, Series VII, George Washington Papers (Manuscript Division, Library of Congress), vol. XXVII; Charles E. Banks, *History of York, Maine* (2 vols., Boston, 1935), I, 420–21, II, 359–60.

20. Joseph Tucker to George Washington, July 15, 1793, Applications For Office Under President Washington, Series VII, George Washington Papers, vol. XXVII; Moses Lyman, et al. to Thomas Jefferson, January 18, 1803, Richard Cutts to Jefferson, November 25, 1803, and passim, Joseph Tucker and Samuel Derby entries respectively, Letters of Application and Recommendation During the Administration of Thomas Jefferson; Banks, *History of York*, II, 354, 359–60, 409. For the more general significance of this removal, see Carl E. Prince, "The Passing of the Aristocracy: Jefferson's Removal of the Federalists 1801–1805," *Journal of American History*, LVII (1970), 572.

21. Joseph Storer et al. to Thomas Jefferson, March 4, 1806, Stephen Thatcher entry, Letters of Application and Recommendation During the Administration of Thomas Jefferson; Edward E. Bourne, *The History of Wells and Kennebunk* (Portland, 1875), 578–79, 585–89, 628, 746, 758–59.

22. Nathaniel Fosdick to George Washington, May 19, 1789, George Thaxter to Washington, undated [1789], Applications For Office Under President Washington, Series VII, George Washington Papers, vols. XI and XXVII respectively; William Wilson to Robert Smith, October 18, 1802, Richard Hunnewell entry, Levi Lincoln to Thomas Jefferson, December 13, 1802. Samuel Bradford entry, James Deering et al. to James Madison, January 21, 1803, Isaac Ilsley entry, and Daniel Davis to Albert Gallatin, April 5, 1803, and Davis to Jefferson, April 20, 1803, Nathaniel F. Fosdick entry, Letters of Application and Recommendation During the Administration of Thomas Jefferson; John Adams to Oliver Wolcott, Jr., August 27, 1800, *The Works of John Adams*, Charles F. Adams, ed. (10 vols., Boston, 1850–56); IX, 78; William Willis, *The History of Portland* (2 vols., Portland, 1883), 462. Francis Cook and John Lee, the collectors of customs in the Maine ports of Wiscasset and Penobscot respectively, were also Federalists.

23. For Robert Earl, William Tobey, and others, see Nathan Wil-

lis to Calvin Chaddock, December 20, 1804, Josiah Dean et al. to Albert Gallatin, August 27, 1805, Isaiah Weston entry, William Almy to Phanuel [Samuel] Bishop, December 3, 1804, Edward Pope entry, Letters of Application and Recommendation During the Administration of Thomas Jefferson.

24. For Ephraim Spooner, William Goodwin, Thomas Matthews, and other Plymouth Federalists, see George Partridge to George Washington, February 21, 1791, Applications For Office Under President Washington, vol. XXII; Henry Warren to Thomas Jefferson, November 10, 1802, Henry Warren entry, Letters of Application and Recommendation During the Administration of Thomas Jefferson; James Thacher to William Eustis, December 30, 1809, William Goodwin, Jr., entry, Letters of Application and Recommendation During the Administration of James Madison, General Records of the Department of State, Record Group 59 (National Archives); Davis, *History of the Town of Plymouth*, 62, 102, 158; Davis, *Ancient Landmarks of Plymouth*, 183, 200, 228, 230, 248–49, 253, 287.

25. For Thomas Fosdick and William Hobby, cf. note 22.

For Stephen Waite, see Rollo Silver, *The American Printer, 1787–1825* (Charlottesville, Va., 1967), 45; Samuel B. Harding, *The Contest Over the Ratification of the Federal Constitution in the State of Massachusetts* (New York, 1896), 37–40; Fischer, *Revolution of American Conservatism*, 415.

26. For William Titcomb, see Theophilus Parsons to John Adams, July 8, 1794, Applications for Office Under President Washington, Series VII, George Washington Papers, vol. XXII. For John Tracy, see Labaree, *Patriots and Partisans*, 88–91, 214; Kenneth W. Porter, *The Jacksons and the Lees* (2 vols., Cambridge, 1937), passim.

27. *The Boston Directory*, 1789, John Naman, Publisher (Boston, 1789); *United States Direct Tax of 1798*, 22nd Report of the Record Commissioners of the City of Boston (Boston, 1890).

28. Parish List, 1792, *Diary of William Bentley*, Essex Institute, eds. (3 vols., Salem, 1905–14), I, 332–38; Phillips, *Salem and the Indies*, 275, and *Salem in the Eighteenth Century*, 327; Morison, *Maritime History of Massachusetts*, 22.

CHAPTER THREE

1. Mark D. Kaplanoff, "Religion and Righteousness: A Study of Federalist Rhetoric in the New Hampshire Election of 1800," *His-*

torical New Hampshire, XXIII (1968), 3–27; Jere R. Daniell, *Experiment in Republicanism: New Hampshire Politics and the American Revolution, 1741–1794* (Cambridge, 1970). The descriptions of state party formations in this and succeeding chapters were aided extensively by the analyses contained in Stephen G. Kurtz, *The Presidency of John Adams: The Collapse of Federalism 1795–1800* (Philadelphia, 1957), a work that continues to hold up well after nearly two decades and many additions to the literature of early party formations.

2. John Langdon to George Washington, July 19, 1789, Applications For Office Under President Washington, Series VII, George Washington Papers (Manuscript Division, Library of Congress), vol. XVII; Joseph Whipple to Alexander Hamilton, October 9, 1790, Hamilton to George Washington, July 26, 1792, Whipple to Hamilton, October 17, 1792, *Papers of Alexander Hamilton*, Harold C. Syrett, ed. (24 vols., New York, 1961–76), VII, 104–5, XII, 117, 588–89 respectively.

3. William Plumer to Jeremiah Smith, December 23, 1794, William Plumer Letterbook, William Plumer Papers (Manuscript Division, Library of Congress); John H. Morison, *The Life of Jeremiah Smith* (Boston, 1845), 69. Alexander Hamilton was instrumental in naming Woodbury Langdon, John's brother and a figure with a checkered political past, to the federal post of commissioner of loans for New Hampshire in 1790. See *Papers of Hamilton*, Syrett, ed., VII, 96–97, 115.

4. For the changeover of customs personnel at Portsmouth between 1795 and 1800, see "List of Civil Officers of the United States . . . October 1, 1792," and "Roll of the Officers, Civil, Military, and Naval of the United States [1801]," *American State Papers, Miscellaneous: Documents, Legislative and Executive of the Congress of the United States*, Walter Lowrie and Walter S. Franklin, eds. (2 vols., Washington, D.C., 1834), I, 60–66, 261. A comparison of the roster of employees circa 1792 with that of 1800 shows that an uncharacteristic wholesale turnover in the lower echelons of the Portsmouth customs service had taken place.

For Whipple on the Jay Treaty and Smith on Whipple et al., see Jeremiah Smith to Oliver Wolcott, Jr., June 14, 1798, Jeremiah Smith entry, Letters of Application and Recommendation During the Administration of John Adams, General Records of the Department of State, Record Group 59 (National Archives).

For Plumer's early recognition of the changes taking place at the

Portsmouth customshouse, see William Plumer to Jeremiah Smith, June 30, 1795, April 19, 1796, William Plumer Letterbook, William Plumer Papers.

5. For a general survey of New Hampshire politics in this period that touches on the roles of both Smith and the Gilmans, see Kaplanoff, "Religion and Righteousness," *Historic New Hampshire*, XXIII (1968), 1–19. See also Lynn W. Turner, *William Plumer of New Hampshire, 1759–1850* (Chapel Hill, 1962). More will be said about Jeremiah Smith in chapter 10.

6. Morison, *Jeremiah Smith*, 66–69, 139.

7. Fisher Ames to Jeremiah Smith, March 13, 1798, Ames to Christopher Gore, July 28, 1798, *The Works of Fisher Ames*, Seth Ames, ed. (2 vols., Boston, 1854), I, 223, 237 respectively.

8. Jeremiah Smith to Oliver Wolcott, Jr., June 8, June 14, 1798, Jeremiah Smith entry, Letters of Application and Recommendation During the Administration of John Adams.

9. William Plumer to Oliver Wolcott, Jr., June 8, 1798 and Eliphalet Ladd to Wolcott, June 15, 1798, Joseph Whipple entry, Jeremiah Smith to Wolcott, June 14, 1798, Jeremiah Smith entry, ibid.

10. Ibid.; William Gardner to Nicholas Gilman, June 14, 1788, Miscellaneous Collection (New-York Historical Society); Alexander Hamilton to Gardner, June 14, 1792, *Papers of Hamilton*, Syrett, ed., XI, 517. Gardner published a pamphlet vindicating his exercise of the office. The loan officer also had to be situated in Portsmouth because he worked closely with the customs collector. For example, all the federal money disbursed in interest payments on federal securities owned by New Hampshiremen derived from customs revenues collected by Whipple.

11. Paine Wingate to ———, June 18, 1798, John Adams entry, Jeremiah Smith to Oliver Wolcott, Jr., June 14, 1798, Jeremiah Smith entry, William Plumer to Wolcott, June 8, 1798, Joseph Whipple entry, Letters of Application and Recommendation During the Administration of John Adams.

12. Hopley Yeaton to George Washington, December 11, 1789, Applications For Office Under President Washington, Series VII, George Washington Papers, vol. XXXII; Hopley Yeaton Petition to Thomas Jefferson, August 1, 1801, Albert Gallatin Papers (New-York Historical Society); John Langdon to Albert Gallatin, August 6, 1802, Hopley Yeaton entry, Letters of Application and Recommendation During the Administration of Thomas Jefferson, General Records of the Department of State, Record Group 59 (National Archives); Joseph Whipple to Alexander Hamilton, October 9,

1790, *Papers of Hamilton,* Syrett, ed., VII, 104–5; Charles Brewster, *Rambles About Portsmouth* (2 vols., Portsmouth, 1869), I, 192. William Gardner is also discussed in chapter 6.

Eleazer Russell, the naval officer in the customshouse at Portsmouth, was replaced sometime in 1798, and was closely identified with John Langdon. It may well be that he was one of Jeremiah Smith's "doubtfuls" who, though not a Republican, found themselves caught between Republicans in Portsmouth and Federalists in control of the state. He perhaps tried unsuccessfully to trim his course between the two camps and was removed as one of a "number of men who halt between the two opinions watching with cowardlike deliberation to join the strongest side." See John Langdon to George Washington, July 19, 1789, Applications For Office Under President Washington, Series VII, George Washington Papers, vol. XVII; Jeremiah Smith to Oliver Wolcott, Jr., June 8, 1798, Jeremiah Smith entry, Letters of Application and Recommendation During the Administration of John Adams.

13. John Langdon to George Washington, July 30, 1789, Applications For Office Under President Washington, Series VII, George Washington Papers, vol. XVII; Samuel Livermore to Oliver Wolcott, Jr., June 28, 1798, Jeremiah Smith to Wolcott, June 14, 1798, Thomas Martin and Jeremiah Smith entries respectively, Letters of Application and Recommendation During the Administration of John Adams; William Plumer to Jeremiah Smith, June 30, October 17, 1795, Plumer Letterbook, William Plumer Papers; Brewster, *Rambles About Portsmouth,* 90, 355.

14. For E. S. L. Livermore's appointment and background, see William Plumer to Woodbury Langdon, March 26, 1791, Plumer to Jeremiah Smith, August 12, 1796, February 9, 1797, Plumer Letterbook, William Plumer Papers; Turner, *Plumer,* 29, 45, 83; Charles Bell, *The Bench and Bar of New Hampshire* (Boston, 1894), 52–53; *Dictionary of American Biography,* Dumas Malone and Allen Johnson, eds. (22 vols., New York, 1928–58), XI, 304. Samuel Adams, an inspector of customs at the port and a "strong Federalist," was promoted to Martin's vacated place as surveyor. Jacob Sheafe to Timothy Pickering, April 13, 1798, Jeremiah Smith to Oliver Wolcott, Jr., June 14, 1798, Samuel Adams and Jeremiah Smith entries respectively, Letters of Application and Recommendation During the Administration of John Adams. John Pierce, later removed by Jefferson, was named commissioner of loans. He was a friend of Plumer's and considered a Federalist "juntoman." Turner, *Plumer,* 42–43.

15. Edward St. Loe Livermore to Samuel Livermore, May 30, 1798, Paine Wingate to ———, June 18, 1798, John Adams entry, Letters of Application and Recommendation During the Administration of John Adams; Jeremiah Smith to Oliver Wolcott, Jr., June 14, 1798, Jeremiah Smith entry, ibid.

16. John Adams to Benjamin Lincoln, March 10, 1800, Mellen Chamberlain Autograph Collection (Boston Public Library).

17. "Roll of the Officers, Civil, Military, and Naval of the United States [1801]," *American State Papers, Miscellaneous,* I, 260–319; Thomas Jefferson's "Anas," March 8, 1801, *The Works of Thomas Jefferson,* Paul L. Ford, ed. (12 vols., New York, 1904–5), I, 363; Hopley Yeaton petition to Jefferson, August 1, 1801, enclosed with Joseph Whipple to Albert Gallatin, October 27, 1801, Albert Gallatin Papers.

One port of entry was established in Vermont: at South Hero, near Burlington, on Lake Champlain. The two collectors there between 1791 and 1801 were both Federalists. Both Stephen Keyes and David Russell were impecunious storekeepers. Keyes, "an ardent Federalist," was an alcoholic who was removed in 1796 and was sued for default. David Russell was "very bitter" against the Republicans and was described by Matthew Lyon as "a petulant, Vain, busy Aristocrat."

For Stephen Keyes, see Jeremiah Wadsworth to ———, February 22, 1791, anonymous memo entitled "Substance of Conversations," undated [1791], Applications For Office Under President Washington, Series VII, George Washington Papers, vol. XXVIII; *The Papers of Alexander Hamilton,* Syrett, ed., VIII, 166n; Franklin B. Dexter, *Biographical Sketches of the Graduates of Yale College* (6 vols., New York, 1885–1912), III, 490–91.

For David Russell, see Stephen Bradley to Albert Gallatin, January 17, 1803, Ebenezer Judd to Bradley, January 1, 1803, Jabez Penniman entry, Letters of Application and Recommendation During the Administration of Thomas Jefferson; Matthew Lyon to Thomas Jefferson, March 3, 1801, Jonathan E. Robinson entry, ibid. Elijah Russell to Jefferson, August 7, 1801, Elijah Russell entry, ibid.; Lewis C. Aldrich and Frank R. Holmes, *History of Windsor County, Vermont* (Syracuse, N.Y., 1891), 211.

18. The historical background for Rhode Island politics is drawn from the following: Mack E. Thompson, *Moses Brown, Reluctant Reformer* (Providence, 1962); Irwin Polishook, *Rhode Island and the Union* (Evanston, Ill., 1969); James B. Hedges, *The Browns of Providence Plantation,* 2 vols. (Providence, 1952–68); David S.

Lovejoy, *Rhode Island Politics and the American Revolution, 1760–1776* (Providence, 1958); Mack E. Thompson, "The Ward-Hopkins Controversy and the American Revolution in Rhode Island: An Interpretation," *William and Mary Quarterly*, Third Series, XVI (1959), 363–75.

19. David H. Fischer, *The Revolution of American Conservatism: The Federalist Party in the Era of Jeffersonian Democracy* (New York, 1965), 277–78. It is difficult to ascertain whether or not the club continued to exist as a formal entity much after 1790. In any event, its leaders continued to be among the most important Federalists in the state throughout the Federalist decade and thereafter. Fischer believes the club continued its existence after ratification: "during the 1780's and 1790's," after "the state's belated entry into the Union, this convivial clique of like minded men gained its reward in the form of federal patronage."

20. Jabez Bowen et al. to George Washington, June 13, 1789, June 19, 1790, John Brown et al. to Washington, June 14, 1790, Applications For Office Under President Washington, Series VII, George Washington Papers, vol. III.

21. Ibid., Jabez Bowen to George Washington, June 19, 1790.

22. Ibid., William Greene to George Washington, June 7, 1790, Welcome Arnold to Washington, June 10, 1790, John Brown and John Francis to Washington, June 11, 1790, vol. XXI.

23. Ibid., Ezra Stiles to David Humphries, undated [1790], vol. XXVI, and Royal Flint to Alexander Hamilton, June 14, 1790, vol. XI; Jeremiah Olney to Alexander Hamilton, August 23, 25, September 10, November 3, 1788, Hamilton to Olney, August 12, October 6, 1788, Olney to Hamilton, February 12, June 7, 12, and passim, 1790, *The Papers of Alexander Hamilton*, Syrett, ed., V, 199–200, 203–5, 215–16, 224, 229–30, VI, 263–64, 458–59, 470.

24. Staughton Lynd's comment on a paper delivered by Forrest McDonald, found in *Fame and the Founding Fathers*, Edmund P. Willis, ed. (Bethlehem, Pa., 1967), 18.

25. Jabez Bowen to George Washington, June 13, 1790, Memo entitled "Information from Mr. Bowen Respecting Characters in the State of Rhode Island," undated [June 1790], Jeremiah Olney's "Memorandum of Sundry persons Suitable Characters to fill the offices . . . in Rhode Island," June 19, 1790, Royal Flint to Alexander Hamilton, June 14, 1790, Applications For Office Under President Washington, Series VII, George Washington Papers, vols. III, XXI, XI respectively.

26. For Theodore Foster, see ibid., Foster to George

Washington, February 18, June 29, 1790, vols. XI, XXVII respectively.

For Moses Brown, see ibid., Brown to Washington, June 6, 1790, vol. XXVII.

For Arthur Fenner, see ibid., Fenner to George Washington, June 9, 1790, vol. XXIV. Fenner's political odyssey during the 1790s remains an enigma. He was at least a moderate Antifederalist and was in the early years of the Federalist decade widely considered a Republican both in Rhode Island and Philadelphia. Yet in 1796 he was an elector for John Adams. In 1800, however, according to important Federalists at least, he was back in the Jeffersonian camp. See Robert Goodloe Harper to John Rutledge, September 4, 1800, folder 10, John Rutledge Papers (Southern Historical Collection, University of North Carolina Library).

27. Arthur Fenner to George Washington, June 9, 10, 1790, Theodore Foster to Washington, June 29, 1790, Applications For Office Under President Washington, Series VII, George Washington Papers, vols. XXIV, XXI, XXVII respectively.

28. George C. Rogers, Jr., *Evolution of a Federalist: William Loughton Smith of Charleston, 1758–1812* (Columbia, S.C., 1962), 212–13. Senator Smith accompanied Washington to Rhode Island and so observed the political interplay evident on the trip.

29. Hamilton's correspondence is rife with evidence of Olney's general incompetence. See the editors' note in *The Papers of Alexander Hamilton*, Syrett, ed., XV, 357–58n.

30. For Olney's political leverage, see John Brown and John Francis to George Washington, June 11, 1790, Jeremiah Olney to Washington, October 7, 1793, and passim, Applications For Office Under President Washington, Series VII, George Washington Papers, vol. XXI. For Biographical data on Olney, see ibid., Olney to Washington, March 16, June 13, 1789, vols. XXI and III respectively; Fischer, *Revolution of American Conservatism*, 281; *George Washington's Correspondence Concerning the Society of the Cincinnati*, Edgar Erskine Hume, ed. (Baltimore, 1941), 388.

31. For Ebenezer Thompson, see "Information from Mr. Bowen Respecting Characters in the State of Rhode Island," undated [June, 1790], Applications For Office Under President Washington, Series VII, George Washington Papers, vol. III; Theodore Foster to Washington, February 18, 1790, ibid., vol. XI; Ebenezer Thompson to Washington, May 21, 1790, Edward K. Thompson to Tobias Lear, January 20, 1790, Theodore Foster to Washington, June 29, 1790,

March 3, 1791, ibid., vol. XXVII; Mack Thompson, *Moses Brown,* 177.

32. This Barton is difficult to pin down because of the frequent allusions to his cousin of the same name. I believe that the editors of *The Papers of Alexander Hamilton* have him confused with the Philadelphia William Barton. See the note in *The Papers of Hamilton,* Syrett, ed., X, 491.

For the Providence Barton, see ibid., VI, 470, X, 12, 257n, 301n; William Barton to George Washington, September 3, 1789, David Rittenhouse to Washington, September 14, 1789, Applications For Office Under President Washington, Series VII, George Washington Papers, vol. II; Royal Flint to Alexander Hamilton, June 14, 1790, and undated [1790], ibid., vol. XI; also *George Washington's Correspondence Concerning the Society of the Cincinnati,* Hume, ed., 407; Forrest McDonald, *We, The People: The Economic Origins of the Constitution* (Chicago, 1958), 342–43.

The complex of customshouses at Newport and its environs were headed by staunch Federalist William Ellery. His responsibilities not only included the major port of entry at Newport proper, but the neighboring customs stations at North Kingston, East Greenwich, Pawtucket, and Warren as well. At each of these towns a Federalist surveyor of customs presided under Ellery's overall supervision.

33. James C. Welling, *Connecticut Federalism; or Aristocratic Politics in a Social Democracy* (New York, 1890); Richard J. Purcell, *Connecticut in Transition, 1775–1818* (Washington, D.C., 1918); James C. Welling, "Connecticut Federalism," *Addresses, Lectures, and Other Papers* (Cambridge, 1904).

34. For biographical data on Huntington, see Jedediah Huntington to Oliver Wolcott, Jr., February 16, 1798, Elisha Hinman entry, Letters of Application and Recommendation During the Administration of John Adams; Ebenezer Belknap to Ephraim Kirby, June 3, 1801, Ephraim Kirby Papers (Perkins Library, Duke University); *The Papers of Hamilton,* Syrett, ed., vol. VI, passim; *George Washington's Correspondence Concerning the Society of the Cincinnati,* Hume, ed., 423–24; Richard J. Purcell, *Connecticut in Transition,* 24–25, 69, 206; Fischer, *Revolution of American Conservatism,* xiii; *Dictionary of American Biography,* IX, 416–17; McDonald, *We, The People,* 144; Clifford K. Shipton, *Sibley's Harvard Graduates, Biographical Sketches of Those Who Attended Harvard College* (16 vols., Boston, 1873–1972), XV, 416–18.

35. Shipton, *Sibley's Harvard Graduates*, XV, 417; McDonald, *We, The People*, 144.

36. Elisha Hyde to Ephraim Kirby, August 13, 1801, Ephraim Kirby Papers; Thomas Seyman to Thomas Jefferson, May 28, 1804, Thomas Seyman entry, Letters of Application and Recommendation During the Administration of Thomas Jefferson; Clifford K. Shipton, *Sibley's Harvard Graduates*, XV, 416–18.

37. Shipton, *Sibley's Harvard Graduates*, XV, 418.

38. Thomas H. Rawson et al. to Joseph Stanton, November 17, 1806, Nicoll Fosdick entry, and Rawson to Stanton, November 26, 1806, Jedediah Huntington entry, Letters of Application and Recommendation During the Administration of Thomas Jefferson,

39. Ibid., Thomas H. Rawson et al. to Joseph Stanton, November 17, 1806, Nicoll Fosdick entry; Thaddeus Burr to George Washington, January 1, 1791, Applications For Office Under President Washington, Series VII, George Washington Papers, vol. XIX; *The Papers of Hamilton*, Syrett, ed., VII, 101–2.

40. Jedediah Huntington to Oliver Wolcott, Jr., February 16, 1798, William Stuart to Wolcott, February 21, 1798, Elisha Hinman entry, George House to Wolcott, February 16, 1798, George House entry, Letters of Application and Recommendation During the Administration of John Adams; Elisha Hinman to Thomas Jefferson, November 16, 1801, Gideon Granger to Jefferson, January 4, 1802, Nicoll Fosdick et al. to Albert Gallatin, January 29, 1803, Elisha Hinman entry, George House to James Madison, May 3, 1801, Nathan Post to Gallatin, March 10, 1803, George House entry, George House to Jefferson, April 7, 1806, Jonathan Palmer entry, Letters of Application and Recommendation During the Administration of Thomas Jefferson.

Other Federalist customs officers in Connecticut included Chauncey Whittlesey at Middletown and Richard Dickinson at Saybrook.

CHAPTER FOUR

1. For New York politics in the Federalist decade, see Alfred F. Young, *The Democratic Republicans of New York: The Origins, 1763–1797* (Chapel Hill, 1967); Dixon Ryan Fox, *The Decline of Aristocracy in the Politics of New York* (New York, 1919); Jabez D. Hammond, *History of Political Parties in the State of New York*, 4th ed. (2 vols., Buffalo, 1850); Alvin Kass, *Politics in New York State 1800–1830* (Syracuse, 1965).

2. John Lamb to George Washington, May 22, 1789, Applications For Office Under President Washington, Series VII, George Washington Papers (Manuscript Division, Library of Congress), vol. XVII; Alfred F. Young, *The Democratic Republicans of New York*, 150–52; Sidney Pomerantz, *New York: An American City 1783–1803* (New York, 1938), 30, 81, 101; Howard Thomas, *Marinus Willet, Soldier-Patriot 1740–1830* (Prospect, N.Y., 1954), 164; Jackson T. Main, *The Antifederalists: Critics of the Constitution, 1781–1788* (Chapel Hill, 1961), 181, 218, 235 and passim; Forrest McDonald, *We, The People: The Economic Origins of the Constitution* (Chicago, 1958), 298.

3. Alexander Hamilton to Richard Harison, July 3, 1790, Harison to Hamilton, July 12, 1790, Box 1, Richard Harison Papers (New-York Historical Society); Arthur Alexander, "Federal Patronage in New York State, 1789–1805" (Ph.D. diss., University of Pennsylvania, 1944), 30.

4. Pomerantz, *New York*, 115; Alexander, "Federal Patronage in New York State," passim.

5. *Longworth's American Almanack, New York Register, and City Directory* (New York, 1789 and 1799); "List of Civil Officers of the United States . . . October 1, 1792," and "Roll of the Officers, Civil, Military, and Naval of the United States [1801]," *American State Papers, Miscellaneous: Documents, Legislative and Executive of the Congress of the United States*, Walter Lowrie and Walter S. Franklin, eds. (2 vols., Washington, D.C., 1834), I, 57–68, 260–319.

6. For the circumstances of Lamb's removal, see Jonathan Burrall entry, passim, Letters of Application and Recommendation During the Administration of John Adams, General Records of the Department of State, Record Group 59 (National Archives); Young, *Democratic Republicans of New York*, 48. Federalist Collectors Benjamin Lincoln of Boston and William Heth of Bermuda Hundred, Virginia, had earlier found themselves in similar straits but kept their customs posts.

7. Benjamin Walker to George Washington, June 1, 1789, Applications for Office Under President Washington, Series VII, George Washington Papers, vol. XXIX; Robert Troup to Oliver Wolcott, Jr., April 22, 1797, William Seton entry, Letters of Application and Recommendation During the Administration of John Adams; New York Chapter, Society of the Cincinnati Papers, passim (New-York Historical Society); George Washington to Benjamin Walker, December 5, 1791, January 12, 1797, *The Writings of George*

Washington, John C. Fitzpatrick, ed. (39 vols., Washington, D.C., 1931–44), XXXI, 435n and XXXV, 363–65 respectively; *The Papers of Alexander Hamilton*, Harold C. Syrett, ed. (24 vols., New York, 1961–76), XI, 500n; Dixon Ryan Fox, *The Decline of Aristocracy in the Politics of New York*, 50.

8. For the affairs of SUM and Scioto, and Walker's deep involvement in both, see Joseph S. Davis, *Essays in the Earlier History of American Corporations* (2 vols., Cambridge, Mass., 1917), I, 197, 222, 242ff., 253, 263, 271ff., 392, 407; Tobias Lear to Alexander Hamilton, August 28, 1790, Benjamin Walker to Hamilton, December 28, 1790, July 12, 1792, Hamilton to Walker, July 20, 1792, *Papers of Hamilton*, Syrett, ed., VI, 575, VII, 388–89, XII, 30–31, 63–64 respectively; Robert Troup to Oliver Wolcott, Jr., April 22, 1797, William Seton entry, Letters of Application and Recommendation During the Administration of John Adams; Benjamin Walker correspondence relating to the Scioto Company, passim, William Duer Papers (New-York Historical Society).

9. For the Adams-Hamilton confrontation over the New York collector's appointment, see Benjamin Walker to Oliver Wolcott, Jr., April 21, 1797, John Laurence to Wolcott, April 21, 1797, Alexander Hamilton to Wolcott, April 22, 1797, Benjamin Walker entry, Letters of Application and Recommendation During the Administration of John Adams; Richard Rogers to Wolcott, April 20, 1797, Richard Rogers entry, *ibid*; William Seton to Wolcott, April 21, 1797, Robert Troup to Wolcott, April 22, 1797, William Seton entry, ibid.

For Joshua Sands, see Caleb Brewster to Wolcott, February 8, 1798, Caleb Brewster entry, ibid.; Sands to Wolcott, May 28, 1798, John W. Leonard entry, ibid.; DeWitt Clinton to Thomas Jefferson, May 31, 1802, DeWitt Clinton entry, Letters of Application and Recommendation During the Administration of Thomas Jefferson. General Records of the Department of State, Record Group 59 (National Archives); Abraham Bishop to Ephraim Kirby, May 25, 1801, Ephraim Kirby Papers (Perkins Library, Duke University); Thomas Jefferson to George Clinton, May 17, 1801, *The Works of Thomas Jefferson*, Paul L. Ford, ed. (12 vols., New York, 1904–5), IX, 254; Young, *Democratic Republicans of New York*, 333; Alexander, "Federal Patronage in New York State," 30; Walter Barrett [pseudonym for Joseph Scoville], *The Old Merchants of New York City* (5 vols., New York, 1863), II, 10–11, III, 299–306.

There were two other small ports in New York State, the harbors at Albany and Hudson near the source of the Hudson River. The collector of the twin ports, joined in a single customs district, was Henry Malcom. He and all his inferior officers, including Surveyors John C. TenBroek, Henry J. Bogert, and Jeremiah Lansing, were important local Federalists. Malcom was a physician, TenBroek a shoemaker, Bogert a storekeeper, and Lansing a clerk in the state court of chancery. TenBroek, not to be confused with Jacob C. Ten Broek, and Lansing were both "poor" relations of powerful upstate political families.

For Malcom, see Ezekiel Gibbs to Oliver Wolcott, Jr., March 21, 1795, Applications For Office Under President Washington, Series VII, George Washington Papers, vol. XIX; Thomas Jenkins et al. to Thomas Jefferson, October 16, 1802, Ambrose Spinat et al. to DeWitt Clinton, February 4, 1803, William Jenkins et al. to Jefferson, January 27, 1804. Henry Malcom entry, Letters of Application and Recommendation During the Administration of Thomas Jefferson.

For John C. TenBroek, see Moss Kent to James Kent, December 10, 1796, May 9, 1799, James Kent Papers (Manuscript Division, Library of Congress); passim, Henry Malcom entry, Letters of Application and Recommendation During the Administration of Thomas Jefferson; Jabez D. Hammond, *History of Political Parties in the State of New York,* I, 56.

For Henry I. Bogert, see Albert Gallatin to Thomas Jefferson, December 10, 1802, Albert Gallatin Papers (Manuscript Division, Library of Congress); Robert Troup to John Jay, May 6, 1792, *The Correspondence and Public Papers of John Jay, 1763–1826,* Henry P. Johnston, ed. (4 vols., New York, 1890–93), III, 423; Alexander, "Federal Patronage in New York State," 39.

For Jeremiah Lansing, see Alexander, "Federal Patronage in New York State," 38–39.

10. For Pennsylvania politics, see Stephen G. Kurtz, *The Presidency of John Adams: The Collapse of Federalism 1795–1800* (Philadelphia, 1957), 183–87; Harry M. Tinkcom, *The Republicans and Federalists in Pennsylvania, 1790–1801* (Harrisburg, 1950); Sanford W. Higginbotham, *The Keystone in the Democratic Arch: Pennsylvania Politics, 1800–1816* (Harrisburg, 1952); Russell J. Ferguson, *Early Western Pennsylvania Politics* (Pittsburgh, 1938).

11. For Jonas Simonds, see Simonds to Thomas Jefferson, April 18, 1801, Thomas Leiper to Jefferson, January 26, 1806, Jonas Simonds entry, Letters of Application and Recommendation During the Administration of Thomas Jefferson.

For Alexander Boyd, see Boyd to Jefferson, March 17, 1801,

Alexander Boyd entry, ibid. As he was an innkeeper in Philadelphia, Boyd's house had served as an informal political headquarters for Antifederalist delegates to the Pennsylvania Ratifying Convention in 1788. He had worked at the customshouse through most of the Confederation on a part-time basis and thus had been kept on in the transition from state to federal customs control. John B. McMaster and Frederick D. Stone, *Pennsylvania and the Federal Constitution, 1787–1788* (Lancaster, 1888), 3–4, 13, 67, 204.

12. Stephen Sayre to Thomas Jefferson, February 5, 1801, Thomas Cooper et al. to Jefferson, May 23, 1801, Stephen Sayre and William Henderson entries respectively, Letters of Application and Recommendation During the Administration of Thomas Jefferson; David H. Fischer, *The Revolution of American Conservatism: The Federalist Party in the Era of Jeffersonian Democracy* (New York, 1965), 340.

13. For Sharp Delany, see Delany to Alexander Hamilton, February 15, 23, 1790 and passim, *Papers of Hamilton*, Syrett, ed., VI, 266, 275–76 and passim; Petition of Philadelphia Merchants to George Washington, April 18, 1789, Richard Peters to Washington, April 22, 1789, Sharp Delany to Washington, April 20, 1789, Applications For Office Under President Washington, Series VII, George Washington Papers, vol. VIII; Donald H. Stewart, "The Press and Political Corruption During the Federalist Administrations," *Political Science Quarterly* LXVII (1952), 441; Henry Simpson, *The Lives of Eminent Philadelphians, Now Deceased* (Philadelphia, 1859), 308.

The original naval officer was Frederick Phile, an aging physician who died in 1793. He was replaced by William McPherson, who was promoted from surveyor to naval officer. McPherson in turn was replaced by Walter Stewart, a prominent Philadelphia Federalist merchant and "gentleman." The latter resigned in 1795 and William Jackson took over the surveyor's office.

For Phile, see Phile to George Washington, March 7, 1789, Applications For Office Under President Washington, Series VII, George Washington Papers, vol. XXII.

For Stewart, see Alexander Hamilton to Walter Stewart, August 5, 27, 1790, Stewart to Hamilton, November 27, 1793, *Papers of Hamilton*, Syrett, ed., VI, 545, 572, XV, 416–17; Ethel E. Rasmusson, "Capitol on the Delaware: The Philadelphia Upper Class in Transition, 1789–1801" (Ph.D. diss., Brown University, 1962), 35, 52, 190; *George Washington's Correspondence Concerning the Society of the Cincinnati*, Edgar E. Hume, ed. (Baltimore, 1941), 15.

14. For Latimer, see Albert Gallatin to William Duane, July 5, 1801, Albert Gallatin Papers (New-York Historical Society); Stephen Sayre to Thomas Jefferson, February 5, 1801, Frederick Frelinghuysen to Jefferson, February 11, 1801, Stephen Sayre and Frederick Frelinghuysen entries respectively, Letters of Application and Recommendation During the Administration of Thomas Jefferson; "Papers of James A. Bayard, 1796–1815," Elizabeth Donnan, ed., in American Historical Association, *Annual Report, 1913* (2 vols., Washington, D.C., 1913), II, 128–29n; Harry M. Tinkcom, *The Republicans and Federalists in Pennsylvania*, 58, 64, 279, 300; Charles Page Smith, *James Wilson: Founding Father, 1742–1798* (Chapel Hill, 1956), 369; Sanford W. Higginbotham, *The Keystone in the Democratic Arch*, 20, 41, 162, 199; Fischer, *Revolution of American Conservatism*, 341; McDonald, *We, The People*, 139, 172; McMaster and Stone, *Pennsylvania and the Federal Constitution*, 737.

15. For William McPherson, see McPherson to George Washington, August 5, 1789, October 23, 1793, Applications For Office Under President Washington, Series VII, George Washington Papers, vol. XIX; Thomas Cooper et al. to Thomas Jefferson, May 23, 1801, Tench Coxe to Jefferson, June 25, 1801, William Henderson and Tench Coxe entries respectively, Letters of Application and Recommendation During the Administration of Thomas Jefferson; *Extracts From the Diary of Jacob Hiltzheimer of Philadelphia, 1765–1798*, Jacob Cox Parsons, ed. (Philadelphia, 1893), 147, 165; *General Washington's Correspondence Concerning the Society of the Cincinnati*, Hume, ed., 382; *The Diaries of George Washington, 1748–1799*, John C. Fitzpatrick, ed. (4 vols., Boston, 1925), IV, 217n; Rasmusson, "Capitol on the Delaware," 163; Simpson, *Lives of Eminent Philadelphians*, 682–83; John Carroll and Mary Ashworth, *George Washington: First in Peace* (New York, 1957), 208n, 227, 575; McMaster and Stone, *Pennsylvania and the Federal Constitution*, 740–41; William H. Egle, "The Federal Constitution of 1787: Biographical Sketches of the Members of the Pennsylvania Convention," *Pennsylvania Magazine of History and Biography* X–XI (1886–87), 250–52; *Directory of the City of Philadelphia* (Philadelphia, 1805, 1807).

For military-civil relations in this period, see Richard H. Kohn, *Eagle and Sword: The Beginnings of the Military Establishment in America* (New York, 1975).

16. For William Jackson, see Jackson to John Adams, June 19, 1798, Applications For Office Under President Washington, Series VII, George Washington Papers, vol. XVI [filed with this collection

in error]; Thomas Willing to John Adams, June 20, 1798, William Bingham to Adams, June 21, 1798, Alexander Hamilton to Oliver Wolcott, Jr., June 25, 1798, William Jackson entry, Letters of Application and Recommendation During the Administration of John Adams; James Simonds to Thomas Jefferson, April 18, 1801, Thomas Leiper to Jefferson, January 26, 1806, Jonas Simonds entry, David Jackson to Jefferson, February 10, 1804, James Gamble entry, Letters of Application and Recommendation During the Administration of Thomas Jefferson; Timothy Pickering to George Washington, vol. VI, Timothy Pickering Papers (Massachusetts Historical Society); John Steele to William Miller, May 22, 1804, *The Papers of John Steele*, Henry M. Wagstaff, ed. (2 vols., Chapel Hill, 1924), I, 434–35; *General Washington's Correspondence Concerning the Society of the Cincinnati*, Hume, ed., 424; Fischer, *Revolution of American Conservatism*, 340; Ashworth and Carroll, *Washington: First in Peace*, 652.

17. John Graff to George Washington, October 21, 1792, November 14, 1793, Sharp Delany to Washington, November 17, 1793, Applications For Office Under President Washington, Series VII, George Washington Papers, XII; Peter Muhlenberg to Thomas Jefferson, August 20, 1807, Peter Muhlenberg entry, Samuel Emery to James Madison, September 17, 1807, Muhlenberg to Albert Gallatin, September 26, 1806, John Graff to Jefferson, September 28, 1807, John Graff entry, Letters of Application and Recommendation During the Administration of Thomas Jefferson; *Directory of the City of Philadelphia*, 1805, 1807.

18. The Federalists described included John Sharp, Jacob Bunner, Isaac Roach, William Milnor, William Gray, William Dunton, Burgess Ball, David Rose, William King, George Hofner, and Lewis Bitting. A wide variety of sources were consulted. In general, the *Directory of the City of Philadelphia* for 1805 and 1807, and Applications For Office Under President Washington, Series VII, passim, George Washington Papers, were the most informative.

19. For Maryland politics, see Libero M. Renzulli, Jr., "Maryland Federalism: 1789–1819" (Ph.D. diss., University of Virginia, 1962); Edward G. Roddy, "Maryland and the Presidential Election of 1800," *Maryland Historical Magazine* LX (1965), 244–268; Frank A. Cassell, "General Samuel Smith and the Election of 1800," ibid., LXIII (1968), 341–59; Dorothy M. Brown, "Maryland and the Federalists: Search for Unity," ibid., LXIII (1968), 1–21; Malcom C. Clark, "Federalism at High Tide: The Election of 1796 in Maryland," ibid., LXI (1966), 210–28.

20. For James McHenry, see McHenry to George Washington, April 17, 1789, January 6, 1791, and passim, Applications For Office Under President Washington, Series VII, George Washington Papers, vols. XIX and VII respectively; McHenry to Alexander Hamilton, May 3, 1791, September 30, 1792, *Papers of Hamilton*, Syrett, ed., VIII, 321–22, XII, 510 respectively.

21. Renzulli, "Maryland Federalism," 151; Brown, "Maryland and the Federalists," *Maryland Historical Magazine* LXIII (1968), 4, 10, 14.

22. For Williams's background, see *Calendar of the General Otho Holland Williams Papers*, Elizabeth Merritt, ed. (Baltimore, 1940), Introduction and passim. See particularly Teresa Williams Davis to Otho Williams, March [?], 1794, and Otho Williams to Elie Williams, March, 1794, pp. 330–31; James McHenry to Alexander Hamilton, May 3, 1791, *Papers of Hamilton*, Syrett, ed., VIII, 321–22; *George Washington's Correspondence Concerning the Society of the Cincinnati*, Hume, ed., 458–59.

23. Otho H. Williams to David Humphries, May 12, 1789, Applications For Office Under President Washington, Series VII, George Washington Papers, vol. V; Williams to Washington, April 18, May 12, July 5, 14, 1789, ibid., XXX; *Papers of Hamilton*, Syrett, ed., vols. VI, XII, passim; *Calendar of the Williams Papers*, Merritt, ed., passim.

24. For indications of the wide-ranging, complex relationship between Williams and Hamilton, see Otho H. Williams to Alexander Hamilton, March 5, April 5, 1792, Hamilton to Williams, June 9, 1792, *Papers of Hamilton*, Syrett, ed., vols. X, XI, passim; Hamilton to Williams, March 28, 1792, *Calendar of the General Otho Holland Williams Papers*, Merritt, ed., 255–56 and passim.

For the Ballard controversy, see Williams to George Washington, undated (1789), Applications For Office Under President Washington, Series VII, George Washington Papers, vol. XXX; Hamilton to Williams, June 18, 1792, Williams to Hamilton, June 28, 1792, *Papers of Hamilton*, Syrett, ed., XI, 601–5; Williams to Hamilton, July 27, 1792, Hamilton to Williams, July 19, August 14, 1792, ibid., XII, 119–22, 46–56, 204–5 respectively.

For the dispute involving Elie Williams, see Otho H. Williams to William Smith, June 26, 1791, Elie Williams to Otho H. Williams, January 23, 1794, and passim, *Calendar of the General Otho Holland Williams Papers*, Merritt, ed., 242, 312, and passim.

25. John Stull to Otho H. Williams, January 9, 1789, March 23, 1794, William Smith to Williams, March 7, 11, 1790, Williams to Philip Thomas, October 16, 1790, October 7, 1791, Williams to

William Smith, June 26, 1791, and passim, *Calendar of the General Otho Holland Williams Papers,* Merritt, ed., 161, 207, 225, 242, 245, 327, and passim; Dorothy M. Brown, "Maryland and the Federalists," *Maryland Historical Magazine* LXIII (1968), 14.

26. For David Porter's forced resignation and its "causes," see Alexander Hamilton to Otho H. Williams, Robert Purviance, and George Gale, January 23, 1794, *Papers of Hamilton,* Syrett, ed., XV, 659–60.

For Robert Purviance's background and politics, see James McHenry to George Washington, April 17, May 24, 1789, William Smith to Washington, undated (1789), Applications For Office Under President Washington, Series VII, George Washington Papers, vols. XIX, XXIII respectively; James McHenry to Alexander Hamilton, September 30, 1792, *Papers of Hamilton,* Syrett, ed., XII, 510; John Glendy to Thomas Jefferson, October 10, 1806, David Porter, Jr., to James Madison, March 23, 1801, Andrew Parks and David Porter, Jr., entries respectively, Letters of Application and Recommendation During the Administration of Thomas Jefferson; John Purviance-James Monroe Correspondence 1800–1802, passim, Purviance-Courtenay Papers (Perkins Library, Duke University).

For Daniel Delozier, see the Diary of William Heth, September 2, 1792 (Manuscript Division, Library of Congress); Albert Gallatin's note appended to Robert Smith to Gallatin, October 10, 1806, and Smith to Gallatin, October 14, 1806, John Stricker entry, Letters of Application and Recommendation During the Administration of Thomas Jefferson; Robert Smith to Gallatin, October 11, 1806, Samuel Smith to Thomas Jefferson, October 11, 1806, Daniel Delozier and John Brice, Jr., entries respectively, ibid.

Robert Ballard, surveyor of customs until his death in 1793, was also an important Baltimore Federalist despite his falling out with Williams. For his political activities, see Ballard to George Washington, January 1, 1789, Samuel Smith to Washington, June 24, 1789, Applications For Office Under President Washington, Series VII, George Washington Papers, vol. II; Ballard to Washington, December 28, 1790, ibid., vol. VII; Otho H. Williams to Washington, undated (1789?), ibid., vol. XXX.

27. For Martin Eichelberger, see Eichelberger to George Washington, undated (1789), August 8, 1793, July 18, 1794, James McHenry to Washington, July 2, 1789, Samuel Smith to Washington, July 17, 1794, Applications For Office Under President Washington, Series VII, George Washington Papers, vol. X; John Kilty to Washington, July 25, 1794, ibid., vol. XVI.

For Alexander McCaskey, see James McHenry to Washington, July 2, 1789, Alexander McCaskey to Washington, July 4, 8, 1789, August 19, 1793, ibid., vol. XIX; William Smith to Otho H. Williams, June 9, 1791, McCaskey to Williams, May 27, 1793, *Calendar of the General Otho Holland Williams Papers*, Merritt, ed., 240, 286.

The other four known Federalists in the lower reaches of the customs service were John Lynch, measurer of customs, and Clement Skerret, Joseph Smith, and John Hamilton, all inspectors of customs. In general, the same sources cited above yielded information on these four.

The Chesapeake Bay and Potomac River areas in Maryland were dotted with a number of small ports, each with a small federal complement of officeholders. Federalists staffed most of these customshouses too. Some of these were Jeremiah and Robert Banning, father and son, at Oxford, James Frazier at Vienna, James M. Lingan at Georgetown, and John Davidson at Annapolis.

CHAPTER FIVE

1. For this overview of Virginia politics, I have relied on Richard R. Beeman, *The Old Dominion and the New Nation, 1788–1802* (Lexington, Ky., 1972); Lisle A. Rose, *Prologue to Democracy: The Federalists in the South 1789–1801* (Lexington, 1968); Norman K. Risjord, "The Virginia Federalists," *Journal of Southern History* XXXIII (1967), 486–517.

2. Virtually the same thing happened to Ebenezer Thompson, incumbent but Antifederalist customs officer at Providence, Rhode Island.

For Daniel Bedinger's background, see Danske Dandridge, *George Michael Bedinger* (Charlottesville, Va., 1909), 1–9; Daniel Bedinger to George Washington, May 20, 1789, Applications For Office Under President Washington, Series VII, George Washington Papers (Manuscript Division, Library of Congress), vol. II.

3. For William Lindsay, see "A List of persons who have . . . requested to be recommended to the President . . . for Appointment," undated (1789), Applications For Office Under President Washington, Series VII, George Washington Papers, vol. IV; James Hunter to ———, April 20, 1797, Francis S. Taylor entry, Letters of Application and Recommendation During the Administration of John Adams, General Records of the Department of State, Record

Group 59 (National Archives); Thomas J. Wertenbaker, *Norfolk, Historic Southern Port* (Durham, N.C., 1931), 100–1.

For Philemon Gatewood, see Samuel Griffin to George Washington, undated (1789), Applications For Office Under President Washington, Series VII, George Washington Papers, vol. XIII; Josiah Parker to Oliver Wolcott, Jr., April 26, 1797, Daniel Bedinger entry, Letters of Application and Recommendation During the Administration of John Adams.

4. Thomas J. Farnham, "The Virginia Amendments of 1795, An Episode in the Opposition to Jay's Treaty," *Virginia Magazine of History and Biography*, LXXV (1967), 82.

5. Daniel Bedinger to Josiah Parker, April 25, 1797, Josiah Parker to Oliver Wolcott, Jr., April 26, 1797, Edward Carrington to Wolcott, September 11, 1797, William Heth to Wolcott, September 19, 1797, Daniel Bedinger entry, Letters of Application and Recommendation During the Administration of John Adams; Charles Lee to Wolcott, September 18, 1797, Otway Byrd entry, ibid.; John Adams to Wolcott, October 4, 1800, *The Works of John Adams*, Charles Francis Adams, ed. (10 vols., Boston, 1850–56), IX, 87.

6. William Heth to Oliver Wolcott, Jr., September 19, 1797, Daniel Bedinger entry, Letters of Application and Recommendation During the Administration of John Adams; Heth to Wolcott, May 20, 1797, Edward Carrington to Wolcott, September 11, 1797, Charles Lee to Wolcott, September 18, 1797, Otway Byrd entry, ibid.; *The Diaries of George Washington, 1748–1799*, John C. Fitzpatrick, ed. (4 vols., Boston, 1925), IV, 259n.

7. Carl E. Prince, "The Passing of the Aristocracy: Jefferson's Removal of the Federalists, 1801–1805," *Journal of American History* LVII (December 1970), 563–75; Dandridge, *George Michael Bedinger*, 1.

8. Alexander Hamilton to Charles Lee, January 18, 1792, Charles Lee to Hamilton, January 29, 1792, *The Papers of Alexander Hamilton*, Harold C. Syrett, ed. (24 vols., New York, 1961–76), X, 522–23, 576–78 respectively. Samuel Hanson to George Washington, March 10, 1792, cited in ibid., 522–23n; Stevens Thomson Mason et al. to Thomas Jefferson, March 3, 1804, Charles Simms entry, Letters of Application and Recommendation During the Administration of Thomas Jefferson, General Records of the Department of State, Record Group 59 (National Archives).

9. For biographical data on Charles Lee, see Irving M. Brant, *James Madison, Father of the Constitution, 1787–1800* (Indianapolis, Ind., 1950), 431; Stephen Hess, *American Political*

Dynasties From Adams to Kennedy (Garden City, N.Y., 1966), 64–67; Rose, *Prologue to Democracy,* 41–42, 157, 188; Stephen G. Kurtz, *The Presidency of John Adams: The Collapse of Federalism, 1795–1800* (Philadelphia, 1957), 274–75; *Dictionary of American Biography,* Dumas Malone and Allen Johnson, eds. (22 vols., New York, 1928–58), XI, 101–2.

10. For Lee's extensive political activity, see Charles Lee to James Iredell, September 20, 1798, James Iredell Papers (Perkins Library, Duke University); Oliver Wolcott, Jr., to Fisher Ames, December 29, 1799, *Memoirs of the Administrations of Washington and John Adams, Edited from the Papers of Oliver Wolcott, Secretary of the Treasury,* George Gibbs, ed. (2 vols., New York, 1846), II, 313–15; Charles Lee to George Washington, December 27, 1796, Washington to Lee, December 27, 1796, *The Writings of George Washington,* John C. Fitzpatrick, ed. (39 vols., Washington, D.C., 1931–44), XXXV, 349–50; *Dictionary of American Biography,* XI, 101–2; Kurtz, *Presidency of John Adams,* 22, 274–75; Rose, *Prologue to Democracy,* 157, 188, 219, 233; John Carroll and Mary Ashworth, *George Washington: First in Peace* (New York, 1957), 276n.

11. John Fitzgerald to George Washington, April 5, 1793, Applications For Office Under President Washington, Series VII, George Washington Papers, vol. XI; George Washington to James Craik, April 9, 1793, Washington to Fitzgerald, April 28, June 3, 1793, *Writings of Washington,* Fitzpatrick, ed., XXXII, 414, 438–39, 485–86 respectively; Washington to Fitzgerald, October 8, 9, 1793, ibid., XXXIII, 114–16; Alexander Hamilton to Fitzgerald, June 30, 1791, *Papers of Hamilton,* Syrett, ed., VIII, 516; Fitzgerald to Hamilton, November 21, 1791, ibid., IX, 515–16.

12. Archibald McLean to Thomas Jefferson, February 22, 1802, Archibald McLean entry, Letters of Application and Recommendation During the Administration of Thomas Jefferson; Stevens T. Mason et al. to Jefferson, March 3, 1804, Thomas Ricketts to Jefferson, March 22, 1804, A. Harrison to Richard Brent, March 22, 26, 1804, Charles Simms entry, ibid.; Henry Moore to Jefferson, March 19, 1804, Cleon Moore entry, ibid.; Beeman, *The Old Dominion and the New Nation,* 163–65; Kurtz, *Presidency of John Adams,* 164–65; Hugh B. Grigsby, *The History of the Virginia Federal Convention of 1788 . . .* (2 vols., Richmond, 1890–91), II, 373; Mary G. Powell, *The History of Old Alexandria, Virginia* (Richmond, 1928), 259–60; manuscript analysis of Virginia Federalists provided by Norman K. Risjord.

13. Josiah Parker to George Washington, May 11, 1792, William Taylor to Washington, May 20, 1792, Edward Carrington to Alexander Hamilton, June 20, 1792, Applications For Office Under President Washington, Series VII, George Washington Papers, vol. XXII; William Lindsay to Hamilton, May 20, 1792, *Papers of Hamilton*, XI, 414–15.

14. Charles Lee to George Washington, July 3, 1789, Richard Henry Lee to Washington, July 27, 1789, Richard Bland Lee to Washington, July 28, 1790, Applications For Office Under President Washington, Series VII, George Washington Papers, vol. XVII; Bushrod Washington to George Washington, March 19, 1789, Richard M. Scott to Washington, June 15, 1789, October 16, 1795, ibid., vol XXV.

15. "A List of Persons who . . . Requested to be Recommended to the President . . . for Appointment," undated (1789), ibid., vol. IV; Samuel Griffin to Washington, undated (1789), ibid., vol. XIII; Hudson Muse to Washington, March 20, 1789, February 1, 1794, ———— to James Monroe, February 3, 1794, ibid., vol. XX; George W. Smith to Washington, February 4, 1794, ibid., vol. XXVI; *The Letters and Papers of Edmund Pendleton, 1734–1803*, David J. Mays, ed. (2 vols., Charlottesville, Va., 1967), II, 459.

16. For the Wrays, see Samuel Griffin to George Washington, undated (1789), Applications For Office Under President Washington, Series VII, George Washington Papers, vol. XIII; Jacob Wray to Washington, May 12, 1790, Samuel Griffin to Washington, April 24, 1790, ibid., vol. XXXI.

For the Rowlands, see Zachariah Rowland to Oliver Wolcott, Jr., November 6, 1797, James Rowland entry, Letters of Application and Recommendation During the Administration of John Adams; Isaac S. Harrell, *Loyalism in Virginia* (Philadelphia, 1926), 57.

17. George Washington to Benjamin Harrison, March 9, 1789, Washington to Samuel Vaughan, March 21, 1789, Washington to Bushrod Washington, July 27, 1789, *Writings of Washington*, Fitzpatrick, ed., XXX, 224, 238, 366 respectively.

18. "List of Civil Officers of the United States . . . October 1, 1792," "A List of the Officers Employed in the Collection of the Internal Revenues of the United States . . . July, 1796," and "Roll of the Officers, Civil, Military, and Naval of the United States [1801]," *American State Papers, Miscellaneous: Documents, Legislative and Executive of the Congress of the United States*, Walter Lowrie and Walter S. Franklin, eds. (2 vols., Washington, D.C., 1834), I, 57–68, 568–73, 260–319 respectively; William Lewis to George Washington, October 22, 1791, Applications For Office

Under President Washington, Series VII, George Washington Papers, vol. XVII; Tench Coxe to Alexander Hamilton, October 31, 1792, *Papers of Hamilton,* Syrett, ed., XII, 635; Douglas S. Freeman, *George Washington, Patriot and President* (New York, 1954), 363n; Leonard D. White, *The Federalists: A Study in Administrative History, 1789–1801* (New York, 1948), 262, 278; Tench Coxe, *A View of the United States of America* (Philadelphia, 1794), 319.

19. For North Carolina politics, see Rose, *Prologue to Democracy;* Henry M. Wagstaff, "Federalism in North Carolina," *Sprunt Historical Publications* IX, no. 2 (Chapel Hill, 1910).

20. "List of Civil Officers of the United States . . . For the Year Ending October 1, 1792," *American State Papers, Miscellaneous: Documents, Legislative and Executive of the Congress of the United States,* Lowrie and Franklin, eds., I, 57–68.

21. Though Hugh Williamson goes virtually unmentioned in most standard accounts of party formations in the Federalist era, he did briefly occupy a place of trust and importance in an informal way. The president frequently consulted him about North Carolina politics and appointments in 1790 and 1791. See the *Dictionary of American Biography,* XX, 298–300; "The Harris Letters," Henry M. Wagstaff, ed., in *The James Sprunt Studies* XIV (1916), no. 1, 16n. These provide background on Williamson's career.

22. Hugh Williamson to George Washington, February 5, December 21, 1790, "The Senators of North Carolina" to Washington, February 8, 1790, Alexander Martin to Washington, February 27, 1790, Applications For Office Under President Washington, Series VII, George Washington Papers, vols. XXX, XXI, XIX respectively. The ten constitutional Federalists were Joshua Skinner, Jr., Hardy Murfree, Levi Blount, Isaac Gregory, Edmund Sawyer, John Walker, James Read, Thomas Callender, John Davis, and Nathan Keais.

It might be of interest to note too that Secretary of State Thomas Jefferson wasn't doing so well with the president in influencing Tarheel appointments in his own department. He suggested three possibilities for nomination to the post of United States district judge, then under the jurisdiction of the State Department, but none of the three were appointed. See Thomas Jefferson to George Washington, June 7, 1790, ibid., vol. XXI.

23. Tench Coxe to Thomas Benbury, July 13, 1792, Alexander Hamilton to George Washington, September 17, 1792, *Papers of Hamilton,* Syrett, ed., XI, 29, XII, 392 respectively.

24. Albert Gallatin's note, undated (1808), Laurence Mooney en-

try, Letters of Application and Recommendation During the Administration of Thomas Jefferson; Samuel Tredwell to Alexander Hamilton, January 15, 1795, Applications For Office Under President Washington, Series VII, George Washington Papers, vol. XX.

25. Gabriel Phillips to Thomas Jefferson, October 18, 1801, Michael Payne entry, Letters of Application and Recommendation During the Administration of Thomas Jefferson.

26. Hugh Williamson to George Washington, March 22, 1790, John Skinner to Oliver Wolcott, Jr., January 27, 1798, Applications For Office Under President Washington, Series VII, George Washington Papers, vol. XXV. The second letter cited above was filed mistakenly with the George Washington Papers rather than those of the Adams administration, apparently because the date on the letter is unclear.

27. Lisle A. Rose, *Prologue to Democracy*, 17–18.

28. Louise I. Trenholme, *The Ratification of the Federal Constitution in North Carolina* (New York, 1932), 11.

29. Hugh Williamson to George Washington, February 5, 1790, Applications For Office Under President Washington, Series VII, George Washington Papers, vol. XXX; William F. Muse to Charles Johnson, October 17, 1801, James L. Shannonhouse entry, Letters of Application and Recommendation During the Administration of Thomas Jefferson; *The Papers of Archibald D. Murphey*, William H. Hoyt, ed. (2 vols., Raleigh, N.C., 1914), I, 336n; Jesse F. Pugh, *A Biographical History of Camden County* (Old Trap, N.C., 1957), 92–97, 129–32; Trenholme, *Ratification of the Federal Constitution in North Carolina*, 103, 151, 163.

30. William Blount to John Gray Blount, January 31, 1790, John Haywood to John Gray Blount, March 18, 1790, Thomas Blount to John Gray Blount, February 6, 1795, October 19, 1795, and passim, *The John Gray Blount Papers*, Alice B. Keith, ed. (2 vols., Raleigh, N.C., 1959), vol. II, passim; Nathan Keais to George Washington, January 2, 1790, Applications For Office Under President Washington, Series VII, George Washington Papers, vol. XVI; William Kennedy to Thomas Jefferson, October 27, 1808, W. J. Sheppard entry, and William Blackledge to Albert Gallatin, November 11, 1801, William Orr entry, Letters of Application and Recommendation During the Administration of Thomas Jefferson.

31. D. Ward et al. to Albert Gallatin, ca. March 15, 1802, Brian Hellen entry, and Gallatin's and Jefferson's annotated comments, ca. April 1803, Benjamin Cheney entry, Letters of Application and Recommendation During the Administration of Thomas Jefferson.

32. James Read to John Haywood, July 14, 1796, September 21, November 24, 1797, August 25, 1798, October 27, 1801, William Campbell et al. to ———, August 12, 1798, and passim, Ernest Haywood Papers (Southern Historical Collection, University of North Carolina Library); Timothy Bloodworth to Thomas Jefferson, December 12, 1803, James Read entry, Letters of Application and Recommendation During the Administration of Thomas Jefferson; John Steele to Edward Jones, March 7, 1798, Steele to James Read, July 2, 1798, and passim, *The Papers of John Steele,* Henry M. Wagstaff, ed. (2 vols., Chapel Hill, N.C., 1924), I, 154–56, 157–58, II, passim. The subordinate employees at the Wilmington customshouse were also Federalists for the most part. See Timothy Bloodworth to Thomas Jefferson, October 6, 1801, John P. Williams entry, Letters of Application and Recommendation During the Administration of Thomas Jefferson.

33. For South Carolina politics, see Rose, *Prologue to Democracy;* George C. Rogers, Jr., *Evolution of a Federalist: William Loughton Smith of Charleston 1758–1812* (Columbia, S.C., 1962); Marvin R. Zahniser, *Charles Cotesworth Pinckney, Founding Father* (Chapel Hill, N.C., 1967).

34. For George Abbott Hall, see Rogers, *Evolution of a Federalist,* 185–86; Charles Pinckney to George Washington, March 2, 1789, William Moultrie to Washington, March 12, 1789, John Matthews to Washington, March 12, 1789, Applications For Office Under President Washington, Series VII, George Washington Papers, vol. XIV.

35. For the circumstances of Holmes' appointment, see Isaac Holmes to George Washington, August 3, 1791, Richard Fruston to Washington, August 3, 1791, Pierce Butler to Washington, August 3, 1791, Applications For Office Under President Washington, Series VII, George Washington Papers, vol. XV. For his peculations, see Donald H. Stewart, "The Press and Political Corruption During the Federalist Administration," *Political Science Quarterly* LXVII (1952), 437; Rogers, *Evolution of a Federalist,* 185–86.

36. For Isaac Motte, see William Moultrie to George Washington, August 10, 1789, August 2, 1791, Charles Pinckney to Washington, August 2, 1791, Applications For Office Under President Washington, Series VII, George Washington Papers, vol. XX; Rogers, *Evolution of a Federalist,* 26, 60, 155, 206; Zahniser, *Charles Cotesworth Pinckney,* 41; Forrest McDonald, *We, The People: The Economic Origins of the Constitution* (Chicago, 1958), 225, 234; Emily B. Reynolds and Joan R. Faunt, *Biographical Di-*

rectory of the Senate of South Carolina, 1776–1964 (Columbia, S.C., 1964), 279.

37. Rogers, *Evolution of a Federalist*, 186.

38. For James Simons, see Samuel Smith to John Rutledge, May 12, 1801, James Simons to Rutledge, June 2, 1801, John Rutledge Papers (Southern Historical Collection, University of North Carolina Library); James Simons to Pierce Butler, February 25, 1795, Butler to George Washington, March 15, 1794 [1795], James Simons to Edmund Randolph, May 20, 1795, Jacob Read to Randolph, May 20, 1795, Butler to Randolph, May 20, 1795, Applications For Office Under President Washington, Series VII, George Washington Papers, vol. XXV; Albert Gallatin's note on James Simons's folder [1801], Anon, to Thomas Jefferson, November 23, 1801, James Simons to John Steele, September 30, 1802, James Symonds [Simons] entry, Albert Gallatin's note filed with Daniel D'Oyley to Gallatin, July 29, 1801, Daniel D'Oyley entry, Letters of Application and Recommendation During the Administration of Thomas Jefferson; *Papers of Hamilton*, Syrett, ed., X, 432n; James Simons to John Steele, December 15, 1802, *Papers of John Steele*, Wagstaff, ed., I, 340–41; Rogers, *Evolution of a Federalist*, 186, 188, 192, 344, 347, 364; George C. Rogers, Jr., *Charleston in the Age of the Pinckneys* (Norman, Oklahoma, 1969), 118.

39. James Simons to John Rutledge, June 2, 1801, John Rutledge Papers; Albert Gallatin's note on James Simons's folder [1801], James Symonds [Simons] entry, Letters of Application and Recommendation During the Administration of Thomas Jefferson; McDonald, *We, The People*, 227.

40. Robert Cochran to George Washington, undated (1789), Applications For Office Under President Washington, Series VII, George Washington Papers, vol. VI; Thomas Pinckney to John Rutledge, August 1, 1798, Benjamin Stoddert to Rutledge, October 12, 1798, John Rutledge Papers; Rogers, *Charleston*, 15; "Roll of Officers, Civil, Military, and Naval of the United States [1801]," *American State Papers, Miscellaneous*, Lowrie and Franklin, eds., I, 278.

41. Cf. note 38. See Particularly James Simons to John Rutledge, June 2, 1801, John Rutledge Papers; Rogers, *Evolution of a Federalist*, 186, 344.

CHAPTER SIX

1. Pierce Butler to Thomas Jefferson, September 3, 1801, Daniel Stevens entry, Letters of Application and Recommendation During

the Administration of Thomas Jefferson, General Records of the Department of State, Record Group 59 (National Archives); Marvin R. Zahniser, *Charles Cotesworth Pinckney, Founding Father* (Chapel Hill, 1967), 102–3, 113–15.

2. For Virginia, see Laurence Muse to James Madison, April 4, 1801, Laurence Muse entry, Letters of Application and Recommendation During the Administration of Thomas Jefferson; Lisle A. Rose, *Prologue to Democracy: The Federalists in the South, 1789–1801* (Lexington, 1968), 25, 40–42.

3. For Connecticut, see Ephraim Kirby to John Chester, July 15, 1801, Timothy Larrabee to Kirby, July 20, 1801, Daniel Crocker to Kirby, August 3, 1801, Ephraim Kirby Papers (Perkins Library, Duke University).

For New Jersey, see Joseph Bloomfield to Aaron Burr, April 8, 1801, William Rossell entry, Letters of Application and Recommendation During the Administration of Thomas Jefferson.

4. For George Clymer, see the Whisky Rebellion Manuscripts, Pennsylvania Miscellany Collection, vol. I (Historical Society of Pennsylvania); George Clymer to Alexander Hamilton, September 28, October 4, 10, 1792, and Alexander Addison to Clymer, September 29, 1792, *The Papers of Alexander Hamilton*, Harold C. Syrett, ed. (24 vols., New York, 1961–76), XII, 495–97, 517–22, 540–542 and passim; Leland Baldwin, *Whiskey Rebels: The Story of a Frontier Uprising* (Pittsburgh, 1939), 87–90 and passim; *Biographical Directory of the American Congress, 1774–1961* (Washington, D.C., 1961), 710.

5. For Henry Miller, see William Findley to Thomas Jefferson, February 26, May 12, 1801, Samuel Bryan entry, Findley to Jefferson, March 5, 1801, William Irwin [Irvine] entry, Letters of Application and Recommendation During the Administration of Thomas Jefferson; Thomas Jefferson's "Anas," March 18, 1801, *The Works of Thomas Jefferson*, Paul L. Ford, ed. (12 vols., New York, 1904–5), I, 364.

6. For John Neville's involvement in the Whisky Rebellion and his Federalist career generally, see John Neville to Alexander Hamilton, October 27, 1791, *Papers of Hamilton*, Syrett, ed., IX, 419ff; Harry M. Tinkcom, *The Republicans and Federalists in Pennsylvania 1790–1801* (Harrisburg, 1950), 54–55, 95, 130; Russell J. Ferguson, *Early Western Pennsylvania Politics* (Pittsburgh, 1938), 84, 151, 164, 267–70; Baldwin, *Whiskey Rebels*, 44–47 and passim.

7. For John Boyd, see John Christ to Thomas Jefferson, June 28, 1801, John Chinn [Christ] entry, Letters of Application and Rec-

ommendation During the Administration of Thomas Jefferson; Rollo Silver, *The American Printer, 1787–1825* (Charlottesville, Va., 1967), 142; John B. McMaster and Frederick D. Stone, *Pennsylvania and the Federal Constitution, 1787–1788* (Lancaster, Pa., 1888), 719–20; Forrest McDonald, *We, The People: The Economic Origins of the Constitution* (Chicago, 1958), 173; William H. Egle, "The Federal Constitution of 1787: Biographical Sketches of the Members of the Pennsylvania Convention," *Pennsylvania Magazine of History and Biography* X–XI (1886–87), 456–57.

For Edward Hand, see the Edward Hand Papers, vols. I–III, passim (Gratz Collection, Historical Society of Pennsylvania); Timothy Matlack to Thomas Jefferson, August 28, 1801, Timothy Matlack entry, William Findley to Jefferson, May 12, 1801, Samuel Bryan entry, Letters of Application and Recommendation During the Administration of Thomas Jefferson; Tinkcom, *Republicans and Federalists*, 254; David H. Fischer, *Revolution of American Conservatism: The Federalist Party in the Era of Jeffersonian Democracy* (New York, 1965), 338.

Thomas Ross and William Nichols, the inspectors of the surveys in the Philadelphia area, were also Federalists.

8. For Richard Morris's appointment and circumstances in 1790, see Richard Morris to Janes Duane, January 21, 1790, Box 8, James Duane Papers (New-York Historical Society); Arthur Alexander, "Federal Patronage in New York State, 1789–1805" (Ph.D. diss., University of Pennsylvania, 1944), 22, 50–51; Richard Morris to Alexander Hamilton, April 13, 1792, *Papers of Hamilton*, Syrett, ed., XI, 274–75. For a biographical sketch, see Franklin B. Dexter, *Biographical Sketches of the Graduates of Yale College* (6 vols., New York, 1885–1912), II, 171–72.

9. For widely differing views of William S. Smith's politics in general and his public role with regard to Jay's Treaty in particular, see the notes in *The Writings of George Washington*, John C. Fitzpatrick, ed. (39 vols., Washington, D.C., 1931–1944), XXXIV, 254n, 272n; Alfred E. Young, *The Democratic Republicans of New York: The Origins, 1763–1797* (Chapel Hill, 1967), 354, 374, 450; Edward P. Alexander, *A Revolutionary Conservative, James Duane of New York* (New York, 1938), 201–5, 209, 252; John Carroll and Mary Ashworth, *George Washington: First in Peace* (New York, 1957), 270.

10. William S. Smith to George Washington, January 11, 1794, Applications For Office Under President Washington, Series VII,

George Washington Papers (Manuscript Division, Library of Congress), vol. XXVI; William S. Smith to Thomas Jefferson, September 5, 1801, Matthew Davis entry, Letters of Application and Recommendation During the Administration of Thomas Jefferson; Young, *Democratic Republicans of New York*, 354; Alexander, "Federal Patronage in New York State," 33. For his office seeking in 1797–1798, and the well-known political consequences and ensuing political embarrassment to President Adams, see William S. Smith to Adams, April 17, 1797, William D. Smith entry, Letters of Application and Recommendation During the Administration of John Adams, General Records of the Department of State, Record Group 59 (National Archives); Manning J. Dauer, *The Adams Federalists* (Baltimore, 1953), 212–13. Katherine M. Roof, *Colonel William Smith and Lady* (Boston, 1929), should be dismissed as an unacceptable source for Smith's politics.

11. For Nicholas Fish's biographical background, see the Nicholas Fish Papers, passim (Library of Congress); Nicholas Fish Papers, passim (New-York Historical Society). For his political activity, see the transcripts of Nicholas Fish's letters, 1801–2, Folder 13, passim, John Rutledge Papers (Southern Historical Collection, University of North Carolina Library); Nicholas Fish to George Washington, February 12, 1791, Applications For Office Under President Washington, Series VII, George Washington Papers, vol. XI; Alexander Hamilton to Oliver Wolcott, Jr., April 22, 1797, Benjamin Walker entry, Letters of Application and Recommendation During the Administration of John Adams; Pierre Van Cortlandt to Thomas Jefferson, May 22, 1801, Pierre Van Cortlandt entry, Letters of Application and Recommendation During the Administration of Thomas Jefferson; Thomas Jefferson to George Clinton, May 17, 1801, *Works of Jefferson*, Ford, ed., IX, 254; Alexander Hamilton to John Armstrong, Jr., April 1, 1793, *Papers of Hamilton*, Syrett, ed., XIV, 269–71; Dixon Ryan Fox, *The Decline of Aristocracy in the Politics of New York* (New York, 1919), 20, 22, 123, 164; Fischer, *The Revolution of American Conservatism*, 301.

12. For Nathaniel Gorham, see Winfred Bernhard, *Fisher Ames: Federalist and Statesman, 1758–1808* (Chapel Hill, 1965), 57, 62, 162; Anson E. Morse, *The Federalist Party in Massachusetts to the Year 1800* (Princeton, 1913), 141n; *The Life and Correspondence of Rufus King*, Charles King, ed. (2 vols., New York, 1894–1900), II, 4; McDonald, *We, The People*, 24, 43, 98, 192. Jonathan Jackson, a United States marshal until his appointment to the internal revenue service in 1796, is discussed in chapter 10.

13. For Leonard Jarvis, see John Hancock to George Washington, May 2, 1789, Jarvis to George Washington, August 10, 1789, Applications For Office Under President Washington, Series VII, George Washington Papers, vol. XVI; Clifford K. Shipton, *Sibley's Harvard Graduates: Biographical Sketches of Those Who Attended Harvard College* (16 vols., Boston, 1873–1972), XII, 213.

For Ebenezer Storer, see Storer to Washington, May 25, 1789, Applications For Office Under President Washington, Series VII, George Washington Papers, vol. XXVI; Edward Dowse to Thomas Jefferson, April 28, 1801, Edward Dowse entry, Letters of Application and Recommendation During the Administration of Thomas Jefferson; Page Smith, *John Adams* (2 vols., New York, 1962), II, 763; Samuel B. Harding, *The Contest Over the Ratification of the Federal Constitution in the State of Massachusetts* (New York, 1896), 56; Shipton, *Sibley's Harvard Graduates*, XII, 208–14.

14. Alexander Hamilton to John F. Mercer, September 26, 1792, *Papers of Hamilton*, Syrett, ed., XII, 488; Libero M. Renzulli, Jr., "Maryland Federalism: 1789–1819" (Ph.D. diss., University of Virginia, 1962), 10, 102n, 167; Dorothy M. Brown, "Maryland and the Federalists: Search for Unity," *Maryland Historical Magazine* LXIII (1968), 4n; McDonald, *We, The People*, 155–57; *U.S. Congress Biographical Directory, 1774–1961*, 924.

15. A. Hanson to George Washington, July 22, 1794, John Kilty to Washington, July 25, 1794 and passim, Applications For Office Under President Washington, Series VII, George Washington Papers, vol. XVI; Kilty to Roger Nelson, July 30, 1801, Charles R. Polk entry, Letters of Application and Recommendation During the Administration of Thomas Jefferson; Kilty to Alexander Hamilton, August 20, 1792, *Papers of Hamilton*, Syrett, ed., XII, 262; Roster of the Maryland Society of the Cincinnati, November 21, 1783, *Calendar of the General Otho Holland Williams Papers*, Elizabeth Merritt, ed. (Baltimore, 1940), 89.

16. For Philip Thomas, see Thomas Scharf, *History of Maryland*, 2nd edition (3 vols., Hatboro, Pennsylvania, 1967), II, 611n; George A. Hanson, *Old Kent* (Baltimore, 1876), 130; *Calendar of the General Otho Holland Williams Papers*, Merritt, ed., passim; Brown, "Maryland and the Federalists," *Maryland Historical Magazine* LXIII (1968), 2; Renzulli, "Maryland Federalism," 51.

For William Richardson, see William Vans Murray to George Washington, December 12, 1792, Applications For Office Under President Washington, Series VII, George Washington Papers, vol. XXIV; Tench Coxe to Alexander Hamilton, December 14, 1792,

Hamilton to James McHenry, April 5, 1793, *Papers of Hamilton,* Syrett, ed., XIII, 322–23, XIV, 288–89; *Calendar of the General Otho Holland Williams Papers,* Merritt, ed., 12; Brown, "Maryland and the Federalists," *Maryland Historical Magazine* LXIII (1968), 2; Scharf, *History of Maryland,* II, 546.

17. The sources illuminating Edward Carrington's political role in the 1790s are extensive. See, for example, *Writings of Washington,* Fitzpatrick, ed., vol. XXXIII, passim; *Papers of Hamilton,* Syrett, ed., vols. X–XV, passim; Rose, *Prologue to Democracy,* passim.

18. For Edward Stevens, see Samuel Griffin to George Washington, undated [1789], Stevens to Washington, March 16, 1789, Applications For Office Under President Washington, Series VII, George Washington Papers, vols. XIII and XXVI respectively; George Washington to Stevens, November 16, 1793, *Writings of Washington,* Fitzpatrick, ed., XXXIII, 153–54; Irving M. Brant, *James Madison, Father of the Constitution, 1787–1800* (Indianapolis, 1950), 240–41; Jackson T. Main, *The Upper Houses in Revolutionary America, 1763–1788* (Madison, Wisconsin, 1967), 127; *Encyclopedia of Virginia Biography,* Lyon G. Tyler, ed. (5 vols., New York, 1915), II, 172–73.

For James Gibbon, see "A List of persons who have requested to be recommended to the President . . . [1789]," and Gibbon to George Washington, January 24, 1790, July 17, 1792, Applications For Office Under President Washington, Series VII, George Washington Papers, vols. IV and VII respectively; Tench Coxe to Oliver Wolcott, Jr., September 18, 1797, James Gibbon entry, Letters of Application and Recommendation During the Administration of John Adams; William Heth to Alexander Hamilton, October 14, 1792, *Papers of Hamilton,* Syrett, ed., XII, 554–56. The one exception among the revenue inspectors was Thomas Newton, Jr., one of "very few" Republicans among Norfolk merchants. At the same time he was "the most respectable and wealthy man in the place." James Monroe to Thomas Jefferson, June 29, November 3, 1802, Littleton W. Tazewell entry, Letters of Application and Recommendation During the Administration of Thomas Jefferson.

19. For Daniel Stevens, see Stevens to Oliver Wolcott, Jr., April 20, 1795, William L. Smith to George Washington, August 29, 1789, and Daniel Stevens to Washington, September 7, 1795, Applications For Office Under President Washington, Series VII, George Washington Papers, vols. XX, XXVI; Albert Gallatin notation [1801], James Symonds [Simons] entry, Letters of Application and

Recommendation During the Administration of Thomas Jefferson; George C. Rogers, Jr., *Evolution of a Federalist: William Loughton Smith of Charleston, 1758–1812* (Columbia, S.C., 1962), 187–88, 346–47; Emily B. Reynolds and Joan R. Faunt, *Biographical Directory of the Senate of South Carolina, 1776–1964* (Columbia, S.C., 1964), 315; McDonald, *We, The People,* 218; "Autobiography of Daniel Stevens, 1746–1835," *South Carolina Historical Magazine* LVIII (1957), 1–18. The three revenue inspectors in the state were also Federalists.

20. For William Polk, see W. Hampton to Polk, April 10, 1794, and passim, Polk Family Papers (Manuscript Division, Library of Congress); Alexander Hamilton to George Washington, February 18, 1792, Tench Coxe to Hamilton, October 19, 1792, *Papers of Hamilton,* Syrett, ed., XI, 40, XII, 600 respectively; William Polk to John Steele, November 28, 1800, *The Papers of John Steele,* Henry M. Wagstaff, ed. (2 vols., Chapel Hill, 1924), I, 190–92 and passim; William Polk to John Gray Blount, January 18, 1794, *The John Gray Blount Papers,* Alice B. Keith, ed. (2 vols., Raleigh, N.C., 1959), II, 347–49 and passim; Mariella Waite, "Political Institutions in the Transappalachian West, 1777–1800" (Ph.D. diss., University of Florida, 1961), 124; Fischer, *Revolution of American Conservatism,* 392.

21. I am indebted to Patricia Watlington for information provided on both James Morrison and Thomas Marshall, as well as several other Kentucky politicians in this period. For Morrison, see Hugh B. Grigsby, *The History of the Virginia Federal Convention of 1788 . . .* (2 vols., Richmond, 1890–91), II, 293; Niels H. Sonne, *Liberal Kentucky, 1780–1828* (New York, 1939), 16. For Thomas Marshall, see George Washington to Thomas Marshall, March 27, 1789, *Writings of Washington,* Fitzpatrick, ed., XXX, 252–53; Rose, *Prologue to Democracy,* 73n.

For John Overton's early political career, see James White to Overton, March 22, 1795, Andrew Jackson to Overton, February 13, 1798, and the introductory sketch, John Overton Papers (Tennessee Historical Society); Thomas P. Abernethy, *From Frontier to Plantation in Tennessee* (Memphis, 1955), 242–70; William H. Masterson, *William Blount* (Baton Rouge, La., 1954), 297 and passim; *Dictionary of American Biography,* Dumas Malone and Allen Johnson, eds. (22 vols., New York, 1928–58), XIV, 115–16; J. W. Caldwell, *Sketches of the Bench and Bar of Tennessee* (Knoxville, 1898), 77–78.

22. For John Neufville, see Peter Freneau to Thomas Jefferson,

July 4, 1804, Adam Gilchrist to Wade Hampton, August 1, 1804, Hampton to Thomas Jefferson, August 11, 1804, Isaac Neufville entry, Letters of Application and Recommendation During the Administration of Thomas Jefferson; Reynolds and Faunt, *Biographical Directory of the Senate of South Carolina*, 282.

For the Harwoods, see Benjamin Harwood to George Washington, December 3, 1792, Thomas Lee to Washington, December 1, 1792, Charles Carroll of Carrollton to Washington, December 1, 1792, Applications For Office Under President Washington, Series VII, George Washington Papers, vol. XIV; John T. Mason to Thomas Jefferson, May 27, 29, 1801, Gabriel Duvall to Jefferson, May 27, 1801, Rose Nelson to Jefferson, May 27, 1801, Thomas Harwood entry, Letters of Application and Recommendation During the Administration of Thomas Jefferson.

23. Main, *Upper Houses in Revolutionary America*, 50–51; John A. Munroe, *Federalist Delaware, 1775–1815* (New Brunswick, N.J., 1954), passim.

24. Jeremiah Smith to Oliver Wolcott, Jr., June 14, 1798, William Plumer to Wolcott, June 8, 1798, Jeremiah Smith and Joseph Whipple entries respectively, Letters of Application and Recommendation During the Administration of John Adams; William Gardner to Nicholas Gilman, June 14, 1788, Miscellaneous Mss. (New-York Historical Society); Alexander Hamilton to William Gardner, June 14, 1792, *Papers of Hamilton*, Syrett, ed., XI, 517, 517n; Jackson T. Main, *The Antifederalists: Critics of the Constitution, 1781–1788* (Chapel Hill, 1961), 166.

25. For Nathaniel Appleton, see Appleton to Timothy Pickering, October 16, 1797, Appleton to John Adams, October 16, 1797, John Lowell to Pickering, October 18, 1797, Thomas Appleton entry, Letters of Application and Recommendation During the Administration of John Adams; Andrew G. Fraunces to Alexander Hamilton, July 1, 1793, *Papers of Hamilton*, XV, 45, and vols. XIV–XV, passim; Bernhard, *Fisher Ames*, 240, 240n; Shipton, *Sibley's Harvard Graduates*, XII, 355–59.

For Thomas H. Perkins, see Perkins to Harrison Gray Otis, March 3, April 21, 1798, Box 4, Harrison Gray Otis Papers (Massachusetts Historical Society); Thomas H. Perkins et al. to Theodore Sedgwick, April 23, 1796, vol. III, Theodore Sedgwick Papers (Massachusetts Historical Society); George Cabot to Oliver Wolcott, Jr., June 19, 1798, Perkins to Wolcott, June 21, 1798, John Lowell to Wolcott, June 23, 1798, Benjamin Lincoln to George Washington, June 27, 1798, Thomas Perkins entry, Letters of Application and Recommendation During the Administration of John Adams; *Boston Gazette,* October 20, 27, November 3, 1800; *Boston Federal Orrery,* November 3, 1794; Samuel Eliot Morison, *The Life and Letters of Harrison Gray Otis, Federalist, 1765–1848* (2 vols., Boston, 1913), I, 94–95, 291, II, 67, 94, 161–71; Fischer, *Revolution of American Conservatism,* 271.

26. Jabez Bowen to George Washington, June 13, 1789, June 13, 14, 19, 1790, and passim, Applications For Office Under President Washington, Series VII, George Washington Papers, vol. 3; *The Providence Gazette,* June 18, 1796; *George Washington's Correspondence Concerning the Society of the Cincinnati,* Edgar E. Hume, ed. (Baltimore, 1941), 388; Mack E. Thompson, *Moses Brown, Reluctant Reformer* (Providence, 1962), 250; Fischer, *Revolution of American Conservatism,* 278; James B. Hedges, *The Browns of Providence Plantation* (2 vols., Providence, 1952–68), I, 190, 312, and passim; McDonald, *We, The People,* 325; Dexter, *Biographical Sketches of the Graduates of Yale College,* II, 452–54; Irwin Polishook, *Rhode Island and the Union* (Evanston, Ill., 1969), 237–38.

27. For John Cochran, see Cochran to Philip Schuyler, August 10, 1791, and the Cochran-Schuyler correspondence, passim, Box 36, Philip Schuyler Papers (New York Public Library); James Duane to Polly Duane, July 19, 1793, Box 8, James Duane Papers (New-York Historical Society); John Cochran to George Washington, July 10, 1789, August 1, 1793, Applications For Office Under President Washington, Series VII, George Washington Papers, vol. VI; William Seton to Alexander Hamilton, April 29, 1792, John G. Worthington to David Ross, November 17, 1792, *Papers of Hamilton,* Syrett, ed., XI, 345–46 and XIII, 220–22 respectively.

For Matthew Clarkson, see Clarkson to Thomas Jefferson, September 18, 1801, Resignations and Declinations Among the Records of the Department of State, 1789–1827, General Records of the Department of State, Record Group 59 (National Archives); Clarkson to George Washington, January 2, 1790, July 16, 1791, October 19, 1793, Applications For Office Under President Washington, Series VII, George Washington Papers, vol. VI; Robert Troup to Oliver Wolcott, Jr., April 22, 1797, Alexander Hamilton to Wolcott, April 22, 1797, William Seton and Benjamin Walker entries respectively, Letters of Application and Recommendation During the Administration of John Adams; *American Minerva,* December 10, 1793; John Jay to Alexander Hamilton, December 22, 1790, Hamilton to James Watson, October 9, 1792,

Papers of Hamilton, Syrett, ed., VII, 377 and XII, 538–39 respectively; John Jay to George Washington, March 13, 1791, *The Correspondence and Public Papers of John Jay, 1763–1826*, Henry P. Johnston, ed. (4 vols., New York, 1890–93), III, 412; Fox, *Decline of Aristocracy*, 19–20; Joseph S. Davis, *Essays in the Earlier History of American Corporations* (2 vols., Cambridge, Mass., 1917), I, 370, 391–95, 456; Sidney I. Pomerantz, *New York: An American City, 1783–1803* (New York, 1938), 221; Alexander, "Federal Patronage in New York State," 88.

28. For Thomas Smith, see Richard Peters to George Washington, May 12, 1789, December 5, 1793, Applications For Office Under President Washington, Series VII, George Washington Papers, vol. XVI.

For Stephen Moylan, see John Moylan to Robert Morris, July 17, 1791, Stephen Moylan to Thomas Jefferson, September 19, 1793, ibid., vol. XX; *Philadelphia Minerva*, July 9, 1796; Stephen Moylan to Alexander Hamilton, October 21, 1793, *Papers of Hamilton*, Syrett, ed., XV, 371–72.

For John Stockton, see "Signers of Jesse Higgins Certificate," undated (1789), Applications For Office Under President Washington, Series VII, George Washington Papers, vol. XV; John Bird to Thomas Jefferson, August 4, 1802, John Bird entry, Letters of Application and Recommendation During the Administration of Thomas Jefferson; Salem [Mass.] *Impartial Register*, July 17, 1800; Munroe, *Federalist Delaware*, 202, 248, 254n; Donald H. Stewart, "The Press and Political Corruption During the Federalist Administrations," *Political Science Quarterly* LXVII (1952), 444.

29. John Hopkins to George Washington, April 10, 1789, Applications For Office Under President Washington, Series VII, George Washington Papers, vol. XV; John Hopkins to Oliver Wolcott, Jr., September 14, 1798, *Memoirs of the Administrations of Washington and John Adams, edited from the Papers of Oliver Wolcott, Secretary of the Treasury*, George Gibbs, ed. (2 vols., New York, 1846), I, 108; Rose, *Prologue to Democracy*, 155–56; Fischer, *Revolution of American Conservatism*, 375.

30. For William Skinner, see Hugh Williamson to George Washington, March 22, 1790, Applications For Office Under President Washington, Series VII, George Washington Papers, vol. XXV.

For Sherwood Haywood, see John Haywood to John Gray Blount, June 14, 1795, and Blount to Haywood, June 20, 1795, Ernest Haywood Papers (Southern Historical Collection, University of North Carolina Library); John Steele to Oliver Wolcott, Jr.,

December 13, 1798, Sherwood Haywood entry, Letters of Application and Recommendation During the Administration of John Adams; *The Papers of John Steele*, Wagstaff, ed., I, 22, 182, 186, 203, 224, 244n, 383.

CHAPTER SEVEN

1. John Steele to Joseph Winston, September 30, 1793, *The Papers of John Steele*, Henry M. Wagstaff, ed. (2 vols., Chapel Hill, 1924), I, 98–99; Jethro Rumple, *A History of Rowan County North Carolina* (Salisbury, North Carolina, 1916), 178, 186, 315; Leland Baldwin, *Whiskey Rebels: The Story of a Frontier Uprising* (Pittsburgh, 1939), 99, 103, 165, 166.

2. James Brice to Thomas Jefferson, December 13, 1808, James Brice entry, Letters of Application and Recommendation During the Administration of Thomas Jefferson, General Records of the Department of State, Record Group 59 (National Archives); "Return of Members of the Society of the Cincinnati," June 10, 1785, *Calendar of the General Otho Holland Williams Papers*, Elizabeth Merritt, ed. (Baltimore, 1940), 121; *The Papers of Alexander Hamilton*, Harold C. Syrett, ed. (24 vols., New York, 1961–76), XVI, 367–68n, 594n; Russell J. Ferguson, *Early Western Pennsylvania Politics* (Pittsburgh, 1938), 133, 135; Baldwin, *Whiskey Rebels*, passim.

3. *The Papers of Archibald D. Murphey*, William H. Hoyt, ed. (2 vols., Raleigh, North Carolina, 1914), I, 200–1, II, 419; *Papers of John Steele*, Wagstaff, ed., I, 84n; Robert O. DeMond, *The Loyalists in North Carolina During the Revolution* (Durham, North Carolina, 1940), 41; Blackwell P. Robinson, *A History of Moore County, North Carolina, 1747–1847* (Southern Pines, North Carolina, 1956), 52–53.

4. For John Wright, see William L. Smith to Alexander Hamilton, April 24, 1793, *Papers of Hamilton*, Syrett, ed., XIV, 340. I am indebted to Norman Risjord for manuscript information provided on the early career of Thomas Carter. See also *Encyclopedia of Virginia Biography*, Lyon G. Tyler, ed. (5 vols., New York, 1915), II, 352; Forrest McDonald, *We, The People: The Economic Origins of the Constitution* (Chicago, 1958), 278.

5. For Kendle Batson, see Nicholas Ridgely, et al. to Thomas Jefferson, February 28, 1803, vol. II, Allen McLane Papers (New-York Historical Society); Kendle Batson to William H. Wells, September 24, 1796, August 27, 1798, Outerbridge Horsey to ———,

September 9, 1799, *Some Records of Sussex County Delaware* (Philadelphia, 1909), 298, 299, 301–2 respectively.

6. D. Ward et al. to Albert Gallatin, March 15, 1802, Albert Gallatin and Thomas Jefferson annotations circa April 1803, Albert Gallatin note [undated, 1801], Brian Hellen, Benjamin Cheney, and Aaron Burr entries respectively, Letters of Application and Recommendation During the Administration of Thomas Jefferson; *Providence Gazette*, June 18, 25, 1796; McDonald, *We, The People*, 343.

7. Robert Smith to Albert Gallatin, October 14, 1806, John Stricker entry, Letters of Application and Recommendation During the Administration of Thomas Jefferson; *Baltimore Daily Intelligencer*, October 7, 1794; *Boston Gazette*, November 3, 1800.

8. For William Coffin, see the William Coffin-James Freeman correspondence, passim, Miscellaneous Collection (Massachusetts Historical Society); Micajah Coffin to Ebenezer Savet, November 14, 1804, Daniel Coffin entry, Letters of Application and Recommendation During the Administration of Thomas Jefferson.

For Comfort Tyler, see John Richardson to Philip Schuyler, May 3, 1795, Box 37, Philip Schuyler Papers (New York Public Library); Asa Danforth to A. Grimes, September 3, 1804, John Swartout entry, Letters of Application and Recommendation During the Administration of Thomas Jefferson; Arthur Alexander, "Federal Patronage in New York State, 1789–1805" (Ph.D. diss., Univ. of Pennsylvania, 1944), 58, 138–39, 153.

For John Armistead, see Alexander Hamilton to George Washington, September 19, 1792, George Washington to Alexander Hamilton, September 24, 1792, *Papers of Hamilton*, Syrett, ed., XII, 392, 424 respectively.

For James Patterson, see the "Letters of William R. Davie," Kemp Battle, ed., *James Sprunt Historical Monographs*, no. 7 (Chapel Hill, 1907), 29n.

9. Joseph Bloomfield o Aaron Burr, April 8, 1801, John Condit to Albert Gallatin, March 8, 1802, William Rossell entry, and Christopher Manning to Condit, February 27, 1802, Andrew Lyle entry, Letters of Application and Recommendation During the Administration of Thomas Jefferson; Carl E. Prince, *New Jersey's Jeffersonian Republicans: The Genesis of an Early Party Machine* (Chapel Hill, 1967), 238; William H. Benedict, *New Brunswick in History* (New Brunswick, N.J., 1925), 44.

10. William Plumer to William Gordon, June 18, 1797, Letter-

book, William Plumer Papers (Library of Congress); Joshua Wentworth to Oliver Wolcott, Jr., January 31, 1798, Joshua Wentworth entry, Letters of Application and Recommendation During the Administration of John Adams, General Records of the Department of State, Record Group 59 (National Archives); Joseph Whipple to Albert Gallatin, August 4, 1802, George Wentworth entry, Letters of Application and Recommendation During the Administration of Thomas Jefferson; Concord *Courier of New Hampshire*, October 11, 1796; Joshua Wentworth to Alexander Hamilton, September 7, 1791, *Papers of Hamilton*, Syrett, ed., IX, 186; Jackson T. Main, *The Upper Houses in Revolutionary America, 1763–1788* (Madison, Wis., 1967), 175–76; Jere R. Daniell, *Experiment in Republicanism: New Hampshire Politics and the American Revolution, 1741–1794* (Cambridge, 1970), 52, 66; David H. Fischer, *The Revolution of American Conservatism: The Federalist Party in the Era of Jeffersonian Democracy* (New York, 1965), xiv.

11. For Jesse Root, Jr., see the Middletown [Conn.] *Middlesex Gazette*, November 14, 1796; Stephen G. Kurtz, *The Presidency of John Adams: The Collapse of Federalism 1795–1800* (Phila., 1957), 410; Richard J. Purcell, *Connecticut in Transition, 1775–1818* (Washington, D.C., 1918), 237–39, 249; *Dictionary of American Biography*, Dumas Malone and Allen Johnson, eds. (22 vols., New York, 1928–58), XVI, 148.

For David Austin, see Austin to Roger Sherman, December 10, 1792 and passim, Baldwin Family Papers (The Sterling Library, Yale University); James C. Welling, *Connecticut Federalism; or Aristocratic Politics in a Social Democracy* (New York, 1890), 37; Purcell, *Connecticut in Transition*, 69; Franklin B. Dexter, *Biographical Sketches of the Graduates of Yale College* (6 vols., New York, 1885–1912), IV, 91–97.

12. For Elijah Brush, Daniel S. Dexter, and Paul Allen, see Samuel Nightingale et al. to George Washington, June 12, 1790, Paul Allen to Washington, June 18, 1790, Petition from the inhabitants of Providence, February 14, 1791, Applications For Office Under President Washington, Series VII, George Washington Papers (Manuscript Division, Library of Congress), vol. I; *Providence Gazette*, July 9, 1796; *George Washington's Correspondence Concerning the Society of the Cincinnati*, Edgar E. Hume, ed. (Baltimore, 1941), 388; Mack E. Thompson, *Moses Brown, Reluctant Reformer* (Providence, 1962), 177; James B. Hedges, *The Browns of Providence Plantation* (2 vols., Providence, 1952–68), I, 203–4;

Historical Catalogue of Brown University 1764–1904, Mary D. Vaughan, ed. (Providence, 1905), 79.

13. For John Ewing, see Ewing to Edward Hand, March 17, 1793, vol. II, Edward Hand Papers (Historical Society of Pennsylvania).

For Thomas Lawrence, see the University of Pennsylvania *Biographical Catalogue of the Matriculates of the College, 1749–1893* (Philadelphia, 1894), 11.

14. For Abraham Low, see Nicholas Fish to Abraham S. Bancker, February 18, 1798, Abraham S. Bancker to Fish, June 22, 1799, folder 1798–1800, Bancker Family Papers (New-York Historical Society); Main, *Upper Houses*, 56.

15. *Papers of Archibald D. Murphey*, Hoyt, ed., I, 1n, II, 409; *The John Gray Blount Papers*, Alice B. Keith, ed. (2 vols., Raleigh, N.C., 1959), II, 136; *Papers of John Steele*, Wagstaff, ed., I, 24n, 438–39; Douglas S. Freeman, *George Washington, Patriot and President* (New York, 1954), 307–8, 363n.

16. For Abel Whitney, see Loring Andrews to Theodore Sedgwick, March 14, 1796, and Abel Whitney to Sedgwick, November 28, 1797, vol. III, Theodore Sedgwick Papers (Massachusetts Historical Society).

For Joseph Storer, see Edward E. Bourne, *The History of Wells and Kennebunk* (Portland, 1875), 572–86.

For George Phillips, see Jeremiah Wadsworth to Oliver Wolcott, Jr., March 23, 1798, George Phillips entry, Letters of Application and Recommendation During the Administration of John Adams; Dexter, *Biographical Sketches of the Graduates of Yale College,* III, 354.

17. For John Berrien, see the John M. Berrien Papers, passim, 1780–86 (Southern Historical Collection, University of North Carolina Library); John Berrien to George Washington, May 10, July 3, 1789, Applications For Office Under President Washington, Series VII, George Washington Papers, vol. III; *Papers of Hamilton,* Syrett, ed., XI, 198; Fischer, *Revolution of American Conservatism,* 406.

For George F. Norton, see Norton to George Washington, February 19, 1791, Edmund Pendleton to Washington, April 9, 1791, Applications For Office Under President Washington, Series VII, George Washington Papers, vol. XXI; Francis N. Mason, *John Norton and Sons, Merchants of London and Virginia* (Richmond, 1937), xxiii, 515–16.

18. Loring Andrews to Theodore Sedgwick, March 13, 1794,

Henry W. Dwight to Sedgwick, February 18, 1796, John S. Hopkins to Sedgwick, February 26, 1798, vols. II and III, passim, Theodore Sedgwick Papers; James M. Banner, Jr., *To the Hartford Convention: The Federalists and the Origins of Party Politics in Massachusetts, 1789–1815* (New York, 1969), 180; Fischer, *Revolution of American Conservatism,* 12, 13, 27n.

19. For Stephen Hussey, see Isaac Coffin to Thomas Jefferson, April 13, 1804, Micajah Coffin to Richard Cutts, May 1, 1804, Daniel Coffin entry, Letters of Application and Recommendation During the Administration of Thomas Jefferson.

For Shubael Breed, see Consider Steny to Ephraim Kirby, July –, 1801, Jonathan Frisbee to Kirby, August 12, 1801, Nathaniel Fosdick to Kirby, September 1, 1801, Ephraim Kirby Papers (Perkins Library, Duke University); Dexter, *Biographical Sketches of the Graduates of Yale College,* IV, 24–25; F. M. Caulkins, *History of Norwich, Connecticut* (Norwich, 1845), 324.

20. See the Nathan Dane Papers, 1789–92, passim (Massachusetts Historical Society); Fischer, *Revolution of American Conservatism,* 247–48; Banner, *To the Hartford Convention,* 104; Samuel B. Harding, *The Contest Over the Ratification of the Federal Constitution in the State of Massachusetts* (New York, 1896), 61–62; *Dictionary of American Biography,* Malone and Johnson, eds., V, 63; Jackson T. Main, *The Antifederalists: Critics of the Constitution, 1781–1788* (Chapel Hill, 1961), 257 and passim; David H. Fischer, "The Myth of the Essex Junto," *William and Mary Quarterly* XXI (1964), 195.

21. Thomas Davis to David Cobb, February 1, 1794, David Cobb Papers (Massachusetts Historical Society); George Cabot to Oliver Wolcott, Jr., June 19, 1798, John Reed to Wolcott, July 5, 1798, Thomas Perkins and Beza Hayward entries respectively, Letters of Application and Recommendation During the Administration of John Adams; William Bacon to Theodore Sedgwick, April 8, 1800, vol. II, Theodore Sedgwick Papers; *Massachusetts Spy and Worcester Gazette,* November 23, 1796; *Life and Letters of George Cabot,* Henry Cabot Lodge, ed. (Boston, 1877), 305; McDonald, *We, The People,* 192–200; Main, *Upper Houses,* 282; Kurtz, *Presidency of John Adams,* 410; Bourne, *History of Wells and Kennebunk,* 503, 584–89, 611–15, 687; Clifford K. Shipton, *Sibley's Harvard Graduates: Biographical Sketches of Those Who Attended Harvard College* (16 vols., Boston, 1873–1972), XIV, 672–73.

22. Moses Robinson to James Madison, March 31, 1801, Anthony

Haswell entry, Letters of Application and Recommendation During the Administration of Thomas Jefferson; Peacham [Vt.] *Green Mountain Patriot,* August 31, 1798; Portsmouth *New Hampshire Gazette,* November 25, 1800; *Calendar of the Ira Allen Papers in the Wilbur Library, University of Vermont* (Montpelier, 1939), 14, 38–39; David M. Ludlum, *Social Ferment in Vermont, 1791–1850* (New York, 1939), 3, 28–29; Chilton Williamson, *Vermont in Quandary: 1763–1825* (New York, 1949), 84, 179; James B. Wilbur, *Ira Allen: Founder of Vermont, 1751–1814* (2 vols., Boston, 1928), I, 471, 499, 566, II, 23, 28, 78, 319–20, 397; Shipton, *Sibley's Harvard Graduates,* XIV, 411–13; Dexter, *Biographical Sketches of the Graduates of Yale College,* II, 576–78.

23. For Joshua Atherton, see William Plumer to Jeremiah Smith, April 28, 1794, February 9, 1797, Letterbook, William, Plumer Papers (Manuscript Division, Library of Congress); Shipton, *Sibley's Harvard Graduates,* XV, 170–72; Main, *The Antifederalists,* 152, 157, 221–22; McDonald, *We, The People,* 238, 249, 285; Charles P. Whittemore, *A General of the Revolution, John Sullivan of New Hampshire* (New York, 1961), 211; Charles Bell, *The Bench and Bar of New Hampshire* (Boston, 1894), 149–52.

For the other New Hampshire appointees, see the *Concord Courier of New Hampshire,* August 9, 30, 1800; *Papers of Hamilton,* Syrett, ed., VII, 188; Lynn W. Turner, *William Plumer of New Hampshire, 1759–1850* (Chapel Hill, 1962), 88, 191–97; Martha M. Frizzell, *A History of Walpole, New Hampshire* (2 vols., Walpole, 1963), I, 20, 23, 658; Whittemore, *John Sullivan,* 213; Jere R. Daniell, *Experiment in Republicanism: New Hampshire Politics and the American Revolution, 1741–1794* (Cambridge, 1970), 189, 209, 218.

24. Theodore Foster to Oliver Wolcott, Jr., June 3, 1798, John L. Boss entry, Letters of Application and Recommendation During the Administration of John Adams; Oliver Whipple to Thomas Jefferson, November 17, 1806, Oliver Whipple entry, Letters of Application and Recommendation During the Administration of Thomas Jefferson; *Providence Gazette,* June 25, 1796; Fischer, *Revolution of American Conservatism,* 284; Providence Typographical Union, *Printers and Printing in Providence 1762–1907* (Providence, 1907), 16; *Historical Catalogue of Brown University,* Vaughan, ed., 69; *Biographical Directory of the American Congress, 1774–1961* (Washington, D.C., 1961), 1473.

25. Andrew Kingsbury to Ephraim Kirby, April 20, 1801, Ephraim Kirby Papers; William Heron to George Washington, July

26, 1790, Applications For Office Under President Washington, Series VII, George Washington Papers, vol. XV; *Connecticut Courant*, May 16, 1796; Purcell, *Connecticut in Transition*, 69, 106, 119, 206; Dexter, *Biographical Sketches of the Graduates of Yale College*, III, 61; Charles S. Hall, *Benjamin Tallmadge* (New York, 1943), 107, 190, 192; Dwight C. Kilbourn, *The Bench and Bar of Litchfield County, Connecticut, 1709–1909* (Litchfield, 1909), 20, 146; *Biographical Directory of the American Congress*, 679.

26. Richard Stockton to Andrew Kirkpatrick, November 3, 1796, Miscellaneous Collection "S" (New-York Historical Society); Jonathan Rhea to Jonathan Foreman, June 8, 1794, July 13, 1795, Folder 78, Jonathan Foreman Papers (New-York Historical Society); Richard Stockton to Jonathan Rhea, October 27, 1801, Box 2, Stockton Family Papers (Princeton University Library); David Ford to Robert Morris, August 21, 1799, Box 7, Robert Morris Papers (Rutgers University Library); Jonathan Rhea to George Washington, January 14, 1793, J. J. Faisch to Washington, August 27, 1795, Richard Howell to Washington, August—, 1795, Applications For Office Under President Washington, Series VII, George Washington Papers, vols. XI, XXIV; Jonathan Rhea to ———, October 31, 1797, Henry Gale entry, Letters of Application and Recommendation During the Administration of John Adams; David Ford, "Journal of an Expedition Made in the Autumn of 1794," *Proceedings of the New Jersey Historical Society*, VIII (1859), 84–86; Kurtz, *Presidency of John Adams*, 410; Irving C. Hanners, *The Society of the Cincinnati in the State of New Jersey* (Bethlehem, Pennsylvania, 1949), 121; Fischer, *Revolution of American Conservatism*, 321.

27. Jacob Radcliff to Abraham Bancker, October 15, 1798, Folder 1798–1800, Bancker Family Papers; Arthur Alexander, "Federal Patronage in New York State, 1789–1805" (Ph.D. diss., University of Pennsylvania, 1944), 147; *Dictionary of American Biography*, Malone and Johnson, eds., XV, 318–19; Alvin Kass, *Politics in New York State, 1800–1830* (Syracuse, N.Y., 1965), 75; Robert W. July, *The Essential New Yorker, Gulian Crommelin Verplanck* (Durham, 1951), 44; John T. Horton, *James Kent, A Study in Conservatism* (New York, 1939), 139.

28. Benjamin Strong to Selah Strong, October 21, 1790, March 19, May 5, June 21, September 8, 1792, June 10, 1796, and passim, Strong Family Papers (New-York Historical Society); New York *American Citizen and General Advertiser*, March 29, 1800; Jabez D. Hammond, *History of Political Parties in the State of New York*,

4th ed. (2 vols., Buffalo, 1850), I, 70; Walter Barrett [pseudonym for Joseph Scoville], *The Old Merchants of New York City* (5 vols., N.Y., 1863), I, 365–66.

29. Moss Kent to James Kent, September 4, 1791, July 21, September 20, 1792, December 25, 1794, May 18, 1795, April 21, December 10, 1796, April 27, 1797, May 13, 1799, August 29, 1800, and passim, vol. I, James Kent Papers (Manuscript Division, Library of Congress); John Van Rensselaer et al. to [Peter] Van Schaack, October 12, 1792, Peter Van Schaack Papers (Manuscript Division, Library of Congress); Alfred F. Young, *The Democratic Republicans of New York: The Origins, 1763–1797* (Chapel Hill, 1967), 267n, 509–13, 517; Hammond, *Political Parties in New York*, I, 130; Horton, *James Kent*, 68, 78, 102, 229.

30. Stephen N. Bayard to John Saunders, August 9, 1800, Stephen N. Bayard Papers (New-York Historical Society); Stephen N. Bayard to Elisha Boudinot, September 7, 1808, March 27, 1810 and passim, Bayard-Boudinot-Pintard Collection (New-York Historical Society); Hartford *Connecticut Courant*, November 14, 1796; Robert Troup to John Jay, May 6, 1792, *The Correspondence and Public Papers of John Jay, 1763–1826*, Henry P. Johnston, ed. (4 vols., New York, 1890–1893), III, 423; "The Reminiscences of James Gordon," Josephine Mayer, ed., *New York History* XVII (1936), 316–24; Young, *Democratic Republicans of New York*, 163, 270, 274; Alexander, "Federal Patronage in New York State," 60, 62, 144; Kurtz, *Presidency of John Adams*, 410; Hammond, *Political Parties in New York*, I, 100.

31. Robert Coleman to Timothy Pickering, June 5, 1798, Robert Morris to Oliver Wolcott, Jr., June 7, 1798, Thomas Murgatroyd et al. to John Adams, June 14, 1798, Robert Waln to Wolcott, May 3, 1800, Israel Whelen entry, Letters of Application and Recommendation During the Administration of John Adams; Harry M. Tinkcom, *The Republicans and Federalists in Pennsylvania 1790–1801* (Harrisburg, 1950), 58, 254; Sanford W. Higginbotham, *The Keystone in the Democratic Arch: Pennsylvania Politics, 1800–1816* (Harrisburg, 1952), 59; Kurtz, *Presidency of John Adams*, 411; Ethel E. Rasmusson, "Capitol on the Delaware: The Philadelphia Upper Class in Transition, 1789–1801" (Ph.D. diss., Brown University, 1962), 168.

32. S. Sitgreaves to Oliver Wolcott, Jr., June 30, 1798, and Theodore Sedgwick to John Adams, August 20, 1797, Seth Chapman and Collinson Read entries respectively, Letters of Application and Recommendation During the Administration of John Adams;

Thomas Jefferson to Benjamin S. Barton, February 14, 1801, *The Works of Thomas Jefferson*, Paul L. Ford, ed. (12 vols., New York, 1904–1905), IX, 177; Raymond W. Albright, *Two Centuries of Reading, Pennsylvania, 1748–1948* (Reading, 1948), 70, 89; M. Luther Heisey, "A Biography of Paul Zantzinger," *Lancaster County Historical Society Papers*, IIIL (1943), 113–19.

In Delaware, Sheriff Joseph Israel of New Castle County was named commissioner. An Adams Federalist, he played a prominent role in the Adams campaign of 1800. Nicholas Ridgely et al. to Thomas Jefferson, February 28, 1803, vol. II, Allen McLane Papers (New-York Historical Society); *Monitor and Wilmington Repository*, October 7, 1800.

33. Samuel Smith to George Washington, September 22, 1794, William Paca to Washington, September 23, 1794, Applications For Office Under President Washington, Series VII, George Washington Papers, vol. XIII; George A. Hanson, *Old Kent* (Baltimore, 1876), 41; McDonald, *We, The People*, 157; *Biographical Directory of the American Congress*, 1592; T. J. C. Williams, *History of Frederick County Maryland* (2 vols., Baltimore, 1967), 127; Dorothy M. Brown, "Maryland and the Federalists: Search For Unity," *Maryland Historical Magazine* LXIII (1963), 11.

Only a little information was uncovered on the politics of the Virginia and South Carolina appointees. Relatives of Virginians Francis Preston, George Keith Taylor, Thomas Nelson, and George Washington were among those granted commissions.

34. Thomas Henderson to Benjamin Hawkins, December 17, 1793, Hawkins to George Washington, January 21, 1794, Applications For Office Under President Washington, Series VII, George Washington Papers, vol. XIV; James Holland to John Steele, September 10, 1798, *The Papers of John Steele*, Wagstaff, ed., I, 161–62; "Letters of William R. Davie," Battle, ed., *Sprunt Historical Monographs*, 26n; Lisle A. Rose, *Prologue to Democracy: The Federalists in the South, 1789–1801* (Lexington, 1968), 175; *Biographical Directory of the American Congress*, 810; Henry Wagstaff, "Federalism in North Carolina," *James Sprunt Historical Publications*, vol. IX, no. 2 (1909), 30.

35. I am indebted to Patricia Watlington for information provided for some of the Kentucky appointees. See also James McHenry to Timothy Pickering, September 6, 1797, and Thomas Davis and John Fowler to Oliver Wolcott, Jr., June 29, 1798, John Caldwell and James French entries respectively, Letters of Application and Recommendation During the Administration of John

Adams; Jonathan and Maud W. Davis, *Glimpses of Historic Madison County, Kentucky* (Nashville, Tenn., 1955), 37; Stephen Hess, *American Political Dynasties From Adams to Kennedy* (Garden City, N.Y., 1966), 240–243, 626; Hugh B. Grigsby, *The History of the Virginia Federal Convention of 1788 . . .* (2 vols., Richmond, 1890–91), I, 7; E. D. Warfield, *The Kentucky Resolutions of 1798* (New York, 1887), 37, 57–59.

36. See the John Overton Papers, passim (Tennessee Historical Society); William H. Masterson, *William Blount* (Baton Rouge, La., 1954), 338 and passim; *Dictionary of American Biography*, Malone and Johnson, eds., XX, 108.

CHAPTER EIGHT

1. Leonard White's conclusion that "there is little evidence that political affiliation was important in making selections" in the post office during the Federalist decade is difficult to understand in light of the sources he examined. See White, *The Federalists: A Study in Administrative History, 1789–1801* (New York, 1948), 179–80.

2. Timothy Pickering to Thomas Robie, March 31, 1792, vol. VI, and passim 1791–94, Timothy Pickering Papers (Massachusetts Historical Society); William Clarke et al. to Wade Hampton, April 6, 1801, William Clarke entry, Letters of Application and Recommendation During the Administration of Thomas Jefferson, General Records of the Department of State, Record Group 59 (National Archives); Timothy Pickering's correspondence, 1791–94 passim, Letters Sent by the Postmaster General, 1789–1836, Records of the Post Office Department, Record Group 28 (National Archives). Pickering had few qualms about aiding his own family. He appointed two cousins to postmasterships during his tenure as postmaster general: Timothy Williams at Huntington, New York, and Moses Wingate at Haverhill, Massachusetts. See John Carroll and Mary Ashworth, *George Washington: First in Peace* (New York, 1957), 266n; White, *The Federalists*, 282–83.

3. Abraham Baldwin to Thomas Jefferson, March 6, 1801, Joseph Habersham entry, and Ephraim Kirby to Jefferson, November 10, 1801, Ephraim Kirby entry, Letters of Application and Recommendation During the Administration of Thomas Jefferson.

4. John Armsrong to Ephraim Kirby, June 2, 1801, Ephraim Kirby Papers (Perkins Library, Duke University); Kirby to Thomas Jefferson, November 10, 1801, Ephraim Kirby entry, Gideon

Granger to Jefferson, April 15, 1801, Elisa [Elizur] Goodrich entry, William Findley to Jefferson, March 5, 1801, William Irwin [Irvine] entry, Findley to Jefferson, February 26, 1801, Samuel Bryan entry, and John Langdon to Granger, December 4, 1801, John Langdon entry, Letters of Application and Recommendation During the Administration of Thomas Jefferson; White, *The Federalists*, 78–79; Wesley E. Rich, *The History of the United States Post Office to the Year 1829* (Cambridge, Mass., 1924), 127–28.

5. For Sebastian Bauman's activities in the 1780s, and an inventory of his meager holdings at his death in 1801, see folder II, Sebastian Bauman Papers (New-York Historical Society). For his politics and official activities in the 1790s, see Jonathan Burrall to William Goddard, June 7, 1791, Joseph Habersham to Bauman, October 10, 1801, and passim, Letters Sent by the Postmaster General, 1789–1836; Bauman to John Jay, undated [1796], Emmet Collection (New York Public Library); the Bauman-Pickering Correspondence, 1792, passim vol. VI, Timothy Pickering Papers; Ashworth and Carroll, *George Washington: First in Peace*, 197, 216; White, *The Federalists*, 182.

6. Timothy Pickering to Rev. John Clarke, November 28, 1791, Pickering to Samuel Blanchard, November 28, 1791, Pickering to Samuel Osgood, November 30, 1791, Pickering to Nathaniel Appleton, November 30, 1791, vol. VI, Timothy Pickering Papers; Petition to James Madison, undated [1801], Benjamin Lincoln entry, Letters of Application and Recommendation During the Administration of Thomas Jefferson.

7. *Philadelphia Minerva*, July 9, 1796; Tench Coxe to Thomas Jefferson, January 25, July 10, 1801, Tench Coxe entry, and Abraham Baldwin to Jefferson, March 6, 1801, Joseph Habersham entry, Letters of Application and Recommendation During the Administration of Thomas Jefferson.

8. Timothy Pickering to John Gardner, November 28, 1791, vol. VI, Timothy Pickering Papers; Charles Goodwin to Thomas Jefferson, April 30, 1801, Charles Goodwin entry, and James Jackson to Jefferson, July 18, 1801, William Stephens entry, Letters of Application and Recommendation During the Administration of Thomas Jefferson; George C. Rogers, Jr., *Evolution of a Federalist: William Loughton Smith of Charleston, 1758–1812* (Columbia, S.C., 1962), 126, 189; Arthur H. Hirsh, *The Huguenots of Colonial South Carolina* (Durham, N.C., 1928), 35.

9. For Jacob Richardson, see Abraham Baldwin to Thomas Jefferson, March 6, 1801, Jacob Richardson entry, Letters of Applica-

tion and Recommendation During the Administration of Thomas Jefferson; Irwin Polishook, *Rhode Island and the Union* (Evanston, Ill., 1969), 175–78.

For Elias Beers, see Gideon Granger to Ephraim Kirby, August 24, 1801, Ephraim Kirby Papers; Abraham Bishop to Gideon Granger, February 4, 1805, Jesse Atwater entry, Letters of Application and Recommendation During the Administration of Thomas Jefferson.

For George Mancius, see W. Mancius to Abraham Bancker, October 11, 1798, Bancker Family Papers (New-York Historical Society); Abraham Baldwin to Thomas Jefferson, March 6, 1801, Joseph Habersham entry, Letters of Application and Recommendation During the Administration of Thomas Jefferson.

For George Craik, see Gay. M. Moore, *Seaport in Virginia: George Washington's Alexandria* (Richmond, 1949) 190–92.

10. Samuel Osgood to Peter Mumford, December 20, 1790, Letters Sent by the Postmaster General, 1789–1836; Timothy Pickering to Samuel Blanchard, November 28, 1791, Pickering to John Gardner, November 28, 1791, vol. VI, Timothy Pickering Papers; White, *The Federalists,* 179, 181.

11. Among the North Carolina postmasters who were followers of John Gray Blount were J. G. L. Schenck of Tarborough, Grover Wright of Greenville, John Harvey of Randolph Court House (a cousin of JG), Benjamin Coakley of Princeton, and William Faulkner of Warrenton.

12. See Lisle A. Rose, *Prologue to Democracy: The Federalists in the South, 1789–1801* (Lexington, Ky., 1968), passim, for an extended discussion of the Blounts' place in the national political spectrum and the motives that caused them to change.

13. Ibid. A plethora of sources must be examined to come to grips with J. G. Blount's wide-ranging political career. In particular, see *The John Gray Blount Papers,* Alice B. Keith, ed. (2 vols., Raleigh, N.C., 1959), vol. II, passim; Blount correspondence in the Ernest Haywood Papers, 1789–1800, Southern Historical Collection (University of North Carolina Library); "The Harris Letters," Henry M. Wagstaff, ed., in *The James Sprunt Studies,* XIV (1916), no. 1; *The Papers of John Steele,* Henry M. Wagstaff, ed. (2 vols., Chapel Hill, 1924), passim; William H. Masterson, *William Blount* (Baton Rouge, La., 1954); Alice B. Keith, "John Gray and Thomas Blount, Merchants, 1783–1800," *North Carolina Historical Review* XXV (1948), 194–205.

14. John H. DeWitt, "General James Winchester," *Tennessee*

Historical Magazine I (1915), 79–105; Louise I. Trenholme, *The Ratification of the Federal Constitution in North Carolina* (New York, 1932), 115, 161; Masterson, *William Blount*, 262–64, 292; Thomas P. Abernethy, *From Frontier to Plantation in Tennessee* (Memphis, 1955), 165, 202, 269; *Dictionary of American Biography*, Dumas Malone and Allen Johnson, eds. (22 vols., New York, 1928–58), XX, 378–79.

15. *Baltimore Daily Intelligencer*, October 7, 1794; Benjamin Galloway to Thomas Jefferson, March 14, 1801, Nathaniel Rochester entry, Letters of Application and Recommendation During the Administration of Thomas Jefferson; Thomas J. C. Williams, *A History of Washington County Maryland* (2 vols., Hagerstown, 1968), I, 109, 136–39.

16. Gideon Granger to John Hollinbeck, January 9, 1802, Granger to Lord Butler, January 10, 1802, Letters Sent by the Postmaster General, 1789–1836; H. C. Bradsby, *History of Luzerne County, Pennsylvania* (Chicago, 1893), 323–27.

17. George Washington to Benjamin Harrison, March 9, 1789, Washington to Samuel Vaughan, March 21, 1789, Washington to Bushrod Washington, July 27, 1789, *The Writings of George Washington*, John C. Fitzpatrick, ed. (39 vols., Washington, D.C., 1931–44), XXX, 178, 238, 366, and passim; *John Gray Blount Papers*, Keith, ed., II, 561–62, 656, 661; Ashworth and Carroll, *George Washington: First in Peace*, 447; White, *The Federalists*, 79, 79n, 282–83; Trenholme, *Ratification of the Federal Constitution in North Carolina*, 70; cf. note 2.

18. Jonathan Trumbull to Tobias Lear, February 18, 1791, Applications For Office Under President Washington, Series VII, George Washington Papers (Library of Congress), vol. XXVII; Franklin B. Dexter, *Biographical Sketches of the Graduates of Yale College* (6 vols., New York, 1885–1912), IV, 445, V, 120–21.

19. Josiah Stebbins to Henry Knox, October 31, 1804, Henry Knox Papers (Massachusetts Historical Society); William Willis, *History of the Laws, the Courts, and the Lawyers of Maine* (Portland, Maine, 1863), 236–42; Dexter, *Biographical Sketches of the Graduates of Yale*, IV, 733–34; Herbert C. Parsons, *A Puritan Outpost* [Northfield, Mass.] (New York, 1937), 213–14, 228.

20. William Plumer to Jeremiah Smith, February 13, 1797, Letterbook, William Plumer Papers (Library of Congress); Lynn W. Turner, *William Plumer of New Hampshire, 1759–1850* (Chapel Hill, 1962), 138, 143–44; David H. Fischer, *The Revolution of American Conservatism: The Federalist Party in the Era of Jeffer-*

sonian Democracy (New York, 1965), 237; J. J. Dearborn, *The History of Salisbury, New Hampshire* (Manchester, N.H., 1890), 407; *Biographical Directory of the American Congress, 1774–1961* (Washington, D.C., 1961), 1710.

21. For James W. Wilken, see Thomas J. Farnham, "The Virginia Amendments of 1795, An Episode in the Opposition to Jay's Treaty," *Virginia Magazine of History and Biography* LXXV (1967), 85; E. M. Ruttenbar, *History of Orange County* [New York] (Newburgh, N.Y., 1875), 150.

For Thomas B. Dick, see Gideon Granger to Thomas B. Dick, January 27, 1802, Letters Sent by the Postmaster General, 1789–1836; Uzal W. Condit, *The History of Easton, Pennsylvania* (Easton, 1885), 180.

For David McKeehan, see William Findley to Thomas Jefferson, February 26, 1801, Thomas Smith to McKeehan, January 30, 1802, Samuel Bryan and David McKeehan entries respectively, Letters of Application and Recommendation During the Administration of Thomas Jefferson.

22. For Samuel Wilds, see John B. O'Neall, *Biographical Sketches of the Bench and Bar of South Carolina* (2 vols., Charleston, 1859), I, 102–5.

For Benjamin Shackleford and Haden Edwards, see Joshua Frey to Thomas Jefferson, October 9, 1803, Haden Edwards to ———, April 25, 1801, Benjamin Shackleford and Haden Edwards entries respectively, Letters of Application and Recommendation During the Administration of Thomas Jefferson.

For William Dickson, see Dickson to John Overton, November 7, 1801, John Overton Papers (Tennessee Historical Society); Trenholme, *Ratification of the Federal Constitution in North Carolina*, 151, 242.

23. For Jonathan Grout, see Winfred E. Bernhard, *Fisher Ames, Federalist and Statesman 1758–1808* (Chapel Hill, 1965), 162–72; Forrest McDonald, *We, The People: The Economic Origins of the Constitution* (Chicago, 1958), 198; Jackson T. Main, *The Upper Houses in Revolutionary America, 1763–1788* (Madison, Wisconsin, 1967), 282; Joseph Charles, *Origins of the American Party System* (Chapel Hill, 1956), 23; *Biographical Directory of the American Congress*, 1216.

For Samuel Dana, see Dana to ——— Richardson, June 28, 1798, Greenough Papers (Massachusetts Historical Society); Samuel Eliot Morison, *The Life and Letters of Harrison Gray Otis, Federalist, 1765–1848* (2 vols., Boston, 1913), I, 286, II, 57, 235.

For Eliab Brewer, see Dexter, *Biographical Sketches of the Graduates of Yale*, V, 63–64.

For Benjamin Whitman, see James M. Smith, *Freedom's Fetters: The Alien and Sedition Laws and American Civil Liberties* (Ithaca, N.Y., 1956), 254; *Historical Catalogue of Brown University, 1764–1904*, Mary D. Vaughan, ed. (Providence, R.I., 1905), 75.

24. For Horatio Seymour, see David Ludlum, *Social Ferment in Vermont, 1791–1850* (New York, 1939), 127; Dexter, *Biographical Sketches of the Graduates of Yale*, V, 306–8.

For John Fay, see Matthew Lyon to Thomas Jefferson, March 3, 1801, Jonathan E. Robinson entry, Letters of Application and Recommendation During the Administration of Thomas Jefferson; Thomas Jefferson's "Anas," *Works of Thomas Jefferson*, Paul L. Ford, ed. (12 vols., New York, 1904–5), I, 363; Dexter, *Biographical Sketches of the Graduates of Yale*, IV, 664.

25. John H. Morison, *The Life of Jeremiah Smith* (Boston, 1845), 45–142 passim; George A. Morison, *History of Peterborough, New Hampshire* (2 vols., Rindge, N.H., 1954), I, 143, 151, 358ff. Other examples of Federalists who operated post offices from their manufactories included William Page of Bellows Falls, Vt., a canal builder and operator of a textile plant; Lemuel Grosvenor of Pomfret, Conn., a woolen manufacturer; and John Reed of Belleville, Pa., a distiller.

26. For John Rogers, see Ezra S. Stearns, *History of Plymouth, New Hampshire* (2 vols., Cambridge, Mass., 1906), I, 450, 466–68.

For Ezra Green, see William Plumer to Jeremiah Smith, May 30, 1797, Letterbook, William Plumer Papers; Charles P. Whittemore, *A General of the Revolution, John Sullivan of New Hampshire* (New York, 1961), 218; McDonald, *We, The People*, 246.

27. Charles Turner to William Cushing, April 9, 1789, William Cushing Papers (Massachusetts Historical Society); Jackson T. Main, *The Antifederalists: Critics of the Constitution, 1781–1788* (Chapel Hill, 1961), 177; Samuel B. Harding, *The Contest over the Ratification of the Federal Constitution in the State of Massachusetts* (New York, 1896), 66, 90–91; Clifford K. Shipton, *Sibley's Harvard Graduates: Biographical Sketches of Those Who Attended Harvard College* (16 vols., Boston, 1873–1972), XIII, 293–99; Samuel Deane, *History of Scituate, Massachusetts* (Boston, Mass., 1831), 361.

28. For Paul Coffin and Nathan Stone respectively, see Shipton, *Sibley's Harvard Graduates*, XIV, 403–9, XV, 298–99.

For Ebenezer R. White, see Dexter, *Biographical Sketches of the*

Graduates of Yale, II, 679–80; McDonald, *We, The People*, 146.

For John Croes, see Mary D. Ogden, *Memorial Cyclopedia of New Jersey* (6 vols., Newark, N.J., 1915), I, 56–57.

For Gottlieb Shober, see the Shober-Timothy Pickering correspondence, 1794–1801 passim, Timothy Pickering Papers.

CHAPTER NINE

1. The only exception was Elijah Russell, postmaster at Gilmantown, New Hampshire, who edited the Republican *Concord Mirrour* and several succeeding Jeffersonian newspapers. His brother was David Russell, the influential Federalist customs collector at Lake Champlain in Vermont. Elijah Russell to James Madison, November 29, 1802, Russell to Thomas Jefferson, August 7, 1801, Elijah Russell entry, Letters of Application and Recommendation During the Administration of Thomas Jefferson, General Records of the Department of State, Record Group 59 (National Archives); Clarence Brigham, *History and Bibliography of Early American Newspapers* (2 vols., Worcester, Mass., 1947), II, 1370.

2. For Senator Burke's remark, see Wesley E. Rich, *The History of the United States Post Office to the Year 1829* (Cambridge, Mass., 1924), 75, 115. For annual fees earned by postmasters, see "Roll of Officers, Civil, Military, and Naval of the United States [1801]," *American State Papers, Miscellaneous: Documents, Legislative and Executive of the Congress of the United States*, Walter Lowrie and Walter S. Franklin, eds. (2 vols., Washington, D.C., 1834), I, 260–319.

3. Gideon Granger to William Hobbey, January 16, 1802, Letters Sent by the Postmaster General, 1789–1836, Records of the Post Office Department, Record Group 28 (National Archives); Rich, *History of the Post Office*, 75.

4. Jonathan Burrall to D. Horton, April 18, 1791, Burrall to David Russell, April 21, 1797, Joseph Habersham to John Wyeth, September 18, 1801, Gideon Granger to William Hobbey, January 16, 1802, Letters Sent by the Postmaster General, 1789–1836; Merriwether Jones to Thomas Jefferson, March 13, 1801, Merriwether Jones entry, Letters of Application and Recommendation During the Administration of Thomas Jefferson; Rich, *History of the Post Office*, 115; Clifford Shipton, *Isaiah Thomas* (Rochester, N.Y., 1948), 50–51.

5. Shipton, *Isaiah Thomas*, 46–47; *Dictionary of American Biography*, Dumas Malone and Allen Johnson, eds. (22 vols., New York,

1928–58), XVIII, 435–36. For a list of newspapers in which Thomas was a partner with former apprentices, see Brigham, *History and Bibliography of Early American Newspapers,* II, 1491.

6. Samuel E. Morison, *Harrison Gray Otis 1765–1848: The Urbane Federalist* (New York, 1969), 254; Rollo Silver, *The American Printer, 1787–1825* (Charlottesville, Va., 1967), 28; David H. Fischer, *The Revolution of American Conservatism: The Federalist Party in the Era of Jeffersonian Democracy* (New York, 1965), 415; Francis M. Thompson, *History of Greenfield* [Massachusetts] (2 vols., Greenfield, 1904), I, 289, 548–50, II, 954–55.

7. For David Carlisle and Alexander Thomas, see David Carlisle to Richard Cranch, December 5, 1797, Cranch Family Papers (Massachusetts Historical Society); Walpole *New Hampshire Journal,* April 11, 18, 25, 1793, July 12, 1797; Walpole *Farmer's Weekly Museum,* January 16, 1798, July 7, 1800, and passim, 1798–1800; Brigham, *History and Bibliography of Early American Newspapers,* II, 1388; Martha M. Frizell, *A History of Walpole, New Hampshire* (2 vols., Walpole, 1963), I, 15ff, 19ff, II, 52–53, 189, 280.

8. Loring Andrews to Peter Van Schaack, October 9, 1792, April 6, 1798, Peter Van Schaack Papers (Library of Congress); Andrews to Theodore Sedgwick, January 28, February 26, March 14, April 18, May 5, 1796, April 29, 1797 and passim, vol. III, Theodore Sedgwick Papers (Massachusetts Historical Society); Stockbridge [Mass.] *Western Star,* passim 1791–97; Richard E. Welch, Jr., *Theodore Sedgwick, Federalist* (Middletown, Conn., 1965), 113–14, 122, 233n, 234n; Richard Birdsall, *Berkshire County: A Cultural History* (New Haven, Conn., 1959), 79, 187–90; Brigham, *History and Bibliography of Early American Newspapers,* II, 1370.

9. Samuel Trumbull to James Madison, December 3, 1802, Joseph Stanton to Madison, December 15, 1802, Samuel Trumbull entry, Letters of Application and Recommendation During the Administration of Thomas Jefferson; Stonington [Conn.] *Impartial Register,* December 31, 1799, April 15, 29, May 6, 27, and passim, 1800; Richard A. Wheeler, *History of the Town of Stonington* (2nd ed., Mystic, Conn., 1966), 156; Brigham, *History and Bibliography of Early American Newspapers,* II, 1494.

10. *Concord Herald,* 1793, passim; Concord *Courier of New Hampshire,* April 11, 25, and passim, 1796, summer and autumn, 1800; George Hough to Alexander Hamilton, July 23, 1793, *The Papers of Alexander Hamilton,* Harold C. Syrett, ed. (24 Vols., New York, 1961–76), XV, 120–21.

Other New England Federalist printer-postmasters included Simeon Butler, printer of the Northhampton [Mass.] *Gazette*, William Wilkinson, printer of the Providence [R.I.] *State Gazette*, and Amos Farley, printer of the Peacham [Vt.] *Green Mountain Patriot*.

11. For T. O. H. Crosswell, see the *Hudson Balance and Columbian Repository*, May 21, July 9, 1801.

For Nicholas Power, see Albert Gallatin's note citing Burr's view of Power [undated, 1801], Aaron Burr entry, Letters of Application and Recommendation During the Administration of Thomas Jefferson; *Poughkeepsie* [*N.Y.*] *Journal*, April 3, 1793; Linda Grant De-Pauw, *The Eleventh Pillar: New York State and the Federal Constitution* (Ithaca, N.Y., 1966), 91, 188; Milton W. Hamilton, *The Country Printer, New York State, 1785–1830* (New York, 1936), 159–60, 218; Frank Hasbrouck, *The History of Dutchess County, New York* (Poughkeepsie, 1909), 217, 242; Brigham, *History and Bibliography of Early American Newspapers*, II, 1468–69.

12. Raymond W. Albright, *Two Centuries of Reading, Pennsylvania, 1748–1948* (Reading, 1948), 116–18.

13. Joseph Habersham to John Wyeth, September 18, 1801, Letters Sent by the Postmaster General, 1789–1836; Robert Harris et al. to Wade Hampton, April 1, 1801, John A. Hanna to S. Harrison Smith, April 4, 1801, John Downey entry, Letters of Application and Recommendation During the Administration of Thomas Jefferson; Henry Simpson, *The Lives of Eminent Philadelphians, Now Deceased* (Philadelphia, 1859), 998–99; Fischer, *Revolution of American Conservatism*, 418; Brigham, *History and Bibliography of Early American Newspapers*, II, 1508.

14. Timothy Osgood to John Scull, February 25, 1790, Letters Sent by the Postmaster General, 1789–1836; Sarah H. Killekelly, *The History of Pittsburgh* (Pittsburgh, 1906), 485; Noble E. Cunningham, Jr., *The Jeffersonian Republicans in Power: Party Operations 1801–1809* (Chapel Hill, 1963), 248. For Scull's anti-Semitic campaign against Israel and the Republicans in general, see Carl E. Prince, "John Israel: Printer and Politico on the Pennsylvania Frontier," *Pennsylvania Magazine of History and Biography* XCI (1967), 46–55.

15. Timothy Osgood to Augustine Davis, July 30, 1790, Gideon Granger to Davis, March 17, 30, 1802, Letters Sent by the Postmaster General, 1789–1836; Merriwether Jones to Thomas Jefferson, March 13, 1801, Jones to Levi Lincoln, March 25, 1801, Merriwether Jones entry, Letters of Application and Recommendation During the Administration of Thomas Jefferson; Dice R. Anderson, *William Branch Giles: A Study in the Politics of Virginia and the*

Nation from 1790 to 1830 (Menasha, Wi., 1914), 91; Merrill D. Peterson, *Thomas Jefferson and the New Nation* (New York, 1970), 706; John P. Little, *History of Richmond* [Virginia] (Richmond, 1933), 88.

16. For Samuel Green, see the Annapolis *Maryland Gazette*, March 28, July 11, 1799; *The Writings of George Washington*, John C. Fitzpatrick, ed. (39 vols., Washington, D.C., 1931–44), XXXI, 228n; James McHenry to Alexander Hamilton, September 30, 1792, *Papers of Hamilton*, Syrett, ed., XII, 511–12; Brigham, *History and Bibliography of Early American Newspapers*, II, 1421.

For Timothy Green, see Libero M. Renzulli, Jr., "Maryland Federalism: 1789–1819" (Ph.D. diss., University of Virginia, 1962), 387–88; Fischer, *Revolution of American Conservatism*, 421; Douglas Southall Freeman, *George Washington, Patriot and President* (New York, 1954), 130, 130n.

17. James Jackson to Thomas Jefferson, July 18, 1801, William Stephens entry, Letters of Application and Recommendation During the Administration of Thomas Jefferson; Gideon Granger to William Hobbey, January 16, 1802, Letters Sent by the Postmaster General, 1789–1836; Lisle A. Rose, *Prologue to Democracy: The Federalists in the South, 1789–1801* (Lexington, Ky., 1968), passim.

18. Leonard White, *The Federalists: A Study in Administrative History, 1789–1801* (New York, 1948), 179.

19. John Lenox to John Steele, August 19, 1799, *The Papers of John Steele*, Henry M. Wagstaff, ed. (2 vols., Chapel Hill, 1924), I, 172–73; *The Papers of Archibald D. Murphey*, William H. Hoyt, ed. (2 vols., Raleigh, N.C., 1914), I, 14n.

20. For Joseph Bliss, see J. Q. Bittenger, *History of Haverhill, New Hampshire* (Haverhill, 1888), 93.

For Benjamin Fearing, see Franklin B. Dexter, *Biographical Sketches of the Graduates of Yale College* (6 vols., New York, 1885–1912), III, 607.

For Ebenezer Whittier, see Fannie S. Chase, *Wiscasset in Pownalborough* [Massachusetts] (Wiscasset, Me., 1941), 123, 165–72, 211, 279.

21. For John Burnet, see James M. Smith, *Freedom's Fetters: The Alien and Sedition Laws and American Civil Liberties* (Ithaca, N.Y., 1956), 270–71; Carl E. Prince, *New Jersey's Jeffersonian Republicans: The Genesis of an Early Party Machine, 1789–1817* (Chapel Hill, 1967), 39; F. S. Urquhart, *A History of the City of Newark* (3 vols., New York, 1913), I, 373.

For Archibald Campbell, see Richard Lenk, Jr., "Hackensack,

New Jersey From Settlement to Suburb, 1686–1804" (Ph.D. diss., New York University, 1969), 127ff.

For John Branson and Reuben Tucker, see Charles S. Boyer, *Old Inns and Taverns in West Jersey* (Camden, N.J., 1962), 89, 131–32.

22. For Micah Lyman, see Moses Robinson to James Madison, March 31, 1801, and Jonathan Rodman to Thomas Jefferson, January 18, 1808, Anthony Haswell and Micah Lyman entries respectively, Letters of Application and Recommendation During the Administration of Thomas Jefferson; Dexter, *Biographical Sketches of the Graduates of Yale College*, IV, 424–25.

For John Holbrook, see Mary R. Cabot, *Annals of Brattleboro, 1684–1905* (2 vols., Brattleboro, Vt., 1921), I, 232–36.

23. For Samuel Batchelder, see Gideon Granger to Samuel Batchelder, December 28, 1801, Letters Sent by the Postmaster General, 1789–1836; Frederic Kidder and Augustus A. Gould, *The History of New Ipswich* [Massachusetts] (Boston, 1852), 122, 128, 255, 335.

For John Stoddard, see Joseph E. A. Smith, *The History of Pittsfield, Massachusetts* (2 vols., Springfield, Mass., 1876), I, 14, 48, 70, 99.

For Thomas Thaxter, see Francis H. Lincoln et al., *History of the Town of Hingham, Massachusetts* (3 vols., Hingham, 1893), I, 323, 384.

24. For Elizur Mosely, see Dexter, *Biographical Sketches of the Graduates of Yale College*, IV, 500.

For James Wilson, see Gideon Granger to the Postmaster at Presqu'Isle, March 26, 1802, Letters Sent by the Postmaster General, 1789–1836.

For John P. Thompson, see William Findley to Thomas Jefferson, February 26, 1801, Samuel Bryan entry, Letters of Application and Recommendation During the Administration of Thomas Jefferson.

25. John F. Verdier to Oliver Wolcott, Jr., November 14, 1797, Thomas Grayson entry, Letters of Application and Recommendation During the Administration of John Adams, General Records of the Department of State, Record Group 59 (National Archives); George C. Rogers, Jr., *Evolution of a Federalist: William Loughton Smith of Charleston 1758–1812* (Columbia, S.C., 1962), 99.

26. Autobiographical Sketch of Richard Cranch, April 11, 1805, John Adams to William Cranch, March 23, 1797, and passim, Richard Cranch Papers (Massachusetts Historical Society); Page Smith, *John Adams* (2 vols., New York, 1962), II, 714–15; Clifford K.

Shipton, *Sibley's Harvard Graduates: Biographical Sketches of Those Who Attended Harvard College* (16 vols., Boston, 1873–1972), XI, 370–76.

27. The postmasters at York, Maine, Peru, New York, and Catawissee, Pennsylvania, were Daniel Sewell, Moses Warren, and Jonathan Shoemaker respectively.

For Sewell, see Charles E. Banks, *History of York, Maine* (2 vols., Boston, 1935), II, 143, 403.

For Warren, see Moses Warren to James Monroe, February 16, 1816, Samuel Green entry, Letters of Application and Recommendation During the Administration of James Madison, General Records of the Department of State, Record Group 59 (National Archives).

For Shoemaker, see Jonathan Shoemaker to Thomas Jefferson, March 31, 1806, William Shoemaker entry, Letters of Application and Recommendation During the Administration of Thomas Jefferson.

For Joseph Horsefield, see John B. McMaster and Frederick D. Stone, *Pennsylvania and the Federal Constitution, 1787–1788* (Lancaster, Pa., 1888), 735–36; William H. Egle, "The Federal Constitution of 1787: Biographical Sketches of the Members of the Convention," *Pennsylvania Magazine of History and Biography* X & XI (1886–87), 217–18; Forrest McDonald, *We, The People: The Economic Origins of the Constitution* (Chicago, 1958), 175.

For Rosewell Billows, see Lyman S. Hayes, *History of the Town of Rockingham, Vermont, 1753–1907* (Bellows Falls, Vt., 1907), 151, 368, 545, 595.

For Dummer Sewell, see McDonald, *We, The People*, 192; Jackson T. Main, *The Upper Houses in Revolutionary America 1763–1788* (Madison. Wi., 1967), 282; Ronald F. Banks, *Maine Becomes a State* (Middletown, Conn., 1970), 376. McDonald elevates Sewell to the occupational category of "capitalistic manufacturer," but Main more accurately decribes him as a "miller."

28. For John Chandler, see Banks, *Maine Becomes a State*, 46–48, 140–41.

For Moses Ames, see McDonald, *We, The People*, 199.

For William Wilson, see Alfred F. Young, *The Democratic-Republicans of New York: The Origins, 1763–1797* (Chapel Hill, 1967), 423.

For Thomas Lewis, see Hugh Blair Grigsby, *The History of the Virginia Federal Convention of 1788* . . . (2 vols., Richmond,

1890–91), I, 76, 338, II, 9, 17–18, 20–22; Niels H. Sonne, *Liberal Kentucky, 1780–1828* (New York, 1939), 59–60. I am indebted to Professor Patricia Watlington for information on Lewis's politics.

For Hugh White, see McDonald, *We, The People*, 234.

For William Richardson, see Louise Trenholme, *The Ratification of the Federal Constitution in North Carolina* (New York, 1932), 70.

29. For Alexander Gilbert, see James Holland to John Steele, September 20, 1798, *The Papers of John Steele*, Wagstaff, ed., I, 163.

For John Bradley, see G. J. McKee to John Steele, November 1, 1798, John Bradley to Steele, November 1, 1798, Joseph G. Wright to Steele, November 1, 1798, John Bradley entry, Letters of Application and Recommendation During the Administration of John Adams.

For Joseph Wales, see ibid., Joseph Wales to Richard Cranch, September 25, 1797, Joseph Wales entry.

CHAPTER TEN

1. The introductory section defining the initial federal court system derives mainly from Julius Goebel, Jr., *History of the Supreme Court of the United States*, vol. I, *Antecedents and Beginnings to 1801* (11 vols., New York and London, 1971), 470–76 and passim.

2. See, for example, Richard E. Ellis, *The Jeffersonian Crisis: Courts and Politics in the Young Republic* (New York, 1971); Donald O. Dewey, *Marshall Versus Jefferson: The Political Background of Marbury v. Madison* (New York, 1970); Kathryn Turner, "Federalist Policy and the Judiciary Act of 1801," *William and Mary Quarterly*, 3rd series, XXII (1965), 3–32.

3. William Ellery to Alexander Hamilton, December 16, 1793, Applications For Office Under President Washington, Series VII, George Washington Papers, vol. XV (Manuscript Division, Library of Congress); Manning Dauer, *The Adams Federalists* (Baltimore, 1953), 153–54.

4. Much of the biographical data and political information on these jurists derives from the following collections: Applications For Office Under President Washington, Series VII, George Washington Papers; Letters of Application and Recommendation During the Administration of John Adams, General Records of the Department of State, Record Group 59 (National Archives); Letters

of Application and Recommendation During the Administration of Thomas Jefferson, General Records of the Department of State, Record Group 59 (National Archives).

The United States district judges in the 1790s were: Richard Law (Conn., 1789–1801), John Lowell (Mass., 1789–1801), David Sewell (Maine, 1789–1801), John Sullivan (N.H., 1789–94), John Pickering (N.H., 1795–1801), Henry Marchant (R.I., 1790–96), Benjamin Bourne (R.I., 1796–1801), Nathaniel Chipman (Vt., 1791–93), Samuel Hitchcock (Vt., 1793–1801), Elisha Paine (Vt., 1801), David Brearly (N.J., 1789–90), Robert Morris (N.J., 1790–1801), James Duane (N.Y., 1789–94), John Laurence (N.Y., 1794–96), John Sloss Hobart (N.Y., 1796–1801), Francis Hopkinson (Pa., 1789), William Lewis (Pa., 1789–92), Richard Peters (Pa., 1792–1801), Gunning Bedford (Del., 1789–1801), William Paca (Md., 1790–99), James Winchester (Md., 1799–1801), Cyrus Griffin (Va., 1789–1801), John Sitgreaves (N.C., 1790–1801), Thomas Bee (S.C., 1789–1801), Nathaniel Pendleton (Ga., 1789–96), William Stevens (Ga., 1797–1801), Harry Innes (Ky., 1791–1801), John McNairy (Tenn., 1797–1801).

5. Richard Law to George Washington, October 10, 1789, Nathaniel Pendleton to Washington, October 13, 1789, John Lowell to Washington, October 15, 1789, Acceptances and Orders of Commissions in the Records of the Department of State, 1789–1820, General Records of the Department of State, Record Group 59 (National Archives); James Duane to Alexander Hamilton, September 24, 1789, Duane to George Washington, April 8, 1794, boxes 7 and 9 respectively, James Duane Papers (New-York Historical Society); Nathaniel Pendleton to William Paterson, July 23, 1796, Box I, Nathaniel Pendleton Papers (New-York Historical Society); Robert Morris notes on the back of Samuel Leake to Morris, May 8, 1800, box 7, Robert Morris Papers (Rutgers University Library).

6. For these specific descriptions, see for Lowell: Clifford K. Shipton, *Sibley's Harvard Graduates: Biographical Sketches of Those Who Attended Harvard College* (16 vols., Boston, 1873–1972), XIV, 650–61; for Sewell: ibid., XIII, 638–45; for Bourne: David H. Fischer, *The Revolution of American Conservatism: The Federalist Party in the Ea of Jeffersonian Democracy* (New York, 1965), 277–78; for Chipman: Chilton Williamson, *Vermont in Quandary: 1763–1825* (New York, 1949), 166, 191, 259–60; Fischer, *Revolution of American Conservatism*, 240; for Duane: Sidney I. Pomerantz, *New York: An American City 1783–1803* (New York, 1938), 41; for Lewis: Sanford W. Higginbotham, *The Keystone in*

the Democratic Arch: Pennsylvania Politics, 1800–1816 (Harrisburg, 1952), 20, 96; for Peters: Richard Peters to John Rutledge, January 14, 1800, folder 9, John Rutledge Papers, Southern Historical Collection (University of North Carolina Library); for Bee: George C. Rogers, Jr., *Evolution of a Federalist: William Loughton Smith of Charleston, 1758–1812* (Columbia, S.C., 1962), 185; for Pendleton: Lisle A. Rose, *Prologue to Democracy: The Federalists in the South 1789–1801* (Lexington, Ky., 1968), 25–26.

7. For Lowell's political involvement, see the Portsmouth [N.H.] *United Oracle of the Day,* July 12, 1800; Fischer, *Revolution of American Conservatism,* 251.

For Laurence, see *The Life and Correspondence of Rufus King,* Charles R. King, ed. (2 vols., New York, 1894–1900), I, 549.

For Pendleton, see George Washington to Nathaniel Pendleton, March 3, 1794, *The Writings of George Washington,* John C. Fitzpatrick, ed. (39 vols., Washington, D.C., 1931–44), XXXIII, 286n.

For Peters, see Charles Page Smith, *James Wilson: Founding Father, 1742–1798* (Chapel Hill, N.C., 1956), 369.

8. For Sitgreaves, see John Sitgreaves to John Gray Blount, January 31, 1790, *The John Gray Blount Papers,* Alice B. Keith, ed. (2 vols., Raleigh, N.C., 1959), II, 11.

For Lewis, see Harry M. Tinkcom, *The Republicans and Federalists in Pennsylvania, 1790–1801* (Harrisburg, 1950), 36, 60, 65.

For Duane, see Alvin Kass, *Politics in New York State, 1800–1830* (Syracuse, 1965), 59; Dixon Ryan Fox, *Decline of Aristocracy in the Politics of New York* (New York, 1919), 122–23; George Dangerfield, *Chancellor Robert R. Livingston of New York, 1746–1813* (New York, 1960), 252–53.

For Sewell, see David Sewell to Theodore Sedgwick, February 19, 1796, and passim vol. III, Theodore Sedgwick Papers (Massachusetts Historical Society).

9. For Chipman, see George L. Montagno, "Nathaniel Chipman's Political Primer," *Vermont History* XXIX (1961), 103–8; Roy J. Honeywell, "Nathaniel Chipman," *New England Quarterly* V (1932), 556–82; Williamson, *Vermont in Quandary,* passim.

For Lowell, see Shipton, *Sibley's Harvard Graduates,* XIV, 650–61.

For Marchant, see Henry Marchant to Alexander Hamilton, December 9, 1793, Applications For Office Under President Washington, Series VII, George Washington Papers, vol. XIX.

For Sewell, see David Sewell to Theodore Sedgwick, February 19, 1796, vol. III, Theodore Sedgwick Papers.

For Hobart, see Fischer, *Revolution of American Conservatism*, 302.

For Peters, see Smith, *James Wilson*, 369.

For Bee, see Melvin H. Jackson, *Privateers in Charleston, 1793–1796* (Washington, D.C., 1969), 51.

10. James Duane to Edmund Randolph, January 15, 1794, Randolph to Duane, January 19, 28, 1794, Duane's draft statement to Randolph, February 11, 1794, Duane to George Washington, April 8, 1794, Richard Peters to Duane, July 26, 1794, Box 9, James Duane Papers; Robert Troup to Alexander Hamilton, December 25, 1793, *The Papers of Alexander Hamilton*, Harold C. Syrett, ed. (24 vols., New York, 1961–76), XV, 588.

11. Jackson, *Privateers in Charleston*, 48–51.

12. A reprinted copy of Judge Sewell's charge to the jury delivered at the district court of Maine on June 21, 1796, may be found in the Walpole *New Hampshire and Vermont Journal*, July 19, 1796.

13. This subject has been ably dealt with from several perspectives other than this one. See James M. Smith, *Freedom's Fetters: The Alien and Sedition Laws and American Civil Liberties* (Ithaca, N.Y., 1956); Leonard Levy, *Legacy of Suppression: Freedom of Speech and Press in Early American History* (Cambridge, Mass., 1960); Dauer, *Adams Federalists;* Stephen G. Kurtz, *The Presidency of John Adams: The Collapse of Federalism, 1795–1800* (Philadelphia, 1957).

14. Smith, *Freedom's Fetters*, 163–64, 200–2, 284, 319–23.

15. Levi Lincoln to Thomas Jefferson, December 13, 1802, Samuel Bradford entry, Letters of Application and Recommendation During the Administration of Thomas Jefferson; Charles Warren, *Jacobin and Junto* (Cambridge, Mass., 1931), 105–6, 111, 111n.

16. For Bee, see Charles Goodwin to ———, April 30, 1801, Charles Goodwin entry, Letters of Application and Recommendation During the Administration of Thomas Jefferson.

For Griffin, see Smith, *Freedom's Fetters*, 348n.

For Hitchcock, see Kathryn Turner, "The Midnight Judges," *University of Pennsylvania Law Review*, CIX (1960–61), 496–500; Smith, *Freedom's Fetters*, 231, 363–66.

17. For Gore's electioneering, see *Rufus King*, King, ed., II, 20–21; Winfred Bernhard, *Fisher Ames, Federalist and Statesman, 1758–1808* (Chapel Hill, N.C., 1965), 159–61.

For Potts, see *Life and Correspondence of Charles Carroll of*

Carrolton, Kate M. Rowland, ed. (2 vols., New York, 1898), II, 182, 188–90, 192.

For McAllister, see Rose, *Prologue to Democracy,* 26, 67; Thomas Jefferson's "Anas," *Works of Thomas Jefferson,* Paul L. Ford, ed. (12 vols., New York, 1904–5), I, 368.

For Daniel Davis, see William Willis, *The History of Portland* (2 vols., Portland, Me., 1883), I, 598.

For Otis, see Harrison Gray Otis to Theodore Sedgwick, November 25, 1796, vol. III, Theodore Sedgwick Papers; *The Life and Letters of Harrison Gray Otis, Federalist, 1765–1848,* Samuel E. Morison, ed. (2 vols., Boston, 1913), I, 57; Kurtz, *Presidency of John Adams,* 60–61.

For Lucius Stockton, see L. H. Stockton to Elisha Boudinot, August 19, 1800, Stimson Boudinot Collection (Princeton University Library); Isaac Smith to John Adams, February 7, 1798, Lucius H. Stockton entry, Letters of Application and Recommendation During the Administration of John Adams; Oliver Wolcott, Jr., to Mrs. Wolcott, January 22, 1801, *Memoirs of the Administrations of Washington and John Adams, Edited from the Papers of Oliver Wolcott, Secretary of the Treasury,* George Gibbs, ed. (2 vols., New York, 1846), II, 468; Carl E. Prince, *New Jersey's Jeffersonian Republicans 1789–1817: The Genesis of an Early Party Machine* (Chapel Hill, N.C., 1967), 57.

18. For Harison's electioneering, see Richard Harison to Peter Van Schaack, February 7, 1797, Peter Van Schaack Papers (Library of Congress); Richard Varick to Harison, March 9, 1801 and passim, box I, Richard Harison Papers (New-York Historical Society); Benjamin Strong to Selah Strong, March 19, 1792, Strong Family Papers (New-York Historical Society); Joseph S. Davis, *Essays in the Earlier History of American Corporations* (2 vols., Cambridge, Mass., 1917), I, 125; John T. Horton, *James Kent, a Study in Conservatism* (New York, 1939), 69; Fox, *Decline of Aristocracy,* 12–13.

19. John Langdon to Thomas Jefferson, May 14, 1802, John Goddard entry, Letters of Application and Recommendation During the Administration of Thomas Jefferson; John H. Morison, *The Life of Jeremiah Smith* (Boston, 1845), 139–40 and passim; Fischer, *Revolution of American Conservatism,* 232–33; Jere Daniell, *Experiment in Republicanism: New Hampshire Politics and the American Revolution* (Cambridge, Mass., 1970), 234; Mark D. Kaplanoff, "Religion and Righteousness: A Study of Federalist Rhetoric in the New Hampshire Election of 1800," *Historical New Hampshire* XXIII (1968), 7–11.

20. William Rawle to James Iredell, September 26, 1798, James

Iredell Papers (Perkins Library, Duke University); *Carlisle Weekly Gazette*, November 26, 1800; Smith, *Freedom's Fetters*, 332n; Tinkcom, *Republicans and Federalists in Pennsylvania*, 58, 248; Higginbotham, *Keystone in the Democratic Arch*, 20.

21. Fisher Ames to Alexander Hamilton, September 8, 1791, *Papers of Hamilton*, Syrett, ed., IX, 187; Warren, *Jacobin and Junto*, 66n; Bernhard, *Fisher Ames*, 125, 179, 184, 246; Davis, *Essays in the Earlier History of American Corporations*, I, 127, 185–86, 255; Kurtz, *Presidency of John Adams*, 276; John Carroll and Mary Ashworth, *George Washington: First in Peace* (New York, 1957), vii, 311; Forrest McDonald, *We, The People: The Economic Origins of the Constitution* (Chicago, 1958), 200.

22. Davis, *Essays in the Earlier History of American Corporations*, I, 319–20, 370, 391, 393; John C. Miller, *Alexander Hamilton, Portrait in Paradox* (New York, 1959), 305–10.

23. For Rawle and Edwards respectively, see: Journal of William Rawle, February 24, 1792, vol. I, William Rawle Papers (Historical Society of Pennsylvania); Nathaniel Hazard to Hamilton, November 25, 1791, *Papers of Hamilton*, Syrett, ed., IX, 529–37.

24. For background on the 1793 privateering controversy, see John C. Miller, *The Federalist Era, 1789–1801* (New York, 1960), 126–39, and *Alexander Hamilton*, 363–78.

25. For Harison, see Alexander Hamilton to Richard Harison, undated [July, 1793], and passim, box I, Richard Harison Papers; Hamilton to Harison, June 12, 1793, *Papers of Hamilton*, Syrett, ed., XIV, 539–40.

For Gore, see Stephen Higginson to Hamilton, August 24, 31, November 22, 1793, *Papers of Hamilton*, Syrett, ed., XV, 273–76, 314–16, 382 respectively; *Rufus King*, King, ed., I, 490–91, 494.

For Rawle, see editor's note, *Papers of Hamilton*, Syrett, ed., XIV, 509–10.

26. For Woods, see John Lockhart to John Haywood, June 30, 1798, Ernest Haywood Papers (Southern Historical Collection, University of North Carolina Library); Benjamin Woods to Timothy Pickering, May 8, 1798, John S. West entry, Letters of Application and Recommendation During the Administration of John Adams.

For Frelinghuysen, see Thomas Jefferson's "Anas," *Works of Jefferson*, Ford, ed., I, 363; Walter R. Fee, *The Transition from Aristocracy to Democracy in New Jersey, 1789–1829* (Somerville, N.J., 1933).

For John Davis, see Davis to Oliver Wolcott, Jr., April 22, July 16, 1798, *Memoirs of the Administrations of Washington and Adams*, Gibbs, ed., II, 45–46, 72–73.

For Marsh, see James Barrett, "Charles Marsh," *Vermont Historical Society Proceedings,* I (1870), 42, 54; Thomas Jefferson's "Anas," *Works of Jefferson,* Ford, ed., I, 363.

For Jeremiah Smith, see Smith to Oliver Wolcott, Jr., June 14, 1798, Jeremiah Smith entry, Letters of Application and Recommendation During the Administration of John Adams.

For Richard Harison, see Harison to Peter Van Schaack, January 7, 1797, box I, Richard Harison Papers; Harison to Van Schaack, February 7, 1797, Peter Van Schaack Papers.

27. Warren, *Jacobin and Junto,* 111; Matthew Lyon to Thomas Jefferson, March 3, 1801, Jonathan E. Robinson entry, Letters of Application and Recommendation During the Administration of Thomas Jefferson; Thomas Jefferson's "Anas," *Works of Jefferson,* Ford, ed., I, 363; Smith, *Freedom's Fetters,* 232–33, 363–64.

28. Timothy Pickering to Richard Peters, August 28, 1798, vol. 10, Peters Family Papers (Historical Society of Pennsylvania); Richard Harison to Peter Van Schaack, February 7, 1797, Peter Van Schaack Papers; Smith, *Freedom's Fetters,* 164, 201, 211, 323.

29. Smith, *Freedom's Fetters,* 319–23, 373–82; *Dictionary of American Biography,* Dumas Malone and Allen Johnson, eds. (22 vols., New York, 1928–58), VI, 43–44.

30. James Barrett, "Charles Marsh," *Vermont Historical Society Proceedings,* I (1870), 42–54, Smith, *Freedom's Fetters,* 363–64.

31. Smith, *Freedom's Fetters,* 338–39, 348–52.

32. Dauer, *Adams Federalists,* 165.

33. Thomas Jefferson's "Anas," *Works of Jefferson,* Ford, ed., I, 363–68; Noble E. Cunningham, Jr., *The Jeffersonian Republicans in Power: Party Operations, 1801–1809* (Chapel Hill, N.C., 1963), 250–51.

34. For Ambrose Gordon, see James Jackson to Thomas Jefferson, July 18, 1801, William Stephens entry, and Charles Harris to John Milledge, August 20, 1801, Charles Harris entry, Letters of Application and Recommendation During the Administration of Thomas Jefferson.

For Samuel Bradford, see Henry Warren to Thomas Jefferson, November 10, 1802, Henry Warren entry, and Levi Lincoln to Jefferson, December 13, 1802, and George Blake to James Madison, December 3, 1804, Samuel Bradford entry, ibid.

For Jabez Fitch, see Matthew Lyon to Thomas Jefferson, March 1, 1801, Joseph Willard entry, ibid.; Smith, *Freedom's Fetters,* 245, 361, 363.

For David Lenox, see Leland Baldwin, *Whiskey Rebels: The Story of a Frontier Uprising* (Pittsburgh, 1939), 113–14, 123, 241.

For John Hall, see Hall to Thomas Jefferson, March 7, 1801, certificates of William Rawle and Richard Peters, March 7, 1801, and passim, John Hall entry, Letters of Application and Recommendation During the Administration of Thomas Jefferson.

For Charles Cochran, see Charles Goodwin to ———, April 30, 1801, Charles Goodwin entry, and Ephraim Ramsey to Thomas Jefferson, May 1, 1801, Alexander Moultrie entry, ibid.

For David M. Randolph, see Smith, *Freedom's Fetters*, 348n.

35. Richard Peters to Timothy Pickering, February —, 1797, Allen McLane entry, Letters of Application and Recommendation During the Administration of John Adams; Kenneth W. Porter, *The Jacksons and the Lees* (2 vols., Cambridge, Mass., 1937), I, 375.

36. For McDowell, see Sam Brown to Thomas Jefferson, January 14, 1801, Charles Wilkins entry, and James Brown to John Brown, February 24, 1801, Samuel McDowell, Jr., entry, Letters of Application and Recommendation During the Administration of Thomas Jefferson.

For Giles, see Alexander Hamilton to Oliver Wolcott, Jr., January 31, 1797, and passim, Applications For Office Under President Washington, Series VII, George Washington Papers, vol. XII; *Carlisle [Pennsylvania] Weekly Gazette*, May 21, 1800.

For Payne, see Benjamin Woods to Timothy Pickering, May 8, 1798, John S. West entry, Letters of Application and Recommendation During the Administration of John Adams; Gabriel Phillips to Thomas Jefferson, October 18, 1801, Michael Payne entry, Letters of Application and Recommendation During the Administration of Thomas Jefferson.

37. For McLane, see Richard Peters to Timothy Pickering, February —, 1797, Allen McLane entry, Letters of Application and Recommendation During the Administration of John Adams.

For Giles, see the *Carlisle Weekly Gazette*, May 21, 1800.

For the Huger brothers, see Thomas Pinckney to John Rutledge, September 23, 1800, folder 10, John Rutledge Papers; Rogers, *Evolution of a Federalist*, 182, 182n.

For Jackson, see Shipton, *Sibley's Harvard Graduates*, XV, 161–63

For Lowry, see Davis, *Essays in the Earlier History of American Corporations*, I, 377–78.

For Cilley, see William Plumer to Benjamin Goodhue, March 2, 1798, Bradbury Cilley entry, Letters of Application and Recommendation During the Administration of John Adams.

For West, see Benjamin Woods to Timothy Pickering, May 8, 1798, John S. West entry, ibid.

38. For Jonathan Steele, see John Langdon to Thomas Jefferson, January 20, 1803, Samuel Sherbourne entry, and John Goddard to Jefferson, March 23, 1803, Jonathan Steele entry, Letters of Application and Recommendation During the Administration of Thomas Jefferson; Charles P. Whittemore, *A General of the Revolution, John Sullivan of New Hampshire* (New York, 1961), 223; Charles Bell, *The Bench and Bar of New Hampshire* (Boston, 1894), 70.

For Robert Boggs, see Boggs to Robert Morris, August 2, 1799, and passim, Robert Morris Papers (Rutgers University Library).

For William Marshall, see John Jay to Alexander Hamilton, June 24, 1793, *Papers of Hamilton*, Syrett, ed., XV, 20.

For Samuel Caldwell, see Caldwell to George Washington, April 14, July 17, 1789, Applications For Office Under President Washington, Series VII, George Washington Papers, vol. V.

For Simeon Baldwin, see Baldwin to Roger Sherman, July 23, 1789, and passim 1789–1801, Baldwin Family Papers (Sterling Library, Yale University); Simeon E. Baldwin, *Life and Letters of Simeon Baldwin* (New Haven, Conn., n.d.), 290.

For Abner Neale, see Neale to John Gray Blount, June 22, August 16, 1793, *The John Gray Blount Papers*, Alice B. Keith, ed. (2 vols., Raleigh, N.C., 1959), II, 273–74 and 298–99 respectively.

For Matthew Pearce, see John Read, Jr., to George Read, Jr., August 3, 1801, and passim 1789–1801, folders I and K, Judge Richard S. Rodney Collection of George Read Papers (Historical Society of Delaware).

CHAPTER ELEVEN

1. For a definition of what constitutes a Federalist, I rely on an explanation offered first in an essay that was in part drawn from these same data: Federalists "were men who electioneered, chaired party meetings, engaged in Federalist propaganda programs, coordinated political activities, or sought systematically and continuously to use their official positions or private influence to affect the politics of others in their respective communities." See Carl E. Prince, "The Passing of the Aristocracy: Jefferson's Removal of the Federalists, 1801–1805," *Journal of American History* LVII (1970), 565. The same definition applies to Republicans.

2. Several recent books adhere to this view, although with different points of emphasis. Among the best of these are Richard E. Ellis, *The Jeffersonian Crisis: Courts and Politics in the Young Republic* (New York, 1971); Jackson T. Main, *Political Parties Before the Constitution* (Chapel Hill, N.C., 1973); Richard Buel, Jr.,

Securing the Revolution: Ideology and Politics, 1789–1815 (Ithaca, N.Y., 1972); Richard H. Kohn, *Eagle and Sword: The Beginnings of the Military Establishment in America* (New York, 1975).

3. See in particular Kohn, *Eagle and Sword*, pp. 277–303, for the linkage between the Continental army and the Federalist party. For an analysis of the ideological unity between revolutionary leadership and the Federalist party, see Buel, *Securing the Revolution*, pp. ix–xii. See also William A. Benton, "Pennsylvania Revolutionary Officers and the Federal Constitution," *Pennsylvania History* XXXI (1964), 419–36.

4. Up to now historians have usually accepted the connection between Constitutional Federalists of the 1780s and the Federalist party of the 1790s as a given fact without really attempting to penetrate the exact nature of that connection. A notable exception that definitively deals with this question for one state is Norman K. Risjord, "Virginians and the Constitution: A Multivariant Analysis," *William and Mary Quarterly,* 3rd series, XXXI (1974), 613–32. Risjord studied 179 of 316 Virginia legislators for whom party affiliations could be determined. Of the 179, 99 favored the Constitution, 80 opposed it; 75 of 80 Antifederalists became Jeffersonian Republicans, 68 of 99 Constitutional Federalists of the 1780s became party Federalists in the 1790s; 31 became Republicans. However, Risjord counts as a Republican any legislator who supported the Jeffersonians either before 1800 or after. A supporter of Washington and Adams, in other words, who converted to Republicanism after 1800, is counted a Republican. Even with this last limitation Risjord found that 68.6 percent of the Constitutional Federalists of the eighties became Federalists in the nineties. Given the limitation, and the fact that Risjord deals with a Republican state and individuals not lured to Federalism particularly by the attractions of appointed federal office, the 68.6 percent figure compares favorably with my finding that 87.3 percent of the known Constitutional Federalists became Federalists in the next decade in the nation as a whole.

5. See in particular Charles W. Roll, Jr., "We, Some of the People: Apportionment in the Thirteen State Conventions Ratifying the Constitution," *Journal of American History* LVI (1969), 21–40.

6. Data interpreted here represent information uncovered for only a part of the first civil service. It is fair to assume that this information is weighted in favor of higher-status individuals, those

who attended college, appeared on local tax rolls, in biographical directories, and occupied local offices. It should be apparent then, that this factor skews percentages in favor of the elite within the civil service. If we could know about all the others, the proportion of "Less Articulate" would almost perforce have to be much higher. This would seem to add significance to the notably high proportion of "Less Articulate" that was discovered in the civil service.

The only existing study that is at all comparable is Sidney H. Aronson, *Status and Kinship in the Higher Civil Service* (Cambridge, Mass., 1964). Aronson studied the appointees of John Adams, selecting only eighty-seven at the top of the federal establishment, all of whom required Senate confirmation and including all nominees of cabinet and subcabinet rank. It is little wonder that this very restricted, highly selective group was found to form a sharply defined social, economic, and status elite. Aronson set out to prove for Adams that "a colonial tradition had developed a legitimizing norm that made political leadership an obligation of high status," and by ignoring the great mass of the civil service below executive level, he was able to do so. See pp. 2, 204–7.

James Kirby Martin, *Men in Rebellion* (New Brunswick, N.J., 1973), provides a much more comprehensive scrutiny of officeholding and the status of officeholders for an earlier generation, that of American revolutionaries. The 487 men in the thirteen colonies who held office in the first governments of the new republic were the subjects of this study. It is clear from Martin's extensive analysis that ruling "elites did exist" in revolutionary America, but they were so restricted socially and economically that, at the time of the Revolution, "a structural crisis in power and political placement among leaders in the colonies" occurred. This crisis helped to precipitate the process of democratization that was a characteristic of American revolutionary political change. The Federalists in the 1790s were mainstream inheritors of this process of change and clearly contributed, in moderate proportions anyway, to broadening the status spectrum of American political leadership and its related federal officialdom. See particularly pp. xi–xiii, 173–96 of Martin's book.

A Note on the Sources

This study has depended heavily on a series of little-used microfilmed manuscript collections, as follows: Applications For Office Under President Washington, Series VII of the George Washington Papers, *Library of Congress* (12 rolls); Letters of Application and Recommendation During the Administration of John Adams (3 rolls), Thomas Jefferson (12 rolls), and James Madison (8 rolls); General Records of the Department of State, Record Group 59, *National Archives.* The above collections, along with those for later presidential administrations, have sometimes been referred to as the "Appointments Papers."

They are poorly filmed and often extremely difficult to use, but are valuable historical sources nevertheless. The collections consist of each administration's appointment file folders and their contents, originally consigned to the Department of State archives. Organized alphabetically by the candidate's last name within each presidential administration, the Letters of Application and Recommendation constitute the accumulated credentials collected for every nominee or applicant for either a domestic or foreign federal appointment. Whenever a person applied for an office, or was so recommended or nominated, a file was created and all of the individual's letters, letters about the applicant, petitions for or against the appointment, and even occasional presidential, cabinet level or congressional notes, or notes on reported oral observations and remarks, were placed in that file. Whether or not the individual gained the office, the file was eventually sent to the State Department and retained as part of the permanent national archives.

These files form a treasure trove of social, economic, political, biographical, and demographic data on individuals great and humble from every corner of the nation. Because the file was established under the applicant's name, still-uncatalogued letters from all sorts of people, again both important and unimportant, might span several years and cover a range of subjects that go far beyond that suggested by the collection title. The Letters of Application and Recommendation are as valuable for state and local politics and life as for national concerns. There are cumulatively thousands of documents in this collection to 1817, and tens of thousands for the remainder of the nineteenth century.

Another obscure filmed *National Archives* collection was also consulted extensively for this study: Letters Sent by the Postmaster General, 1789–1836, Records of the Post Office Department, Record Group 28 (50 rolls), is organized chronologically day by day. It requires sifting, but the reader is rewarded with valuable information that reaches far beyond that which the title suggests, particularly for state and local politics, the development of the postal system, and population expansion and local developments generally.

All of the following manuscript collections are rich in information on Federalists and their lives and politics: *The Massachusetts Historical Society:* Timothy Pickering Papers; Benjamin Lincoln Papers; Harrison Gray Otis Papers; Theodore Sedgwick Papers; Nathan Dane Papers. *Perkins Library, Duke University:* Ephraim Kirby Papers; Purviance-Courtenay Papers; James Iredell Papers. *Library of Congress:* William Plumer Letterbook and the Plumer Papers; James Kent Papers; Diary of William Heth; Peter Van Schaack Papers. Southern Historical Collection, *University of North Carolina Library:* John Rutledge Papers; Ernest Haywood Papers. *New York Public Library:* Emmet Collection; Andrew Bell Papers; Philip Schuyler Papers. *New-York Historical Society:* Richard Harison Papers; William Duer Papers; James Duane Papers; Nicholas Fish Papers; Allen McLane Papers; Bancker Family Papers; Strong Family Papers. *Rutgers University Library:* Anthony Walton White Papers; Robert Morris Papers. *Historical Society of Pennsylvania:* Whisky Rebellion Manuscripts in the Pennsylvania Miscellany Collection; Edward Hand Papers in the Gratz Collection; William Rawle Papers; Peters Family Papers. *Stirling Library, Yale University:* Baldwin Family Papers. *Princeton University Library:* Stockton Family Papers; Stimson Boudinot Collection. *Tennessee Historical Society:* John Overton Papers. *Historical Society of Delaware:* George Read Papers.

Period newspapers, many of them now available on microform, were searched extensively and, as always, remain invaluable sources for early American history. Both city directories and scores of local histories were employed. These took on added value and reliability when used in conjunction with the Letters of Application and Recommendation. The high incidence of historical error in the former works can be minimized by cross-checking information in the latter. I used a large number of printed primary sources, as the notes indicate. For this study I want to single out for mention *The Papers of Alexander Hamilton,* Harold Syrett, ed. (24 volumes, 1961–76), a gold mine of information on the Federalist party. The Hamilton Papers project maintained a remarkably high level of accuracy even as it turned out two volumes a year, making it possible for me to use the printed volumes through the period of Hamilton's stewardship of the Treasury Department.

Index

A *View of the United States of America*, 117

Abbee, Shubael, 175

Adams, Abigail, influence on appointments, 143–44, 234, 283; kinship to, 234

Adams, Abijah, 204

Adams, John (N.H. seaman), 55

Adams, John (pres.): administration of, 42, 53, 71, 93, 96, 107, 151, 203, 217, 236, 247, 356; appointments policy of, x, 10–13, 20, 45, 47–56, 72, 108–10, 112–13, 116, 129, 131, 134, 157, 158, 170–82, 204, 207, 237, 238, 268, 271–72, 278, 283, 357; and Alexander Hamilton, 74, 80–85; as Federalist leader, *xi*; removals from office by, 11, 47–56, 80, 120, 124–25, 127–28, 131–32, 143–44, 150–51, 165, 231–32, 260, 271, 278, 301; and Massachusetts politics, 27–28; as Vice President, 126; kinship to, 140–41, 234; and 1798 land tax appointments, 159, 170–82; foreign policy of as issue, 27, 38, 153, 172, 177, 218, 260–61

Adams, Sam (Ma.), 23

Adams, Samuel (N.H.), 295

Adams Family, 144

Adams Federalists: Md., 197–98; Ma., 28, 152, 217–18, 260; N.H., 255, 266; N.J., 260; N.Y., 13, 84; N.C., 260, 266; S.C., 127; Va., 112; Vt., 260; and land tax of 1798 appointments, 134, 170–82

Addison, Alexander, 136

Albany, N.Y., 19, 191, 216, 301–02

Albemarle Sound region, N.C., 121–24

alcoholism, political allegations of, 52–53, 137, 296

Alexandria, Va., customshouse in, 105, 109, 111–14; post office in, 191

Allen, Joseph, 289

Allen, Paul, 166

American Revolution and appointments to the civil service in the 1790s, *ix–x*, 31, 34, 36, 37–38, 53, 117, 206, 212, 223, 242, 268–70, 273, 276, 357. *See also* Continental Army, Loyalists, Cincinnati, Society of the.

Ames, Fisher, and Ma. politics, 190, 254, 257; and N.H. politics, 50–51, 205

Ames, Moses, 235

Ames, Nathaniel, 251, 261